Cambridge Middle East Library

The Palestinian Liberation Organisation

Cambridge Middle East Library

The Palestinian Liberation Organisation,

People, Power and Politics

HELENA COBBAN

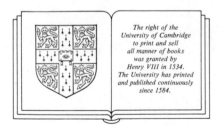

The right of the
University of Cambridge
to print and sell
all manner of books
was granted by
Henry VIII in 1534.
The University has printed
and published continuously
since 1584.

CAMBRIDGE UNIVERSITY PRESS

CAMBRIDGE
LONDON NEW YORK NEW ROCHELLE
MELBOURNE SYDNEY

Published by the Press Syndicate of the University of Cambridge
The Pitt Building, Trumpington Street, Cambridge CB2 1RP
32 East 57th Street, New York, NY 10022, USA
296 Beaconsfield Parade, Middle Park, Melbourne 3206, Australia

© Cambridge University Press 1984

First published 1984
Reprinted 1984

Printed in Great Britain at the University Press, Cambridge

Library of Congress catalogue card number: 83-18915

British Library Cataloguing in Publication Data

Cobban, Helena
The Palestinian Liberation Organisation –
(Cambridge Middle East Library)
1. Palestine Liberation Organisation – History
I. Title
322.4'2'095694 DS119.7

ISBN 0 521 25128 1 hard covers
ISBN 0 521 27216 5 paperback

Contents

Introduction

1 The PLO in the 1980s

Political impact of the 1982 Israeli invasion, 3; antecedents and early origins of Fateh; early life of Yasser Arafat, 6; introducing some other Fateh leaders, 8; relationship between Fateh and PLO; profile of PLO, 10; relations between Fateh and other PLO groups, 15; development of Fateh/PLO leaders' ideology and political goals, 16

Part I: History of the PLO mainstream

2 The phoenix hatches 1948-67

Fateh's founders: the Cairo group, 21; Fateh's founders: the Gulf group, 22; foundation and organisation of Fateh, 23; Fateh's early ideology, 27; impact of PLO's establishment, 1964, 28; Fateh launches its armed struggle, 1965, 31; summary: development of Fateh and PLO down to 1967, 34

3 The joy of flying 1967-73

Arab states' defeat gives guerrilla movement new impetus, 36; Fateh's abortive attempt to stage an uprising in the West Bank, 1967-8, 37; explosion of support for guerrillas from Palestinian refugees; Battle of Karameh, 1968, 39; Fateh takeover of PLO, 1968-9, 42; relations with the Arab states, 1967-70, 45; problems and accommodation in Lebanon, 1968-9, 47; problems and explosion in Jordan, 1968-70, 48; lessons from Jordan events, 1970-1, 52; survival of guerrillas post-1970; activities of the Black September Organisation, 53; the PLO and the 1973 Middle East war, 55

4 Caught in the Lebanon net (1973-76)

The aftermath of the war; Kissinger's diplomacy, 58; the PLO moves towards a political settlement; the PNC opts for a 'mini-state' (1974); formation of the Rejection Front, 60; background to the trouble in Lebanon, 63; first stages of the Lebanese war, spring and summer 1975, 65; Kissinger sets conditions for U.S.-PLO negotiations, 66; winter 1975-6 in Lebanon: the fall of Qarantina and Dbayeh; the start of direct Fateh and Syrian involvement; political developments, 67; Palestinian-Syrian confrontation in Lebanon, summer 1976; the Battle of Tel al-Zaatar, 72; endgame in Lebanon: Arab leaders settle

Illustrations

Preface

This present book was mainly conceived in discussions I had, after leaving Beirut in 1981, with Edward Hodgkin in Milton Abbas, and with Albert Hourani and Roger Owen, past and present Directors of the Middle East Centre at St Antony's College, Oxford. Between them, they convinced me I could write it, and sharpened my ideas of what should go into it. To them are due my first thanks.

The book would never have got any further, however, without the timely help of two fine American universities. I would like to thank Benjamin H. Brown of Harvard's Center for International Affairs for the support the Center afforded me in mid-1982. The Center for Contemporary Arab Studies at Georgetown University then provided a professional home for me throughout the academic year 1982-83, and I am extremely grateful both for the academic insights provided by CCAS Director Michael C. Hudson and other members of the Georgetown faculty, and for the practical help given by Zeina Seikaly and her colleagues in the CCAS's administration. Iman Bibars and Zaha Bustami gave valuable help with some of the Arabic documentary sources, while Sophie Rentz in the Near East Department of the Library of Congress, like Julie Blattner in the CFIA's library in Harvard before her, provided an ever helpful guide to the collections.

Many, many other people have contributed – wittingly or unwittingly, directly or indirectly – to the present work. Two Foreign Editors at the *Christian Science Monitor* were always asking the right sorts of question, and (which is even rarer in the newspaper business) waiting till I felt I had the answers nearly right: they were the late Geoffrey Godsell and David Anable.

In Beirut, far too many people even to name had helped me to look at the Palestinian movement over the years. Souheil Rached of course played a special role, as did many of his friends; Rashid and Muna Khalidi gave countless hours of their time; and Bilal al-Hassan and Mostafa el-Hosseini offered their insights both in Beirut and long after we had all left there.

In a way, I had been gathering material for a book such as this ever since

1979, when the 11-month strike on the London *Sunday Times* forced me, along with what seemed like a majority of my journalistic colleagues there, to think about getting between hard covers. Although most of my researches in that period had a slightly different focus, I did reach the end of 1979 with a number of substantial interviews with Yasser Arafat and Salah Khalaf in my tape-recorder. These provided a depth of background information for the present book which is not reflected accurately in the number of times I have directly quoted from them. Then in early 1983, after I had completed a first draft of the book, pure chance enabled me to find one of its principals sitting still for long enough for me to go back over with him many of the key issues I had by then identified. This was Khaled al-Hassan, and if it seems that he has the last word in some of the chapters here, this is only because it was not until I had done that much groundwork that I even, really, knew which were the questions to ask.

In Washington, many friends helped me to juggle work on the book (including three Middle East visits in the first four months of 1983) with my responsibilities to two very special little people: these friends included Malea Kiblan, Marilyn Mangan and Chris Reynolds.

Throughout my work on the book, the comments, advice and always constructive criticisms of one of the editors of the present series, Roger Owen, were particularly helpful, and Michael Hudson and William Quandt also commented extremely helpfully on the manuscript. At the Cambridge University Press, Robin Derricourt, Liz Wetton and Jane Van Tassel all helped to bring the book into existence. In the end, though, responsibility for all the judgements (and misjudgements) contained herein remains my own. For what it is worth, then, I would like to dedicate this book to my children, both born in Lebanon, and to all the other children of the Levant: may they all one day be able to grow up safely and in peace.

Abbreviations

ADF	Arab Deterrent Force
AHC	Arab Higher Committee for Palestine
ALF	Arab Liberation Front
ANM	Arab Nationalists' Movement
BSO	Black September Organisation
CCAAS	Chinese Committee for Afro-Asian Solidarity
DFLP	Democratic Front for the Liberation of Palestine
JF	Joint Forces
LAA	Lebanese Arab Army
LF	Lebanese Forces
LNM	Lebanese Nationalist Movement
NFLP	National Front for the Liberation of Palestine
NGC	National Guidance Committee
OCAL	Organisation for Communist Action in Lebanon
PASC	Palestinian Armed Struggle Command
PDFLP	Popular Democratic Front for the Liberation of Palestine
PFLP	Popular Front for the Liberation of Palestine
PFLP-GC	Popular Front for the Liberation of Palestine – General Command
PLA	Palestinian Liberation Army
PLF	Palestinian Liberation Front
PLO	Palestinian Liberation Organisation
PNC	Palestinian National Council
PNF	Palestinian National Fund
PPSF	Palestinian Popular Struggle Front
PR	Popular Resistance
UNRWA	United Nations Relief and Works Agency
VOP	Voice of Palestine
WSAG	Washington Special Actions Group

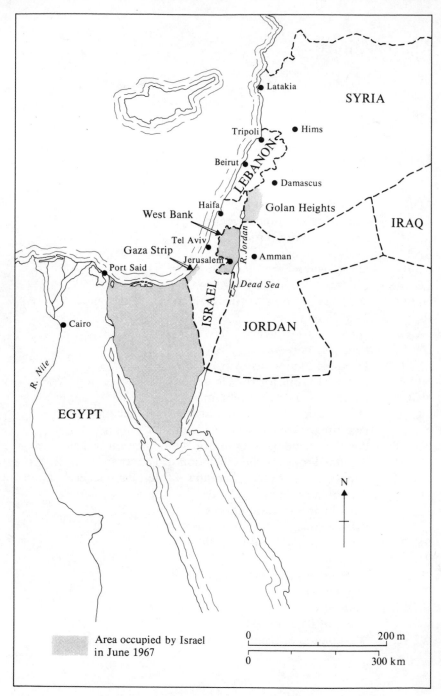

Map 1 Palestine and the surrounding areas

Introduction

Chapter 1

The PLO in the 1980s

In June 1982, the Middle East's most powerful military apparatus, the army of the State of Israel, swept into Lebanon in an operation called 'Peace for Galilee'. As Israeli tanks rolled ever northward, straight through the 40-kilometre limit the Israeli government had originally defined for the operation, heading for the Lebanese capital, Beirut, Israeli leaders spelled out that their principal aim was to destroy the political and military infrastructure of the Palestinian Liberation Organisation (PLO), which had had its unofficial headquarters in Beirut since 1971. They explained that with the PLO 'terrorists' out of the way, they then hoped to be able to impose their own extremely limited form of political settlement on the Palestinian communities in the occupied West Bank and Gaza areas.[1]

By mid-August, the PLO fighters in Lebanon and their local Lebanese allies had successfully repulsed several apparent Israeli attempts to capture Beirut; and despite many near misses, no member of the PLO's top leadership had been wounded or killed there.[2] But civilian losses from the relentless Israeli air, sea and land raids against Beirut, as well as from the total blockade the Israeli army imposed around it, were running so high that the PLO leadership agreed –after receiving strict guarantees from the Lebanese and U.S. governments for the safety of civilians left behind – that the PLO fighters should evacuate the city.

The evacuation, conducted under the eyes of a hastily assembled Multi-National Force with a strong U.S. contingent, started almost immediately. Some 8,000 PLO fighters left the city with their personal arms in their hands, for dispersal to half a dozen different Arab destinations. Many of them immediately became absorbed into the new training courses their leaders devised for them as part of the reorganisation of military activity made necessary by the evacuation.

The PLO's military apparatus was not the only part of the Organisation affected by the Battle of Beirut: its political infrastructure, which had previously displayed a prominent presence in the city, also suffered. The major PLO offices in the city were all badly hit by the repeated Israeli bombardments of June through August, and most of their employees left Beirut with the military convoys.

In mid-September 1982, the PLO political infrastructure was to suffer a further blow when the guarantees under which the PLO leaders had agreed to the evacuation of Beirut proved almost worthless. On September 15th, the Israeli army rolled into West Beirut under the pretext of keeping order there after the assassination of Lebanese President-elect Bashir Gemayyel; and while Israeli troops fired a stream of flares over the Palestinian refugee camps in the Sabra and Shatila districts of West Beirut, the Israelis' Christian Lebanese allies carried out a massacre of innocents there which was to shock the whole world. For the evacuated PLO fighters and employees, many of whom had left their families behind in Sabra and Shatila, the refugee camp massacres provoked a storm of questioning and frustration, and in some cases at least sparked harsh criticism of the PLO leadership for having accepted the U.S. guarantees.

Nevertheless, on balance, the PLO's Chairman, Yasser Arafat, faced the months immediately following the Battle of Beirut with his position in the Palestinian movement stronger than ever before. For Palestinians everywhere, as well as for many of their fellow Arabs, the fact that PLO fighters, equipped only with a few Second World War armoured vehicles, some antiquated anti-aircraft guns and plenty of hand-held bazookas, had been able to hold Israel's ultra-sophisticated military machine out of West Beirut for over two months of almost daily battles, proved a heroic and welcome contrast to what was generally seen as the weakness and timidity of the official Arab regimes at the time. Hailed as 'the symbol of Beirut's steadfastness', Arafat himself was credited with having personally inspired much of the fighters' determination, while he and his co-leaders of the PLO's military apparatus were congratulated for having organised a tough and effective military plan for the defence of the city.

In February 1983, the PLO held the Sixteenth session of its 'parliament-in-exile', the Palestinian National Council (PNC), in Algiers. Arafat and his colleagues in the PLO's dominant constituent group, Fateh, used this occasion to demonstrate to the world that the Palestinian national movement which they had played the principal role in welding together over the preceding quarter-century was still alive and kicking, and that its military and political infrastructures remained intact.

Three hundred and fifty-five delegates gathered from all the corners of the Palestinian diaspora to attend the Sixteenth PNC; they voted in 29 new members (including 23 from a new military list introduced by Arafat) to join in their deliberations. Various reported attempts on the behalf of some Arab governments to stage a delay, a boycott or an interruption of the PNC's proceedings were deflected by the Fateh bosses; and the Algiers meeting saw no significant challenges at all to the Fateh leaders' predominant role inside the PLO, nor to the organisational integrity of the PLO's military and political wings, nor to the PLO's overwhelming support from Palestinian communities everywhere.

Meanwhile, in the other major theatre of direct Israeli-Palestinian confrontation, in the Israeli-occupied areas of the West Bank and the Gaza Strip, the period surrounding the Battle of Beirut also saw no significant political achievements for the Israelis. The Israelis' drive to colonise the West Bank with Jewish settlers forged ahead in top gear. But their attempt to find a credible Palestinian 'Pétain' to deal with there foundered as the overwhelming majority of community leaders inside the occupied areas continued to proclaim their support for the Palestinian 'de Gaulle', Yasser Arafat.[3]

Thus, eight and half months after Israeli Premier Menachem Begin launched the 'Peace for Galilee' war, the Palestinian leadership appeared resilient enough to be able to prove that it had prevented Begin from achieving any of the war's principal *political* objectives.

By the early summer of 1983, however, the picture inside the PLO did not appear so rosy. A rebellion had broken out against Arafat's leadership – and not just from within the PLO, but from within the military cadre of Fateh itself. In a series of statements issued from within the Syrian-controlled areas of eastern Lebanon, the rebels criticised Arafat's continued pursuit of a political settlement to the Palestinian issue and some even questioned his continued right to head the PLO.

The rebellion, which still encompassed only a small proportion of Fateh's officer corps, but which was abetted and encouraged by both Syria and Libya, did more than embarrass Arafat on the world stage he had come to call his own. The depth of the Syrian government's involvement enabled the rebels to deny PLO loyalists any easy access to those areas of eastern Lebanon which in mid-1983 still abutted on the Israeli army's forward lines. Since Jordan, Egypt, western Lebanon and also Syria itself had already over the years been successively 'closed' to Palestinian guerrilla activity, this meant that the 'loyal' PLO now had no military deployment at all in any zone contiguous with its avowed target, Israel.

At the political level, the rebellion also brought to a head a series of immediate criticisms of Arafat's leadership which had simmered inside PLO ranks for some months beforehand, but which had not been adequately resolved in Algiers. More important, it threw the spotlight on issues of far greater strategic impact for the Palestinian national movement: the whole cluster of questions whether the correct balance had been struck between the movement's military and political activities, and between its activities inside and outside 'historic Palestine' (that is, the area encompassed in the British Mandate of the inter-war period there, all now held by Israel).

It remained to be seen, as of June 1983, in what way these larger questions would be resolved. But what was clear was that these were questions which would have to be resolved primarily by the wide-ranging networks of Fateh itself, and that on their resolution, one way or another, would depend the future integrity and effectiveness of Fateh – a movement which had already made a decisive contribution (probably *the* decisive contribution) to the reassertion and renaissance of Palestinian nationalism in our present times. For the roots of the resilience of Palestinian nationalism, as displayed even after the drubbing the PLO fighters took in Lebanon in summer 1982, lay not so much in the history of the PLO's own rather ponderous bureaucratic apparatus as in the development over the preceding quarter-century of its dominant member-group, Fateh.

Fateh's organisational and political bases of support had never been confined either to the dingy series of offices which had constituted the PLO's headquarters in Beirut, or even to the military bases its guerrillas maintained throughout Lebanon. Rather, since the late 50s, Fateh networks had woven through and between the communities of the Palestinian diaspora in all the Arab countries and beyond. The loss of West Beirut was a serious setback for Fateh, certainly; but the group's founders had always viewed Lebanon (as they had viewed Jordan) as a vulnerable forward base, and they had taken care to retain enough of their strategic assets outside the country to enable them to continue to operate even after suffering such a loss.

Fateh, which is a palindromic acronym for *Harakat al-Tahrir al-Filastiniyya* ('the Palestinian liberation movement'), was established in the late 50s and early 60s, through the coalescing of various specifically Palestinian nationalist (as opposed to *Arab* nationalist) networks already active in the refugee camps, in diaspora groupings of Palestinian students, and in the embryo Palestinian communities of the emerging Arab Gulf states. One of the organisers involved was Yasser Arafat.

Arafat, the tireless one-time engineer whose activities were later routinely to span three continents, was born Abdel-Rahman Abdel-Raouf Arafat al-Qudwa al-Husseini, in December 1929. On his mother's side he was connected to the Husseinis, a family prominent in the Sunni Muslim community in Jerusalem. Hajj Amin al-Husseini, the Mufti of Jerusalem, had provided much of the leadership for the Palestinian nationalist movement from early in this century through to the 1948 'disaster' for the Palestinians as represented in the creation of the State of Israel and their own dispersal.

Arafat thus claims Jerusalem as his spiritual home, though it is not known for sure whether he was actually born there, in Gaza or in Cairo.[4] Throughout his boyhood, the territory of Palestine, which was governed by Britain under mandate from the League of Nations, was racked by the successive disturbances provoked by the relentless immigration of Jewish settlers into the country, and the counterposed resistance of the native Palestinian Arabs: the latter saw the Zionist endeavour as different from colonising ventures in other parts of the world only in that, in the beginning at least, it sought to displace the 'natives' from the productive process entirely, by creating an entirely 'Jewish' economy based on purely Jewish labour. Hajj Amin al-Husseini led one influential political wing of that early Palestinian resistance movement, with his cousin Abdel-Qader commanding its military formations. As a youthful member of a less influential branch of the family, it was quite natural in the circumstances that the young Abdel-Rahman should be virtually 'apprenticed' in the national struggle as an assistant to Abdel-Qader. He took the name 'Yasser' as a *nom-de-guerre*, reputedly in memory of a fallen guerrilla hero. (Later, in the 50s, the infant Fateh group's obsession with secrecy induced him to start using another appellation for his activities – 'Abu Ammar' – the name by which most Palestinian militants refer to him to this day.)[5]

Between 1947 and 1949, Hajj Amin's resistance movement was crushed. Britain, weakened and drained by the prolonged struggle against Nazi Germany, handed the increasingly unstable 'Palestine problem' over to the infant United Nations, which decreed that, following a final British withdrawal in May 1948, Palestine should be partitioned into a Jewish and an Arab state. The existing Jewish leadership in Palestine did not reject this proposal outright (though the extremist Jewish group led by Menachem Begin did do so); the Arab Palestinians, seeing the U.N. proposal as seeking to divide the land which they still claimed as theirs, turned it down.

As the British troops pulled out of the country in the weeks leading up to May 1948, the battles between the country's Jewish and Arab communities grew in intensity. Five Arab armies rushed haphazardly to the aid of the Palestinian Arabs. But their intervention resulted in a fiasco: the total number of Arab soldiers mustered came to only 24,000 – far fewer than the number of fighters raised by the Jewish military groups in Palestine; each of the Arab governments involved had its own territorial ambitions in mind, often in competition with the others; and liaison between the Arab armies and the local Palestinian resistance groups was minimal. By the time the interim armistice agreements were signed between Israel and her Arab neighbours in 1949, there was no Palestinian Arab state left at all. Of the areas the United Nations plan had apportioned to such a state, parts had been overrun and retained by the newborn Jewish state (Galilee, Beersheba, etc.); part had been placed under Egyptian military rule (Gaza); and part was held by, and subsequently annexed to, the Hashemite monarchy in Transjordan (East Jerusalem and the rest of the West Bank area).

Not only was there no Palestinian state left, the events of 1948 had also shattered Palestinian society, from its rural and urban bases right up to the highest levels of its leadership. Over a million Arab Palestinians had fled their homes in the areas controlled by the Jewish forces. Hajj Amin al-Husseini tried to keep a leadership grouping called the All-Palestine Government alive from his new base in Gaza: in September 1948 it held a conference called the 'Palestinian National Council', in Gaza. But two months later, Jordan's King Abdullah went on the offensive against this last sign of Palestinian independence, when he convened another conference in Jericho, at which chosen Palestinian community leaders called on him to annex the West Bank to Jordan; the Egyptian government then placed Hajj Amin under virtual house arrest in Alexandria.[6]

Meanwhile, the refugees waited. From the stark and inhuman conditions of the refugee camps scattered in Lebanon, Syria, the East and West Bank sections of Jordan, and in densely populated Gaza, or from the hastily rented lodgings in those areas only the lucky few could afford, they awaited the return which successive United Nations resolutions promised them, to their homes. And as the months of waiting dragged out into years, it was the refugee populations which were to provide the backbone of the Palestinian liberation movement's revival in modern times. Among those waiting in Gaza, in the late 40s and early 50s, for a return to the family properties in Jerusalem, was the youthful Yasser Arafat.

Three more wars raged across the Arab-Israeli frontiers in the three decades which followed 1948, but the refugees of that year and their descendants remained, for the most part, in the refugee camps which they still stubbornly refused to refer to as 'home'. By 1982, the number of Palestinian refugees registered with the specially created United Nations relief body UNRWA had grown to 1,925,726, from a 1950 total of 960,021;[7] many other Palestinian refugees, especially those scattered in corners of the Arab world further from Israel, never registered with UNRWA and therefore never showed up on these UNRWA rolls.

Soon after the creation of Israel, Yasser Arafat left Gaza for Egypt, where he studied engineering at Fuad I University, later the University of Cairo. There he was one of the principal founders of a Palestinian Students' Union, in which capacity, in 1951, he was to make the acquaintance of the son of a former grocer from Jaffa called Salah Khalaf. Another Palestinian grocer's son, Khalil Wazir, orignally from Ramleh, was meanwhile planning his own campaign of revenge against the Israelis. While still a high-school student, Wazir was already organising guerrilla raids behind Israeli lines from Sinai: when the Egyptian intelligence caught him at this in the mid-50s, he was expelled from Egypt; he then took a teaching job in Saudi Arabia, before moving on to the British protectorate of Kuwait. Mean-

Table 1. *Distribution of Palestinians, a 1982 estimate*

	U.S. State Department estimate (000)	PLO estimate (000)
Inside historic Palestine		
Israel	500	530.5
West Bank	700	818.3[a]
Gaza	450	476.7
Outside historic Palestine		
Jordan	1,000	160.8
Lebanon	400	600[b]
Kuwait	320	278.8
Syria	250	215.5
Saudi Arabia	–	127[c]
Iraq	120	20[d]
Egypt	60	48.5
United Arab Emirates	40	34.7
Qatar	20	22.5
Libya	15	23
Oman	0.5	48.2[e]
Elsewhere	424.5	238.3[f]
Total	4,300,000	4,642,900

Comments on large discrepancies above:

a) West Bank: quite possibly the State Department was
not including the 60,000-70,000 Palestinian residents of Jerusalem, whom the Arabs all consider an integral part of the West Bank.

b) The figure for Lebanon has always been only a rough estimate. In the wake of the 1982 Israeli invasion, it has decreased drastically.

c) The State Department figure on this one must be misguided. The PLO probably has a good figure, as it has the right to tax Palestinians in Saudi Arabia.

d) Iraq: hard to know either way.

e) Oman: it is hard to believe the PLO's figure on this one.

f) This discrepancy is the oddest one. The PLO has no interest in minimising this figure, nor the State Department in exaggerating it.

Based on *New York Times*, 4 July 1982, p. IV/1.

while, Khaled al-Hassan, the eldest son of a deceased Haifa property-owner, had already moved to Kuwait in 1952: he spent the next 17 years steering the transformation of the infant city-state's administration into a successful, modern municipality, while building up networks of Palestinian activists and sympathisers throughout the Gulf.

These were the men who were to form the core of the leadership of Fateh at the time of the movement's foundation in the late 50s and early 60s. And though some of the other co-founders of Fateh were to peel away from the movement in the years which immediately followed, and six others to be killed or meet more natural ends, the remaining members of the Fateh core were able to build up layer after layer of disciplined organisers so successfully that by early 1983 these four men were still firmly in the middle of the Fateh web. In fact, all of the 15 members elected to the Fateh Central Committee by a general conference of the movement in spring 1980 had been active in the movement since well before it launched its armed struggle against Israel in 1965.[8]

The stability which marked the composition of the Fateh leadership over the decades thus stood in stark contrast to the notions generally held to in the West about the 'fractiousness' and even 'fissiparousness' of the Palestinian movement. From about the mid-70s onwards, the Fateh bosses were able to bring such a wealth of common political experience and other joint political assets to their enterprise that they were well able to deal with Arab heads of state face to face, even allowing themselves in private to patronise newcomers to the Arab scene such as Colonel Qadhafi (who overthrew the Libyan monarchy only in 1969).

For its part, the PLO was founded, under official Arab auspices, in 1964. It was in January of that year that a summit meeting of Arab heads of state decreed that a 'Palestinian Liberation Organisation' should be formed; and four months later, under the chairmanship of Ahmed Shuqairy, a Palestinian who was a veteran of more than one Arab diplomatic corps, it duly came into existence.

The Fateh leaders more or less ignored the establishment of the PLO: they were concentrating instead on preparations for launching their armed struggle against Israel, a stage which they finally reached on 1 January 1965. But by 1969, in the aftermath of the Arab states' defeat and discrediting in the 1967 Middle East war, Fateh and a coalition of other Palestinian groupings which had emulated it in the guerrilla field were strong enough to take over the PLO apparatus. Yasser Arafat, who had first come to public attention only the year before as Fateh's 'official spokesman', was elected Chairman of the PLO's ruling Executive Committee.

In the years which followed 1969, Fateh strengthened its hold on all parts of the PLO apparatus, while Fateh's own native-born vigour and resilience expanded the PLO's hold over all aspects of Palestinian public life, knitting together the dispersed and demoralised Palestinian communities into a reformed and distinctive national group under the leadership of the PLO.

As formulated in May 1964, the PLO's Basic Constitution vests supreme power in determining PLO policy in a body called the Palestinian National Council (*Al-Majlis al-Watani al-Filastini*; PNC), which has acted with increasing effectiveness since then as a kind of Palestinian parliament-in-exile.[9] The Constitution had laid down that PNC members should be elected by the Palestinian people,[10] but in practice this has never proved possible: participation has, instead, always been the result of lengthy negotiations between the leaders of all major PLO factions prior to each PNC session. In general, existing members of the PNC have retained their seats in the Council from one session to the next, except during the period of rapid change in PNC composition at the time of its Fourth and Fifth sessions, held in July 1968 and February 1969, and except for those few individuals publicly stripped of their PNC membership for some egregious political infraction.

The PNC had held 16 ordinary sessions and one emergency session up to early 1983, with each bringing together a total of between 100 and 450 Palestinians. The Sixteenth session (Algiers, 1983) had a final membership roll of 384 delegates, with a further 120 nominal PNC members unable to attend since they lived in areas under Israeli control. The seats in the Sixteenth Council were distributed as follows: guerrilla groups – a total of 92, with 36 of these going to the largest group, Fateh; Palestinian 'mass organisations' for students, workers, etc. – a total of 63, with 12 of these reserved for the Women's Union; the Higher Military Council (which linked all Palestinian military formations) – 23 seats, newly allocated at this session; and 'independents', including representatives of different refugee communities and geographical areas – 206 seats.[11] In practice, many of the representatives of mass organisations and many Council members who are nominally independent could be expected to be more or less closely linked to one or another of the guerrilla groups.

One of the PNC's main tasks, in addition to laying down the broad lines of PLO policy, has been to elect the PLO's ruling Executive Committee.[12] In practice, this has always been accomplished through protracted negotiations among the different PLO groupings, before and during each PNC session, with the intensity of the debate over the composition of each new Executive reflecting the fact that its final membership largely determines the parameters of PLO policy until the following PNC session. The finally negotiated 'list' of Executive Committee members is presented for ratification at the end of the PNC session, which has generally accepted it with little except symbolic opposition.[13]

After election, the Executive Committee members divide among themselves a number of 'portfolios', which put each of them in charge of a quasi-ministerial PLO apparatus. Thus, after the Sixteenth PNC, for example, Farouq al-Qaddumi was chosen to head the PLO Political Department (its 'foreign ministry'), Issam al-Qadi to head its Military Department ('defence ministry'), Yasser Abed Rabboo its Information Department, and so on (all these appointments were in fact reappointments to positions held before).[14] The real power of the various PLO Departments is limited not only by the facts of Palestinian dispersal but also by the existence of broadly parallel apparatuses maintained by each of the PLO's constituent guerrilla groups; nonetheless, within the parameters of these limitations, several of the PLO Departments have acquired considerable experience over the years in operating as quasi-governmental agencies.

In early 1970, the Executive Committee established a third PLO ruling body, the PLO Central Council, intermediate in level between itself and a fully fledged session of the PNC: it sought thereby to improve coordination with those Palestinian guerrilla groups which were not directly represented in the Executive at that time. Since then, Central Council membership has included all members of the Executive, along with at least an equivalent number of other members directly elected from the PNC.

Throughout its history, the Central Council has played a useful behind-the-scenes role. Its meetings have provided a sounding-board where the policies of the Executive could be discussed within a wider PLO forum; and throughout the successive absences of George Habash's PFLP and other guerrilla groups from the Executive, their continued presence in the Central Council ensured these groups' continued effective participation in PLO affairs and in the PLO's constituency.

In addition to its political organs, the PLO has been able to develop various other aspects of a quasi-state form of organisation. It commands its own regular army (as distinct from the individual forces established by the various guerrilla groups, some of which have at times taken on almost the aspect of regular formations). By 1980 this force, the Palestinian Liberation Army (PLA), numbered 20,000 troops organised into four infantry brigades deployed, at that time, in Lebanon, Syria, Egypt, Iraq and Jordan. The PLA's arms, of mainly East European origin, were reported to include T-34 tanks, *Saladin* and BTR-152 armoured cars, artillery guns and SA-7 surface-to-air missiles.[15] In 1969, Arafat was elected by the PNC as the PLA Commander-in-Chief; but in practice deployment of PLA units has nearly always been subject to the will of its units' various host governments.

The PLO has also fielded an active military police organisation, the Palestinian Armed Struggle Command (PASC), created in 1969, in Jordan.

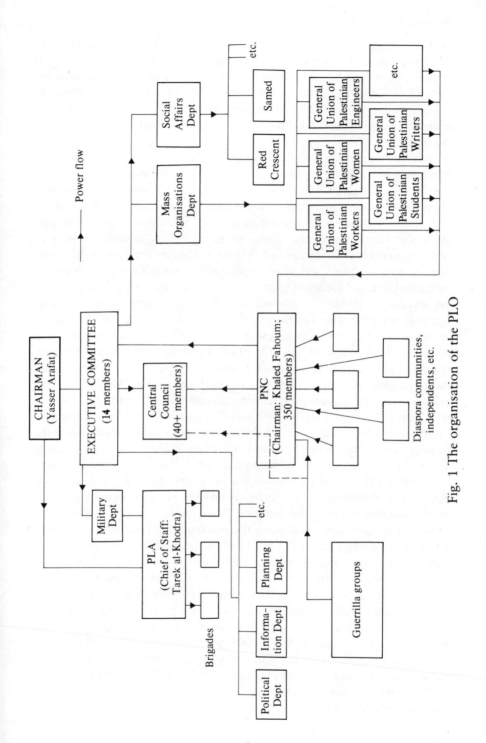

Fig. 1 The organisation of the PLO

As it operated in Lebanon in the 70s and early 80s, the role played by the PASC was twofold: it acted as a civilian police force in those areas deemed by the agreements concluded between the PLO and the Lebanese government to fall under the day-to-day jurisdiction of the PLO (mainly the refugee camps); and it intervened actively to end any dispute between opposing guerrilla groups or factions which threatened to escalate to the use of arms.

On the purely civilian side, the PLO created a whole series of institutions which sought to tie the Organisation directly into many aspects of Palestinian life. The Palestinian Red Crescent Society built and operated a whole network of modern hospitals in areas of high Palestinian population in Lebanon (at least until the operations of many of them were halted by the occupying Israeli forces after the summer of 1982), as well as running clinics in many refugee camps in Lebanon and Syria. The Sons of Martyrs Society, Samed, started off as an orphan-aid project, but rapidly grew to comprise large and modern factories in many manufacturing fields including textiles, carpentry, metalwork and film processing; many of these factories were sited in Lebanon and were destroyed during the Israeli invasion of 1982; others were reportedly dismantled deliberately later on by the occupying Israeli forces. The PLO's Planning Centre has sponsored much social research, especially that relevant to the establishment of any future Palestinian state, and helped to produce curricula for the schools established by the sizeable Palestinian community in Kuwait. The Palestinian Research Center, established in Beirut in 1965 under governmental decree, was able to sponsor much ongoing political research, until its headquarters were levelled by a car-bomb in early 1983. The sophisticated Social Affairs Organisation manages a network of social welfare schemes, which at one stage in the early 80s aimed to reproduce in the Palestinian diaspora the services provided to disadvantaged members of society by the most modern form of welfare state.

Funding for the activities above has come from the Palestinian National Fund, set up alongside the PLO in 1964 for this purpose. While the PNF continues to collect the income tax from Palestinians living in Arab countries which was its original form of revenue (the general level is between 5% and 7% of gross income), its major source of funding from the mid-60s on was the direct subventions from the Arab governments paid to the PLO under the provisions of successive Arab summit meetings since that held in Khartoum in late summer 1967. The Arab summit meeting held in Baghdad in late 1978, for example, allocated an annual subsidy of $250 million to the PLO, alongside another sum of $150 million allocated to 'bolster the Palestinian resistance inside the Israeli-occupied territories', the latter sum to be administered jointly by the PLO and Jordan. But Fateh's continuing

14

dominance inside the PLO was reflected, in the early 80s, in the fact that two-thirds of the money allocated under the Baghdad plan to the PLO was thence dispensed directly to Fateh's own account, with only one-third being distributed among all the PLO's other member-groups.[16]

The allies who had helped Fateh take over the PLO apparatus in 1969 continued to play a significant political role for some years afterwards. In 1974, the Popular Front for the Liberation of Palestine (PFLP), founded by Palestinian physician George Habash, mounted its most ambitious bid yet to challenge Fateh's domination of the Palestinian movement: it spearheaded the formation of the 'Rejection Front' to challenge the decision of the Fateh leadership in the PLO to opt for a political settlement of the Palestinian question.

Four years later, the Rejection Front was in shreds, torn apart both by serious questioning inside the PFLP as to its role and purpose, and by external Arab influences and the pressures of the 1975-76 civil war in Lebanon. In 1980, Habash suffered a debilitating stroke which for many months removed his influence and undoubted charisma from the otherwise disparate strands of the PFLP. By the time he was able to return to a semi-active political life, it was as a respected elder statesman under the patronage of the Fateh bosses, rather than by posing any open challenge to their role.[17]

By 1978, the Fateh bosses' domination of the Palestinian body politic was as total as it could ever be, given the circumstances of a Palestinian diaspora which forced its own inevitable compromises on the Palestinians in their dealings with their Arab 'host' governments. Nearly all of these governments have striven at one stage or another to impose their own control on the Palestinian national movement, either through the guerrilla groupings which they themselves support inside the PLO constellation, or by trying to influence Fateh's own broad apparatus from inside. Indeed, all non-Fateh Palestinian groupings sooner or later arrived at this same conclusion: that the only way to effect real change within the Palestinian national movement was to be able to sway the Fateh leaders' actions from inside their own organisation.

One distinctive aspect of the core of the Fateh founders' ideology – as opposed, for example, to PFLP thinking – had always been the principle of non-intervention in the internal affairs of other Arab states. In 1970, however, the Fateh bosses had not been strong enough to stand in the way of the tide of Palestinian popular resentment against King Hussein in Jordan, and they were forced by their own political base into a confrontation with Hussein. In 1976, again, the pressure of events in Lebanon eventually drew the Fateh leaders into the fighting there, although they had strenuously tried to avoid this, and had managed to stay out of the fighting for the first nine months of the war.

Nevertheless, the Fateh bosses' ability to control their own base was still growing steadily; and this passed a little-noticed test in 1978, in relation to an issue of even deeper fundamental significance to Palestinians than that of intervention or non-intervention in Arab states' affairs. In the spring of that year, the Fateh/PLO leadership proved itself able not only to take the unprecedented step of agreeing to a formal Palestinian-Israeli cease-fire in south Lebanon, but also to impose acceptence of this cease-fire on dissidents inside the ranks of the PLO, including inside Fateh itself.

In the four and a half years which followed, Arafat and his colleagues in the Fateh/PLO leadership proved themselves able to maintain this track record of control over the whole Palestinian armed movement in Lebanon, even through such difficult circumstances as the Israeli air attacks of July 1981, and then throughout the whole siege of Beirut and the evacuation from it.

The Fateh leaders' political thinking had meanwhile been developing in refinement over the years. With its roots firmly dug into the communities of the Palestine exile (as opposed to those Palestinian communities which remained on their ancestral soil in the West Bank and Gaza, and even inside 1948 Israel), the ideological lodestone of the movement from its inception had been the simple but powerful concept of 'the Return'. Since it was the Israeli government which prevented the Return taking place, the Fateh activists were only reflecting community feelings when they argued for the 'liberation of Palestine' from its Israeli/Jewish colonists.

The concept of 'liberation' in those early years was almost exactly analogous to that used by other twentieth-century anti-colonialist liberation movements: the native land would be liberated from foreign oppression and colonialism, and the liberation movement would no more give special consideration to the fate of the colonialists than had the Algerians to the French *colons*, or the Chinese to their former Japanese occupiers.

However, the hard facts of continued Jewish immigration into Israel gradually began to impose themselves on the Fateh organisers. Towards the end of 1967, the Central Committee finally agreed to change the formulation of their eventual goal from the 'liberation of Palestine', to the establishment of a 'secular, democratic state' in Palestine, in which Jews, Palestinian Christians and Palestinian Muslims could live side by side in equality. On 1 January 1968, this new step was made public; but it took the Fateh leaders a further year to change the Charter of the PLO to incorporate the new formulation, and, according to Khaled al-Hassan, even longer than that in some cases to persuade all the other Palestinian groups, and the whole Palestinian public, of the correctness of the change.

There was still much detailed argument over whether all the Jewish population then resident in Israel/Palestine would be allowed to join in this venture, or only those who had moved to Palestine before 1948; and the Fateh organisers were still insistent on pressing for the Palestinian exiles' right to return to their former properties (now largely taken over by Israeli Jewish immigrants under the Israeli governments' 'Absentee Property' laws). But in the aftermath of the Israeli army's stunning military victory over the Arab states in 1967, which now gave them control over all the land of Mandate Palestine, plus parts of Syria and Egypt, the Israeli administration was in no mood at all to discuss any settlement with the Palestinians which might involve diluting the exclusively Jewish character of their state. So the step towards a compromise with Israel that was represented by the Palestinians' 1968-69 espousal of the 'secular democratic state' concept fell on deaf Israeli ears.

By early 1974, the situation had again changed. The October War of 1973 did not result in the 'liberation' of any historically Palestinian lands, but it had badly dented the Israelis' self-image of invincibility and had given the Arab states and their Palestinian confreres more confidence in approaching a settlement. The Fateh leadership of the PLO, having clearly established its dominance inside the Palestinian movement, and having participated to the best of its abilities in the Arab war effort, now hoped to share in the Arab states' diplomatic spoils of war.

At the Twelfth PNC session, held in Cairo in July 1974, the PLO adopted a programme calling for the establishment of 'a Palestinian national authority in any Palestinian areas liberated from Israeli control' (realistically, always thenceforth considered to be the West Bank and the Gaza Strip). Fateh's leaders hoped, on the basis of this new programme, to be able to attend the promised negotiations for an overall Middle Eastern settlement. The 'national authority' concept was another new departure, for it allowed, for the first time ever in the history of the Palestinian national movement, of the possibility of dividing the land of Palestine – even though, as the programme was at pains to point out, this would only be a transitional step towards the creation of a secular democratic state in the whole of Palestine.

In 1977, the 'national authority' concept was spelled out even further, as definitely meaning that the PLO wanted to see the creation of 'an independent Palestinian state' in any of the lands of Palestine freed from Israeli rule. But the Fateh leaders' hopes that their ideological concessions of 1974 and 1977 would lead them to the conference table were to be frustrated: after meeting for one brief session just before Christmas 1973, the Geneva Middle East Peace Conference called for by the U.N. Security Council during the October War was never reconvened. And at the end of

17

1977, Egyptian President Anwar Sadat set all Mideast negotiations on an entirely new footing with his dramatic unilateral initiative towards Israel.

Sadat's initiative elbowed the PLO/Fateh leadership away from their hopes of reaching a peace table; and the 'Palestinian' provisions of the Camp David accords which were concluded the following year among Egypt, Israel and the U.S. proved unacceptable to the PLO/Fateh leadership, which still clung to its call for the creation of an independent Palestinian state in the West Bank and Gaza.

The Fateh leaders appeared ready, in the years which followed 1977, to make many further subsidiary concessions on their programme of 1977. In September 1979, for instance, Yasser Arafat told a visiting delegation of black American community leaders that so urgent was the Palestinians' need to create a state of their own that he would be prepared to establish the future Palestinian state on any part of historic Palestine, however small: 'Even just in Jericho,' was what he said, 'if that were all they would give me.'[18] And in February 1983, Salah Khalaf said that he would support the establishment of a Palestinian state inside the Israeli-occupied territories, 'even if the PLO were denied any role in leading it'.[19] Most PLO/Fateh leaders appeared ready to consider accepting an interim regime inside the occupied territories, under some kind of international (preferably U.N.) control, to supervise the handover of power to the new Palestinian authority; and to consider entering into some kind of confederation with Jordan, as called for by U.S. President Reagan's Mideast peace plan of September 1982, subsequent to the establishment of the independent Palestinian state. Khaled al-Hassan meanwhile even spoke of the possibility of some of the Jewish settlements established during the years of Israeli occupation of the West Bank and Gaza being allowed to remain under the new authority, 'perhaps in return for the rehabilitation of some of our villages inside 1948 Israel'.[20]

But the bottom line for all these concessions still remained the insistence on the need for a Palestinian state, as a refuge and defence for the Palestinians after their decades of travail. And as of early 1983, no such state was yet in sight – indeed, it was expressly ruled out in the Reagan peace plan. Nevertheless, the PLO/Fateh leaders apparently felt that from this demand there were no further concessions they could make. They hoped that, by clinging to this demand and to the political agenda connected with it, they could at least guard the integrity of the national movement for whose entire fate they felt responsible, until such a time as the balance of power in the region changed, and until they could have more chance of talking about their agenda with the only powers able to deliver on it – that is, the U.S. and Israel.

18

History of the PLO mainstream

The leader

My colleague John Cooley and I had spent most of that day, in August 1979, inspecting the terrible damage from the Israelis' latest air and artillery attacks against south Lebanon. In Tyr, I remember, the casualties and the material losses had been particularly shocking.

Yasser Arafat had also, separately, been in south Lebanon that day. When we arrived at his sixth-floor office in the evening for a long-scheduled interview, we found that he had brought his own aide-mémoire back from the south: it was an American-made 175 mm artillery shell – unexploded.

Halfway through the interview, he insisted that this be brought up to prove his point that the Israelis were using American-made weapons against targets in the south. An aide, unconvinced, asked him to reconfirm that he wanted it brought up. 'Yes, yes, the unexploded one,' he insisted. 'Bring it, but be careful!'

A few minutes later, three youths in military dress came in with the metre-long shell. They were sweating profusely, partly from the effort of carrying it up, but also from the clear expectation of what might happen if they should lose their grip on it. And with the Commander-in-Chief right there too!

The Commander-in-Chief tried to be helpful. 'Not that way,' he told them, 'this way. Oh careful, careful! There you go, carefully round here. Careful!'

He seemed to be the only one present unconcerned at the dangers in the shell's manoeuvrings between the furniture towards us, and the youths carrying it just seemed more flustered by his interventions. As we gingerly examined the shell's markings, he turned to us for confirmation: 'This is proof, yes?' he said, triumphantly. We lived to tell the tale.

Chapter 2

The phoenix hatches (1948-67)

The late 40s and early 50s were a time of rapid social and political change for the Arab states bordering on Israel. Egypt saw continued agitation for the ending of Britain's military presence, the overthrow of its monarchy in 1952, and the Israeli-French-British invasion four years later. Syria saw a succession of coups and counter-coups, as more powerful Arab governments contested for influence over Damascus. Lebanon, behind a facade of growing wealth and westernisation, was storing up the discontents which led to the civil war of 1958. And in Jordan, King Abdullah was accused of betraying the Palestinian cause and was shot one Friday prayer-time in 1951 at Jerusalem's Al-Aqsa mosque. His immediate heir, Talal, and later Talal's son Hussein, then took over the task of controlling a population that (East Bank and West Bank) was overwhelmingly Palestinian in origin.

In Cairo, in particular, the years immediately preceding the Free Officers' coup against the monarchy in 1952 were marked by an often clashing ferment of 'universalist' ideas – from communism, to pan-Arabism, to Muslim fundamentalism – each of which sought, in adopting the Palestinian cause as its own, consciously or unconsciously thereby to subordinate it to its own.

Yet in 1951, as Yasser Arafat set about reorganising the Palestinian Students' Union in Cairo, he found several fellow students who agreed with his 'Palestine-first' orientation. Among them was Salah Khalaf, a literature student some four years younger than Arafat whose adolescence had been seared by the experience of the mass flight of the population of Arab Jaffa from their city. Khalaf's family had been able to pack into a crowded ship which took them to Gaza, but he later recalled having seen at least one woman drown in the chaos of the embarkment.[1]

Khalaf was later to emerge, from behind a jovial exterior, as chief of Fateh's security services, and as a powerful orator and organiser for the movement in his own right. As he later recollected his early discussions with Arafat in Cairo:

Yasser Arafat and I ... knew what was damaging to the Palestinian cause. We were convinced, for example, that the Palestinians could expect nothing from the Arab

21

regimes, for the most part corrupt or tied to imperialism, and that they were wrong to bank on any of the political parties in the region. We believed that *the Palestinians could rely only on themselves.*[2]

Thus the Cairo group was already defining what was later to be one of the foundations of Fateh's ideology. By concentrating solely on the question of Palestine, and how to regain it for its original inhabitants, Arafat and Khalaf and the group which developed in collaboration with them in Cairo hoped to cut away all the excess intellectual baggage of the more universalist ideologies and return to what they considered the essentials. Elsewhere throughout the Palestinian diaspora, other similar grouplets were meanwhile coalescing along more or less parallel lines.

The first test of the grouping in Cairo came with the Palestinian Students' Union elections in September 1952; the importance of this vote lay in the fact that, as Khalaf described it, the Union was 'the only Palestinian organisation which held democratic elections'. The 'Palestine-firsters' demonstrated the kind of tactical political acuity which later lay at the heart of Fateh's successes:

Yasser Arafat and I had succeeded in establishing good relations with the students irrespective of their political affiliations. We didn't present ourselves as being against the parties, but rather as being for the Student Union, the name we gave our ticket for the nine seats on the Executive Committee. Six of them, including Arafat and myself, belonged to our group. We gave three seats to members of other parties – to a Muslim Brother, a Baathist, and a communist – to show our democratic and unitary attitude.

Our calculations turned out to be correct. Our ticket was elected with an overwhelming majority.[3]

Four years later, in the 1956 Middle East war, the Israeli, British and French armies overran Gaza, Sinai and the Suez Canal area; the Palestinian student activists in Cairo formed a Palestinian commando battalion to help the Egyptian war effort. According to Khalaf, 'Yasser Arafat, who was a reserve officer at the time, was sent to Port Said as part of the engineering corps to participate in mine-sweeping operations.'[4]

In early 1957, the original members of the Cairo student group started dispersing. Arafat left for Kuwait, where he joined the Ministry of Public Works, later branching out to open his own contracting business there. Khalaf spent a few years teaching in Egyptian-ruled Gaza before joining his old comrades in Kuwait. Some other members of the Cairo group took up positions in the British-controlled Emirate (Princedom) of Qatar.

In the Gulf, the Cairo group members came into direct contact with other Palestinian activists, already installed there for some time, who had developed similar ideas about the need for autonomous Palestinian action. The doyen of these activists was Khaled al-Hassan (Abul-Said), who from

1952 to 1967 served as the Kuwait municipality's chief executive.[5] Hassan had left Haifa in June 1948, travelling to East Africa and then to Egypt, where he was imprisoned for a year, as he described it, 'just for being a Palestinian'. After escaping from the Egyptian prison camp he was reunited with his family in south Lebanon before settling in the Syrian capital, Damascus. In 1950, and again in 1951, he had tried to establish autonomous Palestinian organisations there, but both attempts had failed; and in 1952 he had left Damascus under threat of another spell in prison, making his way thence to Kuwait.

The political atmosphere in Kuwait proved more suitable than either Egypt or Syria for the work of political organising Hassan had in mind, not least because of the flow of people coming and going from there to all the other countries of the Palestinian diaspora: a flow far freer than that among most of the states themselves bordering on Israel. Thus, it was in Kuwait that Hassan first managed to build up a network which struck permanent roots, this time amongst the growing class of Palestinian professionals and businessmen in the Gulf states.

In later years, the commitments many of Fateh's founders had built up in the Gulf states led some on the Palestinian left wing to accuse them of being the creatures of the (generally very conservative) rulers there. In an interview in 1969 with a left-wing Egyptian monthly, Khalaf explained the move the Cairo student leaders made to the Gulf in the mid- and late 50s as having been dictated by the need to earn enough to build Fateh a sizeable organisational war-chest.[6] Hassan used a similar argument, saying that his two previous attempts to found a political organisation had failed 'because we hadn't even a penny to do anything for the movement, because we needed that penny to eat. We were starving at that time.'[7] In addition, all the governments bordering Israel, including that of pan-Arabist Gamal Abdel-Nasser, placed ruthless restrictions on Palestinian political activity right up until 1967; this provided an added impetus for the Palestinian activists to gravitate down to the less politically restrictive atmosphere of the Gulf.

In his autobiography, Khalaf dates the founding of Fateh very precisely, to a meeting held on 10 October 1959, when 'a small group of us met in a discreet house in Kuwait to hammer out the organisational structures of Fateh'.[8] Hassan, however, dated the final unification of the Fateh core only back to 1962, saying that until then all that had developed were independent local groups:

We discovered that wherever there is a concentration of Palestinians at that time, between '58 and '62, there was a Palestinian movement. So Hani [his younger brother, Hani al-Hassan], for instance, and his group were forming a movement in Germany. Hamdan was forming a movement in Austria. Kawkaban was forming a movement in Spain. Abdul-Fattah was forming a movement in Saudi Arabia. Abu Mazen, Abu Yusef – they were forming a movement in Qatar. We were forming a movement in Kuwait. There were some others in Iraq and Gaza and Damascus.

But we [the Kuwait group] were the only ones who managed to have a magazine, called *Filastinuna* [Our Palestine]. It was offered to us by a Lebanese from Tripoli. So through this magazine – and there was a P.O. Box at the magazine – so we became known before the others. So the others started to talk to us, to write to us... So we became the core through the P.O. Box of this magazine. And then we managed to see each other and finally, in '62, we had a conference in Kuwait, and the whole were united in Al-Fateh...

The first man who started Fateh is Abu Jihad [Khalil al-Wazir].[9]

The orientation of the new organisation was that which the refugee activists had already hammered out through years of bitter experience in Cairo, Damascus, Gaza, the Gulf and elsewhere; and it was an orientation which continued as the 'bottom line' of Fateh's activities until at least early 1983. It was based on five principal points of agreement:

1. The common goal of liberating Palestine,
2. The need for armed struggle to attain this goal,
3. Reliance on Palestinian self-organisation,
4. Co-operation with friendly Arab forces, and
5. Co-operation with friendly international forces.

In the years when the Fateh organisation was first crystallising, in the late 50s and early 60s, ideologues throughout the Arab world, including many Palestinians, were still dominating most Arab political discussions with their argument, 'Arab unity is the road to the liberation of Palestine.' The Fateh organisers stressed instead that the liberation of Palestine was itself the most important immediate goal, and that 'Arab unity', insofar as it was important at all, would come about only after the Palestinians' own activity had liberated Palestine. As Khaled al-Hassan described it, 'We reversed the slogan, and this is how we reversed the whole tide of thinking. And we managed to do that. Because when you want to talk about unity, then you have to work against the regimes. When we want to talk about liberation, we have to work on liberation.'[10]

In the beginning, as Hassan admitted, it was uphill work:

Nasser's influence was so strong. So it wasn't easy for us to recruit members... For instance, in Kuwait: usually Kuwait in summer at that time used to become empty [of Palestinians], because most of the Palestinians were teachers. So by the end of the education term they take their leave and go back where they live. And when they came back three months later, we felt that we were going to start again from the very beginning.

The real increase, the real support that comes from the people, and permanently, started in '65 when we started our military action. Then the people realised that we were not just another movement, talking like the others.[11]

The organisational form which emerged from Fateh's earliest efforts proved durable and resilient over the decades which followed. The Fateh founders constituted themselves into a Central Committee, which was to be the seat of the organisation's greatest day-to-day power. Provision was made for the holding on a regular basis of a General Conference to represent the movement's membership. The Conference was designed to be the source of ultimate decision-making power inside the movement. But by early 1983 only four Conferences had been held, with a gap of nine years between the convening of the Third (1971) and the Fourth (May 1980); so in practice, though the Central Committee has had to take into account the views of the Conference – and the Conference does indeed elect the members of the Committee – most of the movement's power is concentrated in the Central Committee's hands.

Between these two levels, an intermediate body called the Revolutionary Council was created. But the Revolutionary Council has had less constitutional power within the movement, and only slightly more effective power in practice, than the Conference: so the development of Fateh since its inception has remained overwhelmingly in the hands of its Central Committee.

Fateh's Fourth General Conference, in 1980, elected a Central Committee of 15 members (their names are listed in Appendix 5; two members of this Committee, Majid Abu Sharar and Sa'd Sayel, had been assassinated as of early 1983). Ten members of the new Committee, including Arafat, Wazir, Hassan, Khalaf and Qaddumi, had constituted the previous Central Committee; the five newcomers included Rafiq al-Natsheh, who had previously served on the Committee as one of the co-founders of Fateh before a spell off the Committee. The Fourth Conference also elected 40 of the Revolutionary Council's 75 members.[12] In addition, the Conference decided for the first time to hold direct elections to the positions of 'Commander-in-Chief of the Forces of the Palestinian Revolution', and 'Deputy Commander-in-Chief': Arafat and Wazir were voted into these positions, reportedly by overwhelming acclamation of the participants.

From the beginning, the harsh circumstances of Palestinian dispersal and Arab repression made their mark on Fateh's internal organisational structure. The vertical political links existing in most conventional, pyramid-structure party organisations were always weak, or even in the view of some virtually non-existent, inside Fateh. What bound the movement together, instead, was the shared pragmatism of its members, as they agreed to overlook their ideological and other differences with fellow Palestinians in the interests of pursuing the common goal. And the general terms in which the goal itself has always been defined, purposely avoiding ideological refinements, itself aided this process. Thus Fateh's internal political map is not marked primarily by cells, local committees, the internal dissemination of 'the party line', formation of ideological factions, and so forth. Instead, it is based on the primary concept of the apparatus (*jihaz*), and the subsidiary concept of the country or regional organisation (*iqlim*).

By the early 80s, Fateh apparatuses spanned all imaginable areas of Palestinian nationalist activity: military, internal political, internal social, relations with the resistance movement in the Israeli-occupied areas, information activities, financial control and other economic activities, relations with Arab states and parties, international diplomacy, and so on. In many of these fields, two, three or even more near-parallel apparatuses may have been at work, each with its special emphasis; and most of the apparatuses had an established transnational base and field of action.

The regional *iqlim* organisations, grouping members of the Palestinian communities existing in each significant Palestinian population centre, would themselves be considered mainly as subsidiaries of the broader internal political apparatus, though their members might also become engaged in the work of the other apparatuses as necessary. From 1971 to 1982, for example, many of the Fateh apparatuses maintained an important presence in Lebanon, so members of the Lebanon *iqlim* (region) could easily be drawn into their activities, though a good proportion of the workers in these apparatuses were still drawn from Palestinians from elsewhere.

The apparatuses and the country organisations each have their own budget and organisational structure, with their lines of control meeting only at the level of the Central Committee. This unique organisational structure was developed by the leadership primarily to ensure the survival of the movement in the face of repeated Arab efforts to infiltrate, split or otherwise undermine it; but it also enabled them to isolate any potential source of ideological ferment, thus keeping the ideological common denominator of the movement at the intentionally low and all-embracing level with which it was founded. As one knowledgeable Palestinian Fateh-watcher explained the resulting situation:

If a Fateh member has a dissident view, then he can disseminate it only in his own apparatus or his own region. Therefore if someone says, 'I represent such and such a current inside Fateh', then in fact he represents it only inside a given apparatus, inside a given region. The leadership can generally co-exist with this, and is not threatened at all by such an expression of views...

Inside any given apparatus, you may find people whose individual beliefs are communist and far rightist working side by side; but they can work together on the

26

common task of the apparatus without creating an ideological storm. Or you may find two people of the same view working together inside the same apparatus, but they are still unable to organise any effective faction from there.[13]

Fateh's organisational and ideological code thus proved extremely durable in the decades following the movement's foundation. But all this was still in the future as Khalil Wazir quietly left his teaching post in Kuwait in 1959 to go to Beirut to start editing *Filastinuna*. Auguring his emergence nine years later as the 'official spokesman' of Fateh, Yasser Arafat put his initials to an article in the journal's first issue, which decried the degradation of life in the Palestinian refugee camps.

Filastinuna continued to come out, at roughly six-week intervals, throughout the next five years. Around it, the secret organisation of Fateh gradually took shape in the refugee camps and Palestinian exile communities throughout the Arab world. Because of the continuity of Fateh's leadership over the next quarter-century, it is interesting to go back and see something of what, back in the early 60s, even before they launched their 'armed struggle', they were aiming for. Given that few copies of the secretly distributed magazine remain in existence in the early 80s, the following account of what *Filastinuna* was saying is taken from a book written in 1964 by the Palestinian writer Naji 'Alush.[14]

According to 'Alush, the writers of *Filastinuna* rejected the idea that what was needed to eliminate Israel was a 'lightning Arab war', for the following reasons:

1. Because the Arab armies are not united and not even mutually supportive, and thus it is not possible for the Arab Republic, for example, to wage a war on its own.
2. The situation of the West Bank is not militarily secure.
3. The Israeli army is on constant alert, and thus we must take this into careful account; and this implies our inability to impose anything on Israel in the way of a lightning war because we would confront the forces of the Israeli militia in every village alongside the Israeli army.
4. Any delay in achieving victory from an attack, beyond a few hours, would expose us to two principal problems: (a) the intervention of the United Nations ... (b) the breaking of the Arabs' power... [15]

'Alush wrote that what *Filastinuna* advocated instead was 'the eruption of a complete guerrilla movement from all the Arab lands'. It based its reasoning on the following points:

1. The building of different groups in each Arab country makes these groups independent of each given Arab front, and no Arab country can find in them any reason to suppress them on the charge that their work is inspired by another Arab country.
2. There are many non-Palestinian Arabs, civilians and military, completely ready

to help any liberation movement created to save Palestine, so long as this movement is far from the atmosphere of inter-Arab wrangling.

3. Israel will have no right, under international law, to take any action against any Arab state, because a revolutionary movement like this would not have at the outset a unified leadership, but would consist of Palestinian groups returning by force to their country to recover their internationally recognised right, which is the right to return.

4. If these groups succeeded in establishing their presence, then they must of necessity unify spontaneously and bring about a genuine Palestinian entity stemming from Palestine, and not an empty political entity imposed from outside – even by the Arab states.

5. And after unity of effort has been achieved, then [this entity] could ask for help openly from Arab and non-Arab countries, and can announce the Free Government of Palestine as existing in action and not just in name, and as fighting for the return of Palestine truly, and through force rather than through words, as is the case now with the groups which seek to impose their tutelage on the Palestinian cause.[16]

Already, by the time this article was written for *Filastinuna* in early 1962, the idea of creating a political 'Palestinian entity' was one which had been discussed for some time, having been since 1959 a pet project of the Iraqi leader Abdel-Karim Qasem. Pan-Arabist ideologues at first firmly opposed such an entity as further solidifying the division of the greater Arab homeland into separate Arab states, a division they were seeking to eradicate. Fateh's concept of a 'Palestinian entity' was, as the quotation above shows, that it should be built in the first instance by the Palestinians themselves, and from the grass-roots upwards; but the 'Palestinian entity' which eventually came into being in 1964 was very different from this conception.

In January 1964, Egypt's President Nasser pulled off something of a diplomatic coup in the Arab arena by gathering 13 Arab kings, emirs and presidents together in Cairo for what was described as the First Arab Summit.[17] The major reason for the gathering – of which the importance can be gauged from the fact that it brought to Cairo even the Saudi monarch, who was waging a bitter war against Egyptian troops in North Yemen at the time – was to discuss Israel's plans for the diversion of much of that valuable Middle Eastern commodity, water, from the Sea of Galilee along an aqueduct to the Negev desert: the Arabs feared Israel could then settle substantial numbers of new Jewish immigrants there, to strengthen their hold on the former lands of Palestine. But the Israelis succeeded in their water-diversion project soon after the summit; the summit decision which therefore proved to have the most lasting effect was that referred to in the official report in the following cryptic terms: 'The necessary practical decisions were taken ... in the field of organising the Palestinian people and enabling them to play their role in the liberation of their country and their self-determination.'[18]

Previous gatherings of Arab officials since 1949 referring to the Palestine problem had called only for 'application of the United Nations resolutions' on the issue; the new tougher formulation of 'the liberation of Palestine', as used above, was therefore not an insignificant departure for the heads of state; and it was on the wings of this new slogan that the new organisation was launched: the Palestinian Liberation Organisation. Veteran Palestinian diplomatist Ahmed Shuqairy, an extravagant orator who had served long years in the foreign services of Syria, Saudi Arabia and the Arab League, was entrusted with putting some flesh on the summit's bare bones of an idea.

Whether the kings, emirs and presidents also intended Shuqairy to breathe life into their new creation was, for many Palestinians at the time, a highly questionable proposition. As Shuqairy busied himself travelling around the Palestinian diaspora to drum up support for the PLO's founding conference, scheduled for May 1964, storms of criticism swirled around his efforts. Particularly vocal in its criticism was the Arab Higher Committee for Palestine (AHC), still led by the venerable Hajj Amin al-Husseini, now living in Beirut. Whatever the reasons for the AHC's hostility – and these may have included continuing contacts between Hajj Amin and his distant younger cousin, Yasser Arafat – soon after the conclusion of the First Arab Summit his Committee was putting out public statements highly critical of Shuqairy's planned organisation.[19]

The opinions of the various pan-Arabist groups about the new entity varied. Most still remained opposed to any hint of Palestinian separatism from the greater Arab cause; but since the PLO's foundation had been supported by a consensus of Arab states, including those officially dedicated to the cause of pan-Arabism (primarily Egypt), there were many reservations in these groups about opposing it outright. On 15 March 1964, a joint communiqué in the names of the Arab Nationalists' Movement (ANM), the Palestinian Liberation Front (Road of Return) and the Palestinian Arab Youth in Lebanon charted out these groups' shared expectations from the embryo entity: they said it should be 'revolutionary', should conscript Palestinians from all Arab countries into the liberation struggle, and should embody elements of democratic practice.[20] Since the ANM, founded by Palestinian physicians George Habash and Wadi Haddad, was one of the most influential proponents of pan-Arabism at that time, its support for the new organisation was seen as important.

The attitude of the group of underground organisers known as Fateh to the First Arab Summit's conception of a Palestinian organisation was more critical than this. According to Khaled al-Hassan, in early 1964 the Fateh leadership still saw a long task of organising in front of it before it could start the armed struggle to which it was dedicated, but

When the PLO was established even those few who were with us, especially the military individuals, they wanted to leave us, saying, 'Well we have the Palestinian Liberation Army; we should join the Army. And now there is the PLO recognised by all the Arab countries, so why not help and support this PLO? Why have something new?[21]

According to Khalaf, he and Yasser Arafat had known Shuqairy since their student days in Cairo back in 1952: Khalaf had been under arrest in Cairo in November of that year after being involved in a student protest, but 'was released thirty-five days later on the personal intervention of Ahmed al-Shukeiry of the Arab League'.[22] Before the PLO's founding Conference, therefore, the Fateh group agreed, despite their reservations about the proposed 'entity', to try to co-ordinate with its appointed leader. According to Khaled al-Hassan, he and Zuhair al-Alami travelled to Cairo to meet Shuqairy, and further discussions were held in Kuwait:

We made so many agreements! But he (Shuqairy) was not able to fulfil any of these because he was so strongly attached to Nasser.

The idea was that he would represent the international political organisation; we would be the military arm – the real functioning military arm, because the PLA was attached to the Arab governments at that time. And then behind the scenes there would be a joint leadership, a secret one, which controls the military and the political activities. [23]

Despite Shuqairy's failure to deliver on these agreements, the Fateh group was anyway able to have around a dozen of its members attend the PLO's founding Conference in May 1964 as delegates. According to Hassan, who was one of these, they were successful in securing a vote for many of the resolutions they sponsored there.[24]

That Conference convened in East Jerusaem, which was still then under Jordanian rule. It brought together 422 members of the Palestinian diaspora, with the basic task of endorsing two documents presented to it by Shuqairy. The first was the Palestinian National Charter, issued on 28 May: its 29 clauses, amended only once since then, in 1968, subsequently became the subject of hot controversy in Western countries.[25] The second document adopted was the Basic Constitution of the PLO, which was thereby, with due attention to pomp and ceremony and messages of support from various Arab leaders, declared inaugurated.

Almost immediately, the organisation was plunged into internal controversy. On 2 July 1964, Shuqairy put out a statement in the Jordanian capital, Amman, claiming *inter alia* that the whole territory of the existing Kingdom of Jordan, including that part lying east of the Jordan river, was part of Palestine.[26] This statement not only offended Shuqairy's Jordanian hosts, but one of the members of his own Executive Committee in the PLO, Dr Fayez Sayegh, also publicly questioned Shuqairy's right to make such statements in the name of the PLO without prior discussion in the Committee.[27]

Shuqairy's altercation with Sayegh was just the first of many disputes which split the leadership of the PLO throughout the next three years. Coming on top of the constraints imposed on PLO activities by those states whose creation the Organisation was, these disputes rendered Shuqairy's Organisation almost completely ineffective. Its major achievement in the period leading up to the 1967 Middle East war was its organisation of some units of the Palestinians' first regular army formations, the Palestinian Liberation Army. PLA units were not allowed to deploy in Jordan, the Arab country with the longest common frontier with Israel; but Palestinian activists later expressed satisfaction that the PLA's presence in Gaza had enabled Palestinian units to contribute to the defence of that sector during the 1967 war – hopeless task though that proved to be against the Israeli onslaught – and the training and infrastructure provided by the PLA proved useful assets for the guerrilla movements when later they took over the PLO apparatus.

For his part, Shuqairy was remembered in later years, even by many Palestinians, as 'the man who gave the Palestinians a bad name by threatening to throw the Jews into the sea'. He himself always strongly denied that that that was, in fact, what he had said on the eve of the 1967 war.[28] But in many ways, the most significant thing is that that is the way he was remembered in his own constituency.

Anyway, back in 1964, the results of the PLO's founding Conference were not received very well by any of the other Palestinian activist groups existing at the time. Hajj Amin's AHC, in a statement dated 10 June 1964, lambasted it as 'a colonialist, Zionist conspiracy aiming at the liquidation of the Palestinian cause'.[29] The Arab Nationalists' Movement distributed a rather bitter little statement calling the newborn PLO 'an organisation which has no relations with the masses'.[30] As for Fateh, following the failure of its leaders' attempt to co-opt Shuqairy into their own schemes, their main preoccupation was now elsewhere, in their continuing preparations for the launching of Fateh's own long-promised armed struggle.

These preparations had been going ahead at least since December 1962, when a heavyweight delegation of Fateh leaders including Arafat, Wazir and Farouq Qaddumi had travelled to Algiers at the invitation of President Ahmed Ben Bella, hero of the newly victorious FLN.[31] But the Algerian President did not want to act openly against the wishes of his more important ally, Egypt's President Nasser, who still feared that any con-

31

certed guerrilla action against Israel would provoke retaliations extremely damaging for Egypt and the other Arab states; so the amount of concrete military aid Ben Bella granted Fateh was severely limited. As Khalaf recalls, 'It was only when Houari Boumedienne came to power in 1965 that Algeria sent us a first arms shipment.'[32] But the Algerians did provide the opportunity for Fateh's first direct contacts in another important direction – with the People's Republic of China, and with North Korea and the Vietcong. Wazir, who had stayed behind in Algiers from the 1962 Fateh delegation to manage the group's new office there, was able to include himself in an official Algerian delegation to Beijing in early 1964: once there, he introduced himself and his groups' ideas to his hosts, and was drawn aside for long discussions with Chinese leaders. Thus was inaugurated Fateh's long relationship with the People's Republic of China.[33]

More important than Algeria, in terms of the concrete contribution made to Fateh's military preparations in the early 60s, was the role played by the regime in Syria at the time. As Khalaf recalled it, two men in Syria's military hierarchy were particularly helpful to the would-be guerrillas: they were air force commander Hafez al-Asad (who was to take over the reins of state power in a military coup in 1970), and the director of military intelligence, Ahmed al-Sweidani. Khalaf wrote, 'It was because of them that we were able to use two training camps in Syria as of early 1964. Other fedayeen [guerrillas] underwent shooting exercises in desert regions, sometimes among the bedouins. Still others, without revealing their membership in Fatah, received training by enlisting in the Palestine Liberation Army.'[34]

For Sweidani, the tactics propounded by the Palestinian group accorded closely with the theory of 'popular liberation war' he had himself worked out for his own country's confrontation with Israel.[35] Syrian officials might also have seen some value in sponsoring Fateh back in 1964 as a counterweight in the Palestinian arena to the influence of the PLO, which they saw as closely associated with the Egyptian regime. For many Fateh thinkers, the alliance with Syria was seen then, and continued to be seen for some years, as an important strategic principle: they considered both Lebanon and Jordan as dangerously exposed to Israeli influence both direct and indirect.[36] Syria, located strategically between these two states but still in direct contact with Israel, was thus seen as providing a pivotal rearguard base.

Finally, Fateh's new military apparatus was ready for action. Or was it? In early autumn 1964, spurred on partly by the PLO's own decision to establish a military wing, the Fateh leadership met in Kuwait. The group was split down the middle on whether the time was ripe to launch military operations. A further, expanded meeting was scheduled for that November, at which the decision was taken by a single vote to go ahead. The date for Fateh's first commando action against Israel was set for 31 December 1964; but in deference to the overruled minority in the leadership which had counselled caution, it was launched not in Fateh's own name, but in that of a fictitious front-organisation, Al-Asifa (The Storm).

'To our great people ... to our struggling Arab nation ... to liberators everywhere,' started Asifa's Communiqué No. 1, issued on 1 January 1965:

From our people, steadfast to the limit, and from the conscience of our battling homeland, our revolutionary vanguards burst out, believing in the armed revolution as the way to Return and to Liberty, in order to stress to the colonialists and their henchmen, and to world Zionism and its financers, that the Palestinian people remains in the field; that it has not died and will not die.[37]

In fact, that first Fateh/Asifa operation appears to have been less successful than claimed. The group of commandos which was due to set out for Israel from Gaza was arrested in its entirety one week before the launch-date, though Fateh leaders claimed that other groups acted successfully from the West Bank area and from Lebanon. Salah Khalaf later claimed that it was the second Asifa operation which was more important than the first, since it directly attacked Israel's controversial water-diversion projects.[38] It was during the latter operation that two events of significance for the group took place: one guerrilla, Ahmed Musa, was shot dead by Jordanian troops as he returned to Jordan from Israel after his mission; and another, Mahmoud Hijazi, was taken prisoner by the Israelis.

By the early 80s, most Fateh leaders were easily prepared to admit that their start in the field of guerrilla action had indeed been modest. Nevertheless, they still saw it as meaningful. In 1982, Khaled al-Hassan explained that between the start of the armed struggle and the 1967 war, Fateh had been hoping to achieve its goal of liberating Palestine

through action and reaction, action and reaction. We will make actions, the Israelis will make reactions. Now the [Arab] governments either will support us against the Israelis, or will fight us. If they fight us, the people will support us. When the people will support us the governments either will support us or they will confront us with their own people...

We wanted to create a climate and the atmosphere of the spirit of struggle in the Arab nation, so that they can have the will of fighting, and I'm sorry to say that we failed.[39]

Throughout 1965, Asifa's military communiqués continued to log up successive guerrilla actions – a total of 39 of them up to the end of the year. But well before that, the Fateh leaders felt confident enough of the success of their venture to associate Fateh's name openly with that of Asifa, which name was subsequently retained as that of the Fateh military apparatus. On 17 June 1965, Fateh addressed an open memorandum, in its own name, to the Secretary-General of the United Nations, U Thant, asking that the prisoner, Mahmoud Hijazi, be considered a prisoner-of-war. In the memorandum, they explained that 'The Asifa forces belonging to the movement [Fateh], in their role as the armed forces of the Palestinian people, began their military operations inside the occupied lands of Palestine.'[40]

Three months later, Fateh was sending an angry memorandum to the Third Arab Summit meeting in Casablanca, Morocco. It complained bitterly about Arab actions against the guerrillas, and added:

In answer to all these [hostile measures], the movement sees a number of steps necessary, among them: calling off the pursuit of the liberation movement by various Arab states bordering and not bordering on Palestine; the release of all prisoners without questioning; lifting the news blackout imposed on the publication of news about the liberation movement in many Arab countries; not opposing the movement's men during the performance of their revolutionary work or when the movement's forces in the occupied territories are forced to take refuge in neighbouring Arab countries; and that the Arab countries should work for the defence of the movement's prisoners in Israel through various well-known means.[41]

By the end of 1965, then, Fateh had already laid down the basis of its activities for the years to come. It had proved itself able to sustain a constant level of guerrilla operations against Israel; and while these certainly did not threaten to bring the Jewish state to its knees overnight, they were a constant irritant to it, whilst acting as a powerful rallying-point for Fateh in the Palestinian communities of the diaspora as well as a potential, and uncontrollable, source of instability for several Arab regimes. Fateh had also already addressed its first appeal to the United Nations, in faint augury of Arafat's triumphant (if not yet triumphing) appearance before the General Assembly nine years later. It had gone to great lengths to make its point of view known to the Palestinian and Arab publics. And in relation to the official Arab state system, it had laid out clearly the terms on which it sought co-operation from the states.

Thus was the picture which was, by and large, to continue up until June 1967 already clearly drawn by the end of 1965. In the intervening months, Shuqairy's PLO suffered continued rifts and schisms, and a few other groups of Palestinian activists tried to follow Fateh's lead onto the battlefield with Israel, but with far less well-sustained success. Fateh meanwhile, with its continuing obsession with secrecy, continued growing only slowly.

Throughout those months of 1966 and the first half of 1967, the pressure was relentlessly building up between the Arab states and Israel. The Syrian-Israeli border was dept turbulent by Israeli attempts to establish *de facto* control of the 1949-ordained demilitarised zone there, and by Syria's sponsorship of intermittent guerrilla raids against Israel — some but by no means all of which were undertaken by Fateh. In their turn, the Israelis retaliated for these with a series of punishing raids against Arab targets in the Jordanian-held West Bank; these prompted clamorous demands from the West Bankers on King Hussein for arms to defend themselves. All of which seemed to point to pressure towards an imminent outbreak of hostilities at least along these two fronts: and one cause, but by no means the only or even the major cause, of this pressure was Fateh's military activities.[42]

The 1967 Arab-Israeli war, when it came, was every bit as devastating for the Arab states as the *Filastinuna* article had predicted, five years previously, would be the case in any encounter between the regular Arab armies and Israel.

But it was in the collapse of the previously existing system of inter-state relations in the Arab world, its checks, balances and interrelated ideologies, that Fateh's most explosively dynamic chance for growth arose, the chance that was to catapult Fateh into the leadership of the PLO.

The joy of flying (1967-73)

Within six days, in June 1967, the Israeli army devastated the armies of Egypt, Syria and Jordan. It had scaled Syria's Golan Heights, whence it threatened to coast along the gentle plains to Damascus; it occupied Gaza and the whole of Sinai and was able to launch offensive strikes deep into the heart of Egypt; it had conquered East Jerusalem and invested the whole of the West Bank with relative ease. All Fateh's earliest fears about the probable course of a regular-army confrontation with Israel were realised, to the profound shock of the whole of the Arab world.

In Egypt, President Nasser, who had for so long and from a position of such apparent authority counselled the Palestinians against precipitate action against Israel, was himself forced to appear, humiliated, before his own people to offer his resignation. Though the Egyptians clamorously refused to allow him to step down, he had to spend long months and years following June 1967 in patiently patching back together Egypt's military hierarchy, its defences and its popular consensus; he was in no position then to dictate tactics or strategy to anyone else, especially the Palestinians. Similarly in Jordan, whose king was now blamed for 'losing the rest of Palestine [i.e. East Jerusalem and the West Bank] to the Zionists'; and to a lesser extent in Syria, whose government had been allowing the Palestinian guerrillas a far freer hand than they enjoyed in Egypt or Jordan, even before the Six-Day War: in all these countries, the military defeat at the hands of Israel had sent their governments' negotiating power *vis-à-vis* the guerrillas plummeting to near zero.

The Fateh leaders, according to some accounts, had not imagined another Middle East war would happen so soon: they had foreseen a gradual build-up of tensions to a war some half-dozen years later. Nevertheless, from the first hours of the 1967 war, they had sought to use to their own advantage whatever developments it might bring. According to Khalaf, Fateh leaders who had hastened to Damascus at the outbreak of the war held a vital conference there on 12 June – even before the eventual cease-fire lines between the opposing armies had been finally stabilised.[1] The debate was long and comprehensive, revolving around the central issue of whether now was the time to launch the next stage of the Palestinians' popular war of liberation, this time inside the newly occupied parts of Palestine. Apparently many of the leadership had reservations, so a two-pronged approach was decided on: Fateh would seek to expand both its military activities against Israel and its political efforts relating to the Arab governments. While Khalaf, Wazir and some other Fateh leaders spent the next two months making dramatically successful tours of Arab countries, amassing political and financial support from governments and people alike, Arafat and a group of other native Jerusalemites and West Bankers slipped back into the occupied territories during July to sound out the possibilities for launching an armed popular uprising there.[2]

On 20 August, the leadership, including Arafat, who rushed over from the occupied territories, convened again to take the final decision: largely on the basis of Arafat's highly enthusiastic reports, it was agreed that guerrilla activities should resume there as from the end of August.

For the next five months, nearly all Fateh's efforts were directed towards this end. They did not have much of an existing organisational base to start from in either the West Bank or Gaza: the activities of the Jordanian intelligence services in the former, and of the Egyptian in the latter, had considerably limited their activities in those districts in the period leading up to the war. (For more details of the development of the resistance movement in the West Bank and Gaza see chapter 8 below.) In the West Bank, the Israelis had been able to take over, virtually intact, the entire political files of the Jordanian intelligence service, along with at least one of the officers in charge who was able to interpret the information in the files in full to Jerusalem's new rulers.[3] But still, access to the West Bank along the many trails fording the River Jordan was considerably easier for the guerrillas in late 1967 than gaining access across the desert sands to Gaza, although the social conditions in Gaza with its high, and highly-concentrated, refugee population were probably riper for the kind of action Fateh planned than were conditions in the West Bank.

Arafat set up his headquarters in the Old Quarter of Nablus, a West Bank town with a long history of Arab nationalist fervour. From Nablus, he travelled in various disguises throughout the West Bank, and even inside the 'Green Line' dividing 1948 Israel from the newly occupied areas. (He was later to recall with some emotion the feelings he experienced one day in early autumn 1967 when he passed by his own childhood home in Jerusalem: his brother, whom he had not seen for many years, was at the door; but the disguised guerrilla organiser could not take the chance of greeting or being recognised by him.)[4] Fateh's aim was to establish guerrilla networks throughout the West Bank: many of their guerrilla operatives were 'infiltrated' into the area across the River Jordan; these included veterans of Fateh's previous two and a half years of guerrilla actions against Israel, along with a growing stream of hastily trained new volunteers. The guerrilla commanders in the various West Bank regions meanwhile also tried to prepare the local population to participate in the popular war, both through organising passive resistance to Israeli military rule and by giving rudimentary military training to recruits from local villages. According to Israeli journalist Ehud Yaari, 'Arafat hoped that the two courses of action – *Fatah*'s terrorism and local rebellion – would finally merge into one movement – a popular armed revolution, led by Arafat and his colleagues.'[5]

The reaction of the Israeli military government in the West Bank was tough. It demolished the houses of suspected guerrilla sympathisers, imposed rigid and economically debilitating curfews on villages accused of harbouring guerrillas, and rounded up network after network of suspected guerrilla activists into Israeli jails – more than 1,000 of them detained without trial before the end of 1967. Once the guerrillas had been hunted out of the villages, the army began making systematic searches of all caves and other hideouts in the region to discover their traces. Finally, by the end of 1967 or the beginning of 1968, Arafat and his remaining commanders had to accept that their plan had failed. According to Yaari again,

[Arafat] transferred his quarters from Nablus to Ramallah to a one-story villa of a supporter. One night in the fall, the Israeli Security Forces encircled the villa and broke into it. They found a warm bed and boiling tea, but Arafat was not there... After the investigators departed, Arafat turned east and crossed the Jordan River for the last time. He left behind him about 1,000 captured terrorists and 200 dead.[6]

What had gone wrong? In retrospect, it seems easy to say that Arafat's idea of embarking on the popular liberation war in the West Bank in 1967 was premature, that the necessary preparations for this arduous task had not been made before he started. In the period preceding the war, Fateh had not succeeded in building strong networks in those parts of Mandate Palestine which remained under Arab control after 1948 – its ideological base and organisational impetus were still directed towards the Palestinians in exile rather than towards those Palestinians who still, in the West Bank and Gaza, remained in their own homes – though in both these areas there was also a large refugee population. It is probably also true to say that in the wake of the 1967 war the established community leaderships in the West Bank, which had been linked to the Jordanian regime for nearly 20 years and continued to receive funding from Amman even after 1967, were still expecting a political settlement between Jordan and Israel to bring an end to the 1967 occupation in the same way Israel's occupation of Gaza and Sinai 11 years before had in its time been ended. These notables therefore wanted nothing as untoward as guerrilla activity to damage the prospects of such a settlement, and in some cases collaborated with the Israelis in rooting out the destabilising elements they still considered to be outsiders.

But the prospects for a political settlement gradually dwindled to near zero as the months of Israel's occupation of the West Bank grew into years, and increasing numbers of the early Israeli 'military outposts' in the occupied region grew into fully fledged civilian colonies. When the West Bankers' own indigenous resistance movement started gaining a strong hold on the population in the early 70s, the example of the 'heroic failures' of late 1967 provided an added bond for many West Bankers with the men who had taken part in them.[7]

Regarding the situation outside the occupied territories, in the despair which permeated the whole Arab world in late 1967 it appeared to many Arabs that the one group trying to do anything at all, with whatever hopes of success, to avenge the June disaster, were the guerrilla activists attacking Israeli targets inside the West Bank and from southern Lebanon. Thus, in early 1968, although Fateh and the other smaller guerrilla groups now had to move their operational bases back to the East (Jordanian-controlled) Bank of the River Jordan and to south Lebanon, with the hope of being able to mount continuing hit-and-run raids against the Israelis from there, nonetheless they continued to attract floods of volunteers from Palestinian and non-Palestinian communities throughout the Arab world.

Who were these volunteers? Certainly, for the most part they were Palestinians, though an Egyptian magazine reported in May 1968 that 12,000 Egyptian youths had contacted the newly opened Fateh office in Cairo to volunteer for guerrilla service,[8] and a similar phenomenon occurred in most other Arab countries. Of the Palestinians who volunteered, the vast majority of those who made their way into Fateh were residents of the refugee camps which still, nearly 20 years after the establishment of the State of Israel, formed a ring of human misery around the Jewish state's borders.

Members of the camp populations had left their homes and farms in the parts of Palestine overrun by the Jewish forces in 1948-49, amidst the collapse of the Arab states' war effort there, hoping for a speedy return. Some Israeli spokesmen have claimed that it was the Arab armies themselves which called on the Palestinians to leave; but a growing and persuasive body of evidence has built up over the years, not least of which is that provided by the detailed stories of both the Jewish/Israeli fighters and the refugees themselves, which points to the Jewish forces having followed a deliberate policy of inciting and terrorising the Palestinians into leaving.[9] Their empty houses were subsequently either used to house the waves of new Jewish immigrants brought into the infant State of Israel or else razed.[10] Festering in their refugee camps throughout the following decades, the refugees stubbornly resisted successive attempts to resettle them somewhere outside their own country on a permanent basis. Consciously or unconsciously blocking out any idea that the village environments they had left behind might have changed significantly, they clung persistently to the single powerful idea of the Return.[11] It was this idea which was the central motive force of Fateh.

Rosemary Sayigh, a former journalist who subsequently studied sociology, has powerfully used the techniques of both professions to chart the fate of those former Palestinian peasant communities which underwent a violent exodus from their villages, followed by two decades of exile in communities which often proved extremely hostile, and which subsequently rallied around the guerrilla movement with practically unbroken unanimity after the 1967 war. She wrote, 'If middle class Palestinians have greater faith in pan-Arabism than working class Palestinians, it is because their experiences in the *ghourba* [the Palestinian diaspora] have been radically different.'[12] Thus, while Palestinian professionals, entrepreneurs and intellectuals were well able to carve out for themselves a new life in the booming economies of the Gulf or elsewhere, and were thus naturally attracted to the forefront of those groups which argued for Arab unity, for the masses of former Palestinian villagers now trapped in the refugee camps – even members of the generation which grew up after the 1948-49 exodus – the sole most important goal always remained Palestine. The camp populations thus became the staunch mainstay of support for the 'Palestine-firsters' of Fateh.[13]

The following brief verbatim testimony, from a Palestinian born three years after the exodus to a refugee family living in northern Lebanon, might go some way to explain why even members of the generation which had never known Palestine flocked to the guerrilla movements in their scores of thousands:

First of all, we live in a very bad situation – in a bare alley between bare walls, you know, and there was nothing else. After, we live near the seashore, there is a land for one woman named Karima Bayasan...And we built two rooms from stones and muds. And after, the owner of the land, she asked for the land. So where? So we refused, and after the bulldozers of the Lebanese authorities came and destroyed the houses of the Palestinians on the seashore, and they gave us tents. I was seven years old. They put us in trucks, and gave us one tent for the family.

At that time some of my brothers wasn't born: we were about nine. So they gave us a tent, and we live in the Bedawi camp. After nine months of the tent, and we were in very bad muds, between muds we lived there! We make a strike, and we enter the schools because it was raining, and what you want with tents? And after, we force the United Nations to build us houses from stones, and still we live in Bedawi camp.[14]

This young man, and the majority of members of his generation from the camp populations, hurried to the mushrooming new training bases Fateh and the other guerrilla groups were able to open once the Arab governments had been forced to lift their restrictions on such activities. By 1970, the guerrillas had trained a total of between 30,000 and 50,000 fighters in Jordan, according to some sources.[15]

By the end of 1967, even those pan-Arabist groups which had hitherto been most strongly opposed to separatist Palestinian ambitions were forced to field their own Palestinian guerrilla groups or lose credibility completely. On 11 December 1967, the Arab Nationalist Movement's weekly *Al-Hurriya* informed readers that the Palestinian branch of the Movement was joining forces with three small existing guerrilla groups to form a new organisation to be called 'the Popular Front for the Liberation of Palestine'. 'Armed resistance,' the statement said, in stark contrast to what the ANM had been arguing shortly before, 'is the one way in which our land can become the major field of battle for the long-drawn-out struggle against the occupations.'[16]

There were recruits aplenty for all the existing groups, and several new ones, to fill the training camps they had hastily organised in Jordan and Syria to more than capacity. But Fateh, with its solid and continuing logistical backing from the Algerians, the Chinese and the Syrians; with its relatively longer experience of sustaining guerrilla activities against the Israelis; and, most important, with its honed and relatively homogeneous command structure which had changed little since the organisation's formal founding nearly a decade before – with all these advantages, Fateh was in a much better position than any of the other hastily cobbled-together guerrilla formations to withstand the strains caused by the guerrilla movements' explosive growth of the late 60s.

Fateh's greatest moment of glory in the months after June 1967, following the smothering of its brief flame of revolt in the West Bank, came on 21 March 1968. Having chased the guerrillas out of the West Bank at the end of 1967, the Israelis were now increasingly making lightning raids against guerrilla positions on the East Bank, inside Jordan proper. Towards the middle of that month, the Jordanian intelligence had passed on to Fateh leaders some information they said they had received from the American CIA.[17] Israel, the Jordanians said, was preparing for a major attack against Karameh, a village about four miles east of the River Jordan where much of Fateh's command network had been established. The Jordanian chief of staff reportedly advised the guerrillas to evacuate the area; but, according to Khalaf, Fateh's reply was, 'The Palestinians, and more generally the

41

Arabs, would never understand if once again we left the field open to the Israelis. Our duty was to set an example, to prove that the Arabs are capable of courage and dignity.'[18] At dawn on 21 March, the attack materialised as expected, with columns of Israeli armour rolling up from the Jordan Valley, supported by helicopters and infantry – a total number of troops estimated at 15,000.[19] The guerrillas had about 300 fighters defending the town, but because they were prepared for the invasion, and because they were able to call in the help of the Jordanian artillery stationed nearby, they were able to inflict relatively heavy losses on the invaders (between 20 and 30 killed, and many more wounded), though at high cost to themselves (about 120 killed).

Karameh is the Arabic word for 'honour'; and as news of Fateh's defence of Karameh was broadcast through the Arab news media, it did indeed seem to much of public opinion throughout the Arab world that the group had also defended *karameh* on behalf of them all. As Khalaf recalled it, 5,000 new recruits applied to join Fateh within the next 48 hours.

Over the two years which followed, the military power of the guerrilla movements grew hugely, primarily in Jordan but also in Lebanon. And while these guerrilla formations never posed any direct threat to Israel's vast and sophisticated military machine, they were nevertheless able to mount hit-and-run raids of increasing effectiveness against targets in the Israeli-held areas, inflicting a steady toll in fatalities and other losses on the Israelis. By May 1969, one British journalist in Israel was describing the guerrillas as 'a real and aggressive component in the Israeli nightmare'.[20]

Hand in hand with Fateh's military efforts after the June defeat went its efforts to gain political recognition in the Palestinian and inter-Arab arenas for the role of guerrilla action in general, and the role of Fateh in particular. On 9 December 1967, Fateh presented a memorandum to a conference of Arab Foreign Ministers then meeting in Cairo, expressing concern at the 'misleading statements' made by Shuqairy, and demanding the closure of Arab information media to him. Shortly thereafter, the newly formed PFLP joined with the General Union of Palestinian Students in demanding his resignation. On 14 December, seven members of Shuqairy's own Executive Committee also requested his resignation, 'because of the way you run the organisation'. Finally, on 24 December, Shuqairy resigned. Khaled al-Hassan recalled that Shuqairy had wanted to 'hand the PLO over to Fateh': Hassan himself had been in agreement with this proposal, but a majority of the other Fateh leaders had preferred to see the PLO as a comprehensive front for all Palestinian groupings – 'the Palestinian people in exile'.[21] Amidst all the political manoeuvrings going on in and around the PLO in those months, a former lawyer called Yahya Hammouda (who before 1948 had supported the Istiqlal Party and Hajj

Amin, and after that date had become active in the Jordanian Communist Party, as well as serving a spell in the Syrian army) took over as acting Chairman of the Organisation until the fundamental debates about the power balances within it could be resolved.

In January 1968, Fateh had convened a co-ordinating meeting of all commando groups, also in Cairo. The only group which failed to participate was the PFLP, which considered the PLO the sole framework for inter-group co-ordination. The groups represented at the January meeting then set up a co-ordinating body called the Permanent Bureau. The PLO hit back two months later by establishing its own guerrilla formation, the Popular Liberation Forces, as an offshoot of the PLA. Thus, when the Fourth PNC was finally convened in Cairo in July 1968, just four months after the Battle of Karameh, the principle of the primacy of guerrilla operations against Israel was agreed by all present. Of the 100 seats at the session, 38 went to the Permanent Bureau and 10 to the PFLP, and 20 were divided between the PLA and the Popular Liberation Forces, with the remainder going to previously serving PNC members.[22]

The Fourth PNC was able to amend the Palestinian National Charter to reflect the new emphases. A total of seven new articles were inserted into the Charter. One of these, Article 9, asserted that

Armed struggle is the only way to liberate Palestine. Thus it is the overall strategy, not merely a tactical phase. The Palestinian Arab people assert their absolute determination and firm resolution to continue their armed struggle and to work for an armed popular revolution for the liberation of their country and their return to it. They also assert their right to normal life in Palestine and to exercise their right to self-determination and sovereignty over it.[23]

Another addition, Article 21, stated, 'The Arab Palestinian people, expressing themselves by the armed Palestinian revolution, reject all solutions which are substitutes for the total liberation of Palestine.' A further significant amendment pointed out, perhaps especially to the pan-Arabists, 'The Palestinian Arab people assert the genuineness and independence of their national revolution and reject all forms of intervention, trusteeship and subordination' (Article 28).

Article 6, which was to become a major focus of interest for the Israelis in coming years, was changed from saying, 'Jews of Palestinian origin are considered Palestinians, providing they are willing to commit themselves to live in order and peace in Palestine', in the original 1964 version, to considering simply, 'The Jews who had normally resided in Palestine until the beginning of the Zionist invasion will be considered Palestinians', without any further conditions. The 1968 text of the National Charter remained unchanged until early 1983, with little prospect that it would imminently be amended to accommodate Israeli or American desires. The Charter stipulates in its own text, 'This Charter shall not be amended save by a majority of two-thirds of the total membership of the National Council of the Palestine Liberation Organisation at a special session convened for that purpose.'

The Fourth PNC was also able to circumscribe the powers of the Chairman of the Executive, which it was felt Shuqairy had abused too freely, and to broaden the powers of the PNC itself.[24] But it was unable finally to resolve the power struggles still raging within its ranks: between the remnants of the PLO old guard and the groups represented in the Permanent Bureau; and between the latter groups and the PFLP. The previous Executive Committee was thus returned to power with the addition of only one new face, Dr Youssef Sayegh, who took over the Planning Department.

The continued growth of the guerrilla organisations, however, soon imposed its own logic on the PLO superstructure. Fateh, the pro-Syrian Saiqa commando group (which had been founded in late 1966) and the PLO established a Military Co-ordination Council in Amman in October 1968; and at the Fifth PNC, convened in Cairo the following February, the guerrilla groups were allotted 57 seats among them, out of the total of 105. Although the PFLP and the PLA both boycotted the session in protest at their share of the seats, it was practically a foregone conclusion that Fateh, with 33 formally allotted seats and many sympathisers in the 'independent' delegations, would be able to impose choice for Chairman on the Organisation. They did: he was the stocky, balding guerrilla organiser, Yasser Arafat. Fateh's Khaled al-Hassan, Farouq Qaddumi and Muhammed Youssef al-Najjar were also elected to the 15-man PLO Executive Committee, where Hassan headed its Political Department ('Foreign Ministry').[25]

The PFLP and some other guerrilla groups did not enter fully into PLO activities until the Seventh PNC in May/June 1970; and a back-room mutiny simmered on in the upper ranks of the PLA until that same year, with some PLA commanders protesting the Executive Committee Chairman's new designation of Commander-in-Chief. But the Fifth PNC had firmly placed Fateh in the control seat in the PLO, which it occupied for the following 14 years. It is therefore instructive to be able to see precisely what the Fateh leaders, whose organisation had its own vibrant dynamic at that time regardless of the PLO, had had in mind when they first decided to 'enter' the PLO, an organisation which a few months previously they had held in such disdain. Here is the view of Salah Khalaf, as told to the Egyptian writer Lutfi Kholi in mid-1969:

It was possible to have a national front in which the PLO would be one of the

parties and not the entire frame of the national front, as its covenant provides...
Fateh would then enter the national front on a level of fundamental equality with
the organisation [i.e., the PLO]. This trend was not opposed by *Fateh*: on the
contrary, we were prepared to follow it to the end. However, there was another
view ... [according to which] the PLO represents for the first time *official Arab
commitment* to the Palestinian Arab people. To regard the PLO as a private force
would result in weakening the PLO itself and dissolving this commitment.[26]

In fact, Fateh was working in two separate directions, in the aftermath of
the June War, to win this vital factor of 'official Arab commitment' to its
version of the Palestinian cause. While pursuing their struggle for predominance in the PLO apparatus, which would enable them to co-opt for
themselves all the 'official Arab commitment' the PLO enjoyed by virtue of
its history and official status, the Fateh leaders had simultaneously been
making direct appeals to the Arab states to broaden the kind of official
support they had already enjoyed *as* Fateh for several years, from Syria and
Algeria.

According to Khalaf, at the very same time Arafat was first setting off to
test the mood in the West Bank in late summer 1967, other Fateh leaders
were despatched to make contact with various Arab heads of state and
government. 'King Feisal,' he wrote, 'who received Abu Jihad [Wazir] in
Geneva, was sympathetic to the cause. He had learned of Fatah's existence
in the early sixties from Zaki al-Yamani, the present oil minister, who was
on friendly terms with one of our militants.'[27] By early 1968, Khaled
al-Hassan had succeeded in persuading King Feisal to enforce the collection of a 'liberation tax' from Palestinians working in the Kingdom, which
thereafter brought between 50 and 60 million riyals a year to the Palestinian movement.[28] Qaddumi and Khalaf went to Libya, still a monarchy,
and left a few days later substantially enriched by contributions to Fateh
from the government and from private donors there. Qaddumi and Khaled
al-Hassan went to Egypt, where Nasser's old suspicions of them still
lingered. They were met only by the Foreign Minister, Mahmoud Riad,
and by Nasser's confidant/chronicler, Mohamed Hasanein Heikal, who
told them, 'We know very little about you... Our intelligence file on
al-Asifah is virtually empty. Your mystery intrigues us, and in the last
analysis your capacity for dissimulation is no doubt an indication of your
seriousness.'[29]

After the guerrillas' success in the Battle of Karameh, the Fateh leadership
thought the time had come to renew their contacts with the principal Arab
governments. Qaddumi and Khalaf returned to Cairo, where this time
Heikal took them to meet Nasser. The Egyptian President cross-
questioned the two Fateh men closely, to allay his previous fears that their
group was linked to his old opponents of the Muslim Brotherhood. Finally

satisfied, he promised to help Fateh with arms supplies and provision of training facilities. But he told them Egypt was in no position to help their finances and suggested they return to King Faisal for help in that field.

The newly forged Egyptian link provided a solid underpinning to much of the growth in Fateh's influence during these years. Once satisfied as to the genuineness of Fateh's intentions, Nasser gave them help in several key fields where their continuing friendship with Syria could not help them as much (and the Syrians, seeing Fateh diversify its sources of support in this way, put increasing emphasis into supporting their co-ideologists of the Palestinian Baathist guerrilla group, Al-Saiqa). Thus Nasser, who still played a continuing behind-the-scenes role in PLO affairs, actively encouraged Fateh's entry into the Organisation. And it was Nasser who first introduced Arafat to the Soviets.

Just as Wazir had first gone to Beijing in an Algerian delegation (whither Arafat afterwards followed him, in 1964 and in 1966), so in July 1968 Arafat travelled with Nasser to Moscow, using an Egyptian passport in the name of Muhsin Amin.[30] In Moscow, Nasser introduced Arafat to Foreign Minister Kosygin, Chairman Brezhnev and President Podgorny; Arafat then had lengthy discussions with Kyril Mazurov, a high-level Central Committee official responsible for relations with national liberation movements, and with two Red Army generals.[31] The relationship thus founded was to build up over the following years to the point where the PLO, with Arafat at its helm, was accorded embassy status for its permanent representative in Moscow in 1981.

The period following the 1967 Mideast war thus saw the majority of Arab government leaders moving towards an alliance with Fateh – an alliance which they doubtless hoped to exploit for all it was worth to shore up their own punctured political fortunes at home. But two Arab leaders were openly dismayed by the growth of the guerrillas' power: these were Jordan's King Hussein and Lebanon's President Charles Helou. Both these countries hosted large Palestinian exile communities, which formed in Lebanon's case about 12% of the total population, and in Jordan's well over one-half. In these communities, the activities of the guerrillas had sparked off a mounting wave of Palestinian nationalist sentiment which threatened to set the delicate power balance in each of these pro-Western countries swinging wildly. Both countries, moreover, shared long borders with Israel, thus providing attractive locations from which the Palestinians might hope to strike at the Jewish state; both countries, too, were nearly defenceless against the thrusting weight of Israeli retaliations.

In 1968 and 1969, the burgeoning power of the guerrillas started clashing openly with the state security forces in both these countries. In Jordan, provocations which were later discovered to have been the work of a palace-sponsored group called 'The Victory Battalions' (Kata'ib al-Nasr) led, on 4 November 1968, to Jordanian troops of the palace guard shelling the Palestinian refugee camps of Wahdat, Jebel Hussein and Schneller.[32] In Lebanon, the guerrillas' relations with the authorities already had a history of bitterness: Fateh commando Jalal Kaawash had been arrested by the Lebanese army back in December 1965, and a Defence Ministry communiqué later announced baldly that he had 'thrown himself out of a window during interrogation'. The following year, the Lebanese security forces laid their hands on no less a haul than Yasser Arafat. But apparently not knowing who he was, they released him three weeks later after the intervention of the Syrians.[33]

As the guerrilla movement gained popular and military power in Lebanon in the late 60s, it increasingly touched off a resonance of sympathetic action from Lebanese leftists and Muslims who, in addition to their ideological sympathy for the commandos, also had their own home-grown grievances against the institutionalised domination of their state apparatus by the country's Maronite Christian minority. The clashes which escalated between the commandos and the Lebanese authorities in 1968-69 thus brought the Lebanese body politic itself to a series of increasingly serious crises. Shortly after Israeli commandos blew up 13 Arab-owned planes at Beirut Airport (in retaliation for the hijack, in December 1968, of an Israeli El-Al plane to Algiers), the Sunni Muslim Premier, Abdullah Yafi, was moved to resign, plunging the country into a political crisis which continued, with only shallow intermissions, until the 1975-76 civil war. But with scores of thousands of Lebanese citizens repeatedly taking to the streets in support of the guerrillas throughout 1969, by October of that year the government and army were forced to come to terms with them. On 2 November 1969, after talks in Cairo between Arafat and the Lebanese army commander Emile Bustany, an agreement called 'the Cairo agreement' was reached between the two sides. Although the agreement's text was never officially published, an unofficial text appeared in the Lebanese daily *An-Nahar* on 20 April 1970, of which the accuracy has never been seriously contested by either side.[34] In effect, what the agreement achieved was to establish principles under which the guerrillas' presence and activities would be tolerated by the Lebanese authorities, but also regulated by them.

For the 300,000 Palestinian civilians in Lebanon, the Cairo agreement brought a significant bonus: the areas of the 16 officially designated UNRWA refugee camps in the country were freed from the heavy hand of the Lebanese army's Deuxième Bureau, which for the past two decades had exercised a rigid control over every tiny detail of day-to-day life in the camps. Everyday camp security was now handed over to the Palestinian

47

Armed Struggle Command, though still under overall Lebanese sovereignty. The refugee camps in Lebanon were thus able to become, in the years following 1969, a key popular base for the guerrilla movement.

In Jordan, no such accommodation between the government and the guerrillas was found possible. The King, after the euphoria of the post-Karameh days when he declared, 'We shall all be *fedayeen* [guerrillas] soon',[35] quickly reverted to his previous fears that guerrilla power in Jordan might undercut his own constituency; and to a certain extent, given Jordan's delicate demographic situation and paucity of historical *raison d'être*, such fears might have seemed justified. The explosive post-1967 growth of the guerrilla movement led to a multiplication of guerrilla groups as each and every political organisation in the Arab world (except for the staid traditionalists of the pro-Moscow Arab communist movements) sought to build up its own group, or grouplet, in the field. Fateh, though the largest and most powerful of all the groups, perhaps did not appreciate the potential dangers of this multiplication of 'competitors'; some members, certainly, tended to the idea that raw overall numbers was what the guerrilla movement needed at the time, regardless of group affiliation; and Fateh was itself 'guilty' of causing at least one new organisational split in the movement when it eased Nayef Hawatma's group out of the PFLP to establish its own new formation, the Popular Democratic Front for the Liberation of Palestine (PDFLP, later, DFLP without the 'Popular'), in early 1969. The core leadership of Fateh was anyway kept pretty busy coping with the problems of its own organisation's enormous growth in these years, and with its parallel policy of winning and cementing official Arab recognition, without having too much time left over for sorting out the overall internal Palestinian body politic in very much detail. In a real sense, then, the Fateh leadership's problems in Jordan in 1970 grew out of the explosive, and unexpected, success of its core concepts of armed struggle, and Palestinian self-activity, in gaining adherents in the preceding years.

The core ideology of Fateh, as we saw in chapter 2, included a stress on Palestinian non-intervention in the internal affairs of existing Arab states; but this concept was not shared by many of the other Palestinian guerrilla groups gaining influence in Jordan in the late 60s.[36] The PFLP still clung to the pan-Arabist ideological approach of its Arab Nationalists' Movement origins; the DFLP, despite Fateh's midwifery at its birth, was soon thereafter calling for the establishment of soviets (workers' and peasants' councils) in some areas of northern Jordan; Saiqa and the Arab Liberation Front were the Palestinian guerrilla sections of respectively the pro-Syrian and the pro-Iraqi wings of the (pan-Arabist) Baath Party, and so on. For all of these groups, a confrontation with Hussein, whom they saw variously as 'reactionary', 'a puppet of Western imperialism' or 'a Zionist tool', was considered not only desirable, but also ideologically necessary. Thus, in direct contradiction to Fateh's long-held ideology, throughout late 1969 and the first half of 1970, the Palestinian guerrillas' challenges to Hussein's authority multiplied as rapidly as their traffic-control roadblocks spread throughout more and more of his capital.

Inside Fateh itself, meanwhile, the Fateh core's own ideology was trickling down only slowly to the movement's thousands of new recruits, some of whom, influenced by the revolutionary outpourings sweeping through Palestinian communities in those days, may have felt inclined to join with the more 'subversive' groups in calling for Amman to be turned into a Palestinian Hanoi from which to assail the Israeli Saigon in Tel Aviv. As Khaled al-Hassan recalled that period,

After Karameh, people started to join Fateh by thousands. So they were not ... brought up, accultured, according to Fateh ideology in a condensed manner. After Karameh, we were forced to make our mobilisation and ideological education to the people in the camps by masses, by lectures, not by cells: and there is a big difference in both ways. There we deal with an individual; here we deal with the masses, with 100 at one time... You can't explain everything; you have no time to explain everything, because it needs one year to make a real member...

But they were all disciplined to the decision. So if you would have said something they would have obeyed it. *But we didn't, and I think we made a mistake.*[37]

It was perhaps not entirely surprising that Hussein should have sought to act decisively against the threat he perceived the guerrillas as posing to his regime; but the build-up to the 1970 crisis in Jordan also had an important international dimension. It was on 9 June 1970, according to the memoirs of Dr Henry Kissinger, then Prsident Nixon's National Security Advisor, that Hussein had succeeded in foiling an assassination attempt, and subsequently assumed personal command of his army, 'but he was reluctant to take on the Palestinians, whom he had ruled since 1967 and hoped to re-unite with his Kingdom'.[38] The reported assassination attempt did, however, provide Kissinger with an opportunity to plan out for the U.S. a decisive role in future developments in Jordan. On 9 June, he convened a meeting of the crisis-oriented Washington Special Actions Group (WSAG), which over the coming two weeks busily commissioned and reviewed plans for an evacuation of American civilians from Jordan, as well as further, unspecified, 'contingency plans'.[39]

After repeated skirmishes on the ground in Jordan between the King's men and the guerrillas, the situation sharpened abruptly again on 6 September 1970, when members of the PFLP flouted Jordanian sovereignty so openly as to bring three hijacked international airliners into the desert airstrip in Jordan which thereby attained brief renown as 'Revolution

Airstrip'. Three days later, in Washington, Kissinger again activated the WSAG machinery. According to his memoirs, the WSAG now commissioned two distinct contingency plans for international intervention in the unfolding Jordanian crisis: in the first of these, prepared at Kissinger's own behest, American forces would act only to ensure the safe evacuation of American civilians from Jordan, while Israel would have the role of reacting to any Syrian or Iraqi moves to help the guerrillas in Jordan. The second plan, prepared in response to President Nixon's declared wishes, would have kept the Israelis right out of it, allowing for direct American military intervention to save Hussein.[40] In preparation for either of these contingencies, and as a warning to the Soviets meanwhile, Kissinger ordered the U.S. military to take several very visible steps towards a higher state of combat-readiness in Europe and the east Mediterranean.[41]

Finally, as Kissinger records it, 'At the end of the second week in September ... whether because our readiness measures had given him a psychological lift or because he was reaching the point of desperation, the tough little King resolved on an all-out confrontation with the fedayeen.'[42] Hussein's loyal bedouin troops went on the offensive against guerrilla positions and refugee camps throughout the Jordanian capital, Amman. The disloyal troops, those who sided with the Palestinians in the ensuing fighting – mainly men of West Bank origin – were later regrouped by Fateh into the Yarmouk Brigade, which was associated with the PLA. The training they had received in the Jordanian army, considered one of the best in the Arab world, proved a considerable asset to the guerrillas' military capability in later years.

On 9 September, the PLO Central Committee had sent an urgent telegram to the Arab kings and heads of state then convening to discuss the Jordan crisis at an emergency summit meeting in Cairo. The Central Committee, the telegram said, 'calls on you to face your historic and national responsibilities, so that the whole of Jordan may not be reduced to ruins by this odious conspiracy'.[43] The hastily arranged summit had been boycotted by Iraq, Syria and Algeria, which all professed support for the Palestinians, as well as by Morocco, which probably supported Hussein.[44] The summit despatched a conciliation committee to Amman, led by Sudanese President Ja'far Numairy; but the successive cease-fires the committee sought to impose there never got off the ground. The actions of Hussein, Kissinger and the Israelis, as well as the PFLP, had all escalated tensions beyond any chance of a compromise.

The Iraqis still had 17,000 regular troops in Jordan in 1970, which had been there since the 1967 Mideast war. But in the September crisis, they noticeably abstained from intervening on the Palestinians' behalf. The only Arab state which did anything on the ground to help the beleaguered guerrilla positions was Syria. According to journalists Marvin and Bernard Kalb, it was on 18 September that Kissinger received first word in Washington that Syrian tanks were crossing into Jordan from the north.[45] Significantly, his informants about this new development were both the Jordanian Ambassador in Washington and the the Israeli Ambassador there, Yitzhak Rabin. As the Kalbs record it, 'Kissinger and Rabin were on the phone several times that night, discussing different aspects of the unfolding crisis.'[46]

Still viewing the Jordan crisis mainly in the light of his preoccupation with great-power relations, Kissinger ostentatiously made some more very visible American military preparations in Europe and the Mediterranean, as a way of 'warning' the Soviets to 'call off' their clients, the Syrians. President Nixon 'backed up these military moves with a stern warning to the Russians to restrain the Syrians and with a private assurance to Hussein not to worry about the Israelis'.[47] Late in the evening of 20 September, according to the Kalbs, Kissinger had an urgent new message for Ambassador Rabin: 'Kissinger's voice seemed tense. He said the Jordanians had asked him to pass on an urgent message: would Israel provide Jordan with air support against the advancing Syrian tanks?'[48] Kissinger himself did not record passing on such a direct request in this call to Rabin. He wrote merely,

I told Rabin of the information we had received from Jordan without specifying the source. After discussion with the President and the Secretary [of State], I could inform him that if Israeli reconnaissance confirmed [a serious Syrian incursion into Jordan], we would look favorably upon an Israeli air attack. We would make good the material losses, and we would do our utmost to prevent Soviet interference.[49]

What passed between the Soviets and the Syrians in those hours of 20 and 21 September is not known. What is known, or at least recorded by Kissinger, is that late on 21 September the Soviet Chargé d'Affaires in Washington informed the State Department's Joseph Sisco that the Soviets were doing all possible to press Syria to withdraw; and by nightfall that same day the Syrian tanks had stopped advancing into Jordan.

The following day, as Israeli army and air force units continued preparations for an intervention in Jordan, Hussein threw his armour and air force against the Syrian tank concentrations near the north Jordanian city of Irbid. The latter, having no air cover, were finally towards the end of the day forced to grind their way back to their own side of the international border: the Palestinians, who on 17 September had called urgently but unsuccessfully on the Iraqi units in Jordan also to come to their aid, were finally left to face their fate alone. Beaten out of Amman, the guerrillas managed to regroup some forces for a few months in the hills and wooded areas of the north of the country; but the following summer Hussein's troops managed to storm their remaining positions there too.

By the time the royalist forces had finally 'purged' Jordan completely of the guerrillas' presence in July 1971, an estimated 3,000 Palestinians, military and civilian, had been killed; several of the refugee camps in Jordan had been reduced to heaps of rubble by the Jordanian artillery; and both Israelis and Palestinians were subsequently to agree that there were even several cases of guerrillas entertaining such fears of what would happen to them should they fall into the hands of Hussein's troops in Jordan that they crossed the River Jordan and surrendered instead to the Israelis.

At the military level, the guerrillas then found themselves unable for the whole of the next 12 years to maintain any presence at all in the Arab country with the longest border with Israel, and the only Arab country enjoying a steady flow of people into and out of the Israeli-occupied West Bank. And politically, relations between Hussein and the PLO leadership remained hostile for the following six years, until the first tentative moves towards a rapprochement were made in early 1977. In 1972, Hussein launched a new political offensive against the PLO when he announced a plan for the creation of a 'United Arab Kingdom' to link the East and West Banks of the Jordan under his crown. The PLO leaders were able to limit the effectiveness of this offensive, partly because of the support they continued to enjoy at the pan-Arab level, and partly because Israel gave no signs of giving up the West Bank anyway. But without a doubt, the defeat they suffered in Jordan in 1970-71 set back by many years their prospects of success in both the military and the political facets of their struggle.

As the dimensions of the defeat in Jordan became clear to the Palestinians throughout 1971, many important questions remained to be answered: about their own tactics and strategy in Jordan, and about those of their supposed friends. Why had the Baath Party regime in Syria, which for so long had supported Palestinian guerrilla action both in theory and in practice, now abandoned its erstwhile allies to the mercies of Hussein's troops? Had the Syrians been persuaded by the Russians to pull out? And what, most crucially, had prevented the Syrian air force from giving air cover to the 300 or so tanks already in Jordan, which would at least have prevented their rout?

The answers to the latter questions are inextricably mixed up in the internal turmoil which Syria's Baath (which means 'Renaissance') Party was then undergoing.[50] The Defence Minister and commander of the air force were one and the same man in Syria in September 1970 – Hafez al-Asad, the same man who had been one of Fateh's earliest patrons inside the Syrian regime. Now he was arguing in Baath Party circles against any 'adventurism' in Jordan; some sources say he had agreed on a joint policy of non-intervention there with the Iraqi Baathist strongman (later President) Saddam Hussein. Anyway, in the midst of the bitter arguments and recriminations which racked the Syrian Baath Party in the wake of the debacle in Jordan, on 16 November 1970, Hafez al-Asad seized power in Damascus in a bloodless coup.[51]

The bitter lessons the Palestinian guerrillas had to learn in Jordan, then, included the stark fact that they could apparently rely on no Arab regime, however friendly otherwise, to allow its commitment to them to supersede what its members finally conceived of as a more pressing *raison d'état*.

This lesson served to convince increasing numbers of Palestinians of the validity of the Fateh leaders' long standing convictions of the need to safeguard the independence of Palestinian political decision-making from reliance on any single Arab regime. But in some other respects, the internal Palestinian debate over the reasons for the defeat in Jordan only tended to accentuate existing divergences of analysis within the nationalist movement. For while 'radical' groups such as the PFLP and the DFLP argued afterwards that the guerrillas' principal mistake had lain in their failure to align themselves wholeheartedly with the Jordanian 'popular forces' against the King, the historic leaders of Fateh argued just the contrary: that the whole confrontation could and should have been avoided by a scrupulous refusal to intervene in internal Jordanian affairs. This debate simmered, unresolved, inside PLO ranks, even as the need to make a similar decision in Lebanon became increasingly pressing throughout the early 70s.

In the three years following September 1970, many Western commentators were already starting to write off the guerrillas and their leadership as an interesting but transient phenomenon, which had reached a brief peak in Jordan in the late 60s but was now plummeting downhill. Veteran Middle East reporter John Cooley, for example (although he did hedge his bets a bit), was writing, 'The odds against [Arafat] looked overwhelming, and younger men less affected by the political attrition of the past years seemed likely to succeed him.'[52] Certainly, the guerrilla movement sustained enormous human, military and political losses during that 'Black September' and the months which followed it; but the enormous fund of popular support it still enjoyed in both Palestinian and non-Palestinian Arab communities nevertheless enabled it not just to survive the defeat in Jordan, but also to regroup with the speed and efficiency which were to send Arafat to the United Nations a bare four years after September 1970.

The semi-official status the guerrillas had acquired at the Arab level, by virtue of their takeover of the PLO apparatus in the years preceding September 1970, was also to play a role in this regard. Throughout and after the Jordan crisis, Arafat was able to deal with the Arab state apparatuses as Chairman of the PLO (their own creation); this was a much stronger position from which to deal than that of a militarily vanquished guerrilla leader. Had a grouping basically unsympathetic to guerrilla aims still been in control of the PLO at this time, the Organisation could easily, in the period of the guerrillas' military weakness, have been turned into a further weapon in official Arab hands against them. As it was, the guerrillas' continuing links, through the PLO, with the Arab regimes acted as a useful safety-net during that period, in which they were able, at the political level, at least, to absorb their rolling defeats at the hands of Hussein's troops.

But the Fateh core, while they still did not change their basic commitment to non-intervention in the Arab states' internal affairs, remained wary of being trapped into a role which would restrict them to being solely the creatures of the regimes in the way they had accused Shuqairy of being. To this end, following the defeats in Jordan, they sought to cover the patient rebuilding of their guerrilla forces, this time mainly in Lebanon, not only through their official PLO connections with Arab state leaders; they also, though it is extremely doubtful if this was a unanimous or even a majority decision inside the Fateh leadership, sanctioned the launching of a selective terror campaign against Israeli and Jordanian targets on a world-wide basis. Salah Khalaf argued in his book that the emergence of the 'Black September Organisation' was a purely spontaneous reaction on the behalf of some embittered rank and filers from a number of existing guerrilla groups, including Fateh, to the events in Jordan.[53] Other sources, mainly Israeli, have linked Black September to Khalaf himself, and to fellow Fateh security officials Mohamed Daoud Awda and Ali Hassan Salameh. Awda, in a much-quoted televised 'confession' made after the Jordanians arrested him in February 1973 while reportedly on a mission in Jordan, said, 'There is no such thing called Black September. Fateh announced its operations under this name so that Fateh would not appear as the direct executor of the operations.'[54]

Throughout the two years following the summer of 1971, a large part of the confrontation between the Israelis and the Palestinians was carried out in the form of a 'war of spooks' in Europe, Asia, even the United States, and of course the Middle East. Black September's most spectacular operation was the seizure of 11 Israeli athletes at the September 1972 Olympic Games in Munich: they killed one of the athletes who tried to resist capture there; the rest, plus five of the eight Black Septembrists, were killed in explosions and a hail of cross-fire as German police tried to ambush the Palestinians at a military airport near Munich. Immediately afterwards, the Israeli armed forces hit back with air raids against Palestinian refugee camps and border villages in Lebanon, killing 14 civilians, and shortly thereafter with a land invasion of the area in which 19 Lebanese troops and 25 civilians were killed, along with an unknown number of Palestinian guerrillas.[55]

Some time in 1972 (and there are some indications that this was almost immediately after the Munich affair) the Fateh leadership reportedly decided to halt the flirtation which some of its members had been carrying out with the Black Septembrists. The necessary instructions were passed down through the Fateh apparatuses; but in two cases, Fateh members who had previously been entrusted by the leadership with the task of liaising with Black September's governmental backers responded to these instructions by effectively defecting to the governments with which they had been liaising. This was what happened to Ahmed Abdel-Ghaffar (Abu Mahmoud), with Libya; and to Sabri al-Banna (Abu Nidal), with Iraq. When these defections had become apparent, the Fateh leadership pronounced a death sentence on both these men. (In autumn 1974, Abdel-Ghaffar was to venture back to see old contacts in Lebanon, and was shot dead 'in mysterious circumstances' in Beirut. Banna, however, continued to evade his death sentence, and was to prove a constant irritant to his erstwhile comrades throughout the following decade.)[56]

In April 1973, the Israelis were able to bring off a significant coup when their commandos landed by night on a Beirut beach and drove to the apartments of Fateh/PLO leaders Kamal Udwan and Muhammed Youssef al-Najjar (Abu Youssef, then serving as the PLO's 'Foreign Minister'), killing them along with the Palestinian poet Kamal Nasir, who was then the PLO spokesman. An Israeli intelligence officer was killed in Madrid; a number of Fateh members and sympathisers were killed in various European capitals; the PFLP spokesman, Ghassan Kanafani, also a prolific writer of short stories, was blown up by a car-bomb along with his young niece, Lamis; and several other officials in the PLO and the guerrilla groups were badly disfigured by letter-bombs.

Nonetheless, while all this was going on, the guerrilla groups were slowly able to rebuild in Lebanon the military formations which had previously been smashed in Jordan. The Israeli secret services were apparently so caught up in their 'war of spooks' against the Palestinians that they failed to take proper account during those years of the gradual build-up of the regular armies' military strength in both Egypt and Syria.

On 6 October 1973, the Egyptian and Syrian armies launched a combined attack against the Israeli troops which had still, more than six years after the June 1967 war, not moved back from the 1967 cease-fire lines deep within these two states' sovereign lands. This was to be, in Egyptian President Sadat's view at least, a limited regular war which could serve as a

55

catalyst for the long-stalled Middle East peace process.

According to Khalaf, Sadat had given a preliminary indication to Qaddumi and himself in mid-August of 1973 that the Egyptian war effort would be imminent.[57] Then, on 9 September, Sadat invited Arafat, Qaddumi and Khalaf to another meeting where he outlined his plan in detail, this time emphasising the postwar phase. He himself would call for the convening of a peace conference. He did not specify that it would be in Geneva, but he listed the countries that would be represented. They were almost the same as those which actually participated in December of the same year: the United States, the U.S.S.R., Israel, Egypt, Syria, Jordan and the PLO.[58]

The Fateh leaders were thus able to prepare some of their own units, and some PLA units, to take part in the coming war. According to Heikal, 'It was on Monday 1 October that some officers of the [Palestinian] resistance and about 120 other ranks had arrived in Cairo to take part in the battle.'[59] These were deployed, along with some Kuwaiti troops who also reached Egypt during the war, in the Canal Zone near the soon-to-be-famous Deversoir Lake. Khalaf wrote that, in addition,

A number of PLA units had been helicoptered behind Israeli lines on the first day of the fighting and seized four hills of Kuneitra in the Golan. From South Lebanon, fedayeen commandos crossed over into Israel to attack the rear lines of the Jewish army in Upper Galilee. Others shelled a number of Kibbutzim beyond the Lebanese border. As of October 6, some 70,000 Palestinian workers employed by Israeli enterprises went on strike in the West Bank and Gaza.[60]

Other guerrilla units, totalling around 1,000 men, made ready to move into Jordan, whence they hoped to be able to cross into the southern Israeli region around Al-Aghwar, but, according to Heikal, King Hussein refused to let them cross and Sadat, when first asked to intervene with Hussein on 11 October, replied that he 'doubted whether there was much he could do'. When, one week later, it became clear the Israelis were getting the upper hand in the battle, Sadat thought the time had come for the 1,000 guerrillas 'to perform some useful functions, such as attacks on Israeli communications'. However, the Egyptian President was now unable to reach King Hussein, whose aides at first kept saying he was out of Amman; when Sadat finally got through to him, Hussein stalled just long enough to render the whole question academic.[61]

In the 1973 war the Arab states' regular armies did not win anything like an outright military victory; nevertheless, they certainly did not meet the fate predicted for any efforts on their behalf by the article in *Filastinuna* 11 years before. But then their aim, in 1973, was never to 'liberate Palestine', merely to regain some of their own occupied lands, at least as a position from which to bargain – an aim which many public figures throughout the world (except in Israel) could understand to one degree or another.

The Palestinians, having contributed to the 1973 war effort, hoped to be able to profit from the diplomatic process which followed it; indeed, in the first flush of Arab self-confidence at the end of 1973 that aim did not seem too far-fetched. The guerrilla movement had come a long way since 1967: it had grown explosively, won a consensus of Palestinian popular support, gained inter-Arab legitimacy, been cut down to size (in Jordan), but nevertheless bounced back with most of its Arab alliances intact. It was therefore with some degree of their own self-confidence that the Fateh/ PLO leaders approached the postwar period.

Chapter 4

Caught in the Lebanon net (1973-76)

On 22 October 1973, the United Nations Security Council passed its first resolution calling for a cease-fire in the 16-day-old Middle East war; but Israeli units commanded by General Ariel Sharon continued their movement southwards from Deversoir, along the *west* bank of the Suez Canal, and within two days had completely cut off supply lines to the Egyptian Third Army now trapped on the *east* bank.[1]

It was on 26 October that Fateh's Salah Khalaf and Farouq al-Qaddumi, who had both stayed in Cairo throughout the war, went to President Sadat's Tahra Palace. The question with which the Egyptian leader confronted them there was one which was to haunt the Fateh leadership for most of the next four years. According to Khalaf 'Before we even had a chance to sit down he asked us point-blank: "Well now, will you agree to participate in the Geneva Peace Conference?"'[2] The two men did not feel they could provide an answer right there and then. The next day, they travelled to Beirut, where they convened an enlarged meeting of the Fateh leadership to discuss Sadat's question. As Khalaf recalled it

A long discussion ensued. Sadat had placed us in a difficult, not to say impossible, situation. Everyone was agreed not to reject the principle of a peace conference out of hand, but it would have been just as imprudent to reply affirmatively... We couldn't simply overlook the fact that the cease-fire had been established on the basis of Resolution 242, which as I said before denies the Palestinians their most elementary rights. So we decided not to reply either way until we received a formal invitation. It was only then that we would be in a position to define our position in a clear and precise manner.[3]

Two weeks later, on 12 November, Sadat received Yasser Arafat, who had been sent to Cairo to explain the answer Fateh had painstakingly hammered out to the Egyptian leader's question. Khalaf wrote, 'Arafat found Sadat's attitude surprising: He seemed distant, practically indifferent as to what decision we had reached. Arafat got the distinct impression that Sadat was no longer concerned by our participation in the Geneva meeting.'[4]

What had happened to change Sadat's attitude in the interim was that the

Palestinians' old adversary from the Jordanian events of 1970, Dr Kissinger – now elevated to the position of Secretary of State in addition to continuing as National Security Advisor to a President Nixon now well on the way down the slippery slope called Watergate –, had been starting on his Middle East 'shuttle diplomacy'. In the five days from 6 to 11 November, Kissinger succeeded in concluding the first bilateral disengagement agreement between Egyptian and Israeli forces.

Over the next two years, the Palestinians were to see Kissinger's successive bilateral approaches to the Middle East problem steadily undercutting the chances of convening the kind of all-party peace conference that Sadat had previously seemed to be promising them. On 31 May 1974, Kissinger succeeded in having Israeli and Syrian negotiators sign an interim agreement which roughly paralleled on the Golan the provisions previously agreed for the Sinai front. On 1 September 1975, the Egyptians and Israelis signed their second agreement, known as Sinai II. It was with a kind of bitter irony that the Palestinians came to realise that a powerful inducement to Sadat to get this step-by-step process under way in the first place had been the entrapment of the Egyptian Third Army east of the Deversoir, of which the Palestinians' own forces stationed in that area had warned the Egyptian High Command back on 12 October, the day General Sharon's men had first reached the Deversoir region. 'The Egyptian officials,' wrote Khalaf of that warning,'... sent no reinforcements to defend this crucial position.'[5]

Kissinger's main aim, during and after the 1973 Middle East war, was simple to describe, if more awesome to contemplate in execution: it was to use the opportunities provided by the war to monopolise for the United States the external diplomatic initiative concerning the Arab-Israeli problem, excluding the Soviets, and if possible also the Europeans, from any meaningful diplomatic role in the region. He had meanwhile somehow to parry the oil weapon which the Arab oil producers had unsheathed towards the end of the October fighting. His attitude to the Palestinians during all this was to try to 'isolate' them.[6] The Secretary of State succeeded brilliantly in realising all his main aims. The Soviet Foreign Minister, Andrei Gromyko, was co-Chairman at the brief one-day session of the Geneva Peace Conference which was held on 21 December 1973, but was deftly kept out of all of the succeeding negotiations, as were the Europeans. On the following 18 March, all Arab oil producers except Libya and Syria lifted the oil embargo against the United States.

In his memoirs of this period, Kissinger's one regret concerning his Middle East policy was that he was unable to win any concessions from the Israelis for his old friend in Jordan, the 'tough little King', Hussein.[7] Hussein's problem was that, on the one hand, he had intentionally not been included in or included himself in the Egyptian-Syrian war effort, and thus could claim none of the diplomatic spoils of war; and on the other, that the Israeli government was far less willing to make territorial or even purely political concessions on the West Bank, which had been the Hashemites' fiefdom from 1948 to 1967, than it was in Sinai or even on the strategic Golan. As Kissinger repeatedly (if somewhat disingenuously) records having told everyone throughout his shuttle diplomacy, his role was simply to transmit and explain the ideas of each side to the other, and not to argue for any American-originated plan. He was not, however, without good advice. For example, he records having told a group of American Jewish leaders on 8 February 1974:

I predict that if the Israelis don't make some sort of arrangement with Hussein on the West Bank in six months, Arafat will become internationally recognized and the world will be in chaos... If I were an advisor to the Israeli Government, I would tell the Prime Minister: 'For God's sake do something with Hussein while he is still one of the players.'[8]

But neither for God's sake, nor for Kissinger's, could the Israelis bring themselves to do this; and Kissinger mistimed his forecast by only two and a half months. For on 28 October 1974, the Seventh Arab Summit meeting in Rabat solemnly affirmed 'the right of the Palestinian people to establish an independent national authority under the command of the Palestine Liberation Organisation, the *sole legitimate representative of the Palestinian people*, in any Palestinian territory that is liberated'.[9] Hussein, who had been imploring Kissinger for any Israeli concession to him in the West Bank, even just a withdrawal from the city of Jericho,[10] was now formally out of the diplomatic ballgame, and the PLO was seeking a way to get in.

The Fateh leadership had prepared the PLO quite thoroughly for the diplomatic involvement which they hoped would follow from the Rabat summit's decision. According to Khalaf, it had been back in July 1967 that Farouq al-Qaddumi had first proposed to his colleagues in the Fateh Central Committee that 'we take a stand in favor of a ministate in the West Bank in the event that Israel would withdraw from these two territories it had just conquered'.[11] But the scheme had been considered too radically conciliatory at that time, and had been shelved: the following year Fateh had enunciated its aim of creating a 'secular democratic state' in Palestine instead. But the fighting in Jordan of 1970-71 provoked yet another reconsideration of goals. According to Khalaf

After the massacres of Amman ... and especially after the expulsion of the last fedayeen from Hashemite territory, it was only too evident that the Palestinian revolution could not count on any Arab state to provide a secure sanctuary or an operational base against Israel. In order to forge ahead toward the democratic, intersectarian society that was our ideal, we had to have our own state, even on a square inch of Palestine. [12]

Khaled al-Hassan, meanwhile, recalled having first himself seriously considered the mini-state solution back in January 1973, when the failure of his call for a revision of Palestinian strategy had led him to resign from the PLO Executive Committee. Then, in the first week of the October War, the Fateh Central Committee had convened a meeting in Shtaura, in eastern Lebanon: Hassan argued there that since King Hussein was not participating in the war,

There was no role now for Hussein in the West Bank, so the West Bank should be ours and we should talk now about the mini-state. To change the main practical strategy, not the aims...

So the idea of having an independent state in the areas freed from the Israeli occupation developed in this way after the '73 war. Because we thought that if there would be a peaceful settlement, the greatest threat would be to our struggle, how to continue. I wrote a small book about it... I said the greatest threat to the Palestinian struggle would come from an Arab victory, because after the war there is either a truce or there is real peace; and if that happens, there will be no room for the Palestinians' struggle... Which is the best thing for the continuation of the struggle?

We came to a decision that the best for us is that the West Bank and Gaza should be a Palestinian state... The way to have a sort of freedom of work either now or after 10 years is when we have our own land; taking also into account that in spite of the fact that we were dominated by our independence in our relation with the Arabs, we also discovered that so long as we do not have our own land, we cannot be 90 or 80% independent when we are working on the land of the others.[13]

Khalaf recorded that the Fateh leaders had hoped to convene a session of the Palestinian National Council immediately after the October War, but they had waited first to obtain a consensus from all the guerrilla groups on a new programme, on the basis of which to enter the postwar diplomatic process.

Early in 1974, the Democratic Front for the Liberation of Palestine (DFLP) started openly espousing the idea of having the PLO call for the establishment of a Palestinian 'national authority' – the euphemism they introduced at this stage for describing a Palestinian mini-state – in the West Bank and Gaza. In a speech delivered on 24 February 1974, to mark the fifth anniversary of the DFLP's foundation, its Secretary-General, Nayef Hawatma, had tried to meet internal Palestinian criticisms of this position by arguing

We are fighting to end occupation and to stand effectively against imperialist solutions. We are fighting for our people's right to establish its national authority on its own land after the occupation has been ended... This national authority would make it possible for our masses in Lebanon and Syria to consolidate, organise and fortify the struggle to return to their homeland and further to wage a long war of national liberation ... no matter how long this takes.[14]

Negotiations which followed, among Fateh, the DFLP and the other guerrilla movements, resulted in the formulation of a ten-point programme, which was adopted *nem con* by the Twelfth PNC, meeting in Cairo in June/July 1974. The most relevant clause of this programme read:

2. The PLO will struggle by every means, the foremost of which is armed struggle, to liberate Palestinian land and to establish the people's national, independent and fighting sovereignty *on every part of Palestinian land to be liberated*. This requires the creation of further changes in the balance of power in favour of our people and their struggle.[15]

In other words, a compromise: the second sentence of the clause indicated that circumstances were not yet officially deemed auspicious for such a move, but when they were it should be taken.

The compromise represented by this wording was, however, so fragile that it fell apart within three and a half months. On 26 September, George Habash's Popular Front for the Liberation of Palestine announced its resignation from the PLO Executive Committee; over the ensuing weeks three other guerrilla organisations also joined the PFLP in its opposition stance. Together they then constituted the 'Front of Palestinian Forces Rejecting Surrenderist Solutions' – the Rejection Front,[16] which was to act as a freewheeling opposition to the Executive Committee for the following four years.

The opposition to the 'national authority' scheme voiced by the Rejection Front represented a widespread grass-roots phenomenon, especially in the refugee camps of the Palestinian diaspora which were Fateh's traditional political base. These refugees, coming originally from villages and towns within Israel's 1948 borders, now saw their dreams of Return postponed to a later stage of the guerrilla struggle, or even possibly quietly forgotten forever; but at huge meetings and in heated discussion groups throughout the Palestinian diaspora, the Fateh (and DFLP) leaders argued out their case again and again.

Fateh and the mainstream of the PLO meanwhile pushed ahead quickly with their post-October War diplomatic initiative: at the end of October 1974, Arafat led a heavy PLO delegation to the Arab Summit at Rabat, and it was on the basis of the PNC's recently agreed 10-point programme that the PLO there received the Arab states' endorsement of its claim to be the 'sole legitimate representative of the Palestinian people'. On 13 November, with Arab League help, Arafat was in New York, addressing the U.N. General Assembly session. But the continuing criticism of the 'national authority' concept back in the resistance movement's home base undoubtedly affected the content of his speech there: he did not mention the 'national authority' scheme at all from the U.N. rostrum, referring instead to 'My dream ... that I may return with my people out of exile, there in Palestine to live ... in one democratic state where Christian, Jew and Moslem live in justice, equality, fraternity and progress'.[17] It was at that session of the U.N. that the PLO acquired the unique 'observer status' with the world body which it enjoyed throughout the following years.

The PLO Chairman had been introduced to the world body by Lebanon's President of four years, Suleiman Franjieh, in a move by the Arab League member-states which was loaded with symbolism. For Lebanon had unimpeachable pro-Western credentials; the proximity of its Christian President to the Palestinian cause would underline that cause's interdenominational nature; and, equally important, Lebanon was by now the main base of the Palestinian military, so the Lebanese had a strong vested interest in helping to secure a solution of the Palestine problem which would simultaneously relieve their country of this burden.

The rebuilding of the Palestinians' military base in Lebanon, following its near-destruction in Jordan in 1970-71, had imposed quite some strain on the fragile political system in that tiny east Mediterranean nation. The Republic of Lebanon, within the boundaries it knows today (formally, at least), is a creation of the French, who from the early 20s till after the Second World War held a League of Nations mandate in Lebanon and Syria, parallel to that held by the British in Palestine, Transjordan and Iraq. Lebanon and Syria remained closely linked to each other up to and even after the French granted their independence in the mid-40s. But the French had gradually strengthened the separate administrations in Beirut and Damascus, giving the former jurisdiction not only over the traditional areas of Mount Lebanon, but also over a wide hinterland which had previously been administered from Damascus.[18] Thus were sown the seeds of the sectarian imbalance which was to plague Lebanon into the 80s: the hinterland was mainly Muslim, and the combined Muslim populations of the new Lebanon had a significantly higher growth-rate than its Christian population; but the political system bequeathed by the French had Christian predominance built into it. Under the 'National Pact' signed in 1943, powerful Maronite and Sunni Muslim community bosses agreed that the presidency and the army command should be in the hands of members of the Maronite Christian sect; the premiership – far less powerful than the presidency – was allotted to the Sunni community; and other state positions were distributed among less favoured segments of the Lebanese mosaic.

Because of the sensitivity of the sectarian issue within Lebanon, no formal census has been taken there since 1932, and each sect and community has postulated its version of demographic developments over the decades since then. One broadly believable set of figures, provided by an outside source, for 1975, the eve of the civil war, put the Lebanese population balance as shown in Table 2.[19]

Table 2. *Christian and Muslim sects in Lebanon, 1975*

Christians	%	Muslims	%
Maronites	23	Sunnis	26
Greek Orthodox	7	Shi'ites	27
Greek Catholics	5	Druze	7
Other	5		
Total	40	Total	60
(1,020,000 persons)		(1,530,000)	

Scores of thousands of Armenian refugees had successfully been absorbed into the Lebanese system following the Turkish massacres of the early decades of this century; but the Armenians were determinedly Christians, and could thus bolster Christian supremacy in the country. The Palestinian refugees who followed them into Lebanon three decades later were, for the most part, Muslims; and of those who were Christians, most were Greek Orthodox, not Maronites.[20] The mere presence of the Palestinians, Muslims and Greek Orthodox alike, tended to strengthen the Arab nationalist current inside Lebanese society. The Maronite-dominated internal security apparatus had therefore kept a tight lid on the Palestinian refugee camps right up until 1969, when rising Palestinian aspirations and the terms of the Cairo agreement blew that lid right off.[21]

Throughout the years following the conclusion of that agreement, Lebanon was the scene of two mounting, and interlinked, popular movements. The Palestinians there, who by then numbered about 400,000, [22] were pouring into their nationalist movement by the thousands, building up not only the guerrilla groups' military strength but also that of their social institutions. Georgetown University's Michael Hudson wrote perceptively back in 1972, 'To a large extent the guerrilla groups did not simply penetrate a national elite but actually reconstituted it.'[23] This process had started tentatively back in Jordan, but had been aborted there by the events of Septmber 1970. It continued to take root as a social process in Lebanon in the years between 1969 and 1982.

Meanwhile, the Lebanese opposition, which had always been an untidy amalgam of Muslim traditionalists (Sunni and Shi'ite), Muslim radicals (left and right), secularists (left and right), pan-Arabists of every brand, socialists, student activists, trade unionists and a tiny sprinkling of marxists, was decidedly on the upswing. One of the few things all these brands of oppositionists could agree on, in addition to their criticism of the Maronite-dominated *status quo*, was their support for the Palestinian resistance movement.

For the Fateh core, these indigenous Lebanese developments represented an opportunity, but also a dilemma; for their own ideology had, since their movement's foundation, stressed the principle of non-intervention in the Arab states' internal affairs. Nevertheless, the Fateh core's ideology had also always laid stress on the demand that the Arab states should, at the very least, use their own security forces to protect the guerrilla movement from Israeli retaliations. As the scale of Israeli actions against targets in Lebanon escalated from 1968 onwards, causing increasing suffering and disruption to the Lebanese as well as to the Palestinian communities there, the Palestinians found their own demands on the Lebanese authorities in this respect running parallel to those of the Lebanese opposition.

The Palestinian professor Walid Khalidi has argued that the Palestinian leadership was moved by its memory of

the Jordanian experience. Never again would the Palestinian revolution face a regular army on its own. The Jordanian catastrophe had occurred precisely because the [Palestinian] revolution had abided by constraining principles of behaviour vis-à-vis the Jordanian masses which had merely played into the hands of the Jordanian authorities, thus facilitating the latter's liquidation task. If the Lebanese Moslem and leftist waters were crying out for the Palestinian fish to jump into them, the Palestinian fish were not going to play coy.[24]

In fact, this was probably true only of a section of the PLO leadership, and certainly not of the historic core of Fateh leaders. For the latter, the prime lesson from Jordan had been the precise opposite: that entanglement in local issues should be strenuously avoided. Khaled al-Hassan's verdict on the 1975-76 fighting in Lebanon, for example, as expressed in 1982, was 'The whole war, we have nothing to do with it. Our men were used in this completely social, Lebanese social problem.'[25] And indeed, the differences within the Fateh leadership on the question of strategy in Lebanon were to become more pointed as the fighting progressed.

The date generally given for the start of the 1975-76 civil war in Lebanon is 13 April 1975, the day on which unidentified assailants reportedly opened fire on Pierre Gemayyel, the leader of the Maronite-dominated Phalangist Party, and right-wing Christian gunmen[26] retaliated by ambushing a bus full of Palestinian civilians in a Christian quarter of Beirut. The clashes which ensued became meshed into other, purely Lebanese, disputes raging at that time. These included one between the small-scale fishermen of the south Lebanese ports (mainly Muslims) and Gemayyel's ally, the former Lebanese President Camille Chamoun, who wanted the government to award a fishing monopoly to a company he owned, as well as the boiling grievances of the various Muslim communities against continued Maronite domination of the Lebanese system.

In the early months of the fighting, the main armed forces involved were the militia of the Phalangist Party, fighting against Palestinian units from the Rejection Front, as well as from the DFLP and the Syrian-backed Saiqa guerrilla group. Fateh, for its part, tried not to commit its forces in any significant numbers to the successive battles of spring and summer 1975, instead seeking to maintain the strength of its fighting forces in the southern areas bordering on Israel while throwing many resources into training those elements of the Lebanese opposition which sought to form or enlarge their militias. Chamoun, a dedicated pro-Westerner, still had not organised much of a militia for his National Liberal Party. The chronically weak Lebanese army was kept out of the fray by the political veto wielded by the Sunni Premier, Rashid Karami, who warned that the army might split down the middle if thrown into the national cauldron at this time – which did indeed happen in 1976.

With monotonous and terrifying regularity, throughout the spring and summer of 1975, successive cease-fires were breached, Lebanon's cities and their mountain hinterland were divided up ever more decisively between the various warring parties, and the scale of the clashes, as well as of the armaments deployed in them, gradually escalated.

Throughout that summer, too, Henry Kissinger – who had survived Watergate and now served the new U.S. President, Gerald Ford, as Secretary of State – was again busy in the Middle East. On 1 September 1975, the official terms of the second Egyptian-Israeli interim agreement, Sinai II, were released; the agreement was signed three days later in Geneva. In return for a further Israeli pullback in Sinai, most significantly this time from the Mitla and Gidi passes and from the Abu Rodeis oilfields, the Egyptians undertook to forswear the use of force against Israel, and to allow cargoes destined for Israel to traverse the newly reopened Suez Canal.

The most significant assurances Israel gained through the agreement were those given by the U.S. in two separate annexes, whose terms remained secret until they were leaked by The *New York Times* in mid-September. The first annexe promised various forms of U.S. economic and military guarantees to Israel; the second, called 'Memorandum of agreement between the U.S. and Israel concerning the reconvening of the Geneva conference', concerned the Palestinians more directly. Clause 2 of this memorandum spelled out that

The United States will continue to adhere to its present policy with respect to the Palestine Liberation Organization, whereby it will not recognize *or negotiate with* the P.L.O. so long as the P.L.O. does not recognize Israel's right to exist and does not accept Security Council Resolutions 242 and 338. The United States Government will consult fully and seek to concert its position and strategy at the Geneva Peace Conference on this issue with the Government of Israel...It is understood that the participation at a subsequent phase of the Conference of any additional state, group or organization will require the agreement of all the initial participants.[27]

This provision not only set tough preconditions for any future U.S.-PLO dialogue, it also implied that the U.S. could not act freely as a mediator in the Arab-Israeli dispute, and gave Israel (as well as the other participants at the Geneva conference's December 1973 session, of course) a veto over any formula for PLO participation at a reconvened conference.

Back in Lebanon, the conclusion of Sinai II only exacerbated tensions. Something of the atmosphere of the Lebanese capital in the weeks after the agreement's signing is given in my own report, written in early November 1975 for the Beirut *Daily Star*:

Of the hotels and buildings in Beirut's major hotel district which were the scene of fierce fighting over the past week, only two buildings remained Wednesday in the hands of the gunmen.

The Phalangists were still in control of the Holiday Inn, and the Nasserite 'Murabitoon' were still in the Murr Tower. Some 350 meters separate the two buildings.

These two buildings have presumably been chosen as bargaining counters because of their immense height, which allows each to overlook the whole district...

[In the Holiday Inn] an unnamed Phalangist official acts as guide, unnervingly clutching a hand-grenade all the time. He stressed that his Party would continue to hold the building until the Murabitoon left the Murr Tower, 'provided we also had other, strong assurances'.

In his own view, these should include that not one foreigner remains armed on Lebanese soil. 'And yes, that includes the Palestinians.'[28]

The Phalangist rank and file were clearly convinced, even at this stage, that their battle was not merely against their Lebanese opponents, but also against the Palestinian resistance organisations, despite the more diplomatic stance still adopted in public by party leader Pierre Gemayyel and some of his colleagues in the party's political apparatus at that stage.

Fateh, meanwhile, was still trying to avoid full-scale involvement in the Lebanese fighting. Their attitude was summed up later that same month by

Salah Khalaf, then one of the chief planners and executors of Fateh's policy in the country:

We are open to all sides. It is in our interest to have the whole of Lebanon standing with us. But now no one can ask us to be angels and not to differentiate between those forces that stand with us and those who are trying to liquidate us...

Our hope lies with dialogue and through dialogue, the only language that can pervade the whole of Lebanon.[29]

Dialogue was, however, unable to prevail. The fragile cease-fire during which the scenes above were recorded broke down rapidly into further intense fighting. In early December 1975, the Christian Lebanese militias stepped up their policy of forcibly expelling the inhabitants of entire Lebanese Muslim, or Palestinian, quarters which remained trapped inside what was emerging as a purely Lebanese Christian enclave east and north of Beirut. The inhabitants of these quarters, not unnaturally, resisted; but their encirclement by the right-wing Christian militias doomed any resistance. On 14 January 1976, the right-wingers were able to storm and sack the small refugee camp for Christian Palestinians located at Dbayeh, north of Beirut; five days later the densely packed Muslim shanty-town at Karantina, next to the Beirut port, fell to them, and the survivors from its former 30,000 population were expelled to West Beirut.[30] These twin developments – plus the right-wingers' imposition of a tight blockade around the remaining Palestinian refugee camps in East Beirut, at Tel al-Zaatar and Jisr al-Basha, which also started in early January – were to have a threefold impact on the course of events.

It was the fall of Dbayeh and the imposition of the siege around Tel al-Zaatar and Jisr al-Basha which were finally to swing the Fateh leadership round to transferring the bulk of their fighting forces in Lebanon, which then totalled around 8,000 well-trained fighters, away from their front-line bases near the Israeli frontier, northwards into the Lebanese war effort. As Khaled al-Hassan explained, 'When they besieged Tel al-Zaatar, we couldn't but go in.'[31] Fateh's prime political base had always been the refugee camp populations, and the leadership could not brush aside the threat that the sacking of Dbayeh might now be repeated at the other two camps. Tel al-Zaatar in particular, with its 'permanent' population of between 50,000 and 70,000 (now also including many poor Lebanese from south Lebanon), was an important constituency for the guerrilla movements. On 20 January, therefore, Fateh reinforcements from south Lebanon joined the Lebanese oppositionists' siege around Camille Chamoun's stronghold in Damour, south of Beirut, enabling the besiegers to break through into the town. From then until the summer of 1982, the fate of the Fateh forces in Lebanon was tied tightly to that of the Lebanese

68

oppositionists, regardless of what Fateh's 'ideological line' might have prescribed.

The second new development sparked off by the fall of Dbayeh and Karantina was that on 21 January a Sunni Muslim lieutenant in the Lebanese army named Ahmed al-Khatib led a rebellion involving around 1,000 officers and men from the army, who then set themselves up as the Lebanese Arab Army (LAA). They accused the 14,000-strong official Army, with its Maronite-dominated officer corps, of intervening illegally to help the right-wing fighters during the battles of Karantina and Damour; and, indeed, some aged Hawker Hunters of the Lebanese air force had tried to relieve the siege of Damour by bombing its encirclers. Khatib's defection brought new, heavier weaponry and matching expertise to the Palestinian/Lebanese oppositionist fighting forces. The process of disintegration the LAA started within the Lebanese army continued throughout the coming months, in a rightwards as well as leftwards direction, until by summer 1976 there was little left of the original army structure.

The third major development signalled by the battle of Karantina was the arrival in Beirut on 21 January of a high-level delegation from neighbouring Syria, comprising Foreign Minister Abdel-Halim Khaddam, chief of staff Hikmat Shihabi and air force commander Naji Jamil. These men were now formally to launch an intervention by their country in the Lebanese civil war which would affect its course decisively over the coming months.

Syria's allies within both the Palestinian resistance and the Lebanese opposition movement had been noticeably distancing themselves from the military activities of the other members of these movements since at least early December 1975 (though few of them could resist the lure of the booty they might win by participating in the last stages of the battle for Damour). The regime of Syrian President Hafez al-Asad was preparing the ground for a diplomatic initiative in Lebanon, which would enable him to emerge as the stern but influential arbitrator among all the parties to the Lebanese conflict; and Khaddam and company duly launched this arbitration during their visit to Beirut the following month. It appeared to succeed with lightning rapidity: on 22 January, the office of Lebanese President Suleiman Franjieh announced an 'overall solution to the Lebanese problem', which Khaddam had negotiated among all the parties. The cease-fire which accompanied this announcement broke down the very next day; but Khaddam persevered in his contacts, and relative calm prevailed in the country by 14 February, the day on which Franjieh announced a (Syrian-brokered) package of moderate internal political reforms known as the 'Programme of National Action'.[32]

The problem with this Programme was that, by spelling out in detail the reform programme the Syrians had tried to put together, it ended up pleasing none of the Lebanese parties concerned. In particular, Syria's assumption of a new stance as a 'neutral' arbitrator upset the enigmatic but immensely popular leader of the Lebanese leftist coalition, Kamal Junblatt, a Druze feudal leader turned socialist pioneer who combined a passion for esoteric oriental philosophies with a paternalistic concern for residents of his mountain fiefdom, along with more than a measure of tough political ambition. Khalaf has spelled out some of the problems which the rift which developed between Junblatt and the Syrians posed for the Palestinians:

Junblatt thought Syria had once again abandoned the National Movement (the leftist wing of the Lebanese opposition movement), which in his view would have been able to impose at least part of its program of institutional, economic, and social reforms if Damascus had supported the left's military strategy a little longer. President Asad, on the other hand, claimed that continued fighting would have hardened the rightist parties and brought about a disastrous foreign intervention, particularly by Israel. In short, *the Palestinian Resistance was torn between the need to maintain its good relations with its Syrian ally and the moral obligation to stand by the Lebanese left.*[33]

For Fateh, especially, this was a real dilemma. The strategic importance the Fateh leaders had always attached to maintaining good relations with Syria was outlined in chapter 2 above. Meanwhile, Junblatt's support for their cause had been important not only within the Lebanese theatre, but also within the wider Arab arena, since he was leader and co-founder of a pan-Arab organisation called the Arab Front for Participation in the Palestinian Revolution which grouped a broad band of political organisations and personalities around the resistance movement, primarily around Fateh. Indeed, so strong were the opposing poles of attraction within Fateh's Syria-Junblatt dilemma, that as the conflict in Lebanon progressed they came near to pulling the Fateh leadership apart.

Whilst the Palestinians were pondering on this harsh problem, at the purely Lebanese level the left-wing and right-wing actors were unable to agree on a formula for implementing the 14 February Programme. The initiative at the Lebanese level then fell to an obscure Sunni brigadier-general in the Lebanese army called Abdel-Aziz al-Ahdab. On 11 March 1976 Ahdab, who was military commander of the Beirut region, suddenly appeared on national television proclaiming himself 'provisional military governor' of the whole country, and calling on Franjieh to resign.

This resignation call had wide support from many Lebanese, who saw the doughty old mountain clansman in the Presidential Palace as a real obstacle to national reconciliation. By 13 March, 68 Lebanese deputies, out of a total House strength of 99, had signed a petition calling on Franjieh to resign, but he stubbornly hung on. Significantly, however, it had not been Lebanese forces, official or unofficial, who had accompanied Ahdab to the television station, but a unit commanded by Fateh security official Ali Hassan Salameh (Abu Hassan). By this gesture, those Fateh leaders responsible for policy in Lebanon appeared to reveal that they had chosen to support Junblatt right down the line, for it was Junblatt who had spearheaded the call for Franjieh to step down even before Ahdab made his move.

On 27 March, Junblatt travelled to Damascus, where during a decisive and prolonged meeting with Asad he continued to insist on Franjieh's resignation as a condition for ending the fighting. Asad then halted all Syrian arms supplies to the Lebanese National Movement (LNM, the coalition of Lebanese leftists led by Junblatt), and on 9 April he underlined his arguments to Junblatt by deploying 1,000 Syrian troops at the Masnaa border post astride the main Damascus-Beirut highway, and in Dair al-Asha'ir, astride the Palestinians' main supply lines to south Lebanon. Three days later, more Syrian units advanced to occupy the strategic Dahr al-Baidar pass in the mountains overlooking Beirut. By then, the crisis between the Syrians and the Lebanese leftists required a speedy Palestinian reaction. On 15 April, Yasser Arafat hurried to Damascus to negotiate a settlement among the LNM, the Syrians and the PLO; the LNM later accepted the agreement he reached, but only 'with reservations'. Under the agreement, Syrian troops dressed in Palestinian Liberation Army uniforms were almost immediately deployed along the 'Green Line' now splitting the Christian-dominated side from the Palestinian/leftist side in Beirut.

The dispute between Syria and the LNM was then briefly diverted into more political channels. The Syrians had agreed, if not to press for Franjieh's resignation, at least to bring forward the elections for his successor from late summer to May (Franjieh's six-year term was due to run out on 23 September, and in the end he did not resign a single day before then). In the elections, the Syrians ran 'their' candidate, Elias Sarkis, the Governor of the Lebanese Central Bank, against one supported by the LNM, lawyer Raymond Eddé. In the first ballot conducted by the House of Deputies on 6 May, in a temporary Chamber protected by Syrian units right on the 'Green Line', Sarkis could muster only 63 of the 66 deputies he needed for an electoral quorum. But then Camille Chamoun, whose voting bloc had until then remained uncommitted, declared for Sarkis; and two days later Sarkis was able to muster a quorum, and won exactly the requisite number of votes. Franjieh had by now openly allied himself with the right-wing 'Lebanese Front' set up by the Phalangists and the Chamounists but he still firmly refused to resign the presidency.

Soon after Sarkis's election, more Syrian troops arrived in Lebanon:

2,000 crossed into north Lebanon on 31 May, and 4,000 into the Beqaa Valley the next day. The government media in Damascus said that the purpose of these deployments was 'to prevent the partition of Lebanon', which the Syrian regime argued would be the consequence if Junblatt were allowed full freedom of action. As the Syrian troops from the Beqaa started advancing towards Beirut and Sidon, the PLO, the LNM and the Lebanese Arab Army established a unified military command called the 'Joint Forces' to try to halt them. On 6 June, this command launched its first major operation, the takeover of all the offices and military bases which Saiqa and the pro-Syrian Lebanese organisations still maintained in the Palestinian/oppositionist areas. This operation succeeded brilliantly: most of the rank and file of these groups were at a loss to explain their Syrian patron's increasingly close alliance with Chamoun and the Phalangists, and they defected *en masse* to the organisations grouped in the new Palestinian/opposition Joint Command. The next day, the Joint Forces succeeded in halting the Syrian troops' advances towards both Beirut and Sidon. In Sidon, a column of 18 Syrian tanks tried to enter the city without any covering infantry forces,[34] and they were destroyed by guerrillas firing rocket-propelled grenades from the city's buildings in a well-planned ambush. In the hills above Beirut, meanwhile, the massed forces of the Joint Command held the Syrians back at Sofar, despite intensive Syrian shelling of the Palestinian refugee camps near Beirut.

The immediate aftermath of the June battles was a stand-off, which immediately translated itself into diplomatic bargaining. On 2 June, the PLO had issued an urgent request for a meeting of Arab Foreign Ministers, and on 8-9 June this duly took place in Cairo. The solution worked out there involved the sending of the (now routine) Arab conciliation commission, but this time backed by an Arab Peace-keeping Force to replace the Syrian force in separating the combatants. The Syrians, who still had a few of their advance units embarrassingly locked in a small pocket near Beirut Airport, were in no position formally to disagree with this. But once these Syrian units had been extricated by the Arab Peace-keepers, Asad affirmed that the rest of his forces would withdraw only at the request of President Franjieh. The Libyan, Saudi and Sudanese troops who had arrived in Beirut on the peace-keeping mission then spent the next four months in the difficult position of having absolutely no peace to keep.

By mid-June, the Syrian troops around Sofar, in the Beqaa Valley and in the north of Lebanon were not moving much, either backward or forward; their only significant movement over the next three months was one which opened a nearly direct mountain route between the Christian rightists' heartland and Damascus. But they did maintain a tight blockade around what had now become a pair of totally enclosed Palestinian/oppositionist enclaves – the one stretching south from Beirut, the other around Tripoli in the north – and while the Syrians tied down a considerable proportion of the Joint Command's forces along the perimeters of these enclaves, down in Beirut the right-wing militias went in for the kill.

(The Israelis meanwhile profited from the available opportunities by launching their own kind of offensive in southern Lebanon: on 24 June, the Lebanese press reported that a crossing-point had been opened in the border with Israel for the first time since 1949, ostensibly for Lebanese citizens who wished to visit Israel. This was the modest start of a process which was to lead, over the months and years which followed, to the consolidation of a significant pro-Israeli bloc in south Lebanon, an area which had previously been only a casualty of Israeli attacks.)

It was on 22 June 1976 that the right-wing militias started unleashing a massive assault against the three Palestinian and Muslim pockets remaining within the otherwise totally Lebanese Christian sector of East Beirut. These were the large Lebanese Shi'ite quarter of Nabaa, and the Palestinian refugee camps at Tel al-Zaatar and Jisr al-Basha. Jisr al-Basha, a small camp, fell to the militias on 28 June, but Nabaa and Tel al-Zaatar held out for longer. On 6 August, Nabaa fell to the Christian militias, with many of the quarter's defenders blaming their defeat on the defection or treachery of pro-Syrian groups in their midst, particularly the Shi'ite groups loyal to Imam Musa Sadr. Six days later, the 30,000 remaining inhabitants of Tel al-Zaatar surrendered after a brutal siege which caused an estimated 300 babies and young children to die of dehydration, in addition to the many more strictly military casualties.

The siege and subsequent fall of Tel al-Zaatar were experiences of lasting impact for the guerrilla movement, replicating for new generations of Palestinians the kinds of horror which had been visited on their forebears by such groups as Menachem Begin's Irgun back in the 40s. This time, however, as in Jordan six years before, the assailants were fellow Arabs; and as the Lebanese rightists launched themselves into the final orgy of killing, which saw at least 1,500 camp residents killed on the single day the camp was finally evacuated, the army of a 'nationalist' Arab regime was sitting idle, if not actually colluding,[35] on the hilltops nearby. This was the scene inside Tel al-Zaatar the day after it fell:

There were corpses of women, children, babies and old people, as well as men of fighting age. Several, cut down in the camp's twisting lanes, had been squashed to sandwich thickness by passing vehicles. On one, only a splayed foot identified it as human remains.

One family group of women and children was heaped together in a small rocky square, their bellies split open. Outside the camp hospital lay a pile of dead old people, one woman with the traditional tracery of blue tattoos on her face, one man with thick, grey stubble on his chin. Throughout the whole area drifted the indescribable smell of rotting bodies.[36]

The day after the fall of Tel al-Zaatar, Arafat addressed an urgent request to the Arab heads of state to convene a summit meeting. The Egyptian government had since June been giving the Palestinians some modest logistical support in Lebanon,[37] seeking through the Palestinians to stem the apparent increase Syria sought in its regional role, as well as to deflect the Palestinians' criticisms of their own successive step-by-step agreements with Israel. But following Arafat's August appeal, it took the Egyptians 13 days to formulate a reply, and this then merely said that it was preferable to postpone the summit until after the fighting in Lebanon had ended.

Nonetheless, some kind of inter-Arab diplomatic effort did seem inevitable once the Arab regimes had absorbed the horrors of the events in Tel al-Zaatar; and all the parties to the struggle in Lebanon devoted the weeks which followed the camp's fall to consolidating a military position on the ground which would give them the best possible negotiating position in the coming talks.

The Fateh leadership's first concern was to work out an appropriate response to the Syrian offensive they foresaw being launched from the Syrian-held parts of Sofar against their positions in the Upper Metn mountain area behind Beirut; and hand in hand with the Syrians' military preparations for such an offensive, they saw the regime in Damascus making increasingly open moves towards the promotion of an alternative, pro-Syrian, leadership for the Palestinian movement.[38] It was at this stage, according to some sources near to the Fateh leadership, that the above-mentioned dilemma of choosing between Junblatt and the Syrians came close to tearing apart the bonds which had kept that leadership together for the past 17 years.

From the time of the Ahdab 'coup', it had been evident that those of the leadership favouring the alliance with Junblatt over that with Syria were directing Fateh policy in Lebanon; and this policy had depended to a certain extent on using discreet help from Syria's Arab rivals in Egypt and Iraq to help bolster the confrontation with Damascus. But by the end of August it had become clear to nearly all the Fateh leaders that this help would not be forthcoming: Sadat's delay in replying to Arafat's appeal was just the latest indication of this. Those of the Fateh leaders who had opposed backing Junblatt against Damascus thus started regrouping to take over control of the movement's Lebanon policy.

Towards the end of September, the Syrians launched their expected offensive against the Joint Forces' positions in the Upper Metn mountains. Within 72 hours, they had pushed the Joint Forces' units out of the whole 13-mile salient which snaked north-east from the mountain town of

Bhamdoun towards Jebel Sannine. This salient had been a key bargaining-counter for Junblatt in his confrontation with the Lebanese rightists. Those Fateh military commanders associated with the 'defeat' in that mountain salient were then demoted or transferred to other postings, and, when Khalil Wazir himself was brought in to direct the defence of the Joint Forces' remaining mountain positions, in part of Sofar, and in Bhamdoun and Aley, it became apparent that a new kind of Fateh policy was under way in Lebanon. The Fateh leaders themselves were to describe this policy as a 'fighting withdrawal':[39] what it meant, in effect, was finding a way to disengage Fateh from its previous partisanship of Junblatt back into a more equitable relationship with Damascus, whilst holding out for what freedom of action they could from the Syrians.

But the Syrians sought to push the advantage they had won in the mountain salient too far. On 13 October, they attacked Bhamdoun. The Palestinian and Lebanese fighters entrenched there then shrewdly used the topography of the town to lay ambushes for the advancing Syrian armour, using the lessons about dealing with tanks which are unsupported by infantry which they had learned the previous June in Sidon and Beirut. They succeeded in holding back the Syrians' advance, as well as a simultaneous offensive launched against the Bhamdoun-Aley axis from the opposite direction by the Phalangist militiamen stationed in Kahhaleh, downhill from Aley.

This gave Arafat the time he needed to despatch more messages, this time to Leonid Brezhnev as well as to the Arab heads of state. On 14 October, as fighting continued in Bhamdoun, according to Khalaf, Arafat

was able to reach Saudi Arabia's Crown Prince Fahd, who said at the end of their conversation: 'I will settle the problem. Give me a few hours.' The next day, an official communiqué was issued by Riyadh announcing a 'minisummit' for October 16 in the Saudi capital. The same day, President Asad interrupted his offensive and proclaimed a cease-fire on all fronts. Under the circumstances, the only way Arafat could get out of Lebanon was to *accept President Asad's offer of a helicopter* to take him to a Syrian airport, from where he flew to Riyadh on a Saudi plane.

Within forty-eight hours, six men – King Khaled (Saudi Arabia), Sheikh Sabah (Kuwait), Presidents Asad, Sadat and Sarkis, and Yasir Arafat – succeeded in bringing the Lebanese civil war to an end.[40]

The participants in the Riyadh mini-summit mapped out the following terms for a settlement in Lebanon: a cease-fire was to go into operation as from 21 October; and those Arab security forces already deployed in Lebanon – that is, the Syrian units there plus the ill-fated units of the previous Arab Peace-keeping Force – were to be reconstituted as an Arab Deterrent Force (ADF) acting under orders from the Lebanese President. Among the tasks listed for the ADF were 'to enforce the [1969] Cairo agreement and its annexes ... to supervise the withdrawal of armed elements to the positions they occupied before April 13, 1975, and ... to supervise the collection of all heavy armaments, including artillery, mortars, rocket-launchers, armoured vehicles, etc.' A committee consisting of representatives of Egypt, Saudi Arabia and Kuwait was formed 'to co-ordinate with the president of the Lebanese Republic on matters related to the implementation of the Cairo agreement and its annexes'. The text of the Riyadh resolutions spelt out that 'The Palestine Liberation Organisation affirms its respect for the sovereignty and integrity of Lebanon, and that it has no intention of interfering in its internal affairs ... and the legitimate Lebanese authorities similarly guarantee the presence and operation of the Palestine Liberation Organisation in Lebanese territory within the framework of the Cairo agreement and its annexes.'[41]

In other words, what the Riyadh mini-summit called for was a return to the *status quo ante* in terms of Palestinian-Lebanese relations; and this was to be achieved under the immediate auspices of the newly constituted ADF. It was not until the participants in the Riyadh meetings repaired to Cairo the following week to receive the endorsement of a full-scale Arab Summit (the Eighth) for their peace plan that it became clear that the ADF would be totally dominated by its Syrian units. Other Arab governments represented in Cairo pleaded that they had no further troops to spare for their ADF assignment, and it may certainly have been true that many of them were unwilling to see their armies bogged down in the dangerous quagmire that Lebanon promised to continue being. But what also emerged clearly in Cairo was the Arab states' general consensus in support of a strong Syrian role in Lebanon. In the end, only token units from South Yemen and the United Arab Emirates were added to those other Arab units already in Lebanon, and all the non-Syrian units quietly drifted out of the ADF assignment over the following couple of years.

The Syrian government's role went through deep and rapid changes throughout and after the Lebanese civil war, swinging from its original alliance with the Palestinians and the Lebanese opposition movement into collusion, or even an informal alliance, with the Lebanese rightwing. At Riyadh, that first swing of the Syrian pendulum appeared to have been halted, and, over the months which followed, despite many manifestations of the bitterness and distrust which still remained between the Syrians and the PLO/Fateh leadership, it was to be reversed. Throughout 1977, both the concrete conditions inside Lebanon and more global political developments outside it acted to push the Syrian government and the PLO leadership back into their former alliance, until by late 1977 they were acting together to lead the opposition to President Sadat's unilateral Middle East peace initiative.

But Asad could never, apparently, forgive Junblatt, whom he continued to accuse of acting as a covert American agent. On 16 March 1977, the leader of Lebanon's Druze and socialist communities was assassinated in the Lebanese mountains in circumstances which pointed heavily to Syrian connivance at some level. Without Junblatt's esoteric but immensely experienced presence, the coalition of leftist parties which he had led lost much of its cohesion and vigour from that day on; while the rightists, despite some bitterly internecine disputes, increased both their military strength and the stridency of their political demands over the following years. The 'balance' in Lebanon between left and right which Asad had claimed throughout the war as one of his key goals thus eluded him. His other major stated goal had been to disentangle the Palestinians from any involvement in internal Lebanese affairs; but despite the misgivings of many Fateh leaders they were forced to play a continuing military/security role in Lebanon in the years which followed 1976, in order to paper over the cracks in the alliance of anti-Israeli Lebanese parties which emerged rapidly after Junblatt's death.

The 19 months of the Lebanese civil war were a punishing period of attrition for the Fateh leadership. They had tried everything possible to avoid being totally drawn into a confrontation there, but finally it was the brutal pressure of events themselves which drew them into the conflict. If, following the fall of Dbayeh and Karantina and the first imposition of the siege around Tel al-Zaatar in January 1976, they had not thrown all available resources into the battle against the Lebanese rightwing, there were only too many hands from the other guerrilla groups hoping to take over from them the banner of leadership in the nationalist movement they had toiled so hard to build. Nevertheless, the Fateh leaders kept their lines of communication open, however tenuously, to the Phalangist leadership, for example through the continuing contacts between Abu Hassan Salameh and others from Fateh on one hand, and Alexandre Gemayyel and others from the Phalangist politburo on the other.

Similarly, the Fateh leaders tried everything possible to avoid being forced to fight the Syrians. There were plenty of outside Arab powers eager for any chance to fish in the Palestinians' muddy waters for any chance to attack the Syrians. Thus, while some Fateh people were moderately grateful for the presence of the few hundred Iraqi 'volunteers'[42] who travelled to Lebanon, via Egypt, in early summer 1976 to fight as part of the Arab Liberation Front in downtown Beirut, at the same time this presence also reminded the Fateh leaders sharply that they could not allow themselves to be seen by most Palestinians at that time as half-hearted in their confrontation with Syria.

In the end, an intricately nuanced policy emerged from the Fateh core. Each individual member of this core certainly had his own assessment of the situation in Lebanon, and his own policy preferences; but as the burden

77

of prime responsibility was shifted between them, the policy which emerged was one which at least allowed the movement to emerge intact from the military challenge and the political pitfalls which strewed those months.

Thus, Khalaf's preference in Lebanon may be seen in general terms as having been to keep all lines open, but ultimately not to endanger the guerrillas' alliance with the Lebanese opposition. When Junblatt was eager to push ahead in the mountains in pursuit of his 'military solution', it was Khalaf who was reported as saying, 'The path to Palestine leads through Jounieh' – the right-wingers' main port and stronghold, which Junblatt argued could have been taken if the Joint Command forces had continued their mountain campaign. At that stage, Khalaf allies such as Nimr Saleh (Abu Saleh), Abu Musa and Abu Khaled al-Amili were in charge of Fateh's military campaign in the mountains. Arafat was meanwhile playing a busy behind-the-scenes political role, trying to prevent any final break between Junblatt and the Syrians.

When it was clear, by the first days of June 1976, that this mediation could not succeed, Arafat had absented himself from the theatre of operations in Lebanon on one of his frequent tours of the Gulf states, and it was Khalaf who was left to make the crucial decision on whether to resist the Syrian troops advancing towards Beirut and Sidon. The fact that it was Khalaf virtually guaranteed that the decision would be to resist the Syrians; but Arafat's main preoccupation throughout this period was apparently to limit the possible adverse consequences of the confrontation with Syria, and to consult with those of the Fateh leaders who were outside Lebanon who had counselled more strongly against getting drawn into a battle with Syria. By early October, this group, which reportedly included Wazir and Hassan, was able to impose its policy, as we have seen above.

The Fateh leadership was thus ultimately able to emerge from the Lebanese civil war itself intact, and with the main bulk of its fighting forces not only intact but also hardened in several different types of battle scenario. The Cairo Arab Summit had allotted Syria a *de facto* mandate to exercise control in the Lebanese theatre; but Fateh still commanded a certain degree of freedom of action there from Damascus, particularly by virtue of its control over those regions in the south of the country from which Israel had expressly excluded the possibility of any Syrian deployment. Fateh's bargaining-power *vis-à-vis* the Syrians was to increase over the months following the Riyadh and Cairo meetings as the Syrians came to understand both the scale of the problem the Lebanese rightists were able (with no small help from Israel) to cause them, and the glaring weakness of the Lebanese left in the absence of Junblatt.

The rigours of the Lebanese civil war, moreover, left Fateh in a considerably stronger position relative to the other guerrilla groups in the PLO spectrum. Saiqa, which had previously represented something of an authentically Palestinian brand of Baathism as well as the interest bestowed on it by Damascus, was completely debilitated by the mass defections of early June 1976. As the Saiqa infrastructure was pieced back together again by its incongruously genial leader Zuhair Muhsin[43] in the aftermath of the war, it was reborn in a much more strictly Syrian mould: the Syrians were wary of giving the rebuilt organisation even the same extremely limited organisational freeway which had led to their embarrassment in 1976. But it was the Popular Front for the Liberation of Palestine which, in a real sense, was the real Palestinian casualty of the war,[44] for the Front had since its creation been marked more by idealism than by any talent for organisation and, though many of its members fought (and died) bravely throughout the war, the fast-changing nuance of the fighting saw its leaders repeatedly outmanoeuvred by the Fateh leaders, particularly by their decision to stage the 'fighting withdrawal' from the mountains.

At the Thirteenth session of the Palestinian National Council, which met in Cairo in March 1977, the PFLP-based Rejection Front was unable to mount more than rhetorical opposition to the Fateh-dominated Executive Committee mainstream, which was able to spell out in the official resolutions of the Council that the PLO's aim was now the establishment of an 'independent national state' in any liberated parts of Palestine, rather than to hide behind the previous phrasing of a 'national authority'.

The mere fact of the survival of the armed Palestinian presence was a matter of prime importance for the guerrilla movement's leadership, especially since this time round, in contrast to what followed the 1970-71 events in Jordan, there was now no further alternative base from which they could operate with any freedom at all. And the Fateh leadership continued to see the presence of an unfettered, armed Palestinian movement as a necessary, if never yet sufficient, condition for the Palestinians' eventual exercise of their political rights inside historic Palestine.

The guerrilla movement's strategic position had nevertheless been considerably weakened by the 19 months of fighting. Many hundreds of its members and supporters had been killed. The uneasy coalition of its allies in the Lebanese opposition emerged bitter, confused and leaderless from the war. The Israelis had won important beach-heads of open support in both central and southern Lebanon. And the Syrian government, which most of the Fateh leadership continued to see – in spite of everything – as a strategic ally in the fight against Israel, found its political legitimacy at home undermined and its military deployments diverted away from the Golan Heights; while even the Syrians' virtual hegemony over Lebanon, which Damascus rulers had historically craved ever since the creation of modern Lebanon, turned out to be a slowly ticking time-bomb which sapped Syria's traditional strength and vitality.

All this had taken place during precisely the period when the PLO (and Syria) might have been expected to launch a strong diplomatic initiative for a move back to Geneva after the vagaries of Kissinger's step-by-step approach to Middle Eastern damage-control. By the end of 1976, the peace-making momentum which had suffused the Middle East throughout the year following the October War had largely dissipated: Israel had rearmed and reorganised its armed forces to make them considerably stronger than ever before, and its colonisation policy had continued making further inroads on the Palestinian lands of the West Bank; and many of the Arab rulers had become more absorbed with spending the new wealth they gained in the wake of the oil embargo than they were with promoting the Palestinians' cause.

At least the Palestinian movement survived. In the months which followed October 1976, its leaders sought to build on the vision of Arab consensus which they thought they had glimpsed at Riyadh and Cairo, in order to try to redirect the Arabs' political momentum back towards the convening of the Middle East Peace Conference, where, they still hoped, they might eventually win the Palestinian state they hoped for.

Chapter 5

The net tightens (1977-80)

The Lebanese war of 1975-76 did not, in the end, prove as damaging for the Palestinian guerrilla movement as the rout they had suffered in Jordan in 1970-71. As the other guerrilla leaders welcomed PLO Chairman Arafat back to Beirut from the Arab summit meeting in Cairo in October 1976, they could at least be relieved that the Arab governments in general, and Lebanon's new President Elias Sarkis in particular, had formally agreed to reiterate the validity of the agreement reached in Cairo eight years previously which allowed and regulated the guerrilla presence in Lebanon. Though Arafat had failed, at the Cairo summit, in his last-minute attempt to limit the role of the Syrian army in the Arab Deterrent Force established for Lebanon by the summit, nevertheless the guerrillas still enjoyed considerably more freedom of military and political action in their principal base in Lebanon than the Syrian government had appeared ready to grant them in the harsh days of the Palestinian-Syrian fighting of summer and autumn of 1976.

The most important decision the Fateh leaders faced in the period following the Lebanese cease-fire was how best to use what freedom of manoeuvre they still enjoyed (in Lebanon and elsewhere) to pursue the national goals from which they saw the 19 bruising months of fighting in Lebanon as having diverted them. Certainly, the Lebanese war had had its effects upon the political balance both inside Fateh and inside the PLO as a whole. Given the complexity of the political process inside Fateh, these changes took quite a time to work through its internal system, and continued to cause controversy inside the movement for the next couple of years. But at the broader PLO level, it was already clear by October 1976 that the Lebanese fighting had significantly weakened the Rejection Front, the coalition of PLO member-groups which in 1974 had criticised the Twelfth Palestinian National Council's endorsement of a diplomatic approach to a settlement. One of the first moves of the Fateh/PLO bosses, therefore, after the Cairo summit meeting, was to start making preparations for the next session of the PNC, at which they could capitalise on this change to strengthen their mandate for the turn towards diplomacy. That session of

81

the PNC, the Thirteenth, was duly convened, in Cairo, in March 1977.

The Riyadh and Cairo summit cease-fires had, however, by no means resolved all the problems the PLO and Fateh leaders faced in Lebanon. The Palestinian leaders saw an urgent need to find a new *modus vivendi* with the Syrian troops who were now deployed under the ADF banner in all parts of the country, except to the south of the 'Red Line' drawn by the Israelis[1] across south Lebanon as the southern limit of ADF deployment. And the first signs of Israel's new forward policy in Lebanon which had appeared in June 1976 (see chapter 4 above) multiplied so rapidly throughout the following months that by the end of 1976 it was already becoming clear that the Palestinians' next major confrontation in Lebanon would be with Israel and not with Syria.

Even as the attention of most of the Palestinian leaders was still turned to the Riyadh and Cairo summit meetings, in October 1976 the Israelis and their local allies were taking steps to establish a new position of strength in south Lebanon. It was in October that the pro-Israeli Lebanese militia led by Saad Haddad, a former Lebanese army major, moved northward from the impoverished hilltop village of Qleiya to occupy the army barracks in the regional capital of Marjayoun, a once-prospering inland market town whose (Christian) population had traditionally tended to support the Palestinians. Control of the Marjayoun barracks gave Haddad control of the strategic road passing through the town, which had long been a key supply-route for the Palestinians between the south Lebanese ports and the guerrilla bases in the hilly Arqoub region[2] to the east.

For their part, the Palestinian leaders lost little time, once it had become apparent that the Arab-sponsored cease-fires of October would take more or less effective hold throughout north and central Lebanon, in trying to redeploy their forces and matériel back to confront the new challenges posed by Haddad's activities in the south. Ever since 1968, the Palestinian guerrilla units operating in south Lebanon had devoted much attention to building up a close alliance with the population there, who were mainly Shi'ite Muslim villagers, living in a social system which had changed little since the days of feudalism. For years these efforts had borne fruit in a generally steady stream of support from the south Lebanese for the Palestinians. But at the same time, it was the poor villagers of the south who had borne the brunt of Israel's successive harsh retaliations against the region since 1968. So when Israel appeared instead, from June 1976 onwards, to be holding out a hand of friendship to the villagers, some of them – at first mainly members of the south's tiny Maronite Christian minority, but later members of other sects too – started to turn against the Palestinians. Combined with the coercive tactics of Haddad, this process was sufficient to start transforming the southern villagers' previously near-unanimous front of support for the guerrillas into a deadly division which pitted village against village and neighbour against neighbour.

Thus, in the months which followed the formal ending of the Lebanese civil war, the area south of the Israeli-drawn 'Red Line' became virtually a free-fire zone between the Israelis and their allies on the one hand, and the Palestinians and their allies on the other. There was no ADF in that area to control the situation; the Lebanese army was still far too weak, as a result of the schisms it had undergone during the civil war, even to consider deploying in an area as tense as the south; and at that stage the United Nations presence in south Lebanon was limited to a handful of observation posts manned by units of the U.N. Truce Supervision Organisation established back in 1949. The tensions which simmered in south Lebanon thus provided a constant backdrop to the Middle East-related diplomatic process from late 1976 onwards, and every so often intruded rudely into it.

The Palestinians still had to face some residual disputes with the Syrian troops now ruling the rest of the country under the ADF banner. In mid-February 1977, Syrian artillery was again pounding Palestinian refugee camps near Beirut, following Syrian requests to enter the Arab University area which the Palestinian Armed Struggle Command had controlled since the early 70s. But problems like this were relatively quickly resolved as the gravity of the situation in the south became apparent not only to the Palestinians but also to the Syrians.[3] The Palestinians also had to take into account the possible effects any confrontation with the pro-Israeli forces there might have on their still-delicate relations with a Syrian government certainly far from being committed to an all-out battle against the Israelis in Lebanon.[4]

Despite these constraints, however, the Palestinians were able, in the early months of 1977, to reinforce their units in the south to the same strength (or in some cases even superior strength) as that which they had enjoyed before the Fateh leadership's decision of January 1976 to build up their military presence further north.

Repeatedly, throughout 1977, the PLO's leaders put on record their readiness to abide by all provisions of the 1969 Cairo agreement, including those limiting the Palestinian military presence in south Lebanon. But the Lebanese government under President Elias Sarkis was chronically weak, and the national army could not hope to become strong enough within the foreseeable future to impose the rule of law either on the country's heavily-armed and battle-toughened militias or on the Palestinian guerrillas. Palestinian leaders, still scarred by the massacres the right-wing Christian militias had wrought in Tel al-Zaatar, and fearful of a repetition elsewhere, continued to argue that the disarming of the Lebanese militias should precede their own full implementation of the Cairo agreement; and that in any case the the this latter process could not go ahead until the Lebanese administration had its own forces ready in place to fulfil its commitments under the Cairo agreement.[5] Since neither of these conditions was fulfilled in the months and years which followed the Cairo and Riyadh summits, the question of the implementation of the Cairo agreement continued to feature on the Palestinian-Lebanese agenda. The Four-Party Arab committee[6] established by the summits met repeatedly over the months following October 1976 to try to find a formula for implementing the provisions of the cease-fire agreement reached at those summits for Lebanon, which included a reimplementation of the Cairo agreement. But, faced with the continuing suspicion between the former combatants of the 1975-76 fighting and the new factor of much more direct Israeli involvement in Lebanon, they failed to achieve this.

These, then, were some of the considerations in the minds of the 293 delegates who made their way, from Lebanon and elsewhere, to the Thirteenth session of the PNC, held in the Stalinist-ornate Nile-side headquarters of the Arab League in Cairo. The central focus of the discussion at the Council, as at that which had preceded it three years earlier, was over the decision to pursue a peaceful settlement, and the best way of doing this.

The negotiating stance held to by the PLO Executive Committee in the period immediately leading up to the Thirteenth PNC session had been outlined by Committee member Farouq al-Qaddumi, head of the PLO Political (i.e. Foreign Affairs) Department, in an interview with the semi-official Egyptian daily *Al-Ahram* at the end of February 1977. Qaddumi explained,

we have said that we reject [Security Council] resolutions 242 and 338, and that we are not prepared to attend the Geneva conference on the basis of these resolutions. The reason for this is that resolution 242 regards our problem as a problem of refugees and not as a political problem... We clearly informed Waldheim of our position, which is as follows:

1. The PLO should be invited.

2. We should attend as an independent delegation.

3. We should attend the conference from the start.

4. We should participate in all its activities without exception.

5. Palestine should be a separate item on the agenda.

6. If we accept the invitation it will be on the basis of General Assembly resolution 3236...

7. The great powers must provide fundamental guarantees for the establishment of an independent Palestinian state in the territories from which Israel withdraws.

8. *We believe that the United States is going through the motions, not really taking action. We do not expect anything from this operation, because it is an American manoeuvre.*[7]

The question of whether, and how, the PNC should alter this policy had come up for intensive discussion among representatives of all the mainstream PLO in the weeks preceding the PNC session. Yasser Abed Rabboo, the DFLP's youthful representative on the PLO Executive Committee, told me in Cairo that these preparatory meetings, mostly held in Beirut, had already resulted in an agreement among Fateh, the Syrian-backed Saiqa organisation and the DFLP to continue the same basic approach as hitherto; and that some of the smaller Rejection Front groupings could also be expected to endorse this agreement, although the PFLP had turned down an invitation to the Beirut talks.[8] In the end, the substance of what Abed Rabboo had said was borne out when the PFLP proved incapable of mustering more than its own 13 votes to oppose the political programme ratified by the Council.

This programme, which consisted of 15 major political clauses, started off with the now routine denunciation of resolution 242. But this time, the previous PNC's call for the establishment of a 'national, independent and fighting authority' on every part of Palestinian land liberated was spelt out specifically as meaning the establishment of an 'independent national *state* on the soil of the homeland'.[9] But the basic approach to a political settlement remained substantially the same: in May 1977, in an interview with the PLO Research Center's monthly, *Shu'un Filastiniyya*, Qaddumi was able to list nearly exactly the same eight points as those quoted above as still forming the guiding policy for PLO diplomacy.[10]

Two other major debates enlivened the proceedings of the Thirteenth PNC. One focussed on the question of PLO contacts with Israeli and other Jewish groups and individuals, following reports of contacts between PLO emissaries and members of the Israeli peace group led by Reserve General Matti Peled. The programme subsequently adopted by the session stated, 'the PNC stresses the importance of relations and coordination with democratic and progressive Jewish forces, inside and outside the occupied homeland, that are struggling against the theory and practice of Zionism', but it had apparently already been decided that the Peled group did not meet the latter criterion.[11]

The other major debate inside the PNC session aroused, in many of the delegates, deeper passions: it was the debate over Yasser Arafat's latest moves towards a reconciliation with King Hussein. The two men had both been in Cairo, in the days immediately before the PNC session, for the first Afro-Arab summit conference. There they had taken the opportunity to hold their first recorded meeting with each other since the victory of Hussein's forces over Arafat's in the fighting in Jordan of 1970-71. The PLO news agency, Wafa, quoted 'a responsible source in the Palestinian delegation' to the summit as having said that the Arafat-Hussein meeting 'took place within the framework of national relations with a view to coordinating Arab efforts at this conference'.[12] But even this heavily bureaucratic formulation could not disguise the enormity of a move to which many PLO activists, still angered by their treatment at the hands of the Jordanian troops, remained bitterly opposed.

In the end, the PNC's programme made no specific mention at all of relations with Jordan. From the point of view of those in the movement who supported a rapprochement with Hussein this was probably a relative victory, given that the previous PNC had called openly for the establishment of 'a national democratic regime in Jordan'. The fact that the new PLO Executive Committee elected at the Thirteenth PNC understood itself to have a mandate to proceed with the overtures towards Hussein was indicated in Qaddumi's later interview with *Shu'un Filastiniyya*, when he argued, 'Certainly, good relations with Jordan are necessary, because Jordan is our strategic depth, and we cannot establish an independent Palestinian state without there being good relations between us and Jordan.'[13]

In political terms, the Fateh leaders scored a significant victory at the Thirteenth PNC by detaching, at least formally, all the PFLP's allies in the Rejection Front from the PFLP, and persuading them to accept seats on the Fateh-dominated list for the Executive Committee elections on political terms which were basically Fateh's own. As I reported at the time,

The Popular Front ... has no place reserved for it in the new 15-member PLO Executive Committee elected by the National Council, whilst its erstwhile rejectionist allies each have one place.

The line-up on the new Executive Committee can be roughly described as: Fateh – five members, pro-Egypt and more or less pro-Moscow – three members each, pro-Syria and pro-Iraq – two members each. A last-minute attempt by the pro-Syrian commando group Saiqa to increase the pro-Syrian contingent was foiled, whilst new members upped the pro-Egyptian representation.[14]

The Fateh leaders did not introduce any dramatic policy changes into the Thirteenth PNC session. The net effect of the session for the Fateh leaders was what they had sought: the PLO Executive Committee's mandate to pursue its existing (and now further refined) diplomatic policy was strengthened, through their own outflanking both of their own internal opposition in the Rejection Front and of the external influence which the Syrian government had apparently hoped to wield inside the session. The political cost the Fateh leaders paid to obtain this result was to increase their links with and indebtedness to an Egyptian regime whose recent policies towards Israel they still distrusted. However, as they were still relying heavily on the Egyptians to help open the door to their own participation in Middle East peace negotiations,[15] this cost was presumably a bearable trade-off. Anyway, moving towards peace negotiations was the task to which the Fateh/PLO leadership principally applied itself in the months which followed the PNC session.

The PLO's turn to diplomacy had registered several significant advances in the years between 1974 and 1977, principally through opening up a near direct dialogue with the governments of Western Europe, and also by establishing formal relations with many Third World states. However, the PLO's diplomatists, including Fateh's Farouq al-Qaddumi, who was in overall charge of the PLO's diplomatic efforts during this period, realised all along that if a peaceful settlement were to be found to the Palestinian problem, this could be achieved only when the PLO was finally able to affect the policies of the governments in Israel and the United States. In early 1977, there were changes of administration in both these countries which had a direct effect on the PLO/Fateh leaders' hopes of achieving a peaceful settlement. In January 1977, Jimmy Carter succeeded Gerald Ford to the U.S. presidency, and four months later the Labour-dominated coalition which had dominated the Israeli government since the establishment of the Jewish state nearly three decades before was ousted at the polls by the Likud coalition headed by former Irgun boss Menachem Begin.

Since September 1975, the U.S.'s Middle East diplomacy had been hamstrung by the commitment Secretary of State Kissinger made to the Israelis, that the U.S. government would not negotiate with the PLO 'so long as the PLO does not recognise Israel's right to exist and does not accept Security Council resolutions 242 and 338'.[16] The very fact of Kissinger's departure from the Department of State in January 1977 thus occasioned some interest amongst the PLO's diplomats. In the immediate aftermath of Jimmy Carter's election to the U.S. presidency the previous November, the President-elect had still been – to the PLO leaders, as even to many Americans – largely an unknown quantity. But the PLO/Fateh leaders were encouraged when they learnt that not only would Kissinger's term in the State Department shortly be coming to an end, but, in addition, his successor there would be the veteran diplomat Cyrus Vance.

As William Quandt, the Middle East specialist who was to sit on Carter's National Security Council, recalled it, members of President Ford's outgoing administration prepared Middle East position papers for the incoming administration which reviewed all the available options for reconvening Geneva, including the idea of including Palestinians in a unified Arab delegation. Menachem Begin's electoral success in Israel, in the spring of 1977, set back many of the new administration's plans, he added, but efforts had continued through Saudi, Egyptian, Syrian and other channels to arrive at the kind of 'acceptable statement' from the PLO which could be interpreted as satisfying the conditions for starting a U.S.-PLO dialogue.[17]

On 16 March 1977, Carter made a declaration in Clinton, Massachusetts, which appeared to constitute a fresh approach in U.S. thinking on the Arab-Israeli question. In Clinton, Carter said,

There has to be a homeland provided for the Palestinian refugees who have suffered for many, many years...

We hope that later on this year, in the latter part of this year, that we might get all these parties to agree to come together at Geneva, to start talking to one another.[18]

Two months later, a delegation of Saudi officials, led by Crown Prince Fahd and including the Foreign Minister, Prince Saud al-Faisal, visited the U.S. They carried with them a memorandum outlining the PLO's view of peace negotiations, written by Qaddumi's predecessor in the PLO's 'Foreign Minister' position, Fateh co-founder Khaled al-Hassan, who was still entrusted by Fateh with many important diplomatic tasks while he presided over the PNC's Foreign Relations Committee. At that stage, there were two major intermediaries between the PLO leaders and the U.S. government: the Egyptians and the Saudis. Subsequently, negotiators from both the U.S. and PLO sides were to report that they felt this arrangement caused a lot of extraneous 'noise' on the diplomatic line, but at the time it seemed that the Saudi mission to Washington was achieving something.

According to Hassan, the Saudi delegation returned to the Middle East from the U.S. capital with a request from the Americans that the PLO should replace its 'negative refusal' of resolution 242 with a 'positive refusal':

that means not just to say that we refuse 242 because it dealt with the Palestinian problem as a problem of refugees: they consider this negative. So they want something positive, saying that we refuse 242 *because it didn't include* so and so and so. Now, maybe because the Egyptians were on the line and the Saudis were on the line, there was more than one interpretation or more than one understanding of the American request...

And we started talking about a phrase: how to write something which refused 242 in a positive way... At that time, we put more than one phrase, saying for instance we would have accepted 242 if it included so and so and so. This was rejected by the Americans. Then we said we *will* accept 242 if it includes so and so and so, and this was also refused by the Americans. Finally, we asked for a commitment, an American commitment to a Palestinian state, either to be made in public or in writing... They also refused: they refused to give any commitment, and they wanted a plain acceptance of 242.[19]

Despite the difficulties, however, indirect negotiations did continue. In the first weeks of June 1977 they seemed to be making such good progress that, according to Hassan, Vance had said that if the PLO could signal its 'plain acceptance' of 242 before the visit he was scheduled to make to

China on 19 June, he would receive the PLO negotiators personally in the State Department. 'Otherwise, Philip Habib would receive us because he [Vance] would be in China.'[20] As it turned out, the PLO leaders were by no means ready to produce a clear and acceptable position on 242 within this time limit. Discussions continued within Palestinian circles on this issue throughout the following five months.

At some stages during the summer and autumn of 1977, it appeared that the sides were close to arriving at an acceptable formula which would allow the U.S.-PLO dialogue to commence and progress to be made towards reconvening the Geneva conference with some sort of Palestinian representation. In mid-August, a meeting of the PLO's 40-member policy-reviewing Central Council listened to a memorandum reportedly passed by the U.S. Ambassador in Damascus, through diplomatic intermediaries, to Central Council Chairman Khaled Fahoum. This memorandum stated that a PLO acceptance of resolution 242 would not necessarily guarantee the PLO a seat at Geneva, but that it would open the way for contacts between the PLO and the State Department. Some of the Central Council members reportedly wanted to pursue this American opening further; but, taken as a whole, the offer enclosed in the memorandum was unanimously rejected. All that those who wanted to keep their lines open to the U.S. could achieve was a decision that the Council should reconvene one month later to discuss further developments.[21]

When the Central Council did reconvene, on 20 September, it had on the table before it an even firmer indication of the American administration's interest in addressing the Palestine question. This was an official State Department statement, issued on 12 September, including the formal analysis that 'the Palestinians must be involved in the peace-making process. Their representatives will have to be at Geneva for the Palestinian question to be solved.'[22] The statement also spelt out that all participants in the Geneva conference should accept Security Council resolutions 242 and 338, but many of the PLO leaders, reportedly including Arafat, nevertheless regarded it as positive enough to want to accord it a clear welcome when the Central Council met in Damascus. One participant in the Central Council session told me shortly afterwards, 'Arafat wanted to lay stress on what he considered a major American step towards the Palestinians.'[23]

But the discussion in that session was also described as 'long and stormy'. It was after that meeting that Arafat appeared briefly with one hand in a bandage, a result, sources inside the Central Council said, of Arafat having broken a glass table-top by banging his fist on it. And the end result was that Arafat and his allies failed to persuade the Central Council to come out with the sort of dramatic political gesture – most probably, a less guarded form of acceptance of 242 – which just might have resulted in a diplomatic breakthrough.

One of the key factors which were reported as ultimately turning the majority of Council members away from endorsing such a gesture was the series of events then occurring in south Lebanon, where American diplomacy had recently failed to persuade the Israelis to allow the deployment of Lebanese army units to pacify a situation of escalating clashes. Sources inside the Council told me, 'One key argument which helped clinch [the result of the meeting] was that if the Americans could not pressure Israel to agree to the stationing of 700 Lebanese peacekeepers in south Lebanon, how could it ever hope to bring about an Israeli withdrawal from the West Bank and Gaza?'[24]

On 1 October, Secretary of State Vance and Soviet Foreign Minister Andrei Gromyko issued a joint statement in New York which announced their intention to achieve the reconvening of the Geneva Conference 'not later than December 1977' – four years to the month after Kissinger had successfully manoeuvred the whole Geneva concept into abeyance. The joint statement outlined several issues which the two superpowers, as co-chairmen of the conference, agreed should be resolved at Geneva: these included 'the resolution of the Palestinian question, including insuring the legitimate rights of the Palestinian people'. It also called for the participation at Geneva 'of the representatives of all the parties involved in the conflict including those of the Palestinian people'.[25]

That evening, Fateh's ruling Central Committee met in emergency session in Beirut. The consensus resulting from their deliberations was most probably reflected nearly verbatim in the statement issued the next day by the PLO news agency, Wafa, which noted that this was the first time the United States had openly recognised the existence of a Palestinian people as such. As I reported at the time, '*Wafa* considered the reference to "legitimate rights" as "reflecting a better understanding of the cause of our Palestinian people" – better, presumably, than previous United States formulations of "legitimate Palestinian interests".'[26]

If the U.S.-Soviet statement was greeted by a markedly unequivocal welcome from the Fateh leaders, it certainly did not get such a reception from the Israelis. Begin's Foreign Minister, Moshe Dayan, who was also in New York at the time, had been shown a copy of the two-power statement on 29 September. The next day, as he recorded it, 'I told Vance that our Prime Minister had ... expressed our objection to any such two-power declaration, and specifically to the contents of this one.'[27]

On 4 October, Dayan and his delegation started their counter-attack against the two-power declaration in a prolonged session of talks with President Carter; the U.S. President later left Dayan with Vance to work out the details of a joint U.S.-Israeli working paper. This was published the following day, under the title 'Suggestions for the resumption of the Geneva peace conference'. Gone now were the references to 'the Palestinian people', or their 'legitimate rights'. Instead, the Israeli-American working paper called for the Arab parties to be represented at Geneva by a unified Arab delegation, 'which will include Palestinian Arabs', after which the conference would split into geographically based working groups. Clauses 3 to 6 of the working paper stated:

3. The West Bank and Gaza issues will be discussed in a working group to consist of Israel, Jordan, Egypt and the Palestinian Arabs.
4. The solution of the problem of the Arab refugees and of the Jewish refugees will be discussed in accordance with terms to be agreed upon.
5. The agreed basis for the negotiations at the Geneva peace conference on the Middle East are U.N. Security Council Resolutions 242 and 338.
6. All the initial terms of reference of the Geneva peace conference remain in force, except as may be agreed by the parties.[28]

In spite of all the gains the Palestinians thought the Israelis had registered in the wording of this working paper, President Carter still apparently considered he had Begin's agreement to a formula – strongly criticised by Dayan – by which the 'Palestinian Arabs' participating in Geneva could be low-level members of the PLO.[29] Meanwhile, according to William Quandt, some of the Arab delegations at the U.N. in New York had been shown some early working drafts of U.S. ideas for Palestinian representation at Geneva which would have accorded the PLO a more visible – though still limited – role, and when they saw the finally published U.S. proposals on this issue, they considered them a step backwards. In Quandt's view, it was this sign of apparent American bad faith which he himself explained as a misunderstanding about the status of the earlier proposals, which then combined with the terms of the U.S.-Israeli joint working paper to stifle the PLO's interest in the negotiations with the U.S. as of mid-October.[30]

On 15 and 16 October, Fateh's Central Committee again convened, though this time Arafat was absent. I reported at the time that

[The Central Committee statement] stressed that, 'The PLO is the sole legitimate representative of the Palestinian people ... and will not accept any maneuvre aiming at taking away this right or sidestepping it.'

A prominent Fateh member confirmed to me today that this formulation represents a firm rejection of working-paper proposals that the PLO be represented in the Palestinian group at any reconvened Geneva peace conference by low-level members. It would also rule out the suggestion that Arafat nominate Palestinian delegates to Geneva who would not represent the PLO there.[31]

The publication of the American-Israeli working paper came as a serious blow to those inside Fateh who had hoped for a speedy opening of talks with the U.S., leading to some kind of PLO participation at Geneva. Their hopes in this regard then received a further blow a bare three weeks later, on 9 November, when Egypt's President Sadat announced to his Parliament that he was willing to travel even to the Israeli Knesset to seek peace with Israel. Thus was launched the famous 'Sadat initiative', whose drama cut through all existing deliberations on the Middle East question, rendering meaningless all the complex discussions of the preceding months among Palestinians, Arab governments, Americans, Russians and Israelis, as a striking new factor of the direct Egyptian-Israeli rapprochement was thrown into the Middle Eastern balance.

The Palestinians had thought, right up until 9 November, that Sadat was arguing on their behalf with the U.S. government for a PLO role *in Geneva*.[32] But in fact, as far back as mid-September 1977, the Egyptian President had responded positively to a suggestion from Morocco's King Hassan that he send an emissary to Morocco to start direct talks with the Israelis, as represented there by Moshe Dayan.[33] His dramatic announcement of 9 November was merely the public follow-up to this process, but it was made even more galling for the Fateh leaders by the fact that Arafat and Qaddumi were actually present, as guests of that session of the Egyptian Parliament, whilst it was made. Despite the fact that these two men in common with the vast majority of other Arabs, did not know at the time whether to take the Egyptian President's announcement absolutely literally, they felt offended enough by the mere mention of visiting Jerusalem under Israeli rule to walk out of the Parliament at that point.

Sadat presented his initiative to Egyptian and Arab opinion as having been undertaken on behalf of all the Arab parties to the Middle East conflict. But during a flying visit to Syria on the eve of his trip to Jerusalem he failed to convince President Hafez al-Asad of the validity of his approach. Once it was clear Sadat was going to continue with the initiative regardless of the fears of his ally of the October 1973 War, it was Asad who pioneered the Arab opposition to him. At that stage, though there were many voices of outrage amongst Palestinian activists, the Fateh leadership seemed momentarily almost too stunned to believe what was happening, and some of its members even harboured apparently irrational hopes that something, anything, would prevent Sadat's visit to Jerusalem from taking place.[34]

But on 19 November, the trip did go ahead. Salah Khalaf wrote, 'Tears were streaming down the cheeks of some of my comrades' as they all sat watching the live television coverage of Sadat's visit to Israel. Once the reality of the Egyptian leader's action had set in, he recorded, Fateh's Central Committee

split into two factions. One believed that we couldn't afford to break with Egypt due to its decisive role in the Arab world, and that we should confine ourselves to criticising the President's move without going any farther.

I took the opposite viewpoint. Naturally, I said, Egypt is a major factor in the equation, but it is only as powerful as the legitimacy and popularity of its regime. In any event, I added, the price of humoring it in this case was too high. I advocated a frontal and sustained attack against Sadat and any states that supported him.[35]

By 22 November, these internal debates had been resolved sufficiently for Arafat to travel to Damascus, where in the name of the PLO he issued a joint communiqué with President Asad in which the two sides declared 'their outright condemnation of this [Sadat's] visit and their readiness to apply all their resources to the elimination of its consequences'. In a clear break from Fateh's traditional ideology of non-intervention in the internal affairs of Arab states, Arafat subscribed in this communiqué to an open joint call 'on the great Egyptian people and its intrepid army ... to resist this treason to the Arab nation'.[36] The following day, Sadat ordered the closure of the PLO office in Cairo, and of the Egypt-based transmitters of the PLO's Voice of Palestine broadcasting house.

The importance of Sadat's move to the Palestinian leaders thus ultimately proved to be twofold. First, and most crucially, Sadat had now set the Arab world's most populous and politically weightiest state firmly on the road to a separate peace with Israel. As Egypt became detached from the Arab-Israeli strategic balance, the Israeli military's position *vis-à-vis* its remaining Arab foes became considerably strengthened, causing immediate strategic worries first and foremost to Syria and the PLO.[37] Secondly, Sadat's initiative forced the Fateh leaders to change the whole strategy they had adopted since 1967 of balancing their policy carefully between the policies of the Arab confrontation states with their own direct grievances against Israel – primarily, Egypt and Syria. Sadat's move forced the Fateh leaders to replace this with a policy of PLO partisanship in inter-Arab quarrels, however much this rankled with some of the Fateh veterans.

On 2 December 1977, the heads of state of Libya, Syria, Algeria and South Yemen, an Iraqi Deputy Premier and Yasser Arafat met in the Libyan capital, Tripoli, to co-ordinate their opposition to Sadat's peace initiative.[38] After a series of preliminary discussions in Tripoli with leaders of other PLO member-groups, Arafat was able to announce the formulation of a joint Palestinian political platform. This was then presented to the other Arab parties present in Tripoli, who modified some of its provisions before endorsing it. The key provision of this platform was that those parties represented in Tripoli should henceforth constitute themselves into a body called the 'Steadfastness and Confrontation Front' (Jabhat al-Sumoud wa at-Tasaddi, more often called simply the Steadfastness Front).

The Iraqis criticised the measures adopted in Tripoli as not tough enough, and soon afterwards announced their decision not to participate in the work of the Front. But Sadat had already been so angered by the convening of the Tripoli meeting that on 5 December he had broken off Egypt's diplomatic relations with all states represented there, giving their diplomats 24 hours to leave the country. His subsequent invitations to all potential participants in the Geneva conference to attend a 'Preparatory Conference' in Cairo in mid-December thus met with little response from the Arab invitees. Not only Syria and the PLO but also Jordan failed to turn up to the seats he allotted them. The diplomatic pattern which dominated the following five years was established when only Egypt, Israel and the U.S. took part in the Cairo meeting.

At the pan-Arab level, Sadat's initiative had forced the PLO into a closer alliance with the 'radical' bloc of states led by Syria; and this new regional factor had its inevitable repercussions on the policy the PLO leaders were to pursue in the months and years which followed, in their last remaining military base, in Lebanon. Already, on the ground in Lebanon, the increasingly aggressive interventions of Israel and its local allies had, as we have seen, provided a strong initial impetus for the PLO leaders' reconciliation with the Syrian government. In the last months of 1977 that tendency was reinforced, as Syrian and PLO military strategists got together to plan the implementation of the secret military decisions taken in Tripoli, which aimed to bolster their defences against Israel in the event of any future Israeli attack. Lebanon was also the place where in the early weeks of 1978 the Fateh leaders set about preparing their own, more direct response to the Sadat initiative.

In the early morning of 11 March, a group of eight seaborne Fateh commandos, led by the 18-year-old female fighter Dalal Mughrabi, landed on the main Israeli coastal highway and hijacked a full passenger bus to take them to Tel Aviv. After a lengthy chase and a bloody shootout with the Israeli security forces, a total of 37 people had been killed, including six of the commandos.

Three days later, the Israeli army struck back, throwing 25,000 troops into a full-scale invasion of south Lebanon which left scores of Lebanese villages devastated and some 700 Lebanese and Palestinians, mainly civilians, dead. Since the Fateh leaders must have understood, prior to launching their own operation, what the likely scale of the Israeli response would be, it is worth questioning just what they had hoped would be achieved through the Mughrabi group's action. One possible indication of an answer was to be provided by Arafat himself four months later, when he spoke to a magazine interviewer:

What have we done after the 1967 war...? We engaged the Zionist enemy militarily and psychologically until the Arab armies were built. We are now playing the same role. *We must keep the area ablaze* until the Egyptian absence [from Arab ranks] is compensated for, either through returning Egypt to the arena of war ... or until balance is restored through building the eastern front.[39]

Certainly, Israel's 1978 invasion of south Lebanon did cause some stirrings of criticism, inside Egypt, of Sadat's peace policy, which Egyptian oppositionists saw as having freed the Israeli military from the long Sinai front to concentrate almost totally on targets along Israel's northern border. But any embarrassment the Egyptian President might have experienced on this score proved only partial and transitory, and was ultimately not sufficient to deflect him from continuing his peace policy with Israel. Indeed, Sadat was probably less embarrassed by the whole affair than was Syria's President Asad, whose troops, deployed actually inside Lebanon and in some cases within clear view of the invading Israelis, took no part whatsoever in March 1978 (with one minor, and apparently accidental, exception) in defending Lebanon's 'sacred Arab land' from the invasion. Sadat was even able to capitalise on Asad's embarrassment by inviting Arab foreign ministers, excluding those of Steadfastness Front countries, to Cairo to discuss the crisis in Lebanon.

On 19 March, the Security Council adopted resolution 425, which called for an immediate Israeli withdrawal from Lebanese territory, and established a new United Nations force to be despatched immediately to southern Lebanon. The official mandate of the force, which operated under the acronym UNIFIL, was defined as 'confirming the withdrawal of Israeli forces, restoring international peace and security and assisting the Government of Lebanon in ensuring the return of its effective authority in the area'.[40]

The first reaction of the PLO leadership to resolution 425 was expressed by a PLO spokesman who told me that, since it made no specific mention of the PLO, 'As far as we are concerned, this is not something that concerns us.' He added, 'Nobody's asked us for a cease-fire, so why should we even discuss the subject?'[41] The Israelis, for their part, continued their operations in south Lebanon for two days after the passage of resolution 425 before they ordered a cease-fire; but no cease-fire was ordered by the Palestinian leadership until after the UNIFIL commander, General Emmanuel Erskine, had met personally in Beirut on 28 March with Yasser Arafat. After that meeting, U.N. Secretary-General Kurt Waldheim was able to announce that Arafat had accepted an overall cease-fire in south Lebanon.

Arafat's decision to co-operate with the UNIFIL command – and thus, by implication, to endorse resolution 425 – marked a turning-point in the history of the Palestinian resistance movement, whose importance has generally been overlooked. It constituted the first open acceptence by the leader of the PLO of a cease-fire agreement with Israel, and his decision to co-operate with UNIFIL was subsequently endorsed by all the official PLO bodies. Arafat had extracted from the U.N. negotiators what he considered a fair price for making this concession: public recognition from them, through their agreement to meet with him openly, of the PLO's interests in and importance to the disengagement process in south Lebanon. His decision to accept this agreement with the U.N. was originally opposed by some groups inside the resistance movement, including his own organisation, Fateh; but over the weeks and months which followed he proved himself able to keep his part of the bargain with the U.N., taking ruthless action against those Palestinian elements, including Fateh elements, who tried to violate the cease-fire.

These Fateh critics of Arafat's cease-fire decision were primarily those organised by the maverick second-level Fateh leader Muhammed Daoud Awda (Abu Daoud).[42] In April 1978, Awda managed to organise cells totalling an estimated 70 or 80 Palestinian fighters, reportedly mainly Fateh people, in south Lebanon. Their purpose was to explode the U.N.-sponsored cease-fire there. The other Fateh bosses heard about the plan, however, and the tough Fateh special police units of 'Branch 17' arrested all those involved, under orders from Arafat and Khalil Wazir.

Awda was accused, in the aftermath of this incident, of having planned it in collaboration with the Fateh renegade Sabri al-Banna (Abu Nidal), who since 1974 had been masterminding operations against the Fateh leadership in close co-operation with the Iraqi intelligence services. At the beginning of 1978, the Baath Party regime in Iraq was still violently opposed to any peaceful settlement of accounts with Israel, and to any PLO moves in this regard. The Baghdad Baathists were also seemingly obsessed with their 15-year-old rivalry with the fellow Baathists ruling in Damascus, and eager to do anything which might weaken the Syrians' links with the PLO and even the Syrians' military stance against Israel.[43] On 4 January 1978, an assassin thought to be associated with Banna and the Iraqis had killed Said Hammami, the PLO's personable and effective representative in London. A long-time Fateh veteran, Hammami had spearheaded Palestinian contacts with Jewish movements and individuals and Israeli oppositionists in Europe, as well as with a broad range of British political groups. His assassination was followed, over the four years ahead, by the killings of nearly a dozen of Fateh's other brightest and most effective diplomats in Europe and Asia, most of which were also thought to have been the work of Banna's networks. At one stage in the early 80s, Banna, who had been expelled from Fateh in 1974 (see chapter 3 above), registered the dubious achievement of apparently being able to continue his anti-Fateh campaign with impunity from parallel bases in Damascus and Baghdad.

In 1978, however, the Fateh bosses were able to pre-empt Banna's apparent attempt to explode the south Lebanese front with Israel. In early May, there were some clashes between French units of UNIFIL and fighters of the Palestinians' and Lebanese leftists' 'Joint Forces'. These clashes, which resulted in the deaths of two French soldiers and the wounding of a dozen more including the commander of the whole French contingent, occurred while French troops were patrolling in the south Lebanese port city of Tyre. However, in discussions soon afterwards with General Erskine, Arafat was able to make clear that since the Israeli army had never been able to enter Tyre and its immediate environs in the March invasion, and since UNIFIL's mandate was 'to confirm the Israeli withdrawal', UNIFIL should be entitled only to staging facilities in Tyre, and not to the establishment of a controlling presence there.

Once all UNIFIL contingents had been apprised of this by Erskine, there occurred only sporadic and limited incidents between PLO units and UNIFIL. UNIFIL's official reports of developments in its zone of operation throughout the next four years gave an apparently clear indication that its units had much more difficulty dealing with the '*de facto* forces' (UNIFIL's code for Major Haddad's men) than it did with 'armed elements' (code for PLO or Lebanese leftist fighters). And the diplomatic representatives in Beirut of some of the Western countries represented in UNIFIL reported that their soldiers' experiences with the Israelis and their allies in south Lebanon acted perceptibly to help shift opinion inside their countries away from their previous general sympathy for Israel.[44]

The first phase of the Israelis' withdrawal from south Lebanon took place on 6 April 1978; it was followed by further partial withdrawals on 14 April and 30 April, with UNIFIL units moving into the positions vacated by the Israelis. Both the latter withdrawals had been effected only after intense diplomatic urging from Western governments, including that of the U.S., and throughout May the Israelis continued to insist on tough conditions if they were to pull back any further. In the end, the Begin government agreed on one final withdrawal: on 13 June, the Israelis handed over only 14 positions to UNIFIL, with a whole strip of land five to ten kilometres wide adjoining the international border retained by Haddad's militiamen.

On 31 July 1978, the Lebanese army was scheduled to undertake its first official deployment in south Lebanon, in accordance with the resolution

425 provision for the return of the Lebanese government's effective authority to the UNIFIL area. After long negotiations, 500 men, commanded by Lieutenant-Colonel Adib Saad, duly set out down the Bekaa Valley. Their route was to take them through UNIFIL lines near Kawkaba, and then through two towns held by Haddad, Khiyam and Marjayoun, before deploying permanently in the UNIFIL-held town of Tibnin, in the central sector.[45] However, UNIFIL officers in Kawkaba told Saad that some of Haddad's fighters had mounted a roadblock up ahead, and as the Lebanese convoy stopped to debate this news, Haddad's rebels lobbed 12 artillery shells into the fields nearby. Saad then decided 'to postpone the movement onward from Kawkaba'.[46] In later months, some symbolic Lebanese army units were finally able to deploy in Tibnin by travelling down the PLO-held Mediterranean coast road; but the army was never, over the four years ahead, allowed any access to the border strip where Haddad ruled with the help of the Israelis and with rotating detachments of Phalangist Party militiamen sent down from the Maronite heartland further north to sharpen their military skills in the south.

The Israeli invasion of south Lebanon in March 1978 did more than upset the balance in the area occupied; it also perceptibly changed the political and strategic balance throughout the country, since it was during that invasion that the almost total control over the country which the Syrians had gained through their preponderance in the ADF was first successfully challenged. The Israelis did nothing at that stage to challenge the Syrian troops in Lebanon head-on; but the fact that the Syrians did not stir from their positions north of the (Israeli-defined) 'Red Line' to help the Lebanese of the south resist Israel was noted throughout the country. Without firing a single shot at the Syrians, the Israelis had as good as proved they could face down the Syrians in Lebanon. Lebanese government members, parliamentarians and even the Lebanese commander of the ADF were among those who reflected the mood wrought in the Lebanese body politic by the invasion when they went on record with statements more or less openly critical of the Syrians and their PLO allies.[47] Then, in April, the right-wing Christian coalition known as the 'Lebanese Front' felt bold enough to start calling openly for the abrogation of the Lebanese government's Cairo agreement with the PLO.

That same month, a dispute between Syrian ADF units and Phalangist militiamen in East Beirut led to the Syrians shelling the Christian suburbs concerned. The same pattern was followed again, with increasing ferocity on both sides, in July and again in September. By the end of the September clashes the Phalangists were able to declare a no-go area throughout East Beirut and the whole Maronite-dominated enclave east and north of the capital, inside which they strengthened their own complete administration, excluding the ADF and the effective writ of the central Lebanese government from its confines.

The *de facto* establishment of the Phalangist mini-state in East Beirut and the adjoining enclave – complete with Phalangist police, military police, social services and tax-enforcers – indubitably affected the whole political balance throughout Lebanon. President Sarkis, a politically and personally colourless man who had been elected under the protection of the Syrians 18 months previously, bent closer and closer towards the views of the assertive Maronite hardliners from mid-1978 onwards, presaging new political problems for the Palestinians and their military presence in Lebanon.

At the broader political level, too, the PLO suffered serious setbacks in 1978, principally through the conclusion of the Camp David treaty among Israel, Egypt and the U.S. in September of that year. Israel's actions against the Palestinians in Lebanon in March 1978 had not deterred Sadat from pursuing his peace initiative with Israel. Indeed, at the time the Fateh leadership launched the Mughrabi operation, the 'peace process' was already in the doldrums, following Sadat's orders to his Foreign Minister to withdraw from a meeting with Israeli representatives two months earlier. But on 18 July 1978, the two countries were back at the negotiating table, at Leeds Castle in England, and thereafter contacts continued between them until the announcement, on 17 September, of the conclusion of President Carter's proudest diplomatic achievement – the Camp David accords.

The Camp David accords consisted of a general Preamble; a lengthy outline of plans for the West Bank and Gaza; a section committing Egypt and Israel to try to negotiate a peace treaty within three months; and a statement of principles which both sides felt should govern future relations between Israel and the neighbouring Arab states.[48] There was no structural linkage between the section dealing with the West Bank and Gaza and that dealing with Egypt-Israel relations, though some of the Egyptian negotiators had reportedly been eager to establish such linkage in order to disprove Arab charges that Egypt was prosecuting a separate peace with Israel. The accord on the West Bank and Gaza called for the establishment of a 'self-governing authority' in these occupied Palestinian areas, which would oversee administrative matters there for a transition period not to exceed five years in length. Once the self-governing authority had been established, 'a withdrawal of Israeli armed forces [of unspecified dimensions] will take place and there will be a redeployment of the remaining Israeli forces into specified security locations'. Then, at a stage not later than three years into the transition period, 'negotiations will take place to determine the final status of the West Bank and Gaza and its relationship with its neighbours, and to conclude a peace treaty between Israel and Jordan by the end of the transitional period'.

On 18 September, Arafat convened an enlarged emergency session of the PLO Executive Committee, which was attended by representatives of all the PLO's constituent guerrilla groups. (For the PFLP, this was the first Executive Committee meeting they had taken part in since 1974.) As I reported at the time,

Sources close to Executive Committee hardliners report that the mood at the meeting ... was one of a unanimity unknown in the past few months of inter-Palestinian faction fights...

The sources noted that even the more moderate PLO figures who had been hoping for some role in the peace initiative launched by Mr Sadat, were convinced by the terms of the Camp David declarations that the initiative offered them no benefits.[49]

The Executive Committee session ended with a call to all Palestinians, inside and outside the areas under Israeli rule, to observe a general strike on 20 September, to express 'their firm opposition' to the Camp David agreements. The public statement containing this call warned, 'Those suspect voices which seek to find a place for themselves within the autonomy conspiracy, and announce their support for the conspiracy of Camp David, will face the will of our people and its just retribution.'[50] The harshness and speed of the Executive Committee's reaction to Camp David, compared with the apparent indecision with which it had greeted Sadat's original decision to go to Jerusalem, clearly indicated that this time the Fateh leadership was unanimous in its opposition to Sadat's diplomacy.

It soon became apparent that the Palestinians were not the only group in the Arab world opposed to Camp David. The whole Camp David process, as envisaged by the Americans, had depended on at least the Jordanian government, and preferably also the Saudis, joining in the diplomatic process started by Sadat. (Significantly, the accords had made no mention of the Syrian territories still occupied by Israel, in the Golan Heights.) But despite the despatch of high-level U.S. emissaries to try to 'sell' Camp David to the other Arab governments, there were no takers. The Jordanians were reported as intensely disliking the police role they saw Camp David as allotting to them in the West Bank, with few compensating political gains on offer. For the Saudis, the omission of any mention of an Israeli withdrawal from Jerusalem was probably a crucial factor, and, in addition, the Saudis' whole diplomatic effort in the Arab world up until September 1978 had been based on the argument that the Arab states should not isolate Sadat too much, in order to be there to stop him signing any bilateral peace treaty with Israel. But now that was what he was going to do.

In the end, the Arab governments' opposition to the Camp David agreements was co-ordinated by a mediator from an unlikely quarter. Throughout 1978, the Baathist government of Iraq had been moving rapidly towards the right in both internal and external policies, in particular strengthening its links with Saudi Arabia. In October 1978, after a flurry of visits between members of the different Arab governments, it was the Iraqis who invited the Arab heads of state to a summit to take the necessary steps to oppose the Camp David process. But before the summit convened, the Iraqis had another trick up their sleeve: a dramatic reconciliation with the Syrian Baathists, effected when the Syrian President visited Baghdad on 24-26 October.

When the Ninth Arab Summit meeting convened in Baghdad at the beginning of November, the Iraqis presented themselves as mediators between (on the one hand) Syria and those of its confreres in the Steadfastness Front who urged immediate sanctions against Egypt and (on the other) members of the conservative bloc led by Saudi Arabia who still hoped they could hold Sadat back from signing a peace treaty by quieter diplomatic means. In the end ten Arab heads of state attended the summit, held on 2-5 November, as did Yasser Arafat leading the PLO delegation, and lower-level representatives of ten other Arab governments. Of all the Arab League member states, only Egypt was not represented.

On 4 November, the summit made one last appeal to Sadat to change his course: it despatched a four-man delegation led by Lebanese Premier Selim al-Hoss to Cairo, but Sadat refused to receive the delegation. The summiteers therefore went straight ahead and agreed a series of measures which would automatically go into effect against Egypt the moment Sadat should actually sign the proposed peace treaty with Israel. These included Egypt's formal expulsion from the Arab League, the transfer of League headquarters out of Cairo, and a boycott against Egyptian state or private bodies which maintained relations with Israel. (The following 26 March, President Sadat did indeed go ahead and sign a peace treaty with Israel, despite the fact that no progress at all had been made on the negotiations concerning the West Bank and Gaza. The next day, Arab foreign affairs and economy ministers met in Baghdad to finalise implementation of the summit decisions. Tunis was designated as the new seat of the Arab League headquarters; a political and diplomatic boycott of Egypt was called for; and the granting of governmental loans to Egypt was suspended. This meeting also issued a condemnation of the U.S. for its role in promoting the bilateral Egypt-Israel treaty.)

The Baghdad summit also created a support fund to funnel approximately $3.5 billion a year in Arab aid to those states remaining on the front line against Israel. The bulk of this would go to Syria, with $800 million earmarked for Jordan, $250 million for the PLO, and $150 million 'to bolster the resistance of the population of the occupied territories'.[51] It was decreed at the summit that the latter sum would be administered jointly by Jordan and the PLO. A subsequent PLO protest against this arrangement, on the grounds that it would undermine the PLO's position as 'sole legitimate representative of the Palestinian people', failed to change it. For at least some in the Fateh leadership, the achievement of keeping Hussein out of the Camp David process was itself sufficient to justify making such concessions at this stage.

In the weeks which followed the signing of the Camp David accords, the U.S. administration stepped up its efforts to persuade other Arab parties to join the peace process, and this time there was also a definite U.S. effort to seek out any Palestinians who might push the self-rule portion of the Camp David process ahead. This effort was directed particularly to community leaders within the occupied territories, and partly also towards seeking some kind of indirect endorsement from the leaders of the PLO. In mid-November 1978, for example, there were many reports in Beirut of new, higher-level contacts between the State Department and the PLO leadership, especially through the Saudi channel.[52] But the Israeli government appeared to be doing everything it could to prevent any meaningful Palestinian involvement. Immediately after the conclusion of the Camp David accords, Premier Begin announced that, in his understanding, the freeze on new Jewish settlements agreed in the accords was to remain in force only for the three-month period envisaged for negotiating the Egyptian-Israeli peace treaty, rather than throughout the whole five-year interim period in the occupied territories, as the Americans and Egyptians had thought would be the case.

In the event, the Israeli settlement programme in the West Bank resumed at full speed once Begin's three-month period was up, despite the failure of the Camp David parties to arrive at anything near agreement on the question of the self-governing authority, and it was accelerated substantially from early 1979 until at least early 1983. This colonisation activity, along with the series of harsh political measures taken against the Palestinians of the occupied territories over the years following Camp David, just about ensured that any of the local West Bank leaders who might otherwise have considered joining the Camp David negotiations refused to have anything to do with them at all. In August 1979, for example, Nablus mayor Bassam Shakaa spoke for a majority in the West Bank when he said, 'We disagree 100 percent with the self-rule scheme... Autonomy can never be acceptable to us since it is a violation of our rights.'[53]

In an interview in mid-March 1979, Fateh's Salah Khalaf explained the PLO's view of the self-rule scheme to me in the following terms:

'It's not just that we won't participate! We will sabotage the self-rule scheme and we will sabotage the whole results of Camp David.'

It was put to Khalaf that the self-rule scheme, even if it stopped short of the self-determination demanded by the PLO, still offered the Palestinians more independence than they had enjoyed before.

'The question is not that this is our first opportunity to administer ourselves,' he replied, 'because the Palestinians are not demanding this form of self-administration. I, for example, want an identity, a homeland, a flag. The self-rule scheme doesn't give me this homeland, this flag, or any independence or self-determination.'

...'I think the demonstrations in the occupied territories during Carter's visit indicate that the Palestinian people don't want this self-rule, nor do they want the results of Camp David, nor do they want anything except the PLO and an independent Palestinian state.'

... He said that even if [the self-rule scheme] were implemented, 'and I don't believe it will be anyway, because the Israelis, and Begin in particular, are not in agreement with it', it would not solve the Palestinian problem.

'Maybe, in form at least, it says that the Palestinians in the occupied territories have self-rule... So *what will they do with the Palestinians who are outside the occupied territories?*'[54]

On 15 January 1979, the Palestinian National Council convened for its Fourteenth session. Significantly, this was the first PNC session ever to be held in Damascus. The 302 delegates were unanimous in their condemnation of Camp David. The major debates centred instead on the exact tactics the PLO leaders should adopt towards Jordan, on which point a general consensus emerged that so long as Hussein stayed out of the Camp David process the contacts with him should be continued, and on internal political matters such as the issue of who should control the Baghdad summit's aid allocation to the PLO, and the distribution of seats in the new Executive Committee. While the Fateh bloc won a more or less clear victory on the first of these internal issues, the Executive Committee question was deadlocked, and the previous Committee was returned to office without change, pending a future agreement on this issue. The final political statement issued by the Fourteenth PNC described the Camp David agreements as 'a conspiracy which should be rejected and resisted by all means'.[55]

During the interview quoted above, Khalaf had questioned whether the Arabs would be wise to tie their cause solely to American diplomacy and interests in the Middle East, in view of the climactic fall, in the early weeks of 1979, of the Shah of Iran, whom Khalaf described as having been 'the summit and citadel of America in the region.' Without a doubt, the victory of the Islamic revolutionaries in Iran had dramatically changed the strategic balance in the whole of the Middle East, though at the time it was hard to gauge the exact dimension of these changes.

The Palestinian guerrillas had had long and close links with the Iranians who now came to power. In some cases these dated back to the early 60s, when some of the Palestinian activists in West Germany who had come into Fateh at around that time (see chapter 2 above) had first made contact with members of Iranian Islamic fundamentalist groups active in West Germany. Throughout the 60s and 70s, many of the Shah's opponents, from both the fundamentalist and the more leftist-oriented organisations, received their military training in the Palestinian guerrillas' training camps. The Palestinians had seen the Shah as a clear ally of Israel in the region.

The victory of the Iranian revolution in early 1979 thus caused much rejoicing in Palestinian ranks: the Palestinian-controlled areas in and near the refugee camps in Lebanon blossomed with huge posters of Iranian leader Ayatollah Ruhollah Khomeini, many of them adorned with the slogan 'Today Iran! Tomorrow Palestine!'[56] On 17 February 1979, Yasser Arafat was the first foreign leader to be invited to Teheran by the Iranian capital's new rulers. He was given a tumultuous hero's reception during his five days there, addressing rallies and prayer-meetings almost as vast as those which had swept Khomeini to power. On 18 February, he inaugurated the new PLO office in Teheran, in the building which had previously housed Israel's diplomatic mission to Iran. Its first 'Ambassador' was the erstwhile head of Fateh's 'German group', Hani al-Hassan.

But the euphoria occasioned by developments in Iran did not last long for the Palestinians. The objective facts of Palestinian dispersal tied the fate of the Palestinian national movement much more firmly to developments in the Arab world than to far-off Teheran, and the situation in the Arab world did not take long to deteriorate from the near-unanimity which had been displayed at the Baghdad summit.

The first major crack in the Baghdad consensus occurred, ironically enough, in that same historic Arab capital. At the end of July 1979, news started emerging of a new purge in Baghdad. Iraqi President Ahmed Hassan al-Bakr, whose hold on power had for some years been merely cosmetic, was elbowed aside by his own strongman, Saddam Hussein. Saddam also executed five of his own strongest supporters in the process. These five, and a couple of dozen other high Baathist officials had been accused of taking the previous autumn's reconciliation with Syria too seriously. The net effect of Saddam's rise to open power was thus that the reconciliation was halted, and it did not take long before the two rival Baathist regimes were back in their years-old posture of mutual antagonism. Any hopes the Palestinian leaders had entertained for building a strong 'eastern front' against Israel (Syria, Jordan, Iraq, themselves) were thereby dashed. Since the Iraqis managed to peel King Hussein away with them as they broke from Syria (he had had a tactical alliance with Damascus since l975), the Palestinians also found themselves over the following months faced with difficult choices to make between Damascus and Amman.

Soon after the Iraq-Syria reconciliation fell apart, relations between Iraq and the revolutionaries in Iran began to worsen rapidly. By September 1980 the two countries were actually at war, in a bloody and debilitating contest which sapped the resources of the entire region while causing yet another deep chasm in the anti-Israeli front. Once again, the Fateh leaders were forced to tread a tricky course between the deadly rivalries of two powers they had hoped would provide them with essential support. Further schisms multiplied rapidly within an Arab world now seemingly cut free from the political gravity which Egypt's vast mass had always provided for it: at one stage in 1981, I identified no fewer than sixteen major disputes dividing the Arab League's 21 members from each other.

The Israelis seemed to understand the weakness of the forces lined up against them in the Middle East in the years from 1979 onwards. They kept up a relentless pressure on the Palestinian guerrillas and their allies in Lebanon. Israeli gunboats and warplanes regularly bombarded guerrilla positions and civilian concentrations throughout the areas to the south of Beirut which were under Palestinian and Lebanese leftist control, and Israeli paratroopers attempted regular forays through UNIFIL lines in south Lebanon against Palestinian encampments. All this was in pursuit of the new, harshly 'pre-emptive', policy declared by Israeli Defence Minister Ezer Weizmann against the Palestinian guerrilla movement in January 1979.[57]

Meanwhile, the strategic control which the Syrians may have hoped to exercise over Lebanon by virtue of their position in the ADF was providing little effective security cover for the Palestinians and their allies in Lebanon. Syrian pilots did, on many occasions from 1978 onwards, attempt to engage the Israeli warplanes as they streaked over Lebanon, but the Syrians never had any effective air-defence cover in the country, and Syrian pilots were again and again from 1977 to 1982 subjected to the indignity – and on occasion fatality – of having their planes shot down by the Israelis. In early 1980, the Syrian command implicitly recognised the weakness of its forces' position in Lebanon when it withdrew them both from the 'Green Line' area still dividing Beirut and from the all the coastal area south of the Beirut suburb of Khaldeh.[58] They then deployed Syrian-controlled units of the PLA along the 'Green Line', but the major coastal artery to the south was left a virtual free-fire zone for the constantly artery to the south was left a virtual free-fire zone for the constantly attacking Israeli air and sea forces, against its poorly armed Palestinian and Lebanese leftist 'defenders'.

While the Israelis roamed the Lebanese skies and coastal waters at will, their allies on the ground in the East Beirut no-go area plotted endlessly to undermine the Palestinian-leftist coalition. Palestinian security sources in those years laid the responsibility for most of the devastating car-bombs which ripped apart West Beirut neighbourhoods between 1979 and 1982 squarely with the 'War Council' set up by Phalangist militia boss Bashir Gemayyel in East Beirut's port district. In addition to all these pressures, all the disputes which racked the Middle East over those years had meanwhile come home to roost inside the Lebanese leftist movement, pitting pro-Iraqis against pro-Iranians, pro-Syrians against pro-Iraqis, and so on, until the movement had effectively splintered into a myriad of terrified and squabbling groups. This, too, weakened the Palestinians' strategic position in Lebanon.

By April 1981, the deterioration of the situation in Lebanon and the threats this posed to the peace of the region had sounded sufficient alarm bells to cause concern even for the three-month-old U.S. administration headed by Ronald Reagan, who had originally come into the White House sharing Israel's views on many Middle Eastern topics (see chapter 10 below). April was the month in which a senior U.S. diplomat in Beirut told me, 'We are desperately trying to keep the lid on the situation here. But we are not sure if we can manage it.' Thus was signalled the start of a new level of U.S. concern over Lebanon, but U.S. diplomacy was hamstrung by the fact that the Reagan administration continued to feel bound by the 1975 commitment not even to talk to the PLO.

The years 1977 to 1981 were tantalising and difficult years for the group of men who by then constituted almost a veteran leadership within Fateh and the PLO. In the years which followed, some of them were to speculate much on just how close they had come, in 1977, to making that vital breakthrough to Washington that they had sought. If they had just made a few more concessions then, could all the heartbreak of the following years have been avoided? But at the time, they had little opportunity for speculation. The challenges posed by Sadat's peace initiative, and the whole train of events which followed it within the Arab world, kept them all incredibly busy. Their major preoccupation throughout the period 1978 to 1981 was just to be able to keep their movement together, and to steer it through all the tricky shoals of inter-Arab politics. This was the period which saw Yasser Arafat, for example, probably clocking up more hours of flying time per month than are allowed even for long-distance pilots, as he hurried to mend whatever holes he was able in the PLO's tearing Arab safety-net. Khalil al-Wazir and Salah Khalaf were kept on their feet in Lebanon, supervising respectively the military and the security aspects of the Palestinians' defence there. Khaled al-Hassan was in the Gulf, steadying the Arab states there in their opposition to Sadat, as he and Farouq Qaddumi tried to keep together the PLO's coalition of international diplomatic support.

It was uphill work, and it was all defensive. From the time that Sadat launched his unilateral peace initiative with Israel there was no opening in sight through which the PLO might enter the peace negotiations to which they had committed themselves since 1974, and, with the Arab states in disarray, there was never any question of brandishing any credible military option against Israel.

The weight of the military and political pressures under which the Palestinian nationalist movement was labouring was certainly apparent at Fateh's Fourth Conference, which brought about 300 key movement organisers to Damascus in May 1980. The political programme they agreed on there still echoed the harsh anger of the early days of the movement. 'Fateh is an independent, revolutionary national movement,' it stressed. 'Its aim is the total liberation of Palestine and the liquidation of the Zionist entity economically, politically, militarily, culturally and ideologically.' The movement's traditional stance towards the Arab countries was reiterated: 'We do not intervene in the local affairs of these states, and we do not permit anyone to intervene in our affairs.' However, those of the historic leadership of Fateh who had been seeking to win it to a more sophisticated political stance received a significant kernel of comfort from the programme when it said it considered PNC decisions 'an integral part' of the programme.[59]

In fact, by 1980, Fateh's far-flung and surprisingly durable organisation was not only still intact, it had also beaten back much of the potential competition it had appeared to face in the early 70s from other guerrilla organisations, principally the members of the Rejection Front. From 1977 onwards, the different strands of the Palestinian exile movement did all seem to be pulling together to a far greater extent than ever before, and the PLO's constituency in the Palestinian diaspora now seemed wedded as never before to its 'invisible constituency' – those Palestinians living under direct Israeli rule. This much, at least, Camp David had achieved.

Chapter 6

The broken wing (1981 – February 1983)

By the spring of 1981, the Palestinian nationalist movement found itself in a complex situation of contrasting strengths and weaknesses. The Camp David accords, with their provisions for self-rule in the occupied territories, had dealt the PLO a harsh diplomatic setback. But the unanimity of the opposition expressed to those provisions by the Palestinians of the occupied territories had stalled their implementation and brought valuable new bases of support from inside the occupied areas into the PLO's constituency. The Arab League's score of member-states found themselves weak and divided as never before. This practically ruled out the chances of arriving at any negotiated settlement with Israel which might satisfy the PLO's already reduced aspirations. But it did leave the PLO/Fateh leaders some room for that inter-Arab manoeuvring which had traditionally been their key to survival; while the very fragility with which many Arab regimes maintained their hold on power gave the PLO/Fateh leaders, with their near-unanimous base of Palestinian support, a relatively stronger position in their bilateral dealings with these regimes. Militarily, meanwhile, the situation in Lebanon had turned into a treacherous stalemate: the Israelis launched repeated and damaging air, land and sea raids against the PLO/Joint Forces[1] positions throughout 1981, but were ultimately unable – short of mounting a really major offensive – to dent them significantly.

By April 1981, there was already a strong expectation that just such an offensive was imminent,[2] and by early June that year, a French reporter was writing from Beirut about expectations of 'an Israeli-Phalangist plan which Yasser Arafat calls the "accordion" plan: its aim is to catch the Palestinian forces in a pincer movement between the Christian militia in Beirut and the Israeli army in South Lebanon'.[3]

In the middle of April 1981, 314 Palestinian delegates travelled to Damascus for the Fifteenth session of the Palestinian National Council. Discussions there reflected the complexity of the Palestinians' situation, in Lebanon, in the occupied territories and elsewhere, but there was little change from previous years in the content of the PLO policy programme which emerged from the session. Camp David, the U.S. and Egypt were roundly denounced; the West European governments' Middle East initiative was welcomed; Soviet President Brezhnev's call for a return to an all-party framework for Middle East peace efforts was supported; and a call for co-operation with all governments opposed to Camp David, including Jordan, was issued.

The most significant occurrences at the Fifteenth PNC concerned negotiations there over membership of the new PLO Executive Committee. It had already been agreed that this time George Habash's PFLP would definitely be returning to the Executive, so the inclusion of the PFLP's Ahmad Yamani in the Executive list came as no surprise. However, the PNC's Syrian hosts had also sought another space in the Executive's 14-man line-up for one of their supporters; after much politicking, the Fateh bosses managed to deflect this demand, and instead succeeded in their own quest to bring Fateh's formal representation on the Executive up from two to three members. This success did not, however, mean that the Fateh caucus at the PNC could immediately agree on who was to fill the new Executive seat. In the end, Fateh Central Committee veteran Mahmoud Abbas, who was absent at the time in Moscow, was nominated.[4]

Less than two weeks after the PNC session ended, the Syrian government made a new move in Lebanon which was to draw the U.S. government into a more direct involvement in that country's tumultuous affairs than it had had at any time since American marines had landed there in 1958.[5] Towards the end of April 1981, the Syrians, who had lost a score of planes in dogfights with the Israelis over Lebanon in the previous two years moved some batteries of SAM-6 air defence missiles forward from Syria into the east Lebanese Bekaa Valley. The Israelis, according to Premier Begin, had originally planned to destroy the SAM batteries at once, with air strikes, but bad weather had delayed them. While the Israeli pilots waited for the weather to clear, the U.S. administration must have become aware of the potential dangers of a direct Israeli-Syrian confrontation in Lebanon. It intervened rapidly to stay the Israelis' hand, promising the Israelis that the U.S. would try to deal through diplomatic channels with the 'threat' the Israelis claimed the Syrian missiles posed.[6] On 6 May, former U.S. career diplomat Philip Habib left Washington for the Middle East at the start of the Lebanese mission with which President Ronald Reagan had entrusted him. The direct U.S. involvement in Lebanon thus initiated was to play a major role in developments there over the following two years, and thereby also in the affairs of the PLO, for which Lebanon still (until August 1982) constituted a major military base.

The man who had despatched Habib as his special envoy to the Levant had occupied the White House only since January 1981. Elected the previous November amidst an uproar of accusations that sitting President Jimmy Carter had represented a failure of U.S. 'leadership' – particularly in dealing with the crisis of the American hostages in Teheran – Ronald Reagan came into office promising a firm, and firmly anti-communist, hand in the U.S. executive branch. His knowledge of Middle East affairs when he entered the White House was, however, perceived by many foreign policy experts in Washington at the time as dangerously slight.

As a candidate, Reagan had repeatedly described the PLO as a terrorist organisation, often expanding this description to refer to its role in a Soviet-dominated international terror network. When he first came into office, therefore, he added to the single precondition that Carter had set for the opening of a U.S.-PLO diaologue – that the PLO accept Security Council resolution 242[7] – the two further preconditions that the PLO 'renounce terrorism' and that it explicitly recognise Israel's right to exist. In early April 1981, however, Reagan's generally hawkish Secretary of State, Alexander Haig, made a fact-finding tour of several Middle Eastern capitals, during which most of his Arab hosts stressed to him the necessity of the U.S. moderating this stance. In his meeting in Riyadh with Saudi Crown Prince Fahd on 7 April, for example, Haig was reported as setting only Carter's single precondition for U.S. recognition of the PLO;[8] and this approach to the question of talking to the PLO appeared to continue to represent U.S. policy at least until June 1982.

Despite such signs of a slight softening in the Reagan administration's attitude towards the PLO, on 8 May the Organisation declared its opposition to the newly despatched Habib mission. A statement issued that day by the PLO news agency, Wafa, said that, because of U.S. support for Israel, the U.S. 'can be neither arbiter nor mediator, for it is one of the foremost parties involved' in the missile crisis.[9] Nevertheless, on 31 May, the U.S. State Department disclosed that it had contacted U.N. Secretary-General Kurt Waldheim 'to convey to all parties to the conflict [that is, including the PLO] ... the need for moderation and restraint'.[10] Indirect contacts thereafter continued between the two sides, dealing mainly with the situation in Lebanon, and conducted both through the U.N. channel and through Saudi, and later on also through Egyptian, mediators.

On 7 June 1981, Habib's delicate web of negotiations among Israel, Syria, Lebanon and the other Arab parties appeared threatened when Israeli jets sped 840 kilometres deep over Jordanian, Saudi and Iraqi territory to bomb Iraq's fast-developing nuclear reactor project just north of Baghdad. On that occasion, however, since Iraq was not directly involved in Habib's negotiations, the American mediator was still able to hold his mission together. In Israel, meanwhile, Premier Begin profited from the popularity of the Iraqi raid to scrape home with a majority of one seat in the general elections held at the end of June. The Habib mission faced a far tougher test the following month, when the continuing cycle of Israeli-Palestinian violence in Lebanon came to one of its most egregious peaks to date.

On 10 July, an Israeli air raid against south Lebanon left one dead and six wounded; the Joint Forces retaliated by shelling a north Israeli settlement, wounding 14. The casualty toll in Lebanon from Israel's responses then soared steeply – 5 dead on 12 July, 10 dead on 14 July, 35 dead on 16 July; and on 17 July, the Israeli air force bombed areas controlled by the Joint Forces in West Beirut itself, levelling one whole building in the Fakhani district and leaving well over 200 dead.[11]

The news from Beirut brought Habib (who had been discussing the Syrian SAMs in Saudi Arabia) hurrying back to the Levant. On 19 July he met Begin in Jerusalem to ask about Israeli conditions for a cease-fire in Lebanon; then he met briefly with Lebanese officials in Beirut before returning to Saudi Arabia, this time reportedly to seek the Saudis' help in obtaining PLO commitment to a cease-fire in Lebanon. The Beirut raid thus served to spur Reagan into broadening Habib's mandate from one centring on the question of the Syrian missiles in the Bekaa to one encompassing the whole wider security issue in Lebanon, in which the increasingly direct Israeli-Palestinian confrontation there was a major factor. But the U.S. mediator still remained unable to undertake any direct contacts with the PLO. Instead, he stepped up his existing indirect contacts with the PLO through the U.N. and Saudi channels.

The same day that Habib returned to the Levant, the PLO Executive Committee held a meeting in Beirut, following which the PLO's Voice of Palestine (VOP) radio station reported, 'The PLO Executive Committee considers the U.S. to be the first responsible party for Begin's crimes against our people and the fraternal Lebanese people.'[12] Soon afterwards, however, Yasser Arafat and Khalil Wazir headed a high-level Palestinian military delegation in talks in Beirut with the UNIFIL commander, General William Callaghan. Although Arafat's statement on emerging from this meeting adopted the same condemnatory tone towards the U.S. and made no mention of cease-fire proposals, it is probable that such proposals were discussed in that gathering, for on 21 July, no less a figure than U.N. Secretary-General Kurt Waldheim sent a message to Arafat asking for PLO agreement to an immediate cease-fire in Lebanon. That same day, too, Reagan was reported as sending a 'very firm' message to Begin making the same request.[13]

By 24 July, Habib's efforts appeared to have been successful in containing the threatened explosion in Lebanon. Speaking in Jerusalem, Habib announced, 'I have today reported to President Reagan that as of 1330 local time [1130 gmt] 24 July 1981, all hostile military actions between Lebanese and Israeli territories in either direction will cease.' Premier Begin thereupon confirmed that 'The Government of Israel endorses the statement just made by Mr Philip Habib.' [14] Five minutes later, the VOP was broadcasting, 'The revolution reaffirms the position conveyed to the U.N. Secretary-General in the wake of his call for a cease-fire, which is to abide by this call, provided the other side abides by it as well.'[15] Despite the cover of a U.N. role which was draped over these negotiations, it nevertheless remains clear that the July 1981 cease-fire represented another watershed for the Palestinians: it was the PLO's most explicit acceptance of a direct U.S. mediating role to date; and conversely, for the U.S., it was their most explicit recognition to date of the necessity of involving the PLO in issues of Middle Eastern war and peace.

At first, there were some fears that the PLO's acceptance of the cease-fire might not be unanimous. On 25 July, Ahmed Jibril's PFLP-General Command distributed a statement saying that it did not consider itself bound by the cease-fire, and over the next few days PFLP-GC units continued to shell areas controlled by Saad Haddad's pro-Israeli militia in south Lebanon. Two days later, Arafat met with Jibril, in the presence of Lebanese leftist Muhsin Ibrahim. The VOP subsequently described the mood of their meeting as 'very frank' but during it 'the cease-fire decision issued by the Lebanese-Palestinian joint command was reaffirmed'.[16] Jibril's infractions of the cease-fire had ceased by 29 July, after what the Lebanese Phalangist Party's radio station described as a clash between PFLP (probably PFLP-GC) units and Fateh units in the south Lebanese town of Nabatiyeh.

Once these initial teething troubles had been dealt with, and despite the varying interpretations placed upon the cease-fire by the PLO and the Israelis – with the former claiming it covered nothing outside southern Lebanon, and the latter claiming it covered any action taken against Israeli targets anywhere in the world – it proved effective for a further ten months in preventing another all-out Israeli-Palestinian confrontation in Lebanon. The reports of the U.N. Secretary-General covering the period from 16 June 1981 to 3 June 1982 noted 47 incidents of the PLO and their Joint Forces allies (in U.N. parlance, the 'armed elements') shooting at or near UNIFIL units during that period, compared with 201 incidents of Haddad's '*de facto* forces' (and more than 17 incidents of the Israelis) doing the same. Meanwhile, the Secretary-General laconically computed that from August 1981 to May 1982 inclusive no fewer than 2,096 Israeli violations of Lebanese airspace had taken place, plus 652 Israeli violations of Lebanese territorial waters.[17] At all events, Habib's cease-fire prevented an all-out clash.

In the weeks following the July 1981 cease-fire in Lebanon, the attention of many of the Palestinian leaders shifted towards the inter-Arab arena. On 7 August, Saudi Crown Prince Fahd Ibn Abdel-Aziz made public the eight points of a new Middle East peace proposal being sponsored by the Kingdom. The 'Fahd plan'called for an Israeli withdrawal from all Arab lands occupied in 1967; the establishment, after a short transition period under U.N. auspices, of a Palestinian state in the West Bank and Gaza; and, in the controversial Clause 7, 'that all states in the region should be able to live in peace'.[18] (The latter clause was generally understood to imply recognition of Israel.) Soon after publishing the plan, the Saudis let it be known that they would be presenting it for endorsement to the next Arab Summit, whose date was subsequently fixed for 25 November, and whose venue was to be the Moroccan city Fez.

Palestinian reactions to the Fahd plan diverged from the beginning. On 8 August, for example, Fateh's Khalil Wazir was quoted as describing the plan as 'positive', while a PFLP spokesman said, 'these proposals represent a direct recognition of the Zionist entity and a call on the PLO to deviate from the revolution's basic course'.[19] The PLO Executive Committee then held a meeting, on 11 August. In the absence of any consensus, it decided not to take any official stand on the Fahd plan, pending the outcome of a meeting Arafat was scheduled to hold with the Saudi Crown Prince.[20]

However, it soon became clear that sharp differences existed on this issue, not only between Fateh and its allies in the PLO but also within the leadership of Fateh itself. Contrasting with Wazir's welcome for the plan when it was first published, on 13 August another Fateh Central Committee member, Majid Abu Sharar, was described as being 'against the plan, because it "links" the solving of the Middle East crisis with the U.S.'[21] Then, four days later, Yasser Arafat gave his first public indication of support for the plan.[22] The final line-up of the Fateh leadership on this issue, as it emerged over the coming weeks, was apparently that Arafat, Wazir, Khaled al-Hassan and at least two other members of Fateh's 12-man Central Committee basically supported the plan; while fellow Committee members Farous Qaddumi, Nimr Saleh, Majid Abu Sharar and Samih Abu Kuwaik all went on record as opposing it. Salah Khalaf's attitude, from his published statements at the time, seems to have been to cover all bases; and Arafat, with his obsession for the unity of the movement, went to great epistemological lengths to qualify his welcome for the plan. It was this split, inside the PLO's predominant constituent grouping, which was to paralyse the PLO's ability to respond politically to the Fahd plan and thus to enable Syrian President Hafez al-Asad, in November 1981, ultimately to force the PLO's hand on the issue.

On 25 September, Arafat returned to Beirut after his promised consultations with Fahd in Saudi Arabia, and three days later Fateh's 75-member policy-reviewing body, the Revolutionary Council, held a meeting. Its results, as regards the Fahd plan, were presumably inconclusive, as the statement issued after the meeting made no mention of the plan at all. A second Revolutionary Council meeting, one month later, also appeared to end inconclusively. Khaled al-Hassan was later to interpret Fateh's position towards the Fahd plan in 1981 as having been: 'There was not a rejection of the plan; there was a sort of understanding of the positive points in it and of the missing points in it.'[23]

By 3 November 1981, Arafat was back in Saudi Arabia, where he told a Kuwaiti press correspondent, 'Once more I stress my welcome for Prince Fahd's proposals.'[24] Then on 6 November the PLO Executive Committee held the first of a series of further debates on the plan. After the 6 November meeting, in a press interview published on 12 November, Arafat appeared to be trying to find some middle ground between the Saudis and those in the PLO and Fateh leaderships who still remained opposed to or sceptical of the Fahd plan. He said, 'I welcomed the plan and said that it constitutes an important basis for resolving the Middle East conflict, but *we do have reservations, and I did convey some remarks to Prince Fahd...* This does not mean that I do not regard it as a positive plan which I have welcomed'.[25] But the PLO Chairman's mediation efforts still bore no fruit. The PLO Executive met again on 13 November, but three days later both the PFLP and the DFLP came out with strong statements against the Fahd plan.

At this point, the Palestinian critics of the Fahd plan were able to bring in their 'big Arab guns' to bear on Arafat and his co-thinkers in the Fateh leadership. At an extraordinary meeting of the foreign ministers of the Steadfastness Front which convened in the South Yemeni capital, Aden, that day, a resolution was passed which appeared to commit the PLO, along with other Steadfastness Front members, to rejection of Fahd's Clause 7.

By 21 November, Arafat was meeting urgently in Damascus with Syrian President Hafez al-Asad, the man who was generally regarded as co-ordinating all the internal Palestinian opposition to Arafat on this issue. Asad's position was not straightforward, however. For example, in a mid-October press interview, Fateh's Khalaf had said, 'The Saudis assured us that Iraq, Jordan and Syria had accepted their proposal';[26] and right on the eve of the Fez summit, on 23 November, Asad's strongman brother Rifaat al-Asad travelled to Saudi Arabia for last-minute negotiations with the Saudi rulers. Meanwhile, several Fateh supporters of the plan pointed out, as the Saudis did, that its contents were based almost entirely on various U.N. General Assembly resolutions which had already been accepted by both Syria and the PLO. But whatever the real basis of Syria's eventual opposition to the plan – as expressed by Asad's absence from the Fez summit – it did seem to provide the government in Damascus with an excellent issue on which to increase its influence inside the PLO at the expense of the PLO's established leadership, at a time when differences between Syria and this leadership were, once again, multiplying.

Arafat's 21 November meeting with Asad seemed to resolve little, though it lasted for three hours. The next day, the PLO Executive Committee met again, this time in Damascus. According to some reports, from Palestinians opposed to the Fahd plan, the results of this meeting were distinctly unfavourable to Arafat. Apparently in his absence, the Executive voted finally to reject the Fahd plan. (Other Palestinian sources, however, say this meeting simply gave Arafat a mandate to go ahead and do what he thought best on the issue.)[27] The result was that when Executive Committee spokesman Abdel-Muhsin Abu Maizar shortly afterwards announced that 'the PLO, Iraq and Syria' had all rejected the Fahd plan, a 'responsible source' in the Palestinian leadership crossly told the VOP, 'Abdel-Muhsin Abu Maizar has not been authorized by the Executive Committee to speak on its behalf about the Fahd plan.'[28]

The drama surrounding the Fahd plan then shifted to another scene: on 25 November the long-awaited Arab Summit did duly open in Fez, in the presence of (among others) Yasser Arafat, Crown Prince Fahd (representing King Khaled), King Hussein of Jordan, South Yemeni President Ali Nasser Muhammed and, of course, the summit's host, King Hassan II of Morocco. The most notable absentee, for whom an official limousine had been waiting at the nearby airport all morning, was Hafez al-Asad. Once it was clear the Syrian leader was going to boycott the session, Fahd surmised that he had no chance of having his plan adopted by the full Arab consensus he sought. Thus, soon after the meeting had convened, he announced he was withdrawing the plan from the agenda, and King Hassan then decided to postpone the summit's proceedings indefinitely.[29]

Some press reports at the time spoke of bitterness in the Fez meeting between Arafat and Fahd,[30] though some participants, including Khaled al-Hassan, later reported there had been none. Hassan did say, however, that there had been a 'misunderstanding' at Fez between Arafat and his 'Foreign Minister', Qaddumi. Arafat was angry that, in the foreign ministers' preparatory discussions before he himself had arrived in Fez, Qaddumi had openly sided with Khaddam and committed the PLO to opposing the Fahd plan.[31]

While the debate over the Fahd plan was still raging in Palestinian and Arab circles, an event occurred which, like the overthrow of the Shah two and a half years earlier, briefly seemed to allow the Palestinians a respite from the gloom which otherwise surrounded them at the Middle Eastern regional level. The 6th of October 1981 was the eighth anniversary of the launching of the October 1973 Middle East war. It was also, by a vagary of the Islamic calendar, the anniversary of the day on which President Sadat had, in 1977, celebrated the Al-Adha Feast in the Al-Aqsa mosque in Israeli-occupied Jerusalem. It was thus a day loaded with symbolism for many Egyptians; and it was on that day that Sadat had decided to stage a huge military parade. As Sadat sat in the reviewing stand not far from Cairo's Tomb of the Unknown Soldier, a junior officer led a posse of soldiers down from the truck they were parading along in, and pumped the President and those around him full of bullets. Vice-President Husni Mubarak, sitting next to Sadat, was saved. Since he would be the successor to the presidency, he was hustled swiftly away from the scene by security men. But Sadat himself had been killed almost instantly.

The real feelings of Egypt's 43 million population by that time towards the man who had claimed to be their 'Father' were revealed a couple of days later, when the heavily guarded funeral cortège taking Sadat's body to its final resting-place passed through almost empty streets. In a gesture of astonishing near unanimity, the Egyptians had turned their backs on Sadat, leaving him to go to his grave in the presence, mainly, of foreign friends such as Menachem Begin, three former U.S. Presidents and Britain's Prince Charles.

The mood which prevailed in Cairo in the weeks following Sadat's killing was one of general, if on occasion studied, calm. The Muslim fundamentalists who had been able to organise the assassination had thereby just about spent their force, and were unable to capitalise on it to impose their own rule on the country. (Indeed, in the days which followed, the security forces were able to arrest nearly all the active members of the different underground fundamentalist movements which had burgeoned in Egypt over the previous decade.) Nor was the secular opposition able to impose its views – which, like those of the fundamentalists, included a general opposition to Camp David – on the Mubarak regime. One of Mubarak's first acts on coming into office was to reaffirm Egypt's commitment to Camp David, and this move was indeed tacitly approved even by many members of the secular opposition, in view of the fact that the last stage of Israel's withdrawal from Sinai was due the following April. However, the manner of his predecessor's passing had obviously left its mark on President Mubarak: his partisanship of Camp David was thenceforth to be far lower-key than Sadat's had been.

Yasser Arafat's first comment on hearing of the death of the man the Palestinians blamed for many of their woes since 1977 was reportedly 'That is what happens to people who betray the Palestinian cause.' Then, shortly afterwards, he wondered openly, 'Why wasn't Mubarak hit? Why was he the only one who wasn't hurt?'[32]

In the Palestinian-controlled parts of West Beirut, the reaction to Sadat's killing was less cautious and more openly joyful. With left-wing newspapers in Lebanon describing the killing as 'an execution', Fateh's Salah Khalaf pursued the same theme when he said, 'It was an execution of all the disgrace and shame which Sadat brought us and the Arab nation, particularly Egypt... This operation by the great people of Egypt through their gallant army has proved that the Palestinian cause lives on in their conscience.'[33]

In the short term, however, Sadat's killing appeared to do little to change the general Arab situation. Throughout October and November 1981 there was much speculation that Mubarak might be able, where Sadat had not been, to 'return Egypt to the Arab fold'. But in the event, Mubarak and those around him were concerned above all with not giving Israel any pretext to postpone the imminent final withdrawal from Sinai. Only after that had been completed almost totally as planned [34] did the Egyptian President make his first tentative gestures towards, for example, Iraqi President Saddam Hussein. Even after April 1982, however, Mubarak continued to stick to the letter of Egypt's commitments under the Camp David agreement. Thus, as of early 1983, the huge political and strategic weight of Egypt still remained tantalisingly out of the Arabs' and the Palestinians' reach.

While the attention of the new ruler of Egypt was centred on Israel's imminent pullback from the rest of Sinai, there continued to be no tangible progress in pursuing that other portion of the Camp David accords which related to the West Bank and Gaza. The Defence Ministry in Begin's new government was now headed by a figure long notorious in Palestinian eyes for his brutality, Ariel Sharon. In the autumn of 1981, he started moving towards a new harsh set of policies both in the West Bank and Gaza, and in the occupied Golan.

In September and October 1981, the Israeli government revealed that it had plans to turn the West Bank and Gaza, which had remained under military rule since 1967, over to what it called 'civilian administration'.[35] On 1 November an Israeli university professor called Menachem Milson was named as new 'civilian administrator' of the West Bank. (No 'civilian' could be found to rule Gaza, so a member of the existing military administration there simply took off his uniform and started ruling in mufti.) The reaction of the Palestinians, both inside and outside the occupied territories, to this innovation was sharp: they saw it as a further step towards transforming the *de facto* occupation of their lands into *de facto* annexation. Nor did the choice of Milson do anything to reassure them. In two

117

recently published articles he had spelt out how Israel should pursue a hard-hitting campaign against the Palestinian nationalists in the occupied territories.[36]

Then, on 14 December 1981, the Israeli government announced the unilateral extension of the rule of Israeli law to the Syrian areas it had occupied in 1967, in the Golan (al-Julan). The Golan's (mainly Druze) residents were ordered to start carrying Israeli identification cards forth-with. The vast majority of them, however, refused, and they launched a general protest strike throughout the Golan which, despite harsh Israeli counter-measures, continued unbroken for several weeks. On 16 Decem-ber, the U.N. Security Council met at Syria's urgent request and declared the extension of Israeli law to the Golan as 'null and void', demanding Israel's immediate abrogation of the measure. Israel refused to comply. Two months later the simmering protests on the Golan erupted into the open again. After the Israelis arrested some Druze community leaders there on 13 February, their followers declared another general strike; yet again, the Israeli military sealed off all the Druze villages from contact with the outside world.

Milson's rule in the West Bank, meanwhile, was bringing no more benefits to the Palestinians there than they had expected. One of the major policies he concentrated on was to foster the development of groups of collaborators in the Palestinian communities, called the 'Village Leagues'. The aim was to cultivate a new community leadership which could even-tually challenge that of the informal network called the National Guidance Committee, which had evolved among those Palestinian nationalist mayors who had been elected in 1976.[37] The most influential Palestinian figure in Milson's scheme was a political maverick called Mustafa Dudeen, who had in previous decades moved across the Middle Eastern scene in guises as various as that of an ardent Nasserite, at one stage, and as a Minister of Agriculture in Amman, at another. Now he emerged as leader of the Hebron area Village League.

On 9 March 1982, the Jordanian Prosecutor-General issued a warning to members of the embryo Village Leagues that they would be charged with high treason under Jordanian law if they did not withdraw their League membership within 30 days. West Bank residents were still able to travel only on the passports which Jordan had issued them during its rule there prior to 1967, and they maintained many business and family links with Amman, so this latest Jordanian ruling (which followed a much earlier ruling from Amman that anyone selling land to Israelis in the West Bank was also committing treason) bore quite substantial weight. Within two weeks, at least 18 League members had quit in response to it.

Then, on 11 March, the Israelis launched a counter-blow by declaring the

National Guidance Committee illegal; and one week later they dissolved the town council in Al-Bireh and dismissed its mayor, Ibrahim Tawil, for having refused to co-operate with the civilian administration. The other West Bank municipalities immediately called for a three-day general strike to protest that action. The strike was observed with near-unanimity throughout the West Bank as a storm of nationalist demonstrations erupted. During these, Israeli soldiers shot and killed six of the demonstrators in at least three separate incidents. The demonstrations and strikes spread to Gaza from 21 March, and on 25 March even reached into some communities of those Palestinians who had remained within Israel in 1948 ('Israeli Arabs'). On 24 March, a Labour-sponsored Knesset motion censuring the Begin government for its policies in the occupied territories resulted in an even vote. The government, which had been reported as considering resignation, then rejected making such a move.

Both Syria and Jordan had meanwhile requested an urgent meeting of the Security Council on the issue, but on 24 March the debate on this issue was adjourned. That day, Milson was quoted as describing the disturbances rocking the occupied territories as 'the most significant battle Israel has had to wage politically since its creation in 1948'.[38] The following day he dismissed two more of the nationalist mayors, Bassam Shakaa of Nablus and Karim Khalaf of Ramallah. (A further half-dozen were to be shut out of their town halls within the following four months.) By the end of the month Israeli counter-measures, such as economically debilitating curfews, wide-scale arrests and the use of firepower against unarmed demonstrators, had sent the population of the occupied areas back to lick its wounds, in expectation of further battles to come.

The next major Israeli-Palestinian confrontation occurred not in the West Bank, however, but once again in Lebanon. On 25 January 1982, Israel's Ambassador to the U.S., Moshe Arens, voiced only what all the PLO leaders were already fearing when he said that an Israeli invasion of Lebanon was just 'a matter of time'.[39] Some thought that that time had come on 3 April, when a Second Secretary at the Israeli Embassy in Paris was assassinated. (A group calling itself the Lebanese Revolutionary Army Faction later claimed responsibility.) The next day, the Israeli government met 'to examine the implications [of the assassination] for Israel's defence'.[40] But the invasion was still postponed. Then, on 21 April, an Israeli soldier was killed by a land-mine planted inside Lebanon. The Israeli government, deeming this an offensive act, sent waves of planes to bomb the Palestinian-controlled coastal town of Damour, killing 23 people there.[41] But still, as in the wake of numerous previous Israeli attacks against Joint Forces (JF) positions and civilian targets in Lebanon since 24

July 1981, the Palestinians continued generally to observe their side of the cease-fire reached on that date.

On 3 June 1982, a gunman in London shot and criticially wounded the Israeli Ambassador.[42] The PLO immediately denied any responsibility for the action, but the next day waves of Israeli F-16 planes bombed Palestinian refugee camps and other targets in Beirut, while further squadrons of planes bombed other Palestinian and Joint Forces positions in south Lebanon. The first Lebanese government casualty reports counted 45 dead and 150 wounded in those raids, though these figures were later revised upward.

This time, the PLO leadership felt it could hold back no longer. As the casualties were still being pulled out of the bombed sports stadium in West Beirut, Palestinian artillery units in south Lebanon started shelling targets inside northern Israel for the first time in over ten months. Yasser Arafat, who had been in Saudi Arabia trying to mediate the Iraq-Iran war, flew back to Beirut, where he was to remain at the head of the JF command until he was evacuated from the city on 30 August.

On 6 June, the Israeli army, whose plans for the invasion had reportedly been ready for more than a year, launched the massive military operation which the Israeli government named 'Operation Peace for Galilee'.[43] The tactics the Israelis followed in that war, in which hundreds of thousands of Israeli army regulars and reservists were to participate over the coming months, showed a sophisticated co-ordination of air, naval and ground activities. In this invasion, unlike the 1978 invasion of Lebanon, the Israelis did not push a solid, massively protected front up through the country; instead they 'leap-frogged' commando units, armour and artillery in over the heads and round the sides of the terrain's JF defenders, using their total air and sea superiority. Without waiting to win complete control of every point in the south the Israelis were thus able to start new battles ever further north, both along the coast and in the inland Shouf mountains. Only after seizing strategic communications points all the way up to the outskirts of Beirut did they finish their 'mopping up' operations in some areas of the south. The battles for total ground control of some of the (heavily defended) refugee camps in the south, for example, lasted for more than a week after they had been totally cut off from Beirut. By 14 June, Israeli units advancing northwards along the western slopes of the Shouf were able to link up with the Phalangist-dominated Christian militias who had been their allies since 1976. The Palestinians and their allies in West Beirut were trapped inside the 'accordion', which could then be squeezed tight.[44]

In later weeks and months, there were to be many questions in Palestinian ranks as to what had happened to the JF's defences in south Lebanon. The answer to this is complex. In chapter 5, we saw how the incessant weight of Israel's retaliations against south Lebanon over the years had started to fracture what, for more than a decade after the Palestinian guerrillas started operating in south Lebanon, had been an almost solid alliance with the local population. Also, the political disputes which had cut into the Lebanese National Movement in all the areas under its control after the 1977 killing of Kamal Junblatt had had their effect on LNM strength in the south; and the majority of Shi'ite villagers there had suffered their own loss of an immediate leader when Imam Musa Sadr disappeared in 1978.[45]

The Palestinians had made mistakes which contributed to the weakness of the JF in south Lebanon, too. Over the years, the ebullience of the revival of their national movement (especially when contrasted to the divergences and doubts pervading much of the LNM) had led on occasion to what some Palestinians and Lebanese described as the beginnings of a Palestinian chauvinism in the dealings of some levels of the guerrilla movement with their Lebanese hosts and allies. Though no one at any level of the Palestinian movement ever harboured the aspiration which the Phalangists were continually accusing them of having, to settle permanently in Lebanon, nevertheless the strength of the PLO's social and political institutions in Lebanon stood in stark contrast to those maintained alongside them by the much more hesitant LNM and the chronically weak Lebanese government.

Strategically, the Palestinian response to the massive Israeli attack of 1982 appeared confused. In July 1981, the Israeli ground thrusts which had accompanied the air bombardments had been met by the JF units in a reportedly pretty effective use of the classic guerrilla response of dissolving into small groups to operate through and behind the Israeli lines. But within a few days, in the 1982 battles, the Israelis' leap-frog advance had forced the JF into the uncomfortable stance, for guerrilla units, of defending a basically static front around the perimeter of Beirut. The effectiveness with which they were to conduct the defence of Beirut perhaps indicated the distance they had travelled from their original guerrilla doctrines, but there were still some in the movement who felt that the old ways would have been better.

At another level, too, many Palestinians afterwards considered that the withdrawal of one of their key commanders in the south – the military commander of the Sidon district, al-Hajj Ismail, whose reported flight from the approaching Israeli assault was the subject of a subsequent internal Fateh enquiry – contributed to the speed with which the Israelis advanced towards Beirut.

According to one well-placed Palestinian source,[46] it was almost immediately after the JF headquarters units in Beirut found themselves

encircled by the Israelis that the PLO leadership started to consider negotiating their forces' evacuation from the city. The fact that they laid no
claim to Beirut or any other part of Lebanon meant that they had to be
guided by the wishes of their Lebanese allies in this matter; and, particularly in the early days of the Israeli invasion, the nerve of many of these allies
appeared to have broken completely.

As the Israelis neared Beirut, however, they suddenly found it much
harder to advance. It had reportedly been clear to the PLO military
command since the first days of the Israeli action that an offensive of such
weight could only be aimed at bringing the Israelis all the way to Beirut.
The PLO's Higher Military Council, which grouped the commands of all
the guerrilla groups plus the PLA, had thus had some short time to prepare
the military defences of the city before the Israelis reached it. Meanwhile,
at the political level, the LNM leaders in Beirut were also able to rally their
own supporters into a spirited defence of their home areas against the
Israelis. The Shi'ites of Ouzai, for example, in contrast to many of their
co-religionists in the south, were reported to have fought toughly to hold
the Israelis out of their strategically located suburb.

The success of the JF defence of the Beirut suburbs thus soon made it clear
to the Israeli command that the city could not be taken without huge Israeli
casualties. Both Palestinians and Israelis were then ready, albeit still hesi-
tantly, for the tortuous negotiations which ensued over the fate of the
besieged city and its hundreds of thousands of inhabitants.

The above-mentioned Palestinian source recalled, however, that the PLO
leaders had considered that the demands made by Ariel Sharon in mid-
June for their unconditional, unarmed evacuation amounted to a call for
their unconditional surrender, and this they continued to reject. The way
they hoped to express this was to try to hold all negotiations for any
evacuation from Beirut with the Lebanese President rather than with
Sharon. But – and this reportedly came as a surprise to the PLO leaders –
President Sarkis refused even to sit at the same table with them. They then
started suspecting him of acting in some kind of co-ordination with
Sharon.[47]

On 8 June, the U.S. mediator Philip Habib had returned to try to deal
with the fighting in Lebanon. The tortuous communications path which
emerged for the negotiations which followed was that the Palestinians
would explain their stand on each issue as it arose to Lebanese Premier
Shafiq al-Wazzan, who had no executive power but who was at least ready
– indeed, willing – to talk with them; Wazzan would relay what they had
told him to Sarkis; then, without intervening or giving his own opinion on
any of the matters raised, Sarkis would relay it to Habib; and Habib would
relay it to the Israelis. 'Thus Sarkis forced the PLO to deal with Habib, and

indirectly with the Israelis,' the same Palestinian source said.

At the first stage of the indirect negotiations, the Palestinians appeared to be offering a dramatic political deal to the Americans. On 16 June, Fateh Central Committee member Hani al-Hassan was reported as saying that the U.S. had the choice of opening talks with the PLO or carrying the responsibility for the destruction of Beirut. The PLO, he said, would be ready to talk about anything in such discussions, 'including laying down [its] arms'.[48] A public denial of this position was issued fairly rapidly by a lower-level PLO official, but by 17 June the first reports were already circulating in Beirut of the terms under which the PLO leaders were saying they were ready to evacuate Beirut.[49]

According to the same anonymous source, the negotiating tactics which the PLO leaders followed throughout the 67 days of the siege of Beirut were as follows:

When we started to negotiate, we had our own scale of priorities. Our first position was that we said we are prepared to leave if there is a disengagement of forces through balanced troop withdrawals by both sides; but the Israelis refused to talk about this completely and replied with a fierce bombardment.

We fell back to another position in the negotiations: we said we will move from Beirut to another point in Lebanon, for example to the Bekaa or to Tripoli. That was another stage in the negotiations; again, it did not succeed.

So we moved to the third stage of the negotiations, through the French-Egyptian project, which was trying through the U.N. to obtain a resolution which would recognise the Palestinians' right to self-determination. And the Palestinian political position was that if this resolution could be issued from the Security Council we would consider it an appropriate political gain from the Battle of Beirut, worth our leaving Beirut for. And [the project] kept alive for many days, as a result of the French-Egyptian activity, but it did not succeed because of the American veto...[50]

The fourth stage was our insistence on overland evacuation to Syria, but Israel said there would be no guarantee that we would not stop off in the Bekaa.

The last stage was that we said, okay, fine, we will leave; but the PLO should retain in Lebanon its political office, and a symbolic brigade of the PLA. This too was rejected, and the rejection came in the atmosphere of the battles, the shelling, the planes and everything. Thus the final point that Yasser Arafat stopped at – and he notified Philip Habib of this, saying that this point is *not* for negotiation, either you accept or we remain to fight till the death in Beirut – this point was that *we are ready to leave without any conditions, but we want an American-international guarantee for the security of the civilians in Beirut.*

And as a result of the negotiations, Habib presented a written undertaking, guaranteeing the security of the Palestinian civilians under the supervision of the international forces. And when this guarantee came through, Arafat agreed to our leaving, and the evacuation started.[51]

The guarantee referred to here was that contained in a document which had been agreed to by the PLO and the governments of Lebanon and the U.S., and was subsequently published by the U.S. State Department.[52] This document provided the ground-rules for the PLO fighters' evacuation from Beirut, and for the deployment of the multi-national force under whose auspices this evacuation would take place; the U.S., France and Italy were all to contribute units to this force. The document also stated:

4. *Safeguards* ... Law-abiding Palestinian noncombatants left behind in Beirut, including the families of those who have departed, will be subject to Lebanese laws and regulations. The Governments of Lebanon and the United States will provide appropriate guarantees of safety in the following ways.

The Lebanese Government will provide its guarantees on the basis of having secured assurances from armed groups with which it has been in touch.

The United States will provide its guarantees on the basis of assurances received from the Government of Israel and from the leadership of certain Lebanese groups with which it has been in touch.

On the basis of these guarantees, on 21 August 1982, the first contingent of PLO fighters set sail from Beirut, bound for Cyprus, still carrying their personal arms to signify that the evacuation was not the surrender Sharon had demanded. Others, and the Syrian units who were also evacuating Beirut, later followed them as the evacuation plan unfolded without any serious hitches.

On 30 August, amidst crushes of people – Lebanese and Palestinians – trying to say a last fond farewell to him, Yasser Arafat travelled down to Beirut port accompanied by Lebanese Prime Minister Shafiq Wazzan, a personal representative of President Sarkis, and LNM leader Walid Junblatt. After a hurried exhange of speeches, the PLO Chairman embarked on a ship to Athens, bringing to an end the whole dramatic 11-year period subsequently referred to by PLO activists as 'Ayyam Beirut' – the Beirut era.

The account above conveys little of the drama or horror of what the Palestinians call the 'Battle of Beirut', a battle in which one of the world's most sophisticated military machines threw all the nasty tricks of ultra-modern military technology against an overwhelmingly civilian concentration of hundreds of thousands of people whose defenders wielded, at best, only hand-held technology, a limited amount of medium artillery, and a few score old-model tanks. The inhabitants of the Lebanese coast had long grown accustomed to living under skies controlled by an alien power, but now the air strikes mounted by that power against them lasted not the fleeting minutes of previous attacks, but for many terrifying hours at a time. The Israelis cut off water and food from the besieged city; they dropped leaflets urging the populace to leave; they mounted a ceaseless 'psy-war' campaign to persuade Beirut's defenders to give themselves up.

124

Yet, according to many of those who lived through those hellish weeks, a tough spirit of militant popular resistance emerged fairly rapidly after the first imposition of the total siege among that majority of West Beirut's residents who remained in the city throughout. The enormity of the Israeli threat looming at the city's entrances seemed to erase the memory of all the factional disputes and problems which had plagued West Beirut since 1977.

As the battle progressed, the dynamics of the relationship between the PLO leaders in Beirut and the LNM began to change. At the beginning of the siege, the shock experienced by many of the LNM's cadres at the rapidity of the Israelis' advance, and at the dimensions of the casualty toll, had led some of them to conclude that further resistance was pointless. But, as the above-mentioned Palestinian source explained it, 'With the continuation of the battle, and from their fear of reprisals by the Phalangists against them, the LNM's activists came to another position: that we should continue to negotiate, and they would continue to support our demand that we exit on our terms and not on Sharon's.'[53]

During the Battle of Beirut, the sophistication of the PLO's decision-making process showed itself at several different levels. At the level of the individual military commanders, many of them were able to explain with clarity afterwards precisely how they had dealt with specific military threats or provocations from the Israelis. The commander of the Museum front, for example, recalled:

We had thrown up huge earth barricades between us and the enemy. But every time there was a cease-fire, the Israelis would bring huge bulldozers right up to the barricades, to try to shovel earth up the barricade from their side and tip it over our heads on our side. Of course, that is an act of considerable tactical significance; but perhaps it is not, strictly speaking, a *military act*, an infraction of the cease-fire, even though the driver and the guard riding on the bulldozer would be well armed. So we could not immediately shoot at the driver and the guard – that would mean we would be breaking the cease-fire!

Instead, we would send out one or two boys with RPGs [bazookas] to try to knock out *the bulldozers*, rather than the soldiers riding on them: and then that is not a military act on our part. We lost some of our best young fighters that way, it is true. But we knocked out 27 Israeli bulldozers on our section of the front alone.[54]

Individual sector commanders such as this one were generally well able, it seems, to keep in touch with the central Operations Room, though it was kept in constant movement around the city for fear of an attack. All military aspects of the siege came under the central direction of the JF Command and, at the purely Palestinian level, the Higher Military Council. As the Israeli forces had closed their ring around West Beirut, the existing JF units there had been joined by other JF units which were able to regroup there from points further south, as well as by Syrian units which had either previously been stationed in West Beirut or regrouped there. The Syrian troops who participated in the Battle of Beirut numbered between 4,500 and 5,000, divided into: 1,500 from the previously Syrian-commanded PLA units; 1,500 from a regular Syrian army formation which had fallen back into the city; and 1,500 other Syrian troops who had previously been distributed throughout the city. Some Palestinians subsequently stressed that these Syrians, who they say fought and died bravely alongside the JF units, did so under JF and not under Syrian command.

Throughout the siege, the Fateh leadership showed itself capable in dividing the many roles required by the situation among its own members. Those in Beirut remained in constant touch with those who were supporting their efforts from elsewhere. Inside Beirut, Khalil al-Wazir and Saad Sayel[55] directed most of the military effort, while Salah Khalaf played an important role in rallying popular morale for the resistance effort, and Hani al-Hassan helped Arafat with many of his political contacts. Outside Beirut, meanwhile, both Khaled al-Hassan and Farouq Qaddumi spent all the period of the siege outside Beirut on various diplomatic missions. But in the view of most of those who participated in the Battle of Beirut, the pivot of all these efforts was the role played by Arafat, as he ceaselessly toured the frontlines, the bread-lines, the refugee camps and hospitals, as well as attending an endless string of political, military and diplomatic meetings.

During the siege of Beirut, too, as he had generally shown himself capable of doing throughout the preceding seven years in the immediate political field, Arafat gathered about himself a group of co-deciders appropriate to the gravity of the political decisions that needed taking. Throughout the siege, all the important Palestinian political decisions in Beirut were reportedly taken by a unified political leadership consisting of the PLO Executive Committee plus all those secretaries-general of the non-Fateh guerrilla groups who had remained in Beirut. In fact, this was all of them, except for the leaders of the Arab Liberation Front and Saiqa, but the latter was represented in Arafat's counsels by a second-level leader. Thus, the final Palestinian decision to evacuate, which was first publicly signalled by Salah Khalaf on 14 August and was confirmed by Arafat the next day,[56] had been taken by the general consensus of all these groups; none of them afterwards was in any position to dispute it.

On 1 September 1982, while the PLO Chairman was still on the high seas, the U.S. President unveiled a comprehensive peace plan for the Middle East – the first over-all Middle East plan to which the U.S. had subscribed since the Camp David project four years earlier, and the first time ever that the head of the U.S. government had laid such a strong claim to world

126

statesmanship as to 'go it alone' in laying out his country's guidelines for peace in that chronically troubled region.[57] The 'Reagan plan' did not call for a complete Israeli pullback to the pre-1967 frontiers, but it did call for further substantial Israeli withdrawals from the Arab lands occupied in that year. It ruled out the possibility of establishing an independent Palestinian state, but it called for the establishment of a Palestinian 'entity' linked to Jordan. The President also launched a strong appeal to the Israeli government, as a sign of its good faith, to halt the establishment of further Israeli settlements in the occupied areas.

On 2 September, Farouq Qaddumi commented that the Reagan plan contained 'positive elements' and, the next day, Yasser Arafat spelt out that 'We do not reject Reagan's proposals, nor do we criticise them; but we are studying them.'[58] Already, the members of the PLO Executive Committee were travelling towards Tunis, which had been the seat of the Arab League since 1979 and was now to offer the PLO a new home for its political apparatus. There, the Executive held its first meeting of the post-Beirut period.

So greatly had Arafat's prestige within the movement been enhanced by his leadership in the Battle of Beirut that this time, in contrast to that stormy series of Executive meetings in November 1981, he was given all that he asked for at the diplomatic level. This amounted to what one participant described as '*carte blanche*'. There was little time for prolonged discussion; there were many arrangements to be made in connection with the Palestinian fighters' new diaspora, and the Arab governments were already well advanced in preparations for a summit meeting due to open shortly, at which the PLO would have to be able to present a decisive and unified stand on the main issue on the Arab table – yet again, with a few changes, the Fahd plan.

The summit duly opened on 7 September. Since it was still officially merely a 'resumption' of the previous year's interrupted session, once again it was held in the Moroccan city of Fez. All Arab League member-states were represented there except Libya. As it now came under discussion at this meeting, the Fahd plan had been significantly amended only in two clauses. Into the fourth clause had been inserted specific mention of 'the Palestinian people's right to self-determination and the exercise of its imprescriptible and inalienable national rights under the leadership of the Palestine Liberation Organization, its sole and legitimate representative'. The controversial Clause 7 now stated, 'The Security Council guarantees peace among all states of the region including the independent Palestinian state.'[59]

This new text of the plan was adopted by a consensus of those meeting in Fez, who included both Arafat and Asad.

On 13 August 1976, the youthful commander of the Lebanese Phalangist Party militia, Bashir Gemayyel, had held a crowded press conference. The day before, his forces and those of Camille Chamoun's 'Tigers' militia had finally succeeded in storming the Palestinian refugee camp in East Beirut's Tel al-Zaatar district. After Gemayyel's press conference, the journalists were to be allowed into the camp to see the results; Gemayyel made a point of telling them, 'We are proud of what you are going to see there.' (Some of the terrible sights which did greet us there are described in chapter 4 above.)

Over the next six years, Bashir Gemayyel grew considerably stronger, thanks mainly to his relationship with the Israelis, and he commanded and educated a whole generation of Phalangist militiamen throughout that period.

On 23 August 1982, Gemayyel had been elected President of Lebanon. The same Parliament which in the 1976 elections had sensed the weight of Syria's presence in the country was now responding similarly to Israel's commanding new presence there. Twenty-two days later, on 14 September, he was dead, killed by a massive explosion in his East Beirut headquarters, which also killed 23 others meeting there.

It had been on 3 September that the Israeli units still encircling West Beirut had committed their first significant violations of the agreement Philip Habib had negotiated, by advancing towards the refugee camps in Sabra and Shatila[60] and clearing minefields which the JF had laid there for the protection of the camps. Then, the day after Bashir Gemayyel was killed, the Israeli army moved in force to occupy the whole of West Beirut. The U.S.-led multi-national force which had supervised the PLO fighters' evacuation from the city had itself departed in the early days of September, ahead of its own schedule, with U.S. officials expressing satisfaction that the PLO evacuation had been completed so successfully.

According to the Israeli journalist Amnon Kapeliouk, Israeli tanks surrounded Sabra and Shatila camps from midday of 15 September 1982 onwards.[61] The camp residents immediately became nervous. According to Kapeliouk, some of them approached Israeli positions around the camp to express their fear that 'armed Lebanese groups' (that is, Phalangists or their allies) might seek to enter the camp. But 'the soldiers reassured them that nothing would happen to them "because they were civilians and not terrorists". They were thus given orders to return to their homes.'[62]

Kapeliouk wrote that the next day

At 3 p.m., the commander of the Israeli forces in Beirut, General Amos Yaron, along with two of his officers, met the Lebanese Forces' intelligence chief, Elias Hobeika, and Fadi Ephram.[63] With the help of aerial photographs provided by

Israel, together they made the arrangements for entering the camps. The Israeli general confirmed to them that his troops would provide all the help necessary 'for cleaning out the terrorists from the camps'. Afterwards, General Drori [Israeli commander in that sector of Lebanon] telephoned to Ariel Sharon to tell him, 'Our friends are going into the camps. We have co-ordinated their entry.' 'Congratulations!' Ariel Sharon replied. 'Our friends' operation is approved.'[64]

From 4 p.m. on 16 September until 10 a.m. on 18 September, the Israeli army units surrounding the camps did indeed give the necessary aid to the LF fighters and those identified by survivors as belonging to Saad Haddad's south Lebanese units, as they went about their business in Sabra and Shatila. As Kapeliouk, who was to be one of the first journalists on the scene after the massacre and who conducted extensive research among the Israeli troops in Beirut at the time, described it,

From the beginning, the massacre assumed huge proportions, according to those who escaped. Throughout those first hours, the Phalangist fighters killed hundreds of people. They shot at anything which moved in the alleys. Breaking down the doors of the houses, they liquidated entire families in the middle of their supper. Residents were killed in their beds, in pyjamas. In numerous apartments, one would find children of 3 or 4 years, also in pyjamas, wrapped up in blood-soaked blankets. But, often, the killers were not content just to kill. In very many cases, the assailants cut off the limbs of their victims before killing them. They smashed the heads of infants and babies against the walls. Women, and even young girls, were raped before being assassinated with hatchets... Sometimes, [the killers] left one single member of the family alive, killing the others before his eyes, so that this unfortunate could afterwards tell what he had seen and been through.[65]

The Israeli soldiers surrounding the camp throughout were given strict instructions not to intervene, and not to go inside the camps. They also blocked the exits from the camps for those many camp residents who at stages throughout the 42 hours of the massacres sought by any means to flee. Kapeliouk mentions the most startling occasion on which this occurred as being when an Israeli tank aimed its main gun at a group of 500 seeking to leave the camps, and forced them to return.[66]

Finally, on the morning of 18 September, the Israelis ordered thé Phalangists out of the camps. The journalists who were then able to enter found scenes of terrifying destruction. Hundreds of bodies lay in the camps' alleys and inside their maze of little houses and apartment blocks; untold numbers of others had clearly been dumped in the mass graves whose newly turned earth marked several areas of the camps; residents' accounts also spoke of many hundreds of Palestinian men being taken away from the area on trucks towards an unknown fate. The total casualty toll of the massacres was almost certainly far higher than the 700-800 figure the Israelis subsequently claimed. Taking into consideration partial figures

129

used by the International Committee of the Red Cross, Kapeliouk arrived at a total figure of 'around 3,000' killed, 'out of a population of 20,000 people in the two camps on the eve of the massacre... It is thought that around a quarter of the victims were Lebanese [camp residents], and the rest Palestinians.'[67]

The uproar which was to follow the disclosure of the massacres led the U.S. hastily to reorganise the despatch of a multi-national force to West Beirut, with strict orders that the Israelis return to the lines they had held at the time of the Habib agreement. In Israel itself, vast demonstrations of shocked Israelis forced the government to establish a judicial enquiry into the massacres, whose publication in early 1983 led to Sharon being shifted sideways out of the Defence Ministry.

For the PLO leaders, as for Palestinians everywhere, the effect of the Sabra and Shatila massacres was traumatic. They had known what to expect if the Israeli army had been able to enter Beirut; yet all the guarantees they had obtained – including that from the U.S. – that this would not happen had proved worthless. Certainly the weeks succeeding the massacres saw much agonised soul-searching from all PLO activists, with only a few of them able immediately to slot this latest outrage against their people into the whole catalogue of previous massacres their people had suffered, from the 1948 massacre at Deir Yassin onwards.

In a speech to the Sixteenth PNC session five months later, Salah Khalaf said that the massacres had had three aims: to cow everyone else in West Beirut into laying down their arms before the Israelis; to 'cheat' the PLO fighters and leaders of the military victory they felt they had registered in the Battle of Beirut; and to terrorise all the rest of the Palestinians in Lebanon into leaving the country.[68] Reflecting previous Western press reports that news of the massacre had provoked anguished criticisms of the PLO/Fateh leaders from many of the PLO fighters now distributed in other Arab countries, Khalaf asserted, 'We know that among the aims of this massacre is our losing confidence in one another.' He accused the Israelis of showing pictures of the Sabra and Shatila massacres to the 7,000-plus Palestinian detainees held in an Israeli concentration camp at Ansar in south Lebanon. 'By showing them they score several points: that these fighters left you behind in Beirut, and that the leadership decided to leave Beirut so that your people could be slaughtered. This is another aim.'[69]

On leaving Beirut, Yasser Arafat had travelled not to Syria, as the Syrians reportedly would have wished, but to Athens.[70] Trouble was brewing between the PLO/Fateh leaders and the Syrian government in the aftermath of the Lebanese fighting, although both sides continued to realise, at least until spring 1983, that the ties between them still constituted a kind of Catholic marriage, from which objective circumstances would permit them no escape. The continuing tensions in Lebanon, where both Syrians and Palestinians continued for some months after September 1982 to fear further Israeli offensives against their remaining forces in the country, served to underline that perception.

In a press interview in early February 1983, Fateh's Khalil Wazir was to sum up the relations between the two sides in the following terms:

Before I outline some of the points of differences between us and Syria, it is necessary to stress that that there is no choice between us – and Syria – except to remain in the same trench in confrontation against the same enemy –imperialism and the Zionist enemy...

I can summarize the differences since the Beirut siege in the following points:

1. The assessment of the situation during the Zionist invasion of Lebanon, and thus the extent of participation in the battles. I don't at this moment want to make something up, but I will recall what Syrian officials themselves said. This was: 'Syria decided to confine the battle to Beirut and to participate with the forces it has there if the enemy decided to confine it there too.' But the matter was different for the Palestinian revolution. We were under siege and in a difficult situation. We were anxious to open other good fighting fronts with the enemy ...

2. The political move in the wake of the exit from Beirut on the Arab and international levels. Here too the difference is a result of the difference between our situation as a revolution and Syria's situation as a state. Without an active and broad political move to bolster the role of the loaded rifle, we will end up in a vacuum. This does not apply to Syria, which is a state that has borders, laws, a flag, an army, and diplomacy.[71]

The political move referred to by Wazir was principally the efforts of the PLO leaders, in conjunction with the rulers of Jordan, Saudi Arabia and other Arab regimes, to test to the full the intentions of the U.S. regarding the Reagan plan. The Fez summit of September 1982 had established a seven-party committee grouping the PLO, the Syrians, Jordanians, Saudis, Moroccans, Algerians and Kuwaitis, with a mandate to visit the capitals of all the Security Council's five permanent members to investigate the chances for further diplomatic movement based on the Fahd plan, now renamed the Fez plan. But even their inclusion on this committee could not, apparently, totally allay the Syrians' fears that they might be left out of whatever diplomatic deal might emerge. In addition, many pro-Syrian members of the PLO constituency expressed fears that Arafat and the other PLO leaders might go as far in their new negotiations with Jordan's King Hussein as to compromise the PLO's claim to be the Palestinian people's 'sole legitimate representative', or as far in their tentative new approaches to the Egyptian regime as to weaken the PLO's opposition to Camp David.[72]

Apparently encouraging the Syrians in their criticisms of the PLO leaders

131

was the Libyan ruler, Muammar al-Qadhafi, who during the Battle of Beirut had called on the PLO leadership to commit suicide rather than leave Beirut, and who subsequently had been the only Arab ruler to boycott the resumed Fez summit.

The PLO/Fateh leaders had realised from the time of their departure from Beirut that the exigencies of the new diaspora being forced on them would require, at least initially the closest possible co-ordination with as many Arab governments as possible. In order to persuade their constituency of this necessity, as well as to reconfirm that the pursuit of a diplomatic solution which had been PLO policy since 1974 would continue to guide the Organisation, they determined that the Sixteenth session of the Palestinian National Council should be convened as soon as possible. In October/November 1982, their plans for this crystallised on a mid-February date, with the location of the meeting to be Algiers – a clear signal to Damascus that the days of Syrian strength within the PLO had now passed.

In a series of meetings which followed, the Syrians and Libyans appeared to be doing everything possible, short of an all-out clash with the PLO, to upset these plans. On 17 January 1983, Qadhafi was able to gather the leaders of five non-Fateh guerrilla groups – the PFLP, the DFLP, the PFLP-GC, Saiqa and the Palestinian Popular Struggle Front – in Tripoli, where they issued a radical-sounding communiqué calling for all-out rejection of the Reagan plan. This was just what the PLO/Fateh leaders did not want to emerge from the forthcoming PNC meeting.

Ten days later, however, the PLO Executive Committee met in the South Yemeni capital, Aden. Arafat held side-meetings there with the PFLP's George Habash and the DFLP's Nayef Hawatma, in which he was apparently successful in persuading them of the importance of 'Palestinian national unity' at that stage of the struggle.

With the PFLP and the DFLP now seemingly defecting from the hard-line Palestinian front they had hoped to sponsor, the Syrians and Libyans presumably gauged that a boycott of the PNC by the other three participants in the Tripoli discussions would have little credibility. The Fateh leaders therefore appeared confident, after the Aden meeting, that the prospects for the holding of the PNC session in much the form they were seeking looked good.

The Syrians had meanwhile been able to persuade one of the co-founders of Fateh itself, Nimr Saleh, who was still a member of the Fateh Central Committee, of the validity of their arguments. From Damascus, throughout the months following the evacuation from Beirut, he had been issuing periodic criticisms of the other Fateh leaders' policies. On 21 January 1983, for example, he issued a statement indirectly accusing Arafat of 'violating the resolutions of the Palestinian institutions and ... endangering the cause of our people'.[73] At a meeting in Kuwait shortly after this, the Central Committee decided to 'freeze' Saleh's positions in both the Committee itself and the command structure of the Al-Asifa forces.

According to one Palestinian source, the Syrians made one final attempt to achieve at least a postponement of the Sixteenth PNC session, when they tried to swing Habash and Hawatma back to their side in the dispute with Fateh at meetings in Damascus on 7 and 8 February. But they failed, and the session opened on schedule and exactly as planned (except that the estimated attendance of 700-800 delegates, observers and vistors had swollen to more than 4,000 by the time the session opened). The members of the remaining 'pro-Syrian' bloc – Saiqa, the PFLP-GC and the Palestinian Popular Struggle Front – all found themselves in the situation of having to take part, or else lose their credibility in front of their remaining Palestinian constituents. They therefore took part. The Fateh leaders, sensing their strength through the unanimity of participation in the session, then apparently decided to pursue their defiance of the Syrian regime to the point where the latter might stop trying to influence the PLO's decision-making.

In his capacity as Chairman of the PLO Executive Committee, Yasser Arafat delivered two rousing speeches at the PNC session. Fateh's own speech ('Kalimat Fateh') was delivered by Salah Khalaf as a late-evening speech which followed two days of intensive Fateh caucusing. Easily the most abrasive challenge to the Fateh leadership at the PNC had been that voiced by the PFLP-GC's Ahmed Jibril. Khalaf used many parts of his speech to respond to Jibril and his backers in Syria and Libya:

Who said that we do not want union or a strategic meeting with Syria? ... Does Syria accept us as we are? Will Syria accept us with our independent national decision, which contradicts my Brother Ahmed Jibril in his interpretation of this decision?... I will be ready to go to Syria and say: Our independent national decision is on the table and your decision is on the table. Our decision and your decision are for both of us, but *our decision is not for you...*

[In the Battle of Beirut] Syria was required to do more. If Syria had opened the door to the fighting, the fighting might have been much greater.

We left Beirut. What did we meet? We met ingratitude. I swear by the honor of this revolution that when I heard that these heroes who left Beirut were called sheep and cattle by the voice of the Libyan Jamahiriyah [government], I nearly began to disbelieve in this entire Arab nation. These heroes are not sheep or cattle. They are men and they are the best of men.[74]

Khalaf thus used this speech to reject any Syrian or Libyan tutelage over the PLO; what he propounded for the substance of the Fateh caucus's policy on current issues was expressed as follows. On the Fez plan, he said,

The Fes [Fez] summit and the Fes resolutions represent the end of Palestinian concessions and not the beginning. This should be understood by all... I have confidence that we are a firm Palestinian leadership. We are all shrewd. We all have fingers in the Arab regimes. If we use all our shrewdness in the Palestinian arena and in the Palestinian revolution, we can achieve what we want... I believe we can come out of this stage and possibly, in a year's time, if we adjust the balance of forces, we may attend another council session and say: No, Fes is not enough. We want more. I am certain of this, but *we have to work in order to reach that stage.*[75]

Khalaf indicated that Fateh had decided to continue the stepped-up contacts with Egypt's President Mubarak which their leaders had been conducting since the Battle of Beirut. He quoted approvingly the dictum of Egyptian opposition leader Khaled Mohieddine, who had told the Fateh caucus, 'if there is a small breach through which the [Camp David] agreements can be dismantled, we should encourage it'.[76] Similarly, he indicated that Fateh favoured continuing the other set of newly stepped-up contacts which had marked their leaders' policy since the previous September: their contacts with Jordan. The latter links were of particular importance in American thinking, given that the Reagan plan had sought to involve Jordan in discussions on the West Bank and Gaza. Some substantial progress had been registered in the contacts in terms of deciding to co-ordinate the Jordanians' and PLO's responses to the Reagan plan, and to conduct preliminary discussions on the form that a confederation between the two sides might be arranged in the future. But many in the 'pro-Syrian' bloc inside the PLO still feared that the Fateh leaders were getting ready to dilute the PLO's claim to represent the Palestinians. Now, Khalaf spelled out that 'if any confederal base is established, *it must be on the basis of an independent Palestinian state.* Frankly, any confederation without a Palestinian state means Reagan and means annexation with Jordan.'[77]

In the event, practically all of the policy points delineated in Khalaf's speech were included in the final political programme which emerged at the end of the Council session. Its text had been jointly drawn up by a six-member committee representing all the major guerrilla groups; Fateh's representative on this drafting commission was Khalil al-Wazir.

The one major topic on which Khalaf had not pronounced directly in his speech was the key question of the PLO's response to the Reagan plan itself. Discussions were still apparently continuing on this subject among some sections of the Fateh caucus, and among them and the other PLO member-groups. The formula which then emerged in the political programme for dealing with the Reagan plan was:

Reagan's plan, in style and content, does not respect the established national rights of the Palestinian people since it denies the right of return and self-determination and the setting up of the independent Palestinian state and also the PLO – the sole legitimate representative of the Palestinian people – and since it contradicts international legality. Therefore, the PNC rejects the considering of this plan as a sound basis for the just and lasting solution of the cause of the Palestine and the Arab-Zionist conflict.[78]

Most of the non-Fateh guerrilla groups in the PLO (but not, strangely, the PFLP) had been working for the programme to contain an open rejection of the Reagan plan. Some of their spokesmen thus expressed satisfaction that the key word *rafd* (rejection) had indeed been included in this clause. But most Fateh leaders considered that by inserting the words 'the considering of' (*i'tibar*) between the words 'rejection' and 'the Reagan plan' they had won enough room to continue, in the months which followed, their exploration of the value of the U.S. initiative.

The period from 1981 to early 1983 was another dramatic era for the PLO/Fateh leaders. They had started 1981 with many apprehensions as to how the coming of the new U.S. President would affect their search for a political settlement to their problem. But by July 1981, Reagan's original hostility to the PLO had been tempered by his experience in office into an indirect involvement with the Organisation through the cease-fire brokered that month between Israel and the PLO by Philip Habib. Though the U.S. government continued to be formally forbidden to have contacts with the PLO, by the summer of the following year a basically PLO-related series of events contributed heavily to the resignation of U.S. Secretary of State Alexander Haig.

Similarly in Israel, in March 1982 and more so in February 1983, it was again a series of PLO-related events which was to affect the fate of decision-makers at the highest levels of government.

It could be argued that neither of these events was in a strict sense a direct result of the PLO leaders' efforts, but the refusal of either the U.S. or the Israeli government to have any direct dealings with the PLO meant that the factors of cause and effect in their relationships with the Organisation were never completely straightforward. What remains true is that by early 1983, decisions taken basically by the PLO/Fateh leaders (to fight on in Lebanon or to seek a cease-fire, to continue resisting in Beirut or to evacuate, to enter the Reagan initiative or not to) appeared to have wider-reaching repurcussions than ever before, and to be able to swing events right inside the cabinet rooms in Washington and Israel.

Not that this had been brought about without tremendous losses and suffering. The victims of the Sabra and Shatila massacres were in one sense victims also of the developing PLO-U.S. relationship, for the Palestinian leadership had left them in Beirut in the care of the U.S. guarantees. At a broader level, nearly the whole of the vast social and political infrastructure which the PLO had built over the years in Lebanon had been lost, with very little compensating gain immediately visible. Although the Palestinian community in Lebanon had for over a decade been the flagship of the Palestinian national movement, it had never been the only ship in the fleet, and throughout this period, as in the whole period since the early 70s, the momentum of the Palestinian national movement continued to shift slowly back towards the struggle being waged on the Palestinians' own land, inside the Israeli-occupied territories.

Sharon, Begin and some other Israelis had hoped openly that their actions against the PLO in Lebanon would somehow cow the nationalists inside the occupied areas into accepting the new political order in the West Bank and Gaza of which Menachem Milson had dreamed. But by the end of the Battle of Beirut, Milson himself had resigned, in implied criticism of Sharon's more militant policies, and, more important, the Village League collaborators in the West Bank and Gaza looked no nearer winning the confidence of the population. Throughout the Battle of Beirut and its aftermath, the Palestinians of the 1967-occupied areas, as well as Palestinians in those areas inside Israel's 1948 borders whose direct relatives peopled the refugee camps of Lebanon, mounted continuous strikes, demonstrations and other signs of solidarity with the PLO's suffering in Lebanon.[79]

Part II

Internal relations

The terrorist

'When I went into the plane, someone hit me from in front. There was a big protest and confusion inside the plane, so I blew it up quickly with a grenade. But I didn't have time to get out of the way properly, and the blast threw me down, and I hit my head on the aircraft stairs. There were about a hundred people in the plane... When I came round there were two people holding me. So I took out my gun, although I thought by that time it was empty... I put it into one of the policemen's stomachs and pulled the trigger, and he died... I was surprised to have found a bullet in the gun.'

This was how 'Ahmed', a self-confessed former member of the Black September Organisation, described his part in an attack which had killed 29 passengers on a Pan Am plane in Rome's Fiumicino airport in December 1973.

Ahmed had been born in 1948. He said that he had joined Fateh in 1968, but that he had left it before signing up for Black September's more exotic operations in the early 70s.

I met Ahmed once, in 1979, in south Lebanon. We sipped coffee amidst the plump velour chairs and tables decorated with lacy mats of a typical Palestinian refugee's tiny, overfurnished living room, as Ahmed discussed the 1973 operation.

I asked him why the operation's planners had picked on an American plane. He replied, 'Because it is America which arms Israel... Because Israel and other nations have no mercy on our people.'

'But even if the American government arms Israel, perhaps the passengers on the plane were opposed to government policy?' I suggested.

'We have people in south Lebanon opposed to our policy too – not the Palestinians, but some of the Lebanese. But they get attacked by Israel too, innocent people.'

'So how did you feel when you blew the plane up, with kids there and women?'

'In south Lebanon –'

'But that's in a battlefield.'

'In south Lebanon, they hit our civilians. Of course, they hit some fighters, that's understood, but they hit civilians too... Isn't that a crime too?'

'But perhaps the kids on the plane were really sweet –'

'And our kids are really sweet too!'

Chapter 7

Non-Fateh guerrilla groups

The two years following the Arab states' June 1967 defeat formed, as we saw above in chapter 3, a decisive period for the Palestinian nationalist movement. It was the period when the idea of independent Palestinian guerrilla action met an explosion of support from Palestinian and non-Palestinian communities throughout the Arab world and when the fathers of that idea – the leaders of Fateh – were able to pull themselves up into the quasi-official status of controlling the PLO.

But the very dimensions of the new support expressed for the guerrilla idea in that period meant on the one hand that Fateh, with its long-engrained habits of slow and careful underground work, was unable to absorb the scores of thousands of new guerrilla volunteers; and on the other, that all the pan-Arabist Arab regimes and parties were eager to stake out their own claim within the rapidly burgeoning guerrilla movement. Thus, the years 1967-69 also saw the growth of a spectrum of other Palestinian guerrilla organisations, which sometimes appeared to outside observers to be jostling with Fateh for overall control of the movement. In 1974, for example, four of the non-Fateh groups banded together in the Rejection Front[1] to co-ordinate their opposition to the PLO/Fateh leaders' pursuit of a diplomatic settlement of the national cause.

In reality, though, Fateh's leadership of the movement was never seriously threatened either by the Rejection Front[2] or by any of the other, earlier challenges Fateh had faced since it had consolidated its hold on the PLO in February 1969. In 1978, the Rejection Front finally disintegrated; its place as the chief internal opposition to the PLO/Fateh leaders was then taken by a grouping of more or less pro-Syrian guerrilla groups. Once again, this grouping was unable to mount anything like an open challenge to Fateh's control of the movement, though until the Battle of Beirut in 1982 the strategic realities of the PLO's relations with Syria gave the pro-Syrian bloc a degree of leverage within the movement out of all proportion to the popular support it could actually count on inside it. Then, after the PLO fighters evacuated Beirut, the Fateh leaders sought to shake off the tutelage they saw Syria and its Palestinian allies as aiming to wield over the Palestinian movement.

139

Nevertheless, despite the longevity and stability of Fateh's predominance within the PLO, the decision of its leaders in 1968 to take the other guerrilla groups with them into the leadership meant that they could never thereafter exercise the degree of monopoly over the national movement which the leaders of most other successful modern-day national liberation movements enjoyed. They therefore had to learn to co-exist with a range of half a dozen other guerrilla movements within the PLO's overall framework. Within that network of relationships, the sheer weight and breadth of Fateh's organisation has enabled its leaders not only, generally, to steer the PLO in the direction they wanted, but also to make converts of many of the other groups' once ardent ideologues, and even – by their own quiet insistence that Fateh is the embodiment of the Palestinian national identity – to extend a kind of paternalistic patronage to some of their most articulate former critics from the other groups.

The Popular Front for the Liberation of Palestine

The origins of the PFLP lay in the meeting, in the late 40s, of the two Arab nationalist figures George Habash and Hani al-Hindi, on the campus of the American University of Beirut where both were students. The two young men had both been seared by their first-hand experience of the Palestinians' 'disaster' of 1948. Habash, a Palestinian medical student, had been expelled from his home in Lydda by the advancing Jewish forces, and Hindi, a Syrian, had served as a volunteer in one of the Arab fighting groups in the 1948 war. Both of them drew the conclusion that the Zionist terror they had experienced could be countered only by counter-terror, and, for a short period between 1949 and mid-1950, they co-operated with a group of Egyptian terrorists working out of Damascus to attack various Western targets there and in Beirut. However, after the Egyptians had been discovered trying to assassinate Syrian President Adib Shishakli, the whole organisation was uncovered; but Habash and Hindi had already, according to the account recorded by Dr Basil al-Kubaisi, decided to turn 'from terrorist politics to mass struggle'.[3]

To pursue this ideal, they returned to their campus in Beirut, to make contact with other Arab nationalists there, and to investigate the many other ideologies then sweeping through campus life. The group they eventually formed, however, stood relatively firm in its opposition to both socialism and communism, seeing these ideologies as divisive in the primary struggle, which they defined as '[eliminating] Zionism and imperialism from the Arab world, and [creating] a united Arab state embracing the Arab people from the Persian Gulf to the Atlantic Ocean'.[4] Campaigning on a platform embodying these ideas, they first won the elections to the

Executive Committee of a key campus literary/nationalist association called Jam͑ iyat al-Urwa al-Wathqa (the Society of the Firm Tie), and then transformed this Committee into the nucleus of a new secret nationalist organisation: the Arab Nationalists' Movement. By the autumn of 1951, the ANM had already scored several victories in confrontations with the university administration and the local police, so the following year they extended their activities off campus, primarily to the Palestinian refugee camps dotted throughout Lebanon. Habash used to tour the camps with a fellow medical student – like himself, a Christian Palestinian – called Wadi͑ Haddad, and by early 1953 they were able to extend their activities to refugee camps in Syria and Jordan. One of their first close contacts in the camps was a schoolteacher called Ahmed al-Yamani, who before 1948 had been a labour activist in Palestine: he was later to rise to the top echelons of the ANM and then of its offspring, the PFLP.

In March 1954, the ANM organised a demonstration on the American University campus to protest the Baghdad Pact, an anti-communist Middle Eastern alliance which the British were trying to develop. One student was killed when the police moved against the demonstration, and 29 were injured; the university authorities then expelled 22 students for their part in organising the protest. The expellees, who included a number of high-level ANM members, were immediately offered places in Cairo University by special order of Egyptian President Gamal Abdel-Nasser, the Baghdad Pact's most ardent opponent in Arab ruling circles. Thus was established the basis for co-ordination between the ANM and Nasser's regime which was to continue until 1967.

By 1967, the ANM had established itself as a wide-flung pan-Arab grouping which could boast a steady, hard-working membership in most of the countries of the Arabian peninsula and the Arab East. These members were mainly people from the professional classes, most of whom had first come into contact with the Movement during their university studies in Beirut, Cairo or Damascus. The high degree of active involvement the Movement demanded from its members limited its ability to attract a working-class membership. Thus, while the ANM came to wield quite wide influence in the realm of ideas, in only one case was it able to command the kind of grass-roots power which took its ideological rivals of the Baath Party to power in Syria and Iraq. The place where the ANM was able to seize state power was in impoverished, backward South Yemen, where the ANM-led National Front participated in the fight for independence from the British; the British handed over power to the Front in 1967. But already, by 1967, the high degree of internal cohesion which had marked the ANM's activities throughout the 50s was starting to erode. It came under pressure from the centrifugal forces pulling at its various far-flung branches. The intense nationalism of the early movement retained a much more socially conservative hue in some cases, such as that of the branch in Jordan, than it did in the case of the South Yemenis or, later, the Palestinians. The ANM's internal cohesion was also racked by a generational struggle within the central leadership.

Most ANM/PFLP sources point to the National (i.e. pan-Arab) Conference held by the ANM in Beirut in May 1964 as marking a key point in this process.[5] One of the major issues debated by the 40-odd participants in this conference was the Movement's continuing relationship with Nasser's regime. The editor of the ANM's official periodical, *Al-Hurriya*, a Lebanese activist called Muhsin Ibrahim, led a campaign there to dissolve the ANM almost completely into the wider Nasserist movement. But Hindi and Yamani considered that Nasserism had suffered a serious setback when Syria had seceded from the Nasser-led union with Egypt in 1961, and they were anyway eager to safeguard the organisational integrity of the Movement they had helped to create while Ibrahim and his (Jordanian) co-thinker Nayef Hawatma were members of a younger generation of Movement activists, and not so personally committed to the continuation of the ANM in its existing form. In this debate, according to some reports, Habash tried to play a conciliatory role: on his advice, the ANM structure was retained in all its existing essentials, but Ibrahim and Hawatma were co-opted onto the 10-member ANM National Command.

The ideological single-mindedness which had held the ANM together for 12 years was by then already dissipating. Ibrahim had been advocating ideas of an increasingly socialist temper in *Al-Hurriya* since the magazine's foundation in 1960, despite the opposition of many ANM founders and old-timers. And as different geographical groupings within the Movement came to confront widely differing local political circumstances, the debates which followed the 1964 conference led to a situation where 'the history of the ANM since 1964 has not been that of a centralized pan-Arab organization, but the record of the political activities of its branches in different Arab countries', as one former ANM member wrote in the early 70s.[6]

The Palestinian branch of the ANM had been formed only in 1964. Before that date, the Movement's many Palestinian members had been expected to shed any 'Palestinian regionalist' sympathies they might have harboured, and to act within the ANM organisations of their places of residence. However, the establishment of the PLO in early 1964, as well as the early organising activities of Fateh, prompted Habash and Haddad to start forming a distinct Palestinian grouping within the ANM, and this move was endorsed by the May 1964 conference. The new grouping was called the National Front for the Liberation of Palestine (NFLP). It had a military wing called the 'Vengeance Youth' (Shebab al-Tha'r), which

142

launched its first cross-border raids against Israel in November 1964.

The NFLP continued to carry out intermittent sabotage against Israeli targets throughout the next two and a half years, though its military activities were sustained with far less regularity than those Fateh was able to mount in this same period. Then came the 1967 war; Nasser's army was smashed by Israel. The man to whose fortunes the ANM had tied its own then stood exposed as a failure who could not even defend his own borders, let alone give advice to others on how to 'liberate Palestine': all the ANM's (and the NFLP's) strategies needed a drastic re-think. This process duly started, and it continued, according to some internal PFLP analyses, right down until 1972. Thus the very period 1967-69 when the Palestinian guerrilla movements registered their most explosive growth saw the ANM and its organisations caught in the throes of rapid internal change.

Nevertheless, the first priority many ANM members saw in the aftermath of the 1967 war was to step up guerrilla activities against Israel. Thus throughout the months when Arafat and his colleagues in Fateh were trying to set up guerrilla bases in the West Bank, some NFLP activists also managed to infiltrate there, but they saw even less success than Arafat. The ANM activists were more successful in Gaza, since, prior to 1967, when the area had still been ruled by Nasser, his security police had been much more tolerant of their activities than they had been of Fateh's. Their previously established networks there were thus able to mount continuing resistance operations against the Israeli military presence in the Gaza Strip right through until 1971 (see chapter 8 below).

In September 1967, Habash and his comrades issued a unity appeal to the other fighting groups. Two months later, this call appeared to have borne fruit when it was announced that the NFLP would join with two other guerrilla groups to form a new organisation to be called the Popular Front for the Liberation of Palestine.[7] The other two groups were the Heroes of the Return (Abtal al-Awda) and the Palestinian Liberation Front (Jabhat al-Tahrir al-Filastiniyya). According to some sources, both these groups had been linked to a former Palestinian officer in the Syrian army called Ahmed Jibril — the former group being the result of his co-operation with PLO Chairman Shuqairy, and the latter, of his co-operation with the Syrian regime.[8] The PFLP's first public statement echoed some of Habash's earlier ideas from the period after the 1948 disaster. 'The only weapon left in the hands of the people ... is revolutionary violence,' it said.[9]

The newly formed PFLP boycotted the meeting to which Fateh had invited all the guerrilla groups in January 1968 — PFLP leaders argued at that stage that the PLO should be the only valid umbrella grouping for the Palestinian movement. But the following month, Habash met in Beirut

143

with Fateh's Khalil Wazir, and the two men worked out a programme for the progressive unification of all their two groups' activities into a single unified movement.[10] However, in March 1968, the Fateh leaders accused the PFLP of having withdrawn its fighters from the crucial Battle of Karameh, and a subsequent commission of enquiry established that the PFLP units in Karameh had indeed, in line with standard procedures for most types of guerrilla warfare, sought to avoid a confrontation there. Fateh then quickly disavowed the Wazir-Habash agreement. Thus, at the stage that Fateh was first establishing its control over the PLO apparatus, in late 1968/early 1969, the PFLP was cast into the role of chief opponent of this process. In the negotiations over membership in the PNC session scheduled for July 1968, the Fateh leaders were able to outsmart the PFLP by ensuring that most of the 'independents' and representatives of the (still then largely notional) 'Palestinian mass organisations' there would be pro-Fateh.[11] The PFLP's reaction was to urge those few 'independent' PNC delegates who would be inclined to support them – mainly intellectuals – to boycott the proceedings in protest. But Fateh was then able to score another point against the PFLP by pointing to the intellectuals as far removed from the groundswell of popular pro-Fateh feeling.[12]

While all these external negotiations continued, relations within the PFLP were also far from harmonious. The debate had raged on inside the PFLP, and particularly among those of its members who had originated in the ANM, over the reasons for the failure of their former ally, Nasser, in 1967. The general trend inside the PFLP was towards an increasingly radical socialist critique of Nasserism, but not all the former ANMers had travelled the same distance along this path. The accusations that Nasserism was a 'petty bourgeois' phenomenon were voiced loudest by those very activists who had formerly idolised Nasser most strongly: the 'new generation' from the ANM, led by Muhsin Ibrahim and Nayef Hawatma. In early 1968, Hawatma moved into the ANM's Palestinian organisation (the PFLP) although he was by origin a Jordanian. There he was able to rally a group of even younger PFLP members into pressing for a conference in August 1968 which issued a 'Basic Political Statement' harshly critical of the 'petty-bourgeois regimes' (i.e. including Nasser's).[13] Habash himself was in jail at the time. The Syrians had imprisoned him in retaliation for the PFLP's sabotage of the Trans-Arabia Pipeline (TAPLINE) where it passed through Syria. He was thus unable to use his conciliatory powers to prevent the leftists from pushing their programme through the August conference.

When the terms of the Basic Political Statement leaked out, they had several serious consequences for the still youthful PFLP. First, Nasser was so incensed by its criticisms that he abruptly cut off all aid to the PFLP.

Two months later, Ahmed Jibril complained of continued ANM tutelage over what was now supposed to be an autonomous Front, and he seceded from the PFLP to continue his military activities under the name of the PFLP-General Command (see below).

In November 1968, Habash managed to escape from his Syrian jail and immediately tried to reassert the supremacy of the ANM traditionalists inside the PFLP. However, the bitterness between the two former ANM factions had now hardened to a point where violence was often used between them. A new PFLP conference was scheduled for February 1969, but amidst an escalating campaign of intimidation against Hawatma's followers, just before the conference was due to open the Hawatma group decided to secede. Receiving physical protection from Fateh units in Jordan, the Hawatma group soon after declared itself to be the Popular *Democratic* Front for the Liberation of Palestine. (In mid-1974, this name was changed to the Democratic Front for the Liberation of Palestine.)

The ANM 'old-timers' meanwhile went ahead with the holding of their PFLP conference. They had moved considerably towards the socialist analyses propounded by the Hawatma group, but still retreated slightly on the August 1968 Statement's outright denunciation of the Arab 'nationalist' regimes.[14]

From 1969 to 1972, PFLP members defined their task as 'building a working-class leadership in the Palestinian movement'. They took as their major model in this Fidel Castro's movement in Cuba, which they considered had been successful in transforming itself from a petty-bourgeois grouping into a viable Communist Party. In the process, however, the PFLP lost many of the more purely nationalist of its former supporters, who felt unable to participate in this transformation. In March 1972, they also lost one further organised faction, which peeled off to the ideological left of the main organisation. This called itself the Popular *Revolutionary* Front for the Liberation of Palestine. It sank almost without trace over the months which followed.[15]

No account of the PFLP's development up to 1972 would be complete without reference to the military options it was pursuing throughout that period – specifically to the hijackings and other international terror operations at which its activists proved themselves masters. These hijackings were to have a great impact not only on and within the PFLP itself, but on the rest of the Palestinian guerrilla movement as well – most notably, when the PFLP's hijackings of three Western aircraft to a desert airstrip in Jordan in September 1970 provided King Hussein with the pretext he needed to clamp down on all the guerrilla groups in Jordan.

The PFLP's first hijacking operation was mounted in July 1968, when three Front members seized a Boeing of the Israeli national carrier, El-Al, while it was in Italian airspace, and forced the captain to land in Algiers. At this stage, the PFLP's reasoning was that since El-Al planes had been used to ferry military personnel and supplies to Israel during the 1967 war, they should be considered valid military targets; that the Arab boycott of Israel made the Jewish state particularly dependent on its international communications; and that the Palestinian communities needed new reasons, after the embarrassment the Battle of Karameh had constituted for the PFLP, to be attracted into PFLP ranks. In the latter respect, the PFLP's operations proved to have some success.[16]

The Front's first hijack also registered some success in immediate tactical terms. The Algerians were embarrassed by the 'gift' the PFLP guerrillas had brought them – as perhaps the PFLP had intended they should be. They quickly flew the plane's non-Israeli passengers to Paris, and soon after released the Israeli women and children. The Israeli government mounted a strong diplomatic campaign against Algeria, which culminated in the International Federation of Air Line Pilots' Associations threatening to boycott Algerian airspace and all Algerian planes. Under this pressure, the Algerians released the remaining Israelis; two days later, in what was described as a 'good-will gesture', the Israelis freed 16 of the 1,200 Arab prisoners whose release the hijackers had demanded.

But if the PFLP planners were to think that the release of further batches of Arab prisoners from Israeli jails could be secured by repeating the process, the Israelis were quickly set to prove them wrong. El-Al's security procedures were immediately tightened considerably, and the Israeli military prepared for a policy of swift retaliations.[17] In December 1968, a PFLP unit attacked an El-Al plane on the ground at Athens airport; two days later, Israeli commando units landed at Beirut airport and blew up 13 Arab-owned airliners there in a clear lesson to the Arab governments to stop allowing the guerrillas to operate from their territory.[18]

As a result of the PFLP's December 1968 operation, and a similar one which followed in Zurich two months later, one guerrilla had been killed (and two Israelis), and five guerrillas consigned to European jails. The PFLP planners then apparently came to consider that the new security procedures protecting Israeli planes made it almost impossible to hijack them and thus seize the hostages the Front needed to trade for the release of their own prisoners. Its notorious 'External Operations' branch (*'amaliyyat kharijiyya*) then took on a momentum of its own whose relevance to the Palestinian cause as such became, in the view of many other members of the guerrilla movement, increasingly attenuated.

In August 1969, a two-person PFLP commando hijacked an American plane flying from Rome to Tel Aviv, diverting it to Syria. There followed a spate of Palestinian hijackings, by the PFLP and sometimes by other groups (but not by mainstream Fateh or the Hawatma group). The aims of these actions could generally be seen as a combination of two factors: a desire to punish Western governments considered supportive of Israel; and the attainment of bargaining-levers to achieve the release of prisoners, even if only those now in European jails as a result of earlier PFLP operations. By July 1970, the Israeli Foreign Minister had spelt out his government's policy of not freeing any further prisoners under such circumstances,[19] but many European governments seemed keen to get rid of guerrilla prisoners in the quickest and least damaging way.

It was on 6 September 1970 that the PFLP mounted the multiple hijacking which was to trigger King Hussein's crackdown in Jordan. By that date, seven PFLP guerrillas were being held in Swiss and German jails: the Front planned the near-simultaneous hijack of a Swiss, an Israeli and an American plane. However, the armed plainclothes guards on the Israeli plane managed to overcome the two hijackers on their aircraft as it made an emergency landing in London. One of these hijackers was mortally wounded in the battle and the other, Leila Khaled, was immediately handed over to the British police. Two other guerrillas, who had planned to board that same Israeli plane in Amsterdam but had been turned back by suspicious Israeli guards, then mounted an autonomous operation by boarding and then hijacking an American plane out of the same airport.

The latter plane, a $20 million jumbo jet, was flown to Cairo, where the passengers were all allowed off and the plane blown up with dynamite. The first American plane and the Swiss plane had meanwhile been taken to a desert airstrip in Jordan which the PFLP had secured against takeover by the Jordanian authorities, christening it 'Revolution Airstrip'. Three days later, another PFLP commando brought a British plane to the same strip, to add to pressure on the British to release Khaled. As the negotiations continued among all the parties concerned, on 12 September the PFLP blew up the three planes at the airstrip, having evacuated the passengers. All but 38 of the passengers were then released: 5 of the remaining hostages were Israeli women; the remainder, men of Israeli and other nationalities.

The whole affair was calculated to embarrass the Jordanian monarch acutely, in the eyes of his own people as well as of his Western friends.[20] On 16 September, Hussein announced the formation of a new military Cabinet, and by dawn the next day his army had started encircling and attacking guerrilla positions around his capital, Amman.

When the first fierce round of fighting died down that September, the PFLP's remaining hostages, who had been kept in 'safe houses' in Amman throughout, were all released unharmed. Immediately afterwards, on 30 September, all the PFLP prisoners in European jails were flown to Cairo.

Thus, although there were subsequently many inside the Palestinian movement who argued that the PFLP's use of the hijack tactic had backfired by
bringing the wrath of the King down on the guerrillas in Jordan, there was
still a strong body of opinion within the PFLP which felt able to justify the
tactic. The debate on this issue raged strongly inside the PFLP as well as
within the guerrilla movement as a whole. As regards Fateh, the disaster
which the battles in Jordan had come to represent by the middle of 1971
was sufficient to persuade a few of the Fateh barons that a limited use of
'external operations' might be used to cover the rebuilding of their military
base in Lebanon over the following months. Some branches of Fateh thus
came to co-operate with the PFLP's experts in this field over the period
1971-72: this was the short-lived terror phenomenon known as 'Black
September' (see chapter 3 above).

Inside the PFLP itself, meanwhile, a body of opinion was building up after
September 1970 which argued that the 'external operations' did not
constitute a Marxist-Leninist tactic, and perhaps even hampered them in
their declared task of building up a 'socialist, proletarian organisation'. By
the time of the 1972 PFLP conference, this point of view had decisively
won out. Immediately afterwards, Habash announced in public that the
Front had decided to stop mounting hijacks, though he dated this decision
as far back as November 1970.[21]

However, Habash's new stand was not supported unanimously within
PFLP ranks: crucially, it divided him from his 20-year comrade in ANM/
PFLP ranks, Dr Wadi' Haddad, who had been the conceiver and organiser
of the whole of the PFLP's 'External Operations' branch. Haddad then left
the PFLP's aegis to continue the operations on his own, with some help
from the Iraqis and other Arab regimes. But when he was buried in
Baghdad in March 1978, after dying of leukaemia in East Germany,
Habash was at the head of the crowd of mourners.

The political results of the PFLP's 1972 conference were that the Front
stepped up its efforts to build a mass support base, and over the next year
and a half it joined in several 'united front' political campaigns with Fateh
and other guerrilla groups in the occupied territories and in the refugee
camps of Lebanon. Having boycotted the Fifth and Sixth PNCs (February
and September 1969), the Front had participated in PNC sessions from
February 1970 on; then, after the battles in Jordan, the losses all the
guerrilla groups had shared there established a fairly firm basis for political
co-operation over the years ahead.

The October War of 1973 changed all that. All the different Palestinian
groups seemed to share a strong expectation that the Geneva Mideast
Peace Conference would convene fairly quickly after the guns of October
fell silent. Fateh and its allies were therefore busy preparing the ground for

148

participation at such a conference, while the PFLP was vehemently opposed to any participation at all in a situation where it saw the balance of power still tipped against the Palestinian cause.

As recounted in chapter 4 above, the 10-point programme produced by the Twelfth PNC in June/July 1974 was conceded by all sides to represent a compromise between the Fateh position and that of the PFLP. Two months later, on 26 September 1974, the compromise fell apart: the PFLP resigned from its membership in the PLO Executive Committee, 'so that it may not be held responsible for the historical deviation in which the leadership of the Organisation [the PLO] has become involved, and so that it may continue to struggle in the ranks of the masses to correct this deviation'.[22] The statement announcing this decision explained that the PFLP

gave its approval to the ten points, although in fact they were a compromise and threadbare formula for national unity, after having placed on record in the minutes of the session our understanding of them to the effect that they involved rejection of the Geneva conference... At the end of the twelfth session of the PNC it was clear what the surrenderist leaderships intended by their acceptance of the ten point programme. They regarded it as legalising their pursuit of the course of deviation and surrender.[23]

This statement also accused the PLO leadership of having engaged in secret contacts with America, 'the imperialist enemy'.[24]

In early October 1974, Habash travelled to Iraq at the head of a delegation representing the PFLP, Jibril's PFLP-General Command, the Iraqi-backed Arab Liberation Front (ALF) and the Palestinian Popular Struggle Front (PPSF). The Palestinian guests and their Iraqi hosts, the National (i.e. pan-Arab) Command of the ruling Baath Party, issued a joint communiqué which spelled out that the two sides

condemned the deviationist trends in the Palestinian arena aimed at enticing the Palestinians to participate in the liquidationist settlements. They agreed that these proposals must be opposed and combated and not be allowed to be pushed through. They also agreed that this requires the establishment, on a firm scientific basis, of a *unified front comprising the sections of the resistance, all mass bodies and organisations and patriotic persons that reject surrenderist solutions.*[25]

Thus was born, on 10 October 1974, in the Iraqi capital, the 'Front of Palestinian Forces Rejecting Surrenderist Solutions'[26], the Rejection Front.

The strength of the Rejection Front's organisation was fairly swiftly put to the test. On 13 April 1975, a bus carrying Rejection Front supporters who had been at a rally in West Beirut was ambushed in the Christian suburb of Ain al-Rummaneh, leaving 27 of them dead. This was subsequently the date used by most Western commentators to mark the start of the Lebanese civil war.

The successive turning-points of the 1975-76 fighting in Lebanon were to bring to the fore, at the strictly Palestinian level, key divergences between the ideological stances of Fateh and the PFLP. For Fateh, the Palestinian cause was all-important. Thus the instinct of the Fateh leadership was to avoid entanglement in the Lebanese fighting as long as possible, and when this became unavoidable to seek to limit it to the minimum necessary to ensure the PLO's survival, while always trying to turn back towards the diplomatic process. For the PFLP, on the other hand, its policy towards the Lebanese war was determined primarily by its pan-Arabist perspective. It saw the Lebanese left as an essential part of the Arab national liberation movement which must therefore be supported throughout. The 13 April attack against their supporters had anyway virtually ensured the participation of all Rejection Front groups in the Lebanese confrontation from that day on.

By the beginning of 1976, as we have seen previously, the Fateh leaders also saw no alternative but to involve their forces in the war, but the differing strategies of the two groups ensured that, at each of the crisis-points which followed, they would still be pursuing differing priorities. The most decisive crisis was that which arose with the mountain battles of September and October 1976. The Fateh leadership had decided that it could not support Lebanese leftist leader Kamal Junblatt any further, and that it had to do a deal with the Syrians, while the PFLP and Rejection Front forces wanted to continue their alliance with Junblatt. The Fateh forces then effected their 'fighting withdrawal' from the Upper Metn region; the Rejectionists and Lebanese leftists who had wanted to remain there were unable to withstand the Syrian advance and fell back in some disarray. The Rejection Front emerged considerably weakened, not only regarding the losses it had suffered in the fighting, but also politically, through the strong reassertion of the Palestine-first ideology which Fateh's moves represented. One long-term side-effect of the whole Lebanese experience had been to convince increasing numbers of former Rejectionists that the establishment of any 'Palestinian entity', however truncated, was preferable to going through yet more tragedies such as those the Palestinians had now lived through in both Jordan and Lebanon. This also weakened the appeal of the Rejectionist cause.

It was thus a severely chastened Rejection Front which made its way to the Thirteenth PNC in March 1977. The Fateh leadership was now able to resolve the 'compromise' represented by the previous PNC's programme in their own favour, and the Rejection Front could mount only 13 votes in the Council to oppose the 194 which voted for the Fateh leaders' formula.

Other developments followed which accelerated the Rejection Front's decline. In April 1977, the PFLP-General Command, which was still nominally (though problematically) in the Rejection Front, saw a violent split between its Secretary-General, Ahmed Jibril, and a former colleague called Abul-Abbas. The latter seceded to form his own guerrilla group, using the name of Jibril's previous creation, the Palestinian Liberation Front (PLF). He managed to ally this group with the Rejection Front and to end Jibril's association with the Rejectionists. But the Abul-Abbas group was far weaker and more difficult an ally for the PFLP to deal with inside the Rejection Front than Jibril had been; and the feuds which continued between Jibril and Abul-Abbas continued to discredit the activities of the Palestinian 'oppositionists' in general (see below).

In November 1977 there followed another development which was decisive in finally unravelling the Rejection Front: President Sadat's visit to Jerusalem. The Rejectionists continued for some time afterwards to accuse Fateh of trying to find some way to insert themselves into the peace process Sadat had launched, but it rapidly became clear that Sadat would not be including them in the peace process. Thus, there was to be no Geneva conference, and no overtures to the PLO to join in the new negotiations which had superseded the Geneva concept: Rejectionism had lost its Palestinian *raison d'être*. In addition, throughout 1978 the Iraqi regime, which had acted as midwife at the birth of the Rejection Front in 1974, was moving rapidly towards a reconciliation with the conservative Arab regimes and away from its former Rejectionist sympathies, and by early August 1978 the PFLP was already perceptibly withdrawing from its former pro-Iraqi stance.[27] So the external Arab pillar of support for the Rejection Front was crumbling too.

The announcement of the Camp David accords in September 1978 sounded the death-knell for the Rejection Front. On 19 September, the PLO Executive Committee convened to consider the Organisation's response to the accords; for the first time in nearly four years, the PFLP was represented at that meeting. The following month, the Rejectionist members of the PLO Central Council, who had not attended any Council meetings since 1974 though they never formally resigned from it, attended a Council meeting in Damascus which endorsed a proposal to amend the Thirteenth PNC's programme significantly. No longer would the call for an independent Palestinian state be tied to other conditions; from now on, the Central Council proposed, this call should be unconditional. The Rejection Front members present reportedly accepted even this formula.[28]

From September 1978 onwards it had been generally agreed that the Rejection Front representatives could return to the Executive Committee. However, at the Fourteenth PNC in January 1979, a continuing objection about internal Executive balance, voiced by Fateh, kept the PFLP out of the Executive until the following PNC, in April 1981, when Ahmed Yamani was included in the Fateh-dominated list elected to the Executive.

With the demise of the 1974-78 Rejection Front, different polarisations became important inside the guerrilla movement, principally those concerned with attitudes towards Syria. George Habash meanwhile seemed to accept the failure of his challenge to Fateh with good grace, from late 1978 on making key appearances in public at Arafat's side as a kind of respected elder statesman of the Palestinian movement. (This relationship was particularly marked during and after the 1982 Battle of Beirut – see chapter 1 above.) Indeed, some PFLP insiders subsequently reported that there had never even been wholehearted agreement inside PFLP ranks over whether the Rejection Front should challenge Fateh for leadership of the movement or merely act to influence Fateh's decision, and at a congress the PFLP held in 1981 there was reportedly much internal criticism of the whole resort to the Rejection Front tactic, which many members said ran counter to the PFLP's concept of the PLO as a 'united front'.[29]

In 1980, Habash suffered what was by all accounts a massive stroke, which left him bedridden for many months. Among reports that, if not nearly dead, he was at all events in no condition to recover his faculties, a bitter succession struggle racked the PFLP. By the middle of 1981, however, Habash had recovered enough to reassert his personal control over his quarrelling subordinates, but he remained physically weak and the months of faction-fighting had already considerably weakened the organisation.

By early 1983, the PFLP had thus mounted two major challenges to Fateh's domination of the guerrilla movement, in the 'growth period' of 1968-70, and in the Rejection Front period of 1974-78. In both periods, the deep external crises the guerrilla movement had to confront soon after the launching of the PFLP challenge (i.e. Jordan in 1970-71, Lebanon in 1975-76) weakened the opposition trend within the guerrilla movement, and showed that Fateh – while it never finally abandoned the Palestinian opposition completely to those outside powers who wished to destroy it – enjoyed sufficient organisational, ideological and political superiority to be able to neutralise the political challenge mounted by the PFLP.

Despite its successive political failures, however, the PFLP had a lasting impact on the whole guerrilla movement in terms of its ideas. Its stress on the need for a pan-Arab liberation movement was always the opposite pole, inside the Palestinian movement, to the Palestine-first ideology of the Fateh leadership, and, though the PFLP was never able to impose its ideas on the movement as a whole, nevertheless the debates it opened up over the years substantially enriched many of the movement's modes of thinking.

The Democratic Front for the Liberation of Palestine

The DFLP was born out of a split within the PFLP in February 1969.[30] By then, many of the PFLP left-wingers who were to form the core of the new group, especially those active in Jordan, had for some months been subject to severe harassment, reportedly including even kidnappings and beatings, from supporters of the PFLP mainstream. Finally, it was only after the intervention of the Fateh leadership that the left-wingers, led by Nayef Hawatma, were able to organise their withdrawal from the parent organisation in some order. The agreement which Fateh brokered between the traditional PFLP leaders and the Hawatma group stipulated that the former's attacks on the Hawatma group should cease, whilst the Hawatma group give up any claim to represent the authentic tradition of the PFLP. (One of Fateh's interests in the whole business was revealed almost immediately, when it became clear that the DFLP would be participating in the Fateh-dominated bodies of the PLO, which were still being boycotted by the PFLP.)

Hawatma had been born in 1935 to a Christian Arab family of modest means living near the Jordanian city of As-Salt. Since the late 50s he had been associated in the ranks of the PFLP's parent body, the Arab Nationalists' Movement, with a Lebanese activist from the same generation called Muhsin Ibrahim, who from 1960 onwards edited the Movement's official periodical, *Al-Hurriyya*. After the 1969 split, the Hawatma group was able to keep control of this periodical, sharing it until mid-1981 with Ibrahim's largely parallel Lebanese grouping, the Organisation for Communist Action in Lebanon (OCAL). The PFLP, meanwhile, was forced to found a new periodical, which it called *Al-Hadaf* (The Target).

With Hawatma in the leadership of the infant DFLP were a group of former ANM/PFLP members, whose average age was around ten years younger than himself. They immediately set about trying to build their group into a 'revolutionary proletarian party' and, in the heady days the guerrilla groups were living through in Jordan prior to the September 1970 crackdown, they even attempted to set up embryo 'workers' and peasants' *soviets'* in some areas of the north of the country. Throughout this period, and even well into the 70s, one of the DFLP's basic doctrines was that Britain's partition of the 'historic Palestine' into two mandate states – Palestine and Jordan – constituted an unnatural division of the area, and that the Palestinian and Jordanian popular movements should therefore unite in a single struggle.

At the purely Palestinian level, the clearest expression of the DFLP's aims came in a draft resolution it presented to the Sixth PNC in September 1969. Contrasting its view with Fateh's year-old advocacy of the establishment of a secular democratic state in Palestine, the DFLP's draft called for 'setting up a *popular democratic Palestinian state* for Arabs and Jews alike ... in which the rights of both Arabs and Jews to perpetuate and develop their indigenous cultures would be respected'.[31] This formulation was not adopted by the PNC; nevertheless, it marked the first signs of a radical innovation in the thinking of the modern Palestinian national movement: an acceptance of some form of Israeli or Jewish cultural nationhood. It was the DFLP's ability to think in these terms which four years later, in mid-1973, made it one of the first Palestinian groups openly to advocate the establishment of some kind of Palestinian entity in the West Bank and Gaza *alongside* the existing State of Israel – a position which in 1974 was adopted by the PNC.

In November 1969, Hawatma had been asked by a European sympathiser to spell out the terms in which the DFLP viewed the Israeli community. He replied that the DFLP

is of the opinion, as an ideological consideration, that Judaism is a religion, pure and simple. The Front does, however, recognise the legitimacy of 'Jewishness' as a culture for Jewish communities, particularly in the case of the Jewish community that is found in the land of Palestine today, with special emphasis on the post-1948 generation that was born and raised in the land of Palestine. We believe that this generation fully has the right to live side by side and enjoy full rights and responsibilities with the Palestinian people.[32]

In the same interview, Hawatma also announced that the Front had already been in contact, in Europe, with representatives of the Israeli leftist organisation Matzpen with a view to developing a joint strategy. In this respect too, the DFLP proved itself to be an early trail-blazer, following a policy of seeking allies on the Israeli left which only afterwards was adopted by other guerrilla groups and, tentatively, by the PLO as a whole.

From its inception in 1969, the DFLP had disagreed with the PFLP's tactic of mounting spectacular operations outside Israeli territory; its emphasis instead was on building grass-roots support for its left-wing approach, primarily among the Palestinian and Jordanian residents of Jordan and the West Bank. As the clashes between the guerrilla groups and the Jordanian government escalated through the summer of 1970, the DFLP became increasingly open in addressing the possibility of a guerrilla takeover of power in Amman. The DFLP's numerical strength was still severely limited, but its slogan of 'All power to the Resistance' echoed the sympathies of many members of the Palestinian community, which formed a clear majority of Jordan's population. When the PNC met in its Emergency Session in Amman in late August 1970, that wave of popular feeling forced the Council to adopt a programme whose terms went a long way towards adopting the DFLP view. It stated, 'Historical, economic, social and political factors all assert the unity of the people of the Jordanian-Palestinian theater... [Our people] emphatically refuse to accept that the country should be partitioned into petty states, one Palestinian the other Jordanian.'[33] After the dimensions of the subsequent Palestinian defeat in Jordan became clear, however, the DFLP engaged in some tentative self-criticism of the tactics it had employed in the period leading up to September 1970, terming these 'political idealism'. From 1971 onwards it turned instead to the more pragmatic path of strengthening relations with Fateh, some of the Arab regimes, and the countries of the socialist bloc.

In its early days as an independent group, the DFLP had had clear pro-Maoist sympathies. (It was not until 1970 that the Soviet Union gave any recognition to the validity of Palestinian guerrilla movement action.) But in the years after 1970, as Soviet support for the guerrillas grew warmer and warmer, the DFLP leadership shifted to a pro-Soviet stance to the extent that by the time the Lebanese civil war broke out it was clearly trying to present itself to the Soviets as an alternative ally within the guerrilla movement which would prove itself more ideologically trustworthy than Fateh. On this basis, the Front was able to build direct relations with several Soviet bloc countries, in addition to the relations it enjoyed with them through its membership in the PLO. However Fateh also had direct relations with all these countries, and Fateh leaders pointed out that the socialist bloc countries always insisted that the PLO representatives to their countries be members of Fateh rather than any other group.[34]

Even after the expulsion of the guerrilla groups from Jordan, the DFLP continued to give emphasis to the situation there, arguing for the need to confront King Hussein in every possible way, but particularly in the ambition he continued to express until 1974, to reassert his own former control of the West Bank. In March 1972, Hussein announced a plan for the establishment of a 'United Arab Kingdom' on the East and West Banks of the Jordan. The DFLP argued that the PLO should produce an alternative to this project, and by August 1973 it had prepared its own proposal to this end. This was to accept the idea of an 'intermediate phase' in the struggle to liberate all of Palestine, which should consist in the establishment of a 'democratic national state on both banks of the Jordan', not including the territories Israel had controlled before 1967. Although the DFLP presented this proposal only as a first step towards the total liberation of Palestine, it aroused much hostility from the other guerrilla groups at that time.

In November 1973, in the new atmosphere prevailing after the October War, the DFLP proposed that, as a preliminary step even before the implementation of the 'democratic state on both banks' idea, the PLO should concentrate on the need to establish a Palestinian 'national authority' just in the Palestinian territories occupied in 1967, i.e. in the West Bank and Gaza. This formulation did find supporters in other guerrilla groups (who had arrived at it from very different reasoning, however), and early in 1974 Fateh, Saiqa and the DFLP jointly presented it as a draft resolution to the PLO Central Council.[35] The proposal became the basis of the programme adopted at the Twelfth PNC in June/July 1974 and thus of the PLO's entire diplomatic initiative from then on.

In March 1974, Hawatma had scored another first in Palestinian ranks by producing a statement for the American writer Paul Jacobs especially for publication in the Israeli newspaper *Yediot Aharonot*.[36] In this statement he spelled out the DFLP's thinking on the 'national authority' concept by referring specifically to the creation of an independent Palestinian state in the West Bank and Gaza – a move which was not enshrined in official PLO policy until 1977.

Some Israeli left-wingers were reportedly encouraged by Hawatma's willingness to speak to the Israeli press, and even to refer therein to the concept of an 'Israeli people', to think that the DFLP might henceforth be content to pursue merely peaceful means in its struggle. But they were shocked two months later when the DFLP mounted a suicide operation in the northern Israeli town of Maalot which led to the killing of 24 Israelis, most of them secondary-school pupils, during the final shoot-out between the three DFLP guerrillas and Israeli paratroopers. The Front launched two other major suicide operations in the months which followed. It continued to argue that the Palestinians must maintain their armed struggle so long as Israel refused to recognise the Palestinian people's rights.[37]

The DFLP's stance in the Lebanese conflict of 1975-76 was different from the one it had adopted five years earlier in Jordan. During the early months of the conflict in Lebanon, the DFLP had been heavily involved on the left-wing/Palestinian side, arguing strongly against Fateh's advocacy of a neutralist position throughout most of 1975, but by early 1976, when the Lebanese leftist leader Kamal Junblatt was advocating pressing home the leftists' and Palestinians' presumed military advantage in a military solution to the conflict, the DFLP at first stood closer than Fateh to the Syrian view that such a course would be unwise. This severely strained the DFLP's relations with many of its former allies on the Lebanese left, including Muhsin Ibrahim's group. Nevertheless, in the fighting which ensued from June to October 1976 between the leftists and Palestinians on one hand and the Syrians on the other, the DFLP did commit its forces to the confrontation on the leftist/Palestinian side, but it argued throughout for the speediest possible rapprochement with the Syrians.

The DFLP was able to score something of a moral victory at the Thirteenth PNC in March 1977, when the goal of the independent Palestinian state was adopted by the PNC with a large majority, and in the following months it appeared keen to see the PLO take part in a Mideast peace conference as a full participant. But following Sadat's visit to Jerusalem, the DFLP was one of the Palestinian groups which argued strongly from the beginning that the PLO would gain nothing from his initiative.

In the five years which followed Sadat's trip, the DFLP maintained a position of more or less loyal opposition to the Fateh leadership in the PLO. Its spokesmen often voiced many of the same criticisms of Fateh policies as those emanating from Damascus throughout that period, but it generally did so in a basically loyal way, since the basic DFLP line continued to support the establishment of an independent Palestinian state in the Israeli-occupied territories. The DFLP's Yasser Abed Rabboo therefore remained on the Executive Committee throughout.

The Vanguards of the Popular War of Liberation, 'Saiqa'

The 'Vanguards' organisation – most usually known by the name of its military wing, As-Saiqa (The Thunderbolt) – was formed as the Palestinian wing of the pro-Syrian Baath Party,[38] in the same way the PFLP had been created as the Palestinian wing of the Arab Nationalists' Movement. In both cases, this act represented a compromise between the well-established pan-Arabist ideology of the parent grouping and the specificity of the Palestinian renaissance starting to sweep through the Palestinian diaspora communities in the mid-60s. But whereas the parent organisation of the PFLP more or less withered on the vine after its Palestinian offshoot had absorbed most of its energies, in the case of Saiqa the offshoot had to continue to live under the tight control of its parent organisation, which throughout the two decades of its control of the state apparatus in Syria from 1963 onwards had its own direct interest in the Palestinian question. Thus, the situation of the Palestinian Baathists of Saiqa has never been particularly easy.

The original decision to found a purely Palestinian Baathist organisation was taken by the Ninth National (i.e. pan-Arab) Conference of the Baath Party, held in Damascus in September 1966.[39] The new formation had little time to organise many activities before the Arab states' defeat in the June War the following year. Nevertheless, the Palestinian Baathists' organisational framework was already in place in time to profit from the surge in Palestinian nationalist feeling in the months following the war, and the solid logistic backing offered by the Syrian regime enabled Saiqa to absorb large numbers of recruits into its induction programmes in those months. At that stage, the leaders of the group were Dafi Jumaani and Mahmoud Maatiyeh, both of them veteran Baathists of senior status in the Baath Party's pan-Arab hierarchy.

157

Saiqa's leaders took part in the conference of representatives of the guerrilla movements which was held in Cairo in January 1968, and from then on allied themselves with Fateh in the bid to capture control of the PLO for the guerrilla movement. When the guerrillas were finally able to achieve this, in February 1969, Saiqa ended up being allotted 12 of the PNC's seats, while Fateh had 33.[40]

Saiqa continued, however, to be caught up inextricably in internal Syrian affairs. From the beginning a high proportion of the group's members were recruited from the vast Palestinian refugee camps which clung close to Damascus and other Syrian cities. This large pool of trained military manpower had no direct lines into the political process of the country in which it existed and was thus always of necessity highly dependent on the whims of the central government regime in Damascus. In the late 60s, this regime was waging its own internal battles with the opposing 'military' wing of the Baath Party (the rulers, in that period, coming from the 'civilian' wing of the party). As the struggle between the two wings of the party heated up through the summer of 1970, the military wing sought to undercut the base of support which Saiqa provided for the ruling civilian wing by closing all branches of the movement outside Damascus.[41] From then on, and throughout the bloody events of the weeks which followed in Jordan, Saiqa found itself nearly paralysed by the turbulent developments in its home base.

On 13 November 1970, these culminated in the takeover by the Baath-ists' military wing which brought air force commander Hafez al-Asad to power. Almost immediately, he carried out a widespread purge of the Saiqa leadership, arresting Jumaani, Maatiyeh and other Saiqa leaders, and bringing the movement firmly under army control. Tabitha Petran outlined Asad's motives in this in the following terms:

General Assad considered *Saiqa* a tool of the [previous] political leadership, but there was a further reason for his action. During the September 1970 fighting in Jordan the bases of the various commando movements gained a new unity and began to pressure their leaders to make a united movement. *Saiqa* pushed this line in Syria, proposing closer links with Fatah. Those arrested were the leaders of this trend. For Assad would not tolerate a Palestinian movement independent of his control.[42]

The man brought in by Asad to head the newly sanitised guerrilla organisation was Zuhair Muhsin, another veteran Baathist, originally from Tulkarm in the West Bank. Muhsin worked hard over the next few years to restore the morale of the Saiqa membership after its traumas of 1970, and also to maintain a balance between Saiqa's activities in the PLO (where he was the member of the Executive Committee responsible for the PLO Military Department) and the state policies of the group's Baathist backers in Damascus. This was difficult at times. For example, in early April 1974 Muhsin was stressing to a reporter, 'The future will show certain Arab leaders the error they committed in turning to Kissinger',[43] but by the end of the following month President Asad had done just that! Nonetheless, until late 1975 Muhsin was able to steer a more or less viable course between the demands of the Fateh-dominated PLO mainstream and those of Damascus.

In the early months of the Lebanese war, Saiqa (like Fateh) sought to avoid the direct participation of the bulk of its more 'regular' full-time forces,[44] but some Saiqa special units do appear to have participated in some of the fighting even in this period. When even Fateh's full-time forces were drawn into the conflict in January 1976, the pressure of events (and perhaps the prospect of loot) also briefly drew Saiqa's forces into the fighting as well, in particular in the siege of Damour. But in line with the policy then developing in Damascus, the Saiqa leadership rapidly sought to limit its part in any fighting after that. By the end of March 1976, the new line being dictated from Damascus for the organisation was saying, 'Proceeding from an Arab and Palestinian position, Sa'iqah opposes any attempt to partition Lebanon *regardless of the source of this attempt*'.[45]

Throughout these months, according to some Palestinian sources, the Syrian regime was building up Saiqa's presence in Lebanon, parallel to that of the pro-Syrian groups in the purely Lebanese spectrum. All this was to no avail, however, as when the final confrontation did come between the Syrians and the members of the Palestinian/oppositionist alliance in Lebanon in early June 1976, the rapidly inflated units of Saiqa in Lebanon, far from aiding the Syrian army's advance, defected *en masse* to the other guerrilla groups.[46]

Muhsin was able to escape to Damascus. His main lieutenant in Beirut, Hanna Bat-heesh, disappeared from the ranks of the guerrilla movement with substantial amounts of the war loot for the acquisition of which he was famed, and once again Saiqa had to be rebuilt from the bottom up. This time, in contrast to 1970, the top leadership did not change hands, but the 'Palestinian' credentials of the organisation had become so tarnished at the grass-roots that its ranks were thrown wide open to any Syrian or Palestinian conscript wanting to benefit from the higher rates of pay it offered relative to the Syrian army or the PLA. By early 1983, some non-Saiqa Palestinian sources estimated that 70 percent of Saiqa's members were actually Syrians.

As of 7 June 1976, Saiqa had had no presence at all in West Beirut. There were still some Saiqa units in the Tel al-Zaatar refugee camp, which had been under siege by the Phalangists since the preceding January, and some of these units played a role there in the bloody battles of July and August which other camp defenders considered little short of treasonous.[47] Thus, even after the majority of the other guerrilla groups were, in early 1977, reconciled to mending their fences with the Syrian government, they still retained considerable resistance to the resumption of Saiqa activities in the areas under their control. The Syrians were, however, able to force the PLO/Fateh leaders to allow this. Then in March 1977, amidst stringent security measures, Muhsin was able to lead a Saiqa delegation to the Thirteenth PNC. In an interview there he gave some first indication of what was to be a tougher new direction in Saiqa policy: 'There will be no Geneva [conference],' he said, 'and there will be no limited settlement to the Mideast conflict in which any decision has to be taken.'[48]

After President Sadat's visit to Jerusalem later that year, Syria and the Fateh leadership in the PLO were forced to co-ordinate their actions even more closely than hitherto, although considerable suspicion still remained on both sides of the relationship. The months which followed Sadat's launching of his peace initiative were therefore relatively easy ones for the Saiqa leaders. But Muhsin apparently wanted to take things too easily; in July 1979 he was killed by an unknown assailant whilst returning to his apartment near Cannes after a visit to a nearby casino.[49] This incident was of some embarrassment to other PLO leaders, since Muhsin was still the head of the PLO Military Department and a member of the Executive Committee. After his killing, his functions inside Saiqa were divided among at least three second-echelon group officials: Isam al-Qadi replaced him as Saiqa Secretary-General; Muhammed al-Khalifa was Saiqa's new nomination for the PLO Executive Committee and Military Department; and Muhsin's brother, Majed Muhsin, took over Saiqa operations in Lebanon.

Meanwhile, as the PFLP's relations with the Fateh leadership eased throughout 1977–79, Saiqa came to represent the new pole of political opposition to Fateh within the PLO, and it was able to attract some other groups to support it. These included Ahmed Jibril's PFLP-GC, the (largely notional) Palestinian Popular Struggle Front, and (to some extent) the DFLP. Saiqa's major criticisms of Fateh from 1979 onwards centred on the links Fateh retained with Saudi Arabia and the other Arab moderates, despite the PLO's membership in the Steadfastness Front, and the overtures the PLO/Fateh leaders were making to Jordan and the U.S. Saiqa and the DFLP lobbied actively and successfully among Fateh members to persuade the PLO to join Syria's boycott of the Arab summit in Amman in November 1980, and again to prevent it backing the Fahd plan the following year.

But Saiqa's ability decisively to influence the Fateh leaders' decisions was always linked to the stature of the group's Syrian backers inside the

Palestinian communities. Just as this had been lowered by successive Syrian actions in September 1970 and June 1976, so it was lowered yet again by the Syrian army's withdrawals from key points in Lebanon during the Israeli invasion there of summer 1982. Thus, as we saw in chapter 6 above, in the period following the Battle of Beirut the Fateh leaders felt able to shake off any challenge from Saiqa's pro-Syrian bloc within the PLO, and, from the quiet tone of his speech to the Sixteenth PNC in February 1983, it seemed that Saiqa Secretary-General Isam al-Qadi recognised this.

The Popular Front for the Liberation of Palestine – General Command

The PFLP-GC had its origins in a group of Palestinian refugees who had served in the Syrian army in the 50s, their leader throughout being a former Palestinian officer in the Syrian army, Ahmed Jibril. According to the PFLP-GC's own account, these activists had worked together since 1959, their aim being to wage a 'war of nerves' against Israel.[50] They thus at first formed themselves into something called the 'Palestinian Liberation Front'; but soon after Fateh had launched its version of the armed struggle against Israel, in January 1965, the Jibril group sought to unite with Fateh. In another version of the same development, the entry of the Jibril group (which was closely allied to the Syrian regime) into Fateh, including into the Fateh Central Committee, of which Jibril was for a short time a member, was a condition the Syrians imposed on Fateh in return for Fateh gaining some logistic support from Damascus for its early military operations.

Whatever the circumstances of Jibril's entry into Fateh, the relationship did not last long. Jibril was apparently canny enough to see that the Fateh leaders were not happy with the relationship with the Syrians, and he found an excuse to leave Fateh rapidly. (Another person who had also been inserted by the Syrians into the Fateh leadership along with Jibril, Youssef al-Urabi, was not so lucky: in February 1966 his body was found riddled with bullets, in circumstances which pointed strongly to a Fateh retaliation.) Jibril's group was meanwhile able to resume its activities under the Palestinian Liberation Front umbrella, until in October 1967 it responded to the appeal for guerrilla unity issued by George Habash's group and thus became one of the founding components of the PFLP.

The relationship with the Habash group, however, proved no happier for Jibril than that with Fateh. After the PFLP conference of August 1968, which issued a statement criticising President Nasser, it was Jibril who was sent by the PFLP leadership to plead with Nasser for a resumption of Egyptian aid to the group. When Nasser refused, Jibril returned to Beirut

161

determined to change PFLP policy. He thought he had achieved this when a PFLP conference in October 1968 decided *inter alia* to dissolve the Palestinian wing of Habash's Arab Nationalists' Movement completely into the PFLP; but in the end that conference marked the departure point between the ANM group in the PFLP and the Jibril group. Jibril then called the grouping emerging around him the PFLP – General Command (*Al-Qiyyada al-'Amma*, PFLP-GC); the group's major publication was called *Ilal-Amam* (Forward!)

The next major alliance in which the PFLP-GC became involved was the Rejection Front, of which it was a founder member in October 1974. But during the latter stages of the Lebanese civil war, some differences started to surface inside the PFLP-GC over the group's links with Syria. In April 1977, this dispute erupted violently into the open, with the secession from the PFLP-GC of a long-time Jibril lieutenant called Abul-Abbas. Abul-Abbas, who was at first thought to have Iraqi backing against Jibril's pro-Syrian line, and who at some stage was taken under Fateh's wing, then took the Jibril group's historic name of the Palestinian Liberation Front. The rivalry between the two groups continued until August 1978, when an entire eight-storey apartment building in Beirut housing Abul-Abbas's headquarters was levelled by a massive explosion, killing over 200 of its occupants. The enormity of this event, which was generally blamed on Jibril, jolted nearly all members of the Palestinian movement, including the PFLP-GC and the PLF, into setting aside the use of force as a means of solving internal Palestinian quarrels.

After the 1978 explosion, the PFLP-GC kept its name alive mainly through the use of novel and extraordinary technological introductions into the realm of guerrilla warfare – the most notable being the group's attempts to cross the border into Israel using hot air balloons and motorised hang-gliders. Behind the stunts, however, the group did retain a small hard core of solid military capability. This enabled it, for example, to capture an Israeli soldier in Lebanon after the 1978 invasion of the country. When he was later exchanged for 83 Palestinian prisoners held by Israel, many of those released belonged to Fateh or other groups; the move thus earned solid credit for Jibril with these organisations.

But Jibril's operations were also to have many negative aspects in the eyes of the PLO/Fateh leaders. In July 1981, he made a short attempt to sabotage the cease-fire agreement they had reached in south Lebanon, but within days Yasser Arafat was able to force Jibril into compliance.[51] The following year, during the Israeli invasion of Lebanon, many Fateh activists expressed considerable bitterness over the inability of the handful of PFLP-GC fighters who actually participated in the fighting even to protect the considerable military stores they had stockpiled near Damour. According to Khaled al-Hassan, the GC had even had (Libyan-supplied) SAM-9s in their stores, but 'The Israelis took everything: we didn't get to use any of it!'[52] The bitterness the Fateh people felt over this issue subsequently spilt over into the hostility they expressed at Jibril's role at the Sixteenth PNC the following February (see chapter 6 above).

Other groups

Just as Saiqa had been formed by a decision of the pro-Syrian Baath Party's National Conference, so was the Arab Liberation Front created by a decision of the pro-Iraqi Baath Party's National Conference.[53] The pro-Iraqi party waited longer before taking this step: in their case, it was taken in April 1969, the year after the Baathists came to power in Baghdad. The ALF has existed continuously since that date, and in 1983 its Secretary-General, Abdel-Rahim Ahmed, was a member of the PLO Executive Committee.

The ALF never had access to a large recruiting pool such as that which Saiqa enjoyed. There are no Palestinian refugee camps in Iraq, and though the sizeable Palestinian population in that country was always as much at the Baathist government's mercy as any other resident of the country, their generally higher level of skill afforded them a broader range of profession-al opportunities than that open to many of their compatriots in Syria. Because of its limited Palestinian constituency, the ALF could never aspire to the same degree of influence within the Palestinian movement that Saiqa often appeared to be bidding for. Therefore the ALF's leaders have gen-erally had to be content to be viewed primarily as instruments of the Iraqi Baathists, without being able to represent much of a Palestinian dimension of their own. While this has limited their influence and effectiveness, it has nevertheless largely saved them from the constantly competing internal tensions (between Baathism and Palestinianism) experienced by Saiqa, although the ALF has seen some degree of attrition of its cadre as a result of faction fighting within the parent party.

Not unnaturally, at the political level, the ALF has always represented a pro-Iraqi line within the PLO. Thus, for example, the ALF was a founder member of the Rejection Front in 1974, although its representative in the PLO Executive Committee at the time, Abdel-Wahhab Kayyali, did not resign outright from the Committee but 'froze' his membership in it instead.[54] At the Thirteenth and Fourteenth PNCs (1977 and 1979), this slot on the Executive was kept open for the ALF, but now for Ahmed instead of Kayyali.

During the Lebanese civil war of 1975-76, the presence of the ALF within

163

the Palestinian movement provided a useful vessel for the Iraqis when they sought to bolster opposition to the Syrians. The few hundred Iraqi volunteers sent to contribute to the defence of West Beirut in the summer of 1976 served under ALF auspices.

As was the case with Saiqa, the real influence of the ALF within the Palestinian movement has always depended to some extent on the stature of the parent regime within the Palestinian communities; and the distance of Baghdad from the scene of the battles with Israel and many of the actions of the Iraqi government have combined to keep this generally low. Though the ideological positions (pan-Arabism, 'socialism', secularism) proclaimed by the Iraqi government since 1968 have enjoyed quite a wide following in Palestinian ranks, Palestinian supporters of these ideals generally tended to associate themselves with the PFLP rather than the ALF.

Apart from the Arab-backed organisations described above, many more authentically Palestinian groups made a brief appearance, particularly in the years 1967-70 before the structure of the resistance movement had crystallised into the form it maintained afterwards. One of the longest-lived, though at a generally minimal level of activity, was the Palestinian Popular Struggle Front, founded in the West Bank before the June 1967 war, by Bahjat Abu-Gharbiyya.[55] After the occupation of the West Bank, the group linked up with the other guerrilla groups and extended its activities to other parts of the Palestinian diaspora. Throughout the 70s it maintained a modest office in Beirut, and it was a founder member of the Rejection Front in 1974. Afterwards, it declined into obscurity, until it re-emerged in late 1982 in the pro-Syrian bloc opposed to Fateh.

Most of the other very small groups which sprang up in the late 60s either later disappeared altogether (like the communist creation Ansar al-Thawra (Partisans of Revolution)) or were absorbed into the larger groups, usually Fateh (like Isam Sartawi's short-lived Action Organisation for the Liberation of Palestine). But after 1971, by which date the entire potential constituency of Palestinian activists had already been organised by one or other of the existing groups, the only new organisations to emerge were either the Arab-backed organisations described above, or 'front organisations' whose names were employed by one or more of the existing organisations for one reason or another (e.g. Eagles of the Palestinian Revolution, Black September Organisation, Arab Nationalist Youth Organisation for the Liberation of Palestine).

Throughout the history of the Palestinian guerrilla movement, too, there have been several unsuccessful attempts by different Arab regimes to create direct alternatives to Fateh from within. These included the Jordanians, with their Keta'ib an-Nasr (Victory Battalions) group in 1969-70; the Syrians, with their unsuccessful attempt called Fateh al-Thawra (Revolutionary Fateh) in 1976, and then their backing of Nimr Saleh (Abu Saleh) against the rest of the Fateh Central Committee in late 1982 and early 1983; and the Iraqis, with their sponsorship from 1974 onwards of the Fateh renegade Sabri al-Banna (Abu Nidal), who often claimed to be acting in Fateh's own name in the years following Fateh's imposition of a death sentence on him in 1974 (see chapters 3 and 5 above).

By early 1983, the failure of all these various attempts to split Fateh from within had left the Fateh leaders still confident of the integrity of their movement. As Khaled al-Hassan judged it,

All those who tried to [split Fateh] find themselves alone. I don't mean that they don't have any supporters: they may have 10 people or 15 people but they cannot split the body of Fateh at all, and they cannot influence the decision at all...

Even if you remember Abu Nidal when he was supported by so many people at the time, he was supported by the Iraqis when they wanted to do military actions against the U.N. peace-keeping force [in March 1978]: in only 12 hours Fateh controlled everything militarily.[56]

Inter-group relations

The successive inter-group negotiations which took place amidst the flurry of Palestinian guerrilla activity of 1968 and early 1969 were to define the broad organisational lines of the guerrilla movement of the Palestinian diaspora in the form they retained at least until early 1983. Yet there is still a fascinating question mark hanging over the issue of the Fateh leadership's decision, in those tumultuous months of the clear vindication of its own theory, to take the other, much smaller, guerrilla groups with it into the leadership of the PLO: for that decision was to have a profound impact over the 15 years ahead not only on relations within the Palestinian movement, but also on the Palestinian leadership's relations with the Arab regimes, and indeed on its entire ability to wage its national struggle effectively.

Not all in the Fateh leadership had agreed on that decision. Khaled al-Hassan, for one, had argued strongly at the time that Fateh could and should take over the PLO on its own, without the other groups being involved at all. As he was later to recall,

When Nasser decided to get rid of Shuqairy, Shuqairy asked us, Fateh, to take over the PLO; and the negotiator was Hani [al-Hassan]. Then finally Shuqairy resigned, and delivered the responsibility to the Executive Committee which elected Yahya Hammouda...

Then the new Executive Committee came and said, 'Look, we ... are going to resign and we will deliver you everything, but we advise you not to allow the [other] organisations to enter the PNC *as organisations*. Because we are now in power, give us all the names you want from Fateh, and the rest we will choose from the independents, and then you will be in control without talking about the organisations.'[57]

In Hassan's view, Fateh had certainly been strong enough in 1968, at both the Palestinian and Arab levels, to succeed in taking over the PLO apparatus alone. This would not, at that time, he considered, have necessitated engaging in the physical liquidation of members of the non-Fateh groups,

because at that time they were weak enough, and as long as we keep them far from the PLO, they will finish. They will not be legal. *We gave them the legality...* At that time we could have escaped [full-scale liquidations of the other groups]; now we could not. Because at that time we were so much stronger than the [Arab] regimes, and the regimes needed us more than we needed them – Syria, Jordan, Iraq.[58]

Hassan said that he had also received firm promises of support for his plan for Fateh to take over the PLO, from the PLO's main financers – Saudi Arabia, Kuwait and Qatar – as well as its key supporter among regimes, Egypt. Indeed, by 1969, he said, the Arab regimes were *asking* Fateh to exert a monopoly in the PLO:

It was suggested in the Arab Summit conference in 1969 in Rabat that Fateh *be recognised as the PLO*; and it was Arafat who said No. There would have been full recognition; I had arranged that before... It was suggested by King Faisal [of Saudi Arabia], as a matter of fact.[59]

The arguments of the majority in the Fateh leadership which had opposed Hassan on this point were later explained by Salah Khalaf in the following terms:

We were new in the arena. We were afraid of the PLO, because it was the creature of the Arab regimes... So we said, Let some of the other organisations come in with us.

Don't forget: we are not on our own land. If we were on our own land, we could make unity by force, like the Algerians... But Fateh is still in overall control.[60]

The thinking of this Fateh majority had also been explained in an internal Fateh organisational document published in 1969, which said,'In case the revolution is faced with difficulties which require it to retreat to less developed positions, it should establish relations with different forces and groups to be in a better position to protect itself while preparing for a counter-attack.'[61]

Over the years which followed the Arafat group's decision to take the other groups into the PLO along with Fateh, the 'front-line' Arab regimes were able, as we have seen, to rebuild much of the legitimacy and internal cohesion which had been shattered by the 1967 war. Once they had done so, there was no longer any possibility of Fateh confronting their protégés within the Palestinian movement — at least, not without engaging in a massive blood-bath which might have had devastating effects on the movement. They thus had to live with the decision they had made back in 1968, and with the constant presence of an organised internal opposition and of petty inter-Palestinian battles which this entailed.

By 1978, the ability of the Fateh leaders to retain their own purely Palestinian patch of political turf within the movement was most probably reflected pretty accurately in the allocations decided among the different groups for the funds received by the PLO under the Baghdad summit resolutions: Fateh received two-thirds of these.[62] But after the new en-hancement of their position within the movement with which the Fateh leadership initially emerged from the 1982 Battle of Beirut, Khaled al-Hassan and other Fateh leaders felt able to renew the argument that PLO decision-making should henceforth be conducted on a majority basis and not by consensus: that is, that Fateh should be able to overrule the other smaller groups.However, Yasser Arafat, the most visible symbol of Fateh's new relative strength, was still evincing the magnanimous attitude he had displayed to me in late 1979 when he said, 'It is true that Fateh is the biggest organisation, but we are all of us PLO.'[63]

Chapter 8

The movement inside historic Palestine

This study has already documented at some length the extent to which the Arabs' 1967 defeat marked a turning-point in the politics of the Palestinian diaspora: how much more decisive a development was it for those Palestinians who had remained within the boundaries of Mandate Palestine! Eight hundred thousand Palestinian inhabitants of East Jerusalem and the West Bank and 400,000 residents of Gaza were now brought under direct Israeli military rule. These figures include both traditional Palestinian inhabitants of the two areas and their substantial populations of refugees from within the boundaries Israel had staked out in 1948-49. Almost overnight in 1967, these Palestinians' relationship to Israel was transformed from a more or less remote, more or less idealistic, and generally indirect confrontation into the daily question of survival under an occupying power. For those Palestinians who had remained in their homes inside 1948 Israel, too (the 'Israeli Arabs', who now numbered about a half a million), Israel's occupation of the new areas was to have far-reaching consequences over the years ahead. For the first time in two decades they could reach out from the social and political isolation to which their citizenship of Israel had confined them and come into contact with virtually intact Arab societies in the West Bank, Gaza and (to a lesser extent) the Golan and Sinai.

These by-products of Israel's resounding military victory in 1967 were to have profound effects, over the 15 years which followed, on the goals, tactics and political make-up of the Palestinian national movement, which at the time of its revival in the late 50s had been based primarily on the struggle of the Palestinian exiles to return to their homes. An important key to understanding the development of the Palestinian national movement in the post-1967 period therefore lies in seeing the extent to which the exiles and the still-resident sections of the movement managed to move towards effective co-ordination of their activities and their goals, in a situation where the Israelis, reluctant to give up the occupied areas, did everything possible to frustrate such co-ordination.

The West Bank

When the Israelis occupied the West Bank in 1967, they found a population which had already been thoroughly pacified for over a decade by the omnipresent security police of King Hussein's pro-Western monarchy. The West Bank had been formally annexed by Jordan in April 1950, and over the following 17 years the administration in Amman had worked assiduously to integrate it with the (also mainly Palestinian-populated) East Bank area of Jordan proper. In 1955-56, the youthful Hussein had tried to open up Jordanian public life a little. For a brief period, party political activities were allowed, and general elections were held which returned a moderately Arab nationalist Premier, Suleiman Nabulsi, to power. A high proportion of activists, in nearly all the parties across the Jordan political spectrum, in that short period of liberalisation were residents of the West Bank. But in 1957, the King clamped down again: he dismissed the Nabulsi government and closed the party offices. Those party activists who wanted to continue their work were then forced to do so underground, but in the event the only ones with enough sense of organisation to maintain their political infrastructure more or less intact over the following ten years were the few hundred communists.[1]

Hussein's police meanwhile kept an efficient watch both on the West Bank's sinuous frontier with Israel and on any groups of people in the West Bank's interior – specifically, in its vast Palestinian refugee camps – who might even be thinking of violating that frontier. The Fateh leaders were not to forget that the first 'martyr' of their armed struggle against Israel fell to a Jordanian bullet in 1965.

The foundation of the PLO, in May 1964 at a conference in their own East Jerusalem, caused some interest among West Bank community leaders. But few of them appear to have acted on any assumption at that time that the new organisation could provide a realistic alternative to rule from Amman. One year later they were proved right, when Hussein curtailed even the limited political activities he had originally allowed the PLO office in Jerusalem. Then in November 1966, the Israeli army mounted a bloody reprisal raid against the West Bank village of Samu', leaving scores of civilians dead and wounded. Much of the West Bank erupted into clamorous demonstrations, as its residents demanded arms and protection from the Jordanian regime. King Hussein sent in his East Bank bedouin troops to try to crush the demonstrations, while his police arrested hundreds of community leaders from the region.

In June 1967, the Israelis were able to seize the West Bank without having to face any of the harsh battles which marked their entry into Gaza and the Golan. Some units of Hussein's army fought staunchly for defence of West Bank strongpoints, but their commanders had no strategic plan for participation in the war, and the Jordanians' reputedly effective training and discipline proved no match at all for the superior Israeli weaponry. In the aftermath of the fighting, the new Israeli military governors of the region thus felt able to demand a speedy resumption of 'normal' administration and public services in the West Bank. A certain number of community leaders, most notably in Jerusalem, refused to comply with these orders, and West Bank schoolteachers mounted a strike which lasted several weeks. But the Israelis deported those figures in the Jerusalem administration they saw blocking their plans, including the Mayor and the President of the Islamic Council, and they were able to finesse a solution to the education problem which took the teachers and their pupils back to their classes and off the streets.

The 'armed struggle' which Yasser Arafat and his Fateh colleagues had brought into the West Bank in the weeks following the June War was meanwhile beaten back out of the towns and villages – on occasion, with some help from community leaders. The West Bankers then appeared more or less resigned to having their future decided through negotiations between the Israelis and Hussein.

The Battle of Karameh in March 1968 started to change this situation. Muhammed Milhem, later to be elected mayor of the West Bank town of Halhoul, considered that Karameh 'gave a big boost to those on the West Bank: it showed that the Palestinians were able to hold out in front of the Israeli army, which had defeated three Arab armies'.[2]

Other factors also eroded the seeming resignation to their fate which many West Bankers had evinced in the immediate post-June period. The passage of time itself, with no progress visible towards any peace negotiations, indicated that trust in a negotiated 'liberation' might prove illusory, and these early months and years of the occupation were filled with ominous signs of permanent Israeli ambitions in the area. In 1968, East Jerusalem was formally 'united' with West Jerusalem, that is, annexed to Israel;[3] and in the Jordan Valley and elsewhere throughout the West Bank, the Israelis started fencing off wide tracts of land both for military outposts and, increasingly, for paramilitary co-operatives and civilian settlements.

It took the West Bankers some time, however, to start organising their own resistance to Israeli rule. One of the main reasons for this was the Israeli practice – which runs directly counter to the Fourth Geneva Convention concerning treatment of civilian populations of territories occupied in time of war – of summarily deporting any community leader who raised his (or, on several occasions, her) head in resistance to Israeli military rule. One researcher has documented the cases of 671 individual West Bank residents, and two entire tribes, deported to Jordan or Lebanon over the period 1967-78;[4] further investigation of a sample of the deportees listed revealed that 25% of them were educators, 22% were students, and 15% were non-teaching professionals.[5] Taken together with the Israelis' widespread use of 'emergency regulations' which enabled them to imprison anyone in the occupied territories for up to six months without a trial, these deportations caused a steady attrition of the Palestinian leadership in the West Bank. The deportations did, however, bring one unintended benefit over the years to the PLO leaders operating from outside the Israeli-ruled areas: most of the deportees immediately started working with the PLO upon arrival in Jordan or Lebanon. They brought with them fresh experience of resistance activities 'on the inside', and did much to help cement the two wings of the national movement. By the early 70s, the PLO Executive Committee lists drawn up by successive PNCs included a minimum of three deportees from the occupied territories each time.

King Hussein meanwhile continued to try to exercise his influence on the West Bank. Municipalities and other administrative bodies continued to be financed and directed from Amman, leading to a situation where in 1981 an Israeli researcher, writing about the early years of the occupation, could refer openly to

the existence of common interests between Israel and Jordan in day-to-day activities. These common interests led to a tacit agreement between the two countries. Israel's activities were directed toward the normalization of daily life, while the Jordanian government was mainly concerned with precluding new political realities in the area...

Cooperation between Israel and Jordan in instrumental matters strengthened the West Bank elite's pragmatic patterns of action, especially among the veteran circles.[6]

The 'veteran circles' referred to here were that majority of West Bank community leaders from the days of the preceding Jordanian administration who rapidly learnt to co-exist with the Israeli occupation. These figures used the patronage their municipal and other positions continued to give them under the occupation to try to generate continued community support for the regime in Amman.

At some stages in the early years of the occupation, the Israelis appeared to be coming close to trying to create an alternative leadership in the West Bank to that of the pro-Jordanian 'veteran circles'. In June 1968, the Military Command of Judea and Samaria – the Israelis had changed their name for the West Bank to this dual appellation in December 1967 – started discussing plans for a limited self-rule scheme in the West Bank. One Israeli participant in these discussions later stated,

To avoid any false expectations, [Israeli Premier Levi] Eshkol insisted that the other side [in any self-rule negotiations] understand that it was discussing an

171

agreement *with* Israel, not one to *replace* Israel. Israel had no intention of evacuating its forces from the area; furthermore, complete responsibility for foreign affairs and security would rest with Israel. Another clarification was that neither Jerusalem nor the Gaza Strip would be subject to negotiation. His last clarification dealt with the autonomous area's financial dependence on Israel, emphasizing that operations within the West Bank would not be financed by Jordan.[7]

The Mayor of Hebron, Skeikh Ali Ja'bari, was reportedly drawn into these discussions, but details of the plan leaked out, causing Ja'bari to withdraw.[8]

It is entirely possible, of course, that in 1968 the Israelis were not really committed to any policy of self-rule in the West Bank, from their recognition of the worth of the existing Jordanian link there, but that they sought to increase their own leverage over the Jordanians within that relationship by suggesting the possibility of an alternative to the existing set-up. However, the continuing effect of the 1968 self-rule affair was that it made many Palestinians very wary of schemes to decide the fate of the West Bank on its own, in isolation from a more comprehensive solution, out of the fear that such schemes could easily be dominated by the Israelis, and it forced them, later, to clarify their ideas of the terms under which an interim solution, in the West Bank and Gaza, for instance, might become acceptable.

In 1970, Jordanian influence among West Bankers plummeted with news of the Jordanian-Palestinian fighting of Black September. Two years later, a plan Hussein published for the establishment of a 'United Arab Kingdom' on both banks of the Jordan, following liberation of the West Bank, did not attract many West Bank supporters in addition to the known pro-Jordanians. By 1973, the Jordanians were facing another challenge to their influence in the West Bank: this time it came not from the Israelis but from the PLO.

In January 1973, the Eleventh PNC had taken a secret decision to establish a new body inside the occupied territories to co-ordinate the activities of the different resistance organisations there. In August 1973, the Palestinian National Front in the Occupied Territory (PNF) issued its first communiqué, which affirmed that the PNF was 'an integral part of the Palestine national movement as represented by the Palestine Liberation Organisation'.[9] The communiqué also explicitly rejected Jordan's claim to represent the Palestinian people.

The PNF almost immediately received a strong boost to its organising momentum, with the immense psychological lift Palestinians and Arabs everywhere experienced during the October 1973 war. After the war, the PLO's turn towards a political settlement further boosted the PNF's popularity and activities inside the West Bank. Indeed, the PNF organisers could congratulate themselves that they had made some contribution to the Twelfth PNC's decision, in June/July 1974, to pursue a political option based on the call for establishing a 'Palestinian national authority' on any parts of Palestine evacuated by Israel. The PNF had sent its own message to the PNC arguing, 'The present stage requires agreement on an interim program of action affirming the *authority of the revolution*, as embodied in the Palestine Liberation Organization, over every inch of territory from which the Zionist presence is dislodged.'[10]

Inside the West Bank, meanwhile, the PNF demonstrated its growing influence in early December 1973, when it was able to persuade the traditionally pro-Jordanian Higher Muslim Council in Jerusalem to come out in open support of the Algiers Arab Summit's recognition of the PLO.[11] One week later, the Israelis deported eight PNF members to Jordan. These included the Mayor of al-Bireh and the member of the Muslim Council who had organised its pro-PLO statement. But the deportations only triggered further demonstrations and protests.

The culmination of the PLO's turn towards a diplomatic solution in this period was Yasser Arafat's appearance at the United Nations in New York in November 1974. This development unleashed a storm of support for him on the West Bank. According to Ann Lesch's description

Students took to the streets in the main towns on November 16: 2,000 pupils demonstrated in Jenin and, when Israeli soldiers killed a teenage girl, thousands of residents of Jenin attended her funeral. The sit-ins and demonstrations continued to spread, even affecting small villages... Five men were deported to Lebanon, including a member of the Ramallah Chamber of Commerce and the President of Bir Zeit College, Dr Hanna Nasir. Nasir's deportation led to further demonstrations at Bir Zeit... Thus, demonstrations that were originally triggered by Arafat's speech took on their own momentum during the following weeks.[12]

The momentum of this mass movement in the West Bank carried the pro-PLO resistance movement to a new peak in April 1976, when pro-PLO personalities took part in municipal elections and swept nearly all the pro-Jordanian local councils out of office.

The Israelis had organised one previous round of local elections in the West Bank, in 1972. At that stage, the PLO had argued for a boycott, but, when it became clear that many West Bankers would exercise their vote, the PLO had quietly argued for returning the existing local councils, as a block, so as not to introduce any changes 'under Israeli sponsorship'. In 1976, however, the pro-PLO community leaders inside the West Bank argued strongly for participation on their terms, and were able to persuade the PLO leaders outside of the value of this course. According to West Bank sociology professor Selim Tamari, the PLO's aims in participating

173

were 'to create solid loci of political power which would back the political demands of the PLO for independence and also act as barriers against compromises with an "autonomy" which would preserve the West Bank and Gaza under Israeli sovereignty'.[13] In the event, the results of the elections had wide-reaching social as well as political significance, for the newly elected council members belonged to a younger generation of men with a solid professional background, who now replaced the traditionalist pro-Jordanian veterans.

The year 1976 was, however, a troubled year for the Palestinian movement outside the occupied territories, as it suffered successive blows during the fighting in Lebanon. It was towards the end of that war that the relationship between the two wings of the movement inside and outside the occupied territories evinced a new maturity. The mayors of five leading West Bank municipalities sent an urgent message to the participants in the Arab mini-summit in Riyadh in late September calling on them to 'stand against the horrible conspiracy in Lebanon'.[14] Now, for the first time, the leaders inside the occupied areas were seeking to extend their political protection over the leaders outside, rather than vice versa. The following year brought two events which buffeted the West Bankers' hopes of an imminent settlement of their problem through their alliance with the PLO. The spring that year saw the coming to power in Israel of Menachem Begin, a man who had repeatedly claimed that 'Judea and Samaria' were integral parts of the Land of Israel, and six months later President Sadat broke Arab ranks to visit Jerusalem.

According to some observers of events on the West Bank in 1977, the response there to Sadat's visit to Jerusalem showed that the political development of the new generation of leaders of the national movement had been so rapid as to take them in advance of their own constituencies, for the mayors' opposition to Sadat's move was not echoed by unanimous popular condemnation. Political scientist W. F. Abboushi, who was then teaching at Bir Zeit, reported, 'In terms of population, the mayors represent the majority of the people of the West Bank... On the issue of Sadat's visit, however, the mayors did not represent the majority. The general sentiments of their own cities and towns, as well as of the rural population, were for Sadat's peace initiative.'[15] However, Abboushi wrote that publication of the final terms of the Camp David accords in September 1978 swung the population back behind the mayors again:

After a lively discussion of the two agreements, it became clear that West Bankers would not accept the one affecting the West Bank and Gaza. They saw in this agreement a great deal of ambiguity, and they suspected the ambiguity was intentional.

174

Two factors did not help the new situation. First, Begin's public statements made clear that he did not intend to withdraw from the occupied territories nor to discontinue, let alone dismantle, the Jewish settlements. Secondly, Hussein's opposition persuaded many people that the agreement was so bad that America's best friend in the region could not accept it.[16]

The West Bank municipal leaders were vehemently against the self-rule scheme proposed at Camp David. Nablus Mayor Bassam Shakaa said, 'We disagree 100 percent with the self-rule scheme. The idea for it did not originate with the Palestinian people or the Arab people... Autonomy can never be acceptable to us since it is a complete violation of our rights.' Halhoul Mayor Muhammed Miehem said, 'Autonomy in the political context means a certain status for a minority within a state. Thus, it does not lead to statehood for the minority. Autonomy cannot lead us to an independent Palestinian state.' And Hebron Mayor Fahd Qawasmeh said, 'If Israel and America really want an independent Palestinian state then why don't they announce it now? We are ready now. We cannot accept that our future can only be placed under discussion five years from now.'[17] But perhaps the most telling comment, in terms of popular perceptions of how Camp David affected life in the West Bank, was Milhem's remark, '*After Camp David, the Israelis felt able to use live ammunition against our demonstrators.*'[18]

It was after Sadat launched his peace initiative that the West Bank mayors and other community leaders organised themselves into an informal grouping called the National Guidance Committee (NGC). Conceived primarily as a support network among the different West Bank communities, it sought to avoid the mistakes made by the Palestinian National Front founded in 1973, which it now largely replaced: first, its members agreed to keep the NGC within a purposely low profile, to try to protect its members from the deportations which had struck the original organisers of the PNF soon after it had been formed; secondly, they agreed to restrict the NGC to the principal aims of countering Camp David and supporting the PLO, in order to avoid the competition and arguments between rival ideologies which had also sapped the PNF's strength. For a short while, the Israelis – who had their own objections to the autonomy plan as agreed at Camp David – appeared to tolerate the NGC. In late 1978 they allowed it to organise a number of large rallies held to protest the autonomy agreement. But soon enough they felt threatened by its continued stress on the PLO's representativeness. In May 1980, they deported Milhem and Qawasmeh from the West Bank (and the following month Shakaa lost both legs in a bomb attack, whose perpetrators were never brought to trial), and in late 1981 they declared the NGC illegal and dismissed all the remaining activist mayors from their positions (see chapter 6).

175

Camp David's American, Israeli and Egyptian sponsors were unable to find any personalities from either the West Bank or Gaza to take part in the 'autonomy talks'. This fact, taken in conjunction with the Israelis' determination to make no concessions on their desire to retain ultimate control of the occupied territories, ensured that the talks could achieve nothing. After halting construction of new settlements in the occupied areas for three months, the Begin government stepped up its settlement programme dramatically, to the extent that at the end of 1982 Meron Benvenisti, a former member of the Israeli administration of Jerusalem, predicted that at the current rate of development there would be 100,000 Israeli settlers in the West Bank by 1987.[19] (This figure excludes East Jerusalem, which already had more than 60,000 Israeli settlers by the early 80s.)

In autumn 1981, the Begin government confirmed that, rather than waiting for results from the Camp David autonomy talks, it would start implementing its own version of 'civil administration' in the West Bank and Gaza. On 1 November, the head of the new administration in the West Bank was named as Menahem Milson, a professor of Arabic literature from the Hebrew University of Jerusalem. Milson had already, in two articles published earlier that year, spelt out his analysis of what was wrong with the situation in the occupied territories. In one of these, he had argued, 'The PLO's political dominance in these territories is not a "natural" development, but rather is at least in part a result of certain acts of omission and commission by both Israeli and American officials.' The PLO was able to exercise twofold pressure on the population of the territories, Milson argued, through 'the offer of patronage money on the one hand, and on the other hand physical terror and intimidation'. What Israel and the U.S. should do, he said, was to 'create conditions within which moderates in the territories will be able to express their views openly'. He considered that without some legitimation from within the occupied territories, King Hussein would not go against the Arab consensus of opposition to the Camp David autonomy talks.

How is such legitimation to be achieved? by *freeing the population of the territories from the grip of the PLO*. This must be done by Israel, with the support and cooperation of the U.S....

Continued political domination of the territories by the PLO will guarantee that organization's continued legitimacy within the Arab world, not to mention its power to veto any Arab move in the direction of Camp David.[20]

Once in office, Milson immediately moved to counter what he saw as the sources of the PLO's influence inside the West Bank. He blocked the funds allocated by the joint PLO/Jordanian committee which had been flowing into the West Bank for the past three years, and he instituted a new strong-arm tactic of insisting that municipal leaders deal with his new administration on his own terms. Those who refused were summarily dismissed. Meanwhile, in line with his idea of cultivating and protecting 'the moderates', he worked quickly to build up the Village Leagues as alternative focuses of power and patronage to those previously supplied by the municipalities. One reporter described the results of this latter policy:

With a half-dozen Israeli soldiers in two armored cars guarding his home, Bishara Qumsieh could relax. He talked about helping his fellow Palestinians, about his admiration for Anwar Sadat and about the need to sit down and negotiate autonomy with Israel.

In the eyes of Palestinian nationalists who want independence, Qumsieh is a quisling, rejected by his people, who could help Israel legitimize its occupation. Last Tuesday the Palestine Liberation Organization (PLO) claimed responsibility for shooting Qumsieh's counterpart in Ramallah and warned he could meet the same fate.[21]

There is little doubt, too, given the tone of the Israeli leaders' statements as their army raced towards Beirut in the summer of 1982, that the idea of severing that link between the national movement outside and the movement inside the occupied territories was one of the principal aims of that summer's Israeli invasion of Lebanon. However, throughout that summer, the West Bank saw repeated demonstrations in support of the PLO leaders and fighters besieged in Beirut. In a demonstration held in Nablus on 5 July, two people were killed, and in another in Jerusalem on 28 September an 18-year-old girl was killed.[22]

Thus, in 1982 as in 1976, the difficulties being experienced by the movement outside did not result in any immediate weakening of the commitment to it expressed by activists and supporters of the movement inside the territories. In fact the opposite was the case, as both wings of the movement shared the pain of direct confrontation with the Israeli military, and the elation of resisting it.

At the end of 1982, the Israelis planned to cap their destruction of PLO 'dominance' in the West Bank by organising a convocation of all the Village League members they had organised, and in many cases also armed. In the event, despite intensive lobbying efforts, they could attract only 500 people to the meeting, held in Hebron. To Muhammed Milhem, speaking from exile in Amman, this paltry figure proved the failure of the Israelis' attempt to wean support away from the PLO: 'The leaders of the Village Leagues are colonial agents, those who accept to collaborate with the colonisers... Yet less than 1% of the West Bankers attended the Hebron meeting: this shows our people are among the cleanest, the least tainted by treachery, of any in the world!'[23]

The first 15 years of Israel's occupation of the West Bank were marked by a profound transformation of the area's internal political balance. Generally quiescent in 1967, and often reluctant to stress their Palestinian-ness to the extent that this might compromise their chances of being freed of the occupation through an Israeli accommodation with Jordan, by 1982-83 the West Bankers had moved into a position of effective co-leadership of the Palestinian national revival.

Of course, some stresses remained in the relationship between these two wings of the movement, a result of the different environment in which each had to operate and of the variations in their levels of political experience. Some indication of the areas in which these stresses lay was given by left-leaning Bir Zeit professor Selim Tamari in the following terms:

Initially, and to some extent yet today, the resistance [i.e. the movement outside the territories] made a cult of militarism, elevating armed struggle as a catchword... After 1974, and especially after 1976, we witness a noticeable change in the strategy of almost all resistance organizations. They began to seriously consider political mobilization as a form of struggle and understand the severe limitations on activities within the occupied territories...

Another weakness – this comes mainly from the right although left organizations also fall prey to it – is a reliance on traditional individuals and groups as opposed to organizing people at the grassroots.[24]

Amplifying Tamari's comments, Muhammed Milhem also criticised the PLO leaders for having no overall framework for co-ordination among all the various different resistance groupings inside the West Bank.[25]

For their part, very conscious that their role as 'head of the tribe' should rule out any open criticism of other 'tribe members', some Fateh activists nonetheless at times in the mid-70s expressed impatience with what they considered the political naivety of some of their supporters on the West Bank. But they expressed understanding that this had been brought about by the successive Israeli deportations from the West Bank. As the decade came to a close they were starting to evince admiration for the rapidity with which the remaining West Bank leaders had learnt to master techniques of mass struggle which were new to the movement as a whole and to afford the resistence struggle inside the West Bank and the other Israeli-controlled areas a new importance in their strategic view.

Within the West Bank Palestinian community itself, the debates which continued inside the Palestinian diaspora communities also found their place, albeit in a differently refracted form. Inside the West Bank, only a slightly larger proportion of Palestinians than outside argued for an unconditional accommodation with Israel. In both cases, proponents of this view formed a tiny proportion of the whole, and in the terms of the nationalist movement they were always considered beyond the pale of rational debate. Inside the West Bank, a larger proportion of the population than in the diaspora supported the idea of creating an independent Palestinian state in the occupied territories: West Bank 'rejectionists' were a relatively rare phenomenon. But inside the West Bank the opposite ideological pole to that of the Fateh leadership's Palestine-first strategy was occupied not by pan-Arab-type 'rejectionists' but by the region's tightly organised Communist Party and its left-wing, rigidly anti-Jordanian allies – all of whom still supported the idea of the independent Palestinian state. It was the competition between the pro-Fateh and the pro-Communist wings of the movement which rendered the PNF virtually impotent after its overwhelming victory in the 1976 local elections. This competition re-emerged to a degree in late 1982, after it had become clear that the Fateh leadership's response to President Reagan's September 1982 Mideast peace plan was to consider the feasibility of regaining the occupied areas for the Arabs through some kind of accommodation with Jordan.[26]

Throughout the years after 1974, however, two linked factors served to cement the relationship between the West Bank movement and the PLO leaders outside. The first of these was the West Bankers' new stress on their Palestinian-ness. This feeling was fed by their memory of what the Jordanians had done to the Palestinians in Jordan in 1970-71, and by the continued mobility of the West Bankers, many of whom travelled to work in the Gulf or elsewhere, keeping them in close touch with their brothers, cousins and friends on the outside. The second factor cementing the two wings of the movement was the shared political goal of creating an independent Palestinian state in the occupied territories. These solid socio-political facts meant that after 1974 the vast majority of West Bankers did not view the PLO, in the way Israeli 'experts' such as Menahem Milson did, as simply another participant in the three-cornered patronage struggle (Israel, Jordan and the PLO) for influence over them; for them it was their partner or, as the municipal leaders elected in 1976 never tired of repeating, their 'sole legitimate representative'.

Gaza

The Egyptian army units which participated so disastrously in the 1948 fighting in Palestine/Israel stayed on in Gaza after the armistice, keeping tight Egyptian control over the 80-square-mile Strip, with its majority population of refugees from inside Israel's 1948 frontiers and its densely populated patchwork of towns, sprawling refugee camps and citrus groves. Many of the earliest Fateh activists and leaders, especially those connected with the Palestinian Students' Union in Cairo in the early 50s, had grown up in the teeming climate of despair of the post-1948 years in

Gaza. These included Wazir, Khalaf, Kamal Udwan and Selim al-Zaanoun; Yasser Arafat also retained extensive family connections there.[27]

The Egyptians exerted tight control over the Gaza population from the very beginning. Hajj Amin al-Husseini, the Mufti of Jerusalem, was briefly allowed to run his 'All-Palestine Government', but in 1949 was taken to Egypt and placed under house arrest in Alexandria. Egyptian army and intelligence units meanwhile did all they could to prevent 'infiltration into Israel' (that is, in most cases, back to their own homes and farms) by the vast numbers of uprooted Palestinians in the Gaza refugee camps, lest this should threaten the armistice signed with Israel in 1949 in Rhodes. This ban on infiltration was lifted only briefly, and still under tight Egyptian control, in 1955-56 (see chapter 9 below).

By 1967, the Gazans, unlike the West Bankers, had already been exposed to one four-month period of direct Israeli occupation, during the Israeli-French-British invasion of Egypt in 1956. When that invasion started, some of the former Students' Union leaders from Cairo who had already graduated were already working back in Gaza. They established an underground organisation to resist the occupation, called the Popular Resistance (PR; Al-Muqawama al-Shaabiyya). As Selim al-Zaanoun, one of the leaders of the PR, later explained it, there had been two main resistance groupings in 1956 in Gaza: the PR and another network called the National Front, which was led by Haidar Abdel-Shafei. While the National Front had been more leftist-oriented, he said that at the beginning the PR had been an expression more of Muslim Brotherhood and Baathist feelings, but 'The experience of the resistance in Gaza in 1956 was that there was no need for parties: so long as the land was occupied there should be no parties. The Muslim Brother should become a Palestinian, the Baathist should become a Palestinian, and the Arab Nationalist should become a Palestinian.'[28] The experience of the PR in Gaza, under the extremely harsh conditions of actual daily struggle against the Israeli occupation, thus served to underscore the ideas the Students' Union had been developing at a more theoretical level over the past few years.

The conditions of the 1956 occupation of Gaza were indeed harsh. According to a Western journalist covering the 1956 war, 'at least' 275 Palestinians had been killed in an Israeli combing operation in the Gazan town of Khan Yunis, and a further 111 in a refugee camp near Gaza.[29] Zaanoun's account of the former incident was that

When they first came in, they killed 1,200 youths in Khan Yunis. They took them out into the streets and killed them in front of their fathers and their mothers ... because Khan Yunis had resisted them. Gaza City was not exposed to such events because the U.N. observers were there, and because the administration of the town handed it over to the Israelis.[30]

The head of the U.N. observer force in Gaza, Lieutenant-Colonel R. F. Bayard of the U.S. Army, reported on 13 November 1956 that the Israelis were trying to prevent his men from seeing actions they were taking against the civilian populace, and that

Many Israeli soldiers have robbed civilians, taking watches, rings, fountain pens, etc., away from the Arabs either in their homes or on the streets. Every vehicle and every bicycle has been confiscated. Private workshops and machine shops have been stripped of all mechanical tools. Many mules and horses have been taken and cloth has been taken from the stores.[31]

The Gazans' resistance organisations had had no chance, before the 1956 Israeli invasion, to prepare themselves to resist, to stockpile weaponry and so on, so their fight was unequal from the very beginning, and their relief was correspondingly huge when Egyptian and American diplomacy managed to relieve them of the occupation. Nasser soon clamped down on all the former resistance activists, however, once again with the aim of not endangering his cease-fire with Israel. Zaanoun said that many of the former leaders of the PR then 'went down to the Gulf states where they became involved in the founding of Fateh. They kept in touch with their old comrades in Gaza, however, especially through their yearly summer visits back there.'[32]

In the light of their memories of 1956, and as the likelihood of another Egyptian-Israeli confrontation increased in the mid-60s, the population of Gaza started making its own preparations to resist. The PLA already had units in place in Gaza, and in early 1967 those which had been stationed in Iraq and Syria moved into Gaza, which was the only Palestinian area in which they were allowed to deploy. By June, the PLA troops there totalled around 5,000 men. Their training was considered quite good, but the level and variety of their armament limited their ability to take on a regular army. In addition to the PLA, in the weeks leading up to June the general population also started arming, taking handguns, rifles and assault rifles, and some rudimentary training, from makeshift militia centres that mushroomed throughout the Strip. The Egyptian authorities, preparing for their own war effort, allowed the Gazans to prepare their resistance.

During the war, the PLA and such Egyptian units as remained in Gaza put up a stiff fight. For two days, they managed to prevent the Israelis from controlling the whole of the Strip. Once the Israelis did find themselves in control, they set about pacifying the population with a vengeance, though this time the general population's widespread access to stockpiled arms made the Israelis more wary of using the kinds of tactics they had used in

181

1956. Instead, over the weeks which followed their entry into Gaza, they rounded up thousands of Gazan males between the ages of 16 and 40, put them on trucks and summarily deported them to Egypt. According to one of the deportees, their number reached well over 15,000. But armed resistance to the occupation continued in every town and refugee camp for the next four years. A large proportion of this was co-ordinated by the remaining Arab Nationalists, whose organisation had been allowed by the Egyptian authorities to flourish in Gaza in the years leading up to 1967, and which therefore commanded a wide following. In 1968, they became an important component of the Arab Nationalist offspring, the PFLP.

In summer 1971, the Israelis determined to put an end once and for all to the resistance which continued to simmer in Gaza. The new security regime introduced by the military commander of the area, Ariel Sharon, included a tough 'shoot-first' policy towards anyone even remotely suspected of links with the armed resistance, and the forcible deportation of 14,700 refugees from the three largest refugee camps. Their shelters were then demolished to make room for broad new security avenues which sliced the camps into more controllable units. A special report of the UNRWA Commissioner-General later recorded:

Israeli soldiers arrived in the camp (on some occasions, at least, at night), marked shelters for demolition and gave the inhabitants notice ranging from two to forty-eight hours to leave with all their belongings. The refugees were told that there was good accommodation available for them in El Arish (in central Sinai), but that if they preferred, they could go to the West Bank of Jordan, or remain in Gaza if they could find unoccupied accommodation there.[33]

The administrative set-up which the Egyptians had left behind in Gaza differed from that left by the Jordanians in the West Bank. In Gaza, there were no elected municipalities; the four towns, led by Gaza City, instead had appointed mayors. After the 'pacifications' of the summer of 1971, the Israelis sought to reinstate the Gaza municipality, and they brought in veteran Gaza businessman Rashad al-Shawwa to be the new mayor. Shawwa tried to bring some order back into the Gazans' daily lives by opening an export route to Jordan which could stimulate the citrus business and other trade, and he publicly denounced Israeli declarations voiced at that time that Israel would never leave Gaza. But, nevertheless, he was trapped between the strong demands of the Israelis and of his own constituency, many members of which had criticised him for accepting the job in the first place. They criticised him again in early 1972, when he expressed some enthusiasm for the 'United Arab Kingdom' plan King Hussein was then proposing, to bring the West Bank and Gaza under some kind of rule from Amman. On this occasion, the criticism of Shawwa came not only from the nationalists in the Strip, but also from those close to the traditional pro-Egyptian administration there. Then in October 1972, the Israelis asked Shawwa to extend municipal services to the nearby Shati refugee camp the following year. He refused, seeing this as a prelude to liquidating the refugees' right to return to their original homes, whereupon the Israelis abruptly dismissed him and returned the city to direct military rule.

In October 1975, the Israelis reinstated the civilian administration in Gaza, again under Shawwa. For the next seven years he was to play a pivotal role in the politics of the Gaza Strip and in the diplomatic moves over its fate. That he himself appreciated the nature of this role was revealed by the frequency with which he would travel among Gaza, Cairo, Amman and Beirut to consult with his own people, the Egyptians, the Jordanians and the PLO – and, of course, the Israelis – before making any major move.

Popular reactions in Gaza to Sadat's visit to Jerusalem in 1977 broadly paralleled those in the West Bank. The consensus reached between those who were for it and those who were against was to adopt a generally wait-and-see attitude. In Gaza, as in the West Bank, the terms of the Camp David accords when they emerged met with hostility from the population. Two large meetings were held in Gaza in the weeks after the war, to discuss the response to Camp David. At one of these Shawwa himself was in the chair.

Soon afterwards, Sadat started floating the idea of a 'Gaza-first' solution, under which the self-rule provisions prescribed in the Camp David accords would be implemented first of all in Gaza, and only afterwards in the West Bank. But, according to Ann Lesch, 'the Israeli government seemed to be only interested in the Gaza option if it meant splitting Gaza from the West Bank'.[34] Sadat soon thereafter seemed to drop the idea. The only prominent Gazan who had openly embraced it was the elderly Imam Hashem Khuzundar, a traditional pro-Cairo figure. On 1 June 1979, he was assassinated, apparently by a PFLP execution squad.

By early 1983, Gaza remained what it had been a decade earlier, a ticking time-bomb of resentment against the Israelis, and Mayor Shawwa accurately reflected this in his continued opposition to Camp David and his repeated statements of support for the PLO – which were only slightly qualified by his continued links with Hussein.

The lengthy period of large-scale armed resistance to the occupation which the Gazans had sustained in the years following 1967 had been beaten back by Sharon's tough counter-measures, but the resistance movement had shown itself capable of mounting a carefully targeted series of more limited armed operations in Gaza over the decade which followed, of which Khuzundar's assassination (which was denounced by Fateh as unnecessary) was only one instance. The Gazans' resistance meanwhile also assumed many of those features of mass political struggles which were simultaneously being developed in the West Bank.

In the early years of the occupation, the PFLP had registered much success in its campaign to prevent Gazans from working inside Israel. Over the years, and especially after 1971, this success had eroded substantially. But in Gaza, as in the West Bank, direct exposure to Israeli society and the stimulation of the area's cash economy through wages from Israel did not soften the residents' resentment of the Israeli occupation, as some more liberal Israelis appeared at times to have hoped. In both areas stimulation of the cash economy was a result not only of the inflow of wages from Israel, but increasingly throughout the 70s also of remittances from family members outside, especially in the Gulf countries.

The Gazans started off their life under the 1967 occupation with a richer history and popular culture of direct resistance to Israel to look back on than that obtaining in the West Bank. The structure of Gaza's communities, with their heavy refugee component, meant that they saw relatively fewer fixed interests of their own at risk in any confrontation with Israel. But the four years of punishment the Gazans took at the beginning of the occupation hurt them badly, and another factor which had a stifling effect on their resistance movement was their sheer physical and social isolation from the Arab countries after 1967. Even after Gazan students were allowed in 1971 to start travelling to other Arab countries to complete their studies, and other limited types of visits were allowed, the population as a whole still lacked the daily contact with friends and relatives in the Arab world which the West Bankers' window on Jordan allowed them.

Throughout the years of Israeli occupation, Gaza's residents, like the West Bankers, felt themselves under heavy Israeli economic pressures to emigrate, but despite a lower overall level of local educational, social and administrative institutions than those in the West Bank, they proved themselves better able than the West Bankers to resist such pressures. In the terms set by the Palestinian national movement as a whole, this in itself was no small achievement.

The Palestinians of 1948 Israel: 'Israeli Arabs'

The exodus of the Palestinian Arabs from the areas brought under Israeli/ Jewish control in 1948 was a widespread phenomenon, yet as the Jewish state set down roots it became clear that around 150,000 Arabs remained within its frontiers. By the early 80s, the number of these Palestinians had grown, through one of the highest rates of natural increase in the modern world, to over 500,000.

The situation of the 'Israeli Arab' community was unique and difficult from the start. That small fraction of the area's original Arab residents which remained after the 1948 exodus found itself transformed within a few weeks from being part of the indigenous majority population into being an ever suspect minority; it had also been stripped of nearly all of its significant community leaders.

The formal declaration of the State of Israel in 1948 promised equal treatment to the new state's Arab citizens, but those areas of Israel which supported a substantial Arab population were placed under a military regime for the following 18 years. Omnipotent and arbitrary, the Military Government in Galilee, the Little Triangle and the Negev exerted careful control over every aspect of the Israeli Arabs' life. At the political level, this even included the Military Government's (and its successors') direct intervention in what were supposed to be the democratic processes in the Arab areas. The American researcher Ian Lustick has written that during elections to the highest organ of Israeli democracy, the Knesset,

the Military Administration, and after its abolition other agencies responsible for the affairs of the Arab sector, made it a practice to distribute differently-printed ballots to different hamulas [clans]. Knowing that the results would be carefully tabulated and recorded, the leaders of the hamulas would strive to ensure that hamula members voted strictly according to instructions.[35]

Lustick also printed an example of three of these distinctive ballot papers, all for the same pro-Labour Party list, issued for Knesset elections as late as 1973.[36]

The Military Government was far more than merely an Israeli party-political device, however. Under its auspices, the Israeli rulers also continued at full speed with the traditional Zionist mission of Judaising the land. The lands of those Palestinians who had fled were all brought under the administration of the new state's 'Custodian of Absentee Property', who was then able to apportion it among the waves of new Jewish immigrants the state was bringing in.[37] Neither was the land of those Palestinians who had stayed sacrosanct. Under the pretext of 'state security', which was only later to become a catchword for Jewish colonising activities in the West Bank, since 1948 the State of Israel had been fencing off, seizing and colonising the lands of its own Arab citizens. This practice continued until the early 80s. In March 1983, for example, a headmaster in the Little Triangle village of Taibeh told a *Washington Post* reporter the total land area his village controlled had dwindled to under 3,000 acres from the total of about 17,000 acres it had controlled in 1948; the village population had meanwhile increased from 4,000 to 20,000.[38]

The political status of the Arab community in Israel had been overturned by the events of 1948, and its transformation from a mainly peasant society into a subproletarian class in the Israeli wage economy effected broad changes in its social composition in the years which followed. At the cultural level, meanwhile, the newborn Jewish state campaigned at full speed to assimilate all its citizens into its heavily Jewish-dominated cultural mainstream. Writing in 1966, for example, the then Israeli Arab Sabri Jiryis said of the government-supervised curricula in Israeli Arab schools, 'In the whole of the four years of secondary education only 32 periods are devoted to Arab history, the Arab conquest of Spain and the Arab civilisation that made that country so brilliant during the 700 years of Arab rule. In contrast, 384 hours are devoted to the study of Jewish history.[39] Jiryis also quoted a one-time Advisor on Arab Affairs to the Israeli Premier as saying in 1961, 'If there were no pupils the situation would be better and more stable. If the Arabs remained hewers of wood it might be easier for us to control them. But there are certain things that are beyond our control.'[40]

The results of Israeli government policies towards the Israeli Arabs did nevertheless appear, by the mid-60s, to be offering some hope, to some Israeli commentators, that these Arabs had become resigned to their fate. A major factor which reversed that trend – if indeed it really existed – was the Israeli Arabs' sudden exposure, after 1967, to the virtually intact Arab societies of the West Bank and Gaza. In many cases, particularly in Galilee and the Little Triangle, which abut on the north of the West Bank, the effect on the Israeli Arabs' ways of thinking was electrifying. By 1974-75, one American social scientist researching the attitudes of Arabs in 'the north of Israel' – that is, Galilee and the Little Triangle – asked them how they would identify themselves. Sixty-three percent of the respondents said that the description 'Palestinian' suited them 'very well', while only 14% said the same of the description 'Israeli'.[41] A survey taken a decade earlier would most likely have shown very different results.

The growth of the Israeli Arabs' nationalist consciousness was not the only factor causing concern to the Israeli authorities by the mid-70s; the sheer growth in their numbers was also a cause of intermittently expressed Israeli disquiet. Moreover, the effects of the growth of the Israeli Arabs' numbers were felt most keenly in the two above-mentioned northern parts of the country, which had not, under the United Nations Partition Plan for Palestine, formed part of the Jewish state. Several Israeli commentators expressed fears that an Arab majority in these areas might seek in the future to secede from the Jewish state to join a Palestinian Arab state, if one was created. A glance at a map outlining those administrative regions of northern Israel which already had an overall Arab majority indicated that these regions formed an almost unbroken chain between the West Bank and southern Lebanon.[42]

186

The most open official expression of this Israeli demographic fear was that enclosed in a report written by Israel Koenig, the governor of the Northern District, which was made public in September 1976. Pointing to the fear that the Israeli Arabs might very soon form an overall majority in Galilee, the 'Koenig memorandum' argued for an accelerated campaign to Judaise the area, which would include large investments in new Jewish settlements there, a differentiation of official incentives to Jewish and to Arab citizens to have large families, and the introduction of policies designed to encourage Arab emigration.[43] The Labour government in power in Israel at the time disavowed the memorandum. But after its publication, successive Israeli governments did put renewed emphasis into encouraging Jewish settlement in Galilee, and in early 1983 Menachem Begin's government was discussing the introduction of precisely the kind of discriminatory child allowances that Koenig had argued for.

In 1948, most Arab community leaders had fled those parts of Palestine which were overrun by the Jewish units. The only ones who managed to return were some of the Communist Party leaders, who, through their links with the Jewish communists and on the basis of the Soviet Union's early recognition of the State of Israel, managed to return to their homes in Haifa and Nazareth. Over the decades which followed, and from within the framework of a party which offered continued recognition to the State of Israel, they were to play a significant role in keeping alive some spirit of national culture and feeling for the Arabs of Israel. For many years, the only Arabic-language cultural outlet available at all in Israel was that provided by the communist newspaper *Al-Ittihad* (The Union); and several of the Arab communist leaders, including Knesset members Emil Habibi and Tawfiq Zayyad, were themselves poets whose work was loved and renowned throughout the Arab world.[44] A number of factors, however, contributed to the weakening of the communists' support from the Israeli Arabs in successive elections in the first decade of the State of Israel's existence. First among these were the heavy controls on political life exerted by the Military Government. And, in their attempt to cling to what few known cultural and social norms remained to them, the Israeli Arabs may also have been susceptible to the ruling party's standard anti-communist arguments. Thus, the proportion of the Arab vote cast for the Communist Party in general elections slipped from 22.2% in 1949 to 15.6% in 1955.[45]

In 1956, at the height of the Soviet Union's alliance with Egyptian President Nasser, the Israeli Communist Party entered into what was named a 'Popular Front' with some pro-Nasser Arab nationalists in Israel. But two years later, the strains between the two sides broke the Front apart. The Arab nationalists then tried to continue their activities under the name of Al-Ard (The Land). Sabri Jiryis was one of the founders of Al-Ard, as were Habib Qahwaji, who was later to leave Israel and sit on the PLO Executive Committee, and a teacher called Saleh Baransi.

According to Baransi, Nasser's 1952 coup in Egypt had awakened the Arabs in Israel out of the 'state of shock' 1948 had left them in. After 1952, 'They began to follow the events in Egypt and all over the Arab world with a great sense of hope.'[46] Nevertheless, until the founding of the Popular Front in 1956, 'our struggle was an individual struggle. There was no leadership. The people who were ready to become leaders didn't know each other and couldn't contact each other even when they did. We were very isolated. Every village, every town was a closed area. No one was allowed to leave or enter without permission.' [47] Baransi offered some praise to the communists for their role in increasing the Israeli Arabs' political awareness: 'Without the communists, this would have taken a very much longer time. They taught us very much.' But he explained that the main difference between the communists and the Arab nationalists inside Israel 'always concerned the Palestine problem'.[48]

When the nationalists established Al-Ard in 1958, its constitution did not describe the struggle of the Arabs in Israel, as the communists at that time did, as a struggle merely for civil and human rights. According to Baransi,

We put the greatest stress on the struggle for our *national* rights as a people. The first article [of the group's constitution] said that we are an inseparable part of the Palestinian people, who are an inseparable part of the Arab nation, which is an inseparable part of the world liberation movement. This was too much for the communists and the Zionist liberals to accept, those who had cooperated with us in the Popular Front.[49]

It was also too much for the Israeli state to accept. The Al-Ard group went through various legal battles to establish its existence over the years which followed. Forbidden to set up a party, they tried to organise themselves as a commercial venture. When that too was outlawed they tried to put up their own list of candidates for the elections of 1965; that was also ruled illegal, and Baransi was exiled from his home village.

The same year that Al-Ard was finally quashed, however, saw a new split in the Communist Party, over the very same issues which Al-Ard was raising. According to Ori Stendel, who until 1971 was Deputy Advisor on Arab Affairs in Israel, the Jewish leaders in the Communist Party felt they 'could not shrug off responsibility for the sharp anti-Israel statements that appeared in *Al-Ittihad* or in the manifestos circulated among Arab settlements'.[50] The split between these Jewish leaders and those Arabs and Jews who supported the *Al-Ittihad* line deepened, and in the end the *Al-Ittihad* group seceded to form 'The New Communist List', Rakah.

Because Rakah's secession had enabled its members to resolve some of the ideological problems they had been facing from within their mother party, the new party was able to occupy a stronger position in the Arab body politic in Israel than Maki (the orthodox Communist Party) had before it. Rakah activists worked much harder in defence of what they saw as Arab civil and human rights inside Israel than Maki had, and Jewish Rakah lawyers such as Felicia Langer and Lea Tsemel became virtual folk heroes and heroines for Palestinian nationalists inside and outside the Israeli-ruled areas for their defence of nationalist prisoners in the Israeli courts. In 1975, the Rakah-led list came first in the municipal elections in the key Galilee Arab town of Nazareth, and Tawfiq Zayyad became mayor.

Nevertheless, the political demands of Rakah concerning the Palestinian question still remained within limits consonant with the continued exist-ence of the State of Israel. As spelt out by Zayyad in a 1976 speech, Rakah's position was as follows:

Land expropriation has to be stopped, and confiscated Arab land must be given back to its legal owners. In addition the right of the Arabs to exist and to develop on their land and in their homeland must be recognized. The Arabs must have the right of due respect to their culture and national dignity, the right of full representation in the various official and public institutions, and the right of participation in remolding the general policy of the state and the future relations with the Jewish people, which they want to be based on mutual understanding, cooperation and respect.[51]

Such a stand was not sufficiently nationalistic for some of the younger Israeli Arabs, who in the years after 1967 sought to organise around more purely nationalist demands, as Al-Ard had before them. The new genera-tion of activists had learnt some lessons from the trials and tribulations of the Al-Ard group. One of the chief of these was apparently that it would be wiser not to hope to create a single centralised nationalist grouping im-mediately, but to build up more informal groups across a wider geographic and social base. The best-known of these new groups was Abna' al-Balad (Sons of the Village), founded in 1970 in the large Triangle village of Umm al-Fahm, but broadly parallel groups also mushroomed in most sizeable Israeli Arab communities throughout the 70s.[52]

According to one of the founders of Abna' al-Balad, the lawyer Moham-med Kiwan, his group differed from Al-Ard in that the latter had centred its programme on the question of Arab unity, but 'The problem for us is not how to create Arab unity, but the question of the Palestinian people. So the most important thing for us now in Abna' al-Balad is our Palestinian identity.'[53] This formulation, it may be noted, almost exactly mirrored Fateh's own earliest ideological innovation, and that Abna' had drawn the same conclusions as Fateh from this original premise was indicated by its emphasis (as expressed by Kiwan): 'We say that the only true legitimate representative of the Palestinian Arab people is the Palestine Liberation Organization... This is the first principle. Secondly, that all the Palestinian people, everywhere, constitute one identity.'[54]

In fact, despite the remaining ideological divergences, the trend over the late 70s and early 80s was that the Rakah communists and the more informal nationalist groupings found they could work effectively together on a whole range of issues affecting the Arabs in Israel. One major symbol of this co-operation, in the years from 1976 onwards, became the Israeli Arab community's annual observance of the 'Day of the Land', held to protest land seizures. The first Day of the Land was held on 30 March 1976, with its major rallies and demonstrations hosted by Tawfiq Zayyad's newly installed municipal administration in Nazareth. Six participants in the demonstrations were killed by the Israeli police that day, and, far from scaring the Israeli Arabs away from further nationalist activities, the killings acted as a kind of 'baptism by fire' for many thousands of Israeli Arabs back into the mainstream of the modern-day Palestinian national movement. Successive Days of the Land over the years which followed 1976 not only served as focuses for the Israeli Arabs' own nationalist renaissance but also became an important link between the Israeli Arabs and the population of the 1967-occupied territories, who started observing the same Day of the Land in the succeeding years. On 30 March 1983, for example, despite heavy Israeli curfews, one Palestinian was reported killed in Hebron, in the West Bank, in connection with observance of the Day of the Land in that city.[55]

In September 1982, the Israeli Arabs' reactions to the mass killings in the two Beirut refugee camps provided a further demonstration of the revival of Palestinian national sentiment amongst the Israeli Arabs. On 22 September, a general strike was called in Nazareth in condemnation of the Beirut killings, and clashes between the police and the city's residents that day left 42 residents wounded and 60 arrests.[56] Arab communities throughout Israel observed the same strike that day, and in many of the demonstrations which accompanied the strike the slogans which were reportedly shouted were of a tone never heard from the Israeli Arabs in public before. In Haifa the demonstrators shouted, 'Oh martyr, rest in peace, we will finish the struggle.' In Shafa Amr they shouted, 'From your blood, oh children of Sabra, the free state will arise.' In the village of Kabul they shouted, 'There can be no negotiations except with Yasser Arafat', and in Sakhnine, 'There is no alternative to the PLO'.[57]

At some levels, perhaps, it was easier for some of the Israeli Arabs to feel an immediate affinity for the Palestinian nationalist movement outside the Israeli-ruled areas than it was for some West Bankers. The refugees in

Lebanon and Syria who formed a major constituency for the guerrilla groups were after all the former neighbours and in many cases close relatives of the Israeli Arabs. At the political level, however, the distance of their immediate interests from those of the PLO was probably greater, from 1974 onwards, than that of the West Bankers and Gazans. For example, if an independent Palestinian state were to be created in the West Bank and Gaza, what effect would that have on the status of the Israeli Arabs? (One answer to this question came from the 1974-75 survey mentioned above, which found that a stunning 29% of the Israeli Arab respondents said they would 'definitely' move to such a state, and only 33% said they would 'definitely' not do so.[58])

Despite such tactical divergences as may exist, the strength of the Palestinian revival spearheaded by the nationalist movement outside the Israeli-ruled areas appeared to have been sufficient to sweep the Israeli Arabs' indigenous movement into its orbit. In Saleh Baransi's view,

In the first phase [after 1948], the Arabs who remained in Israel were the main force because only they symbolized the existence of the Palestinians in our country, in their country. But after the establishment of the PLO, and, especially, after the eruption of the Palestinian revolution in 1967, I think the main force is the Palestinians who are living outside [in] the Arab world.[59]

For their part, the Fateh leaders also appeared, by early 1983, to be seeking some way of building on such expressions of allegiance to the mutual benefit of both sides. In a report presented to the Sixteenth PNC in February 1983, and sponsored by Fateh's Khalil al-Wazir, the writer said explicitly,

We should put forward two questions, the first to ourselves and to the Arab nation as a whole, and that is: how much longer shall we continue to ignore the struggle of more than 500,000 Palestinians who had Israeli nationality imposed on them? ...

We do not ask of these citizens to challenge the racist state, because that is *not within their powers*. But they are capable of playing an effective political role in the service of their Palestinian cause.[60]

The possible difficulties in store for the Palestinian national movement as it faced the problems involved in integrating the Palestinians of 1948 Israel into the larger movement were pointed up (indirectly) by Ian Lustick. 'The regime,' Lustick wrote in 1979, 'has experienced a real decrease in its ability to manipulate the [Israeli] Arab population.' Having already examined the hard-line policies advocated publicly by such men as former Israeli Defence Minister Ariel Sharon and former head of the Labour Party's Arab Department Amnon Linn, Lustick warned,

If control over the minority [i.e. the Israeli Arabs] breaks down ... a radical reassessment of the position of Arabs in Israel will be required. Under such circumstances pluralist or consociational futures could become relevant; so might the possibility, now discussed publicly only in [Israeli] ultranationalist circles, of *eliminating the problem through mass expulsions.*[61]

While the 'pluralist or consociational futures' referred to here could conceivably include the Fateh/PLO formula of a single 'secular democratic state', the other alternative Lustick raised also looked distinctly possible.

External relations

The political base

It was a windy night in early 1983 at the plush new seaside hotel in Kuwait. The local branch of the General Union of Palestinian Women was holding an $80-a-plate benefit for educational programmes the Union was running in Lebanon and Syria, and all the tables on the pool-side plaza were full. The scheduled troupe of folklore dancers was late, so conversation drifted around and between the tables as the diners awaited them. Much of it concerned a recently reported incident in the West Bank, where hundreds of young Palestinian girls had been struck by a mysterious illness. Those with close relatives on the West Bank huddled frequently to exchange information.

There were quite a few familiar faces from Beirut there, but we ended up at a table with strangers – Palestinians recently returned to the Arab world after 17 years in Brazil, speaking mostly Portuguese to each other. The girls of this family, like many others at the dinner, were in strict but decorative Islamic cover-up. 'Nice to be back,' said one of the younger ones, 'back in the Arab world, that is!'

After quite a bit of fussing by the entirely worthy-looking woman from the Union (ten to one, a schoolmistress), the troupe finally gets set up. Mostly teenagers, male and female, all in military outfits with a lively but ragged series of songs and dances on nationalistic themes. One stirring number about the Battle of Beirut. Somebody is recording them simultaneously on no fewer than three video cameras, for subsequent distribution.

The Fateh Central Committee has been meeting here this week. Near the beginning of the show, Committee members Salah Khalaf and Farouq Qaddumi edge in to a front table, with the DFLP's Nayef Hawatma and Yasser Abde Rabboo behind them. Many informal greetings; the Union lady looks flustered with honour at their presence. One of the heavily scarved girls from our table shyly takes up a bouquet to Khalaf, comes back blushing.

After the show, the business: a man in charge here now. Donations! Names and pledges handed up on scruffy bits of paper. Mostly 100 dinars each($400); quite a few 1,000 dinars; the name of a prominent banker is read out with a pledge of 5,000 dinars. The total eventually goes over 25,000 dinars ($100,000).

The compere then announces that Qaddumi has donated his set of worry-beads for an auction. Bidding starts at 200 dinars, rises rapidly, tossed between two jovial Palestinian contractors present, to a final total of 7,200 dinars. $30,000 for a set of beads! Someone suggests the loser (only 7,150 dinars) be given Khalaf's beads as a consolation.

Afterwards, Khalaf and Qaddumi stride out rapidly (Hawatma and Abed Rabboo still in tow). The Central Committee is still deadlocked on the latest phase of the Reagan peace plan but coming along to the dinner had clearly been important for them. Looking after the base.

Arab relations

From the very start of their association with each other, Fateh's leaders had explicitly rejected any idea of espousing a pan-Arabist ideology, or any other 'universalist' ideology. Yet from the earliest days of its emergence the Palestinian resistance movement's development was intricately, even symbiotically, bound up with the course of events in the Arab states. There were many reasons, both objective and subjective, for this. First, following the Palestinian disaster of 1948, the Palestinian nationalists were unable to operate from any 'liberated area' inside their own country. Those parts of Mandate Palestine which remained free of Israeli control between 1948 and 1967 were kept under tight control by the Jordanians and the Egyptians throughout that period. The Palestinian refugees who dreamt of Return therefore always had to work for its realisation from under the watchful eye of an Arab government (until 1967, that is, when the refugees in camps in the West Bank and Gaza came under direct Israeli rule). The Arab governments, meanwhile, and especially those in the four Arab countries bordering directly on Israel which were host to the greatest numbers of refugees, have always had their own compelling *raisons d'état* to consider when addressing the question of Israel, and thus also the Palestinians' aims towards Israel.

In addition, the 'Palestinian question' was always a vibrant factor in the internal politics of the Arab states. Once again, this factor was especially important in the four states directly bordering Israel, although it was also a factor of undoubted importance in the internal politics of all those other countries which consider themselves Arab, 'from the [Atlantic] Ocean to the Gulf', as the Arab nationalists described their territory.

Palestine, within the borders the Palestinians and the other Arab states today consider valid, was carved out of the Ottoman Empire by the British only in the aftermath of the First World War. These borders were then enshrined in the 1920 Treaty of San Remo, through which the infant League of Nations assigned a mandate over the country to the British government. The only boundary of Mandate Palestine which had any validity prior to 1920 was that with Egypt – and even then it was not strictly speaking an international boundary, but one between two parts of the Ottoman Empire coming under different forms of administration. It had been drawn up in an agreement between the Ottomans and the British in the first half of the nineteenth century. In other directions, the relations between the Palestinians and their neighbours in the period leading up to and including the First World War were those simply of co-subjects of the Ottoman Empire. The *sanjaq* of Jersualem extended to the East Bank of the Jordan, for example, and the *wilayet* of Acre to much of present-day south Lebanon. The leading families of the big cities were meanwhile linked by ties of trade, culture and marriage to other leading families throughout the Fertile Crescent and even in Egypt. The Salams and Sursocks of Beirut owned extensive lands in Palestine, and the Khalidis and Nashashibis of Jerusalem exercised an intellectual influence far beyond what was to become Mandate Palestine. Throughout most of the latter centuries of the Ottoman period, the majority of the inhabitants of what the 1920 Mandates defined as Lebanon, Syria, Transjordan and Palestine would have described themselves first perhaps as 'Muslims' or 'Christians', and after that simply as 'Arabs', though the word 'Palestine' was in use in Arabic-language publications well before 1914.

In 1920, the inhabitants of Palestine found themselves closed inside the new borders drawn by the British, and closed in there, moreover, with all the problems of the escalating influx of Jewish colonists which had been prescribed by the British government's Balfour Declaration of 1917. (The Balfour Declaration had been endorsed by the League of Nations when it awarded the British their Mandate.) The specificity of the problems caused to the Palestinians by the Jewish immigration over the succeeding decades probably served to accelerate the formation of a specifically Palestinian strand to their more general Arab self-identity, faster than, for example, most Jordanians in that period came to consider themselves Jordanian rather than Arab, or most Lebanese to consider themselves Lebanese rather than Syrian or Arab. The national trauma of 1948 only hardened this process. R. Sayigh has poignantly documented how acutely the Palestinian refugees who streamed into Lebanon in 1948 were made to feel themselves alien to the surrounding culture, and thus to emphasise their self-identification as Palestinians rather than as Arabs.[1]

The Palestinians placed a large share of the blame for their defeat and trauma in 1948 on the leaders of the Arab states whose promises to come to their aid had weakened their own self-reliance. This same judgement against the rulers in Egypt, Syria and Jordan was also delivered by their own citizens, who cited it as a prime reason for the overthrow of the 1948 regimes in those countries during the four years following the disaster. But the Palestinians' own ruling class was demoralised, weakened and divided by the defeat, the intricate social structure which it had headed in Palestine smashed by the dispersal of the Palestinian communities. It was unable either effectively to protest the other Arab regimes' incompetence during the 1948 debacle or even, in the years which followed, to protect its own communities from the harsh treatment meted out to them by their unwilling Arab hosts – let alone ever hope to redress the Palestinian issue as a whole.

In the leadership vacuum which obtained in Palestinian diaspora society from 1948 until 1967, the dispersed Palestinian communities were left, on the one hand, ripe for the emergence of radical movements but, on the other hand, disenfranchised and at the total mercy of the host governments. Political radicals of all ideological colourings made successive bids to rally the leaderless Palestinian constituencies around their cause. This only aggravated the fears which the host regimes already harboured of the Palestinian communities in their midst. But up until 1967, and even after that date, the host governments were always able to confine Palestinian radicalism within easily manageable limits by exploiting to the full the inherent social, political and economic weaknesses of the Palestinian refugee communities. The precarious situation which resulted was aptly described by Sayigh in the following terms:

Often depicted as a 'threat' to precarious governments, it has not been as often noticed that Palestinians have been recruited in large numbers to *support* regimes. Their disenfranchisement, combined with their desperate need for a solution to their crisis, made them for a time the most easily manipulated constituency that Arab politicians possessed.[2]

In this respect, the role the Palestinians of Saiqa played in propping up the Salah Jadid regime in Syria up to 1970 has already been remarked in chapter 7 above, but the effect that Sayigh was describing was evident in other Arab states too.

The particular innovation that Fateh introduced into this pattern was that it rejected both kinds of reaction resorted to by Palestinian activists up till then. On the one hand, Fateh's founders rejected the idea of tying the Palestinians' fortunes to those of any one existing regime. Khaled al-Hassan summed up the reasons for this decision when he said, 'We have suffered from kings, republics, leftists, rightists, progressives, reactionaries – we have suffered from all.'[3] On the other hand, they purposely cut themselves loose from the universalist ideologies which were often directed against the regimes, and which abounded in the Palestinian communities throughout the 50s. As Hassan, again, described this step,

This was something that we decided, to avoid a lot of problems. And you shouldn't forget that most of us had previously been members of political parties. So we know what kinds of clashes will take place which will lead finally to a situation where, instead of working to our cause, we will work how to defend ourselves or how to defeat the others. We wanted to avoid that.[4]

Farouq al-Qaddumi, meanwhile, who had made his personal odyssey through the avowedly socialist Arab nationalism of the Baath Party, defended the new 'anti-ideology' ideology of Fateh in the following terms:

If the Palestinian revolution represented by Al-Fateh is said to be bourgeois, this implies that there should be factories, capitalists, and workers, in other words specific classes. We cannot say that there is a bourgeois class if there is no working class. What is this class? *Because of the evacuation of the Palestinians, Al-Fateh represents the refugees.* It is the only revolutionary movement which has transcended the Arab movements, Arab parties and Palestinian regional movements, and it has done this because it depended on the refugee class.[5]

In the years which followed 1948, the Arab states bordering Israel all imposed strict controls on the refugee communities to prevent any infiltration back into Israeli-held territory which might, through the heavy reprisals Israel was wont to respond with, draw the states into a war with Israel which they felt ill prepared to face. The only exception to this rule occurred in Egyptian-held Gaza, for a few months in 1955-56. In February 1955, the Israelis had mounted a particularly savage raid against an Egyptian police post in Gaza which left over three dozen Egyptians dead, and afterwards the Egyptian government sanctioned the establishment of some Palestinian infiltration units under strict Egyptian control. But this action did indeed help to draw Egypt into the war with Israel of the following year and, after the war, the Egyptians again halted the infiltration groups' activities.[6]

The strict controls maintained on autonomous Palestinian organising activities by all the 'front-line' states bordering Israel helped to persuade many of the activists from Egypt, Gaza and the other front-line areas to move down to the booming economies of the Arab Gulf states in the late 50s. The opportunities they could find there to help finance their organising activities provided another powerful motivation. In Kuwait, Qatar and to a lesser extent Saudi Arabia, they found many of the freedoms and facilities the Palestinian activists were looking for. Indeed, from the point of view of basic organising (as opposed to actual fighting), these countries offered some important advantages over the front-line states. The continuous flow of immigrant workers and professionals between the new oil states and their homes in the front-line states meant that cross-border communications were easier than was the case across the tightly controlled borders between most of the front-line states at the time.

In addition, some of the most influential of Fateh's eventual founders

198

found the general political atmosphere in the Gulf states much more congenial than in the front-line states. In the view of Khaled al-Hassan, for example,

There are two kinds of Arab regimes. There are those who believe that they represent the leadership of all the Arab world – including everybody, including even the animals! – and this monopoly type of thinking means that they think that they have the right to take the decision and nobody else has the right to take the decision... Those who saw in Fateh a real competitor to themselves, either regimes or political parties – those are the main source of our trouble. Even those whom we supported into power, when they came into power they turned against us. Like the Iraqi Baathists...

The same with the Arab Nationalist Movement; the same with the communists: those always decided to infiltrate us in order to control us.

The *other* regimes only believe in their own small countries, and they don't want anyone to interfere and they don't interfere in the affairs of the others: like the Moroccans, the Tunisians, the Algerians, the Sudanese, the Gulf – the Saudis.[7]

Thus it remained true that the formative years of the coalescence of Fateh into a unified movement were passed by most of the movement's top leaders in the Gulf states. These states, with their sizeable populations of Palestinians whose longing for Return was little diminished by their move – which they all saw as temporary – to the rapidly developing city-states of the Gulf, always thereafter provided a stable rearguard base for Fateh. As Hassan summed up the record of Kuwait and its neighbours,

We never had a problem with the Kuwaitis. As a matter of fact, I got the agreement of the government here to allow us [Fateh] to have an official office here in 1963; and just before we were ready to open the office, the PLO was announced, so we were asked to have our office here secretly, because they couldn't allow two public offices at the same time. But the co-operation was always with us more than the PLO. Even the money, we raised from the Sheikhs before we really started with the people.

This was not a surprise for me: those people [the Sheikhs] are not so highly educated, perhaps they are not so 'progressive' in the modern meaning of the word; *but they are sincere nationalists*. It is not easy to convince them but when you do convince them they are so sincere and they keep their word of honour more than we. With the Kuwaitis for example, or the Saudis or the Qataris, we never had to remind them to send what they have promised.[8]

As their rearguard base in the Gulf states was coalescing behind them, the Fateh leaders also never forgot the imperative of organising the Palestinian refugees in their areas of greatest concentration, that is in the refugee camps ringing Israel's borders. Their own personal links with the camp populations as well as their solid political instinct dictated this move to them. But they were always cognisant of the problems involved in this

199

enterprise. They saw the necessity of co-ordinating with the authoritarian, but avowedly nationalist, regimes in Egypt and Syria, but always guarded against the attempts these regimes would make to rob them of their freedom of action. Whilst the actual regimes in Jordan and Lebanon might not be so strict, the Fateh leaders always saw the security services of both of these countries as dangerously infiltrated by the Israelis.

In 1961, the union between Egypt and Syria, which for the three years of its existence had been proclaimed by Nasser as his finest achievement in the field of Arab unification, broke up with the secession of Syria. The ideological underpinnings of Nasserism, with its stress on Arab unity, were shattered. Specifically, and crucially for the Fateh leaders, it now became clearer than ever that the Nasserite approach would not be able to offer any immediate prospect of the regular Arab armies liberating their land: Nasser himself confirmed this in 1962, when he told a gathering of refugees in Gaza that he had 'no plan' for his army to redress their greivance against Israel. The Fateh people were thus able to attract more credibility than ever before for the ideas of Palestinian self-organisation which they were developing through their Beirut magazine *Filastinuna*.

By 1964, the Fateh leaders felt confident enough to approach the rulers of one of the front-line states – still not Egypt, the power of whose security services they continued to fear might overwhelm them, but Syria – to seek its help in launching their armed struggle against Israel. In the years leading up to 1967, as we have seen above, Syria's rulers espoused a military theory of 'popular liberation war' against Israel, and they were in any case wary of Egypt's influence inside the PLO after it had been formed in 1964. They thus responded favourably to the overtures of the Fateh leaders, and it was with some logistic support from Syria that Fateh's armed struggle against Israel was duly launched at the beginning of 1965.

The relationship between this armed struggle and any contribution the front-line Arab states could make was summed up in an article which appeared in *Filastinuna* in November 1964, even as Fateh's preparations for launching the armed struggle neared their completion:

The revolutionary vanguards of the Palestinian Arab people [i.e. Fateh] see that the true starting-point in the battle of liberation and return, which represents the first stage of our struggle, is as follows:

– That the Palestinian revolutionary vanguards should not be opposed, and that the way should be open for them to grow and to prepare for the launching of the armed Palestinian revolution inside the occupied lands on the basis of the independence of the Palestinian personality; that it should not sell itself to anyone; and on the freedom of its leadership in its work and in determining its zero hour.

– Opening the way for the Palestinian revolutionary vanguards to work with the Arab masses so they may be a support for them...

– The continuation of the official Arabs' military preparations to defend Arab land and oppose any Jewish attempt to attack the land adjacent to the already occupied lands.

– Continuation of Arab preparations for the organised, offensive Arab war against Israel if the circumstances should call for this; and in this case the circumstances would be concerned not only with Israel, but also with all the forces of world colonialism. Therefore the whole of the Arab world should stand absolutely together to undertake its decisive battle for total liberation from all the forces and means of colonialism.[9]

A year and a half after the Fateh leaders launched their armed struggle, their relationship with Syria came to a crisis point when Ahmed Jibril, whom the Syrians had put into Fateh's military command as part of the co-operation deal, clashed with Yasser Arafat.[10] The pro-Syrian officer Youssef al-Urabi was killed in the clash which ensued, as was a Fateh commander called Major Hishmi, and Arafat was thrown into jail by the Syrians.[11] He was fairly quickly released and Fateh as a whole emerged practically unscathed from the whole encounter, vindicating its leaders' original assessment that they were now strong enough to work with Damascus without totally sacrificing their own freedom of action.

In the meantime, the Fateh leaders had been able to cement the links they had started building with the Algerian government in 1962. Over the decades ahead this relationship was to prove to be one of the stablest and most helpful the guerrillas were to enjoy with any Arab regime. But the solid backing which the Algerians (quite actively) and some of the Gulf rulers (more passively) could offer from afar did little to mitigate the fact that, for most of the period up to 1967, the Fateh leaders continued to feel at least as vulnerable to hostile actions from the front-line Arab regimes as they did to the actions of the Israelis.

The defeat the front-line regimes suffered in 1967, which had far-reaching social and political, as well as military, consequences inside their own societies, abruptly reversed the power balance between them and the Palestinian guerrillas of Fateh. Now, suddenly, the Palestinian movement could grow in relative freedom from the interference of the weakened front-line regimes, and this growth certainly was of explosive dimensions. The regimes, meanwhile, desperately searching for any political position which could shore up the shattered legitimacy of their rule at home, to this end seized on what may at first have been a largely rhetorical commitment to the Palestinian resistance movement. The Fateh bosses were made welcome in Cairo, Damascus and all other Arab capitals and, once present in the presidential palaces and royal *diwans*, they proved themselves tough enough negotiators to be able to turn the verbal support of their hosts into the solid logistics and matériel their rapidly burgeoning movement needed.[12]

If the developments which followed June 1967 – with King Hussein saying 'We are all fedayeen now', Nasser giving Fateh a leg-up into the saddle of the PLO, and even the Lebanese government forced to concede considerable powers to the guerrillas in Lebanon – looked like a reconciliation between the guerrilla movement and the front-line Arab regimes, then it soon proved to be only a temporary truce in a relationship where contradictions as well as coincidences of interest are deeply built in.

The complexities of the interaction between Fateh and the different Arab regimes arise not only from the divergences between the potentially destabilising effects of guerrilla action and the Arab states' more cautious *raisons d'état*, but also from the complexities of the modes of intervention the regimes on one hand, and the guerrilla leaders on the other, can utilise inside each other's internal political constituencies.

Fateh had since its inception been committed to the principle of non-intervention in the internal affairs of the existing Arab states, and its leaders always tried to uphold that principle in practice, though on occasion their efforts in this regard proved less than totally successful. In Jordan in 1970 they found themselves unable to control the wave of anti-regime feeling which engulfed many even of their own members; and in Lebanon in early 1976 they eventually felt they had to join the fighting if their credibility within the Palestinian communities was to be saved. However, it should also be noted that Fateh has repeatedly throughout its history (if usually in private) been reproached by members of the Arab left for not reciprocating the support the left so abundantly offered the Palestinian movement.[13]

Yet even a general commitment to non-intervention has not left Fateh without any means of affecting the balance within the various Arab countries inasmuch as it affects their own Palestinian cause. The very existence of an autonomous Palestinian organisation would always – at least until the time when the Palestinians too could enjoy the benefits of statehood – stand as a reproach to the regimes for their inability to muster their huge resources effectively against Israel. In addition, as shown above, Fateh's founders realised from the start that they needed the help and support of the other Arab peoples, and preferably also the other Arab states (and especially their armies), if they were to be able to reach their goals.

What the Fateh leaders relied on in their dealings with the Arab world was the strong national/cultural/religious attachment which the citizens of all the Arab countries shared for the Palestinian cause.[14]. Whereas Fateh organisers could commit themselves quite willingly to not speaking to Arab citizens about their own states' internal policies, the states generally found it hard to stop them speaking to them about Palestine, and the Fateh leaders were always adept at using the pro-Palestinian popular sentiments thus kept alive to lever the regimes into giving them a large measure of the kinds of official support they needed. No Arab ruler needs reminding that Jordan's King Abdullah was shot in 1951 because of his alleged treachery to the Palestinians; or that Egypt's King Farouq was toppled three years later by officers raising his poor performance in the 1948 war with Israel high in the list of charges against him; or that in more modern times Anwar Sadat, the only Arab leader ever formally to make peace with Israel, was dealt with even more harshly by members of his own military.

Fateh's original conception, at the time of the coalescing of its leadership in the early 60s, had been that their organising work would lead to the creation of a Palestinian National Council among the Palestinian communities (the original Fateh concept of this Council was distinct from that of the Council which in 1964 became the PLO's governing body) *and an Arab National Council among the non-Palestinian Arab communities.* The two bodies would then come under a joint leadership. As Khaled al-Hassan explained it, the aim of the Arab National Council would be 'to mobilise the Arab masses in support of the liberation of Palestine. And in that way, either they would contradict with the regimes and there would be a revolution and we would have Arab leaders with the real will to fight, or the Arab leaders would change and fight'.[15]

In the end, however, this was not the strategy the movement followed. What deflected Fateh from the course its original leaders had charted was precisely the explosion of popular support for its guerrilla ideology which occurred in the period after the 1967 war. This upsurge of support catapulted the Fateh leaders into regional prominence in the leadership of the PLO, without allowing them time to build up the intricate twin base organisations they had originally planned. The resulting dilution of the Fateh leaders' effectiveness at the Palestinian level, especially during the Jordan crisis of 1970, was chronicled in chapter 3 above. At the Arab level, the diversion from their original strategy meant that the Fateh leaders ended up dealing with the Arab governments without being able to utilise the kind of disciplined pan-Arab support network they had originally visualised.[16]

Thus was established the internal dynamic within the Fateh leadership between those such as Hassan or Kamal Udwan, who advocated a kind of 'principled pragmatism' in their dealings with Arab governments, and those such as Nimr Saleh and Salah Khalaf, who seemed to advocate a more strictly populist approach to Palestinian-Arab relations. In 1973, for example, Udwan was to explain, 'You deal with this or that regime while you know full well that its position is wrong: but you gamble on being able to change this position through the new realities that you create... There is a difference between error and treachery. For us, treachery is when the wrong position becomes irremediable.'[17] For his part, Khalaf was to say in the late 70s, in the epilogue to the book he produced with Eric Rouleau, that this kind of approach advocated by Udwan had led to a situation where 'we came to be seen less as revolutionaries than as politicians. It goes without saying that this change in our image was very damaging for us among the Arab masses, who had expected more from us.'[18]

If the Arab rulers were always sensitive to the Palestinians' ability to arouse the pro-Palestinian sentiments of their own citizens, then for their part most of them had few qualms about 'intervening' in the Palestinians' own internal affairs. This they sought to achieve both through traditional means of political and financial patronage and through their sponsorship of various client guerrilla groups, and also to a lesser extent, though trying to sponsor dissident movements favourable to their cause within Fateh itself (see chapter 7 above).

Throughout the 70s, these last kinds of intervention only made much headway in two cases. On each occasion this occurred when the representative Fateh had sent to a particular Arab capital became so convinced by the arguments of his hosts that they were able to 'turn' him against his former bosses. This is what happened to Ahmed Abdel-Ghaffar in Libya and to Sabri al-Banna in Iraq, with both defections taking place in the early 70s. But neither Abdel-Ghaffar nor Banna came from the highest echelons of Fateh's organisational framework. Banna, prior to his defection, had been a member of Fateh's 50-person Revolutionary Committee; Abdel-Ghaffar, not even that. The historic leaders of the movement, however (that is the people who had guided it ever since it first coalesced in the early 60s),seem to have been unified enough by their common experiences at the hands of the various Arab regimes never to fall for the blandishments of any of them, as these two men apparently did. In both cases referred to above, the historic leaders were quite easily able to limit to manageable proportions the damage caused to the fabric of their organisation by the defections.

It was in 1968 and early 1969 that a formula was first arrived at for mediating and institutionalising the complex tangle of relations between the Palestinian guerrilla movement, with Fateh at its head, and the consensus of the many strands of the existing Arab state system. The formula consisted in the regimes handing over most of the real power within the PLO – their own creation – to the guerrillas. This solution proved remarkably durable in the 14 years which followed. Throughout that period, the PLO had a double face: on the one hand, through the logistic and political support the Arab states continued to accord it, it represented their continuing commitment to the guerrillas' cause; and on the other, it repre-

sented the commitment of at least the mainstream of the guerrilla movement – and from 1970 onwards, the 'oppositionist' guerrillas as well – to
work in conjunction with rather than against the official Arab state
system. In 1973/4, five years after these ground rules were established, they
were merely capped off by the Arab states' agreement, at the Algiers and
Rabat summits, to recognise the PLO (with its leadership still vested in
Fateh) as the 'sole legitimate representative' of the Palestinian people.

The guerrilla groups' takeover of the PLO in 1969 coincided with, and
was entirely consonant with, a significant shift in Fateh's thinking at that
time. For the dimensions of the disaster the Arab countries had suffered at
the hands of the Israeli army in 1967 had led the Fateh leaders to think that
the 'action and reaction' strategy they had adopted hitherto was somewhat
rash, given the Israelis' strategic superiority and the apparent unreadiness
of the Arab societies to take the measures necessary to redress this balance,
as the Fateh people had hoped would happen. As Khaled al-Hassan
explained this policy shift,

After '67 we had to change the strategy ... because Syria was involved anyway [in
the direct problem of the Israeli occupation of part of her land], Jordan was
involved anyway, and Egypt was involved anyway. And when these three are
involved, all the other other Arabs are involved. So continuing our military actions
– it means *we are with these three*, because they have to fight at least to take back
their own land.

So we continued with another strategy: a strategy of condensing this climate of
hope by our fighting, *to enable Nasser to rebuild his military power, and the
Syrians and the Jordanians: to enable the Arabs to rebuild their power*.[19]

Thus, if in the period prior to 1967 the Fateh leaders had viewed guerrilla
action as a challenge as much to the Arab states as it was to Israel, then in
the months after the June defeat they saw the need to tie their strategy,
including their military strategy, closely into alliance with the military
strategy of the Arab regimes. To some in the Fateh leadership, this switch
represented an ideologically unwelcome accommodation with the Arab
regimes, but even they saw it as a necessary tactical retreat, in view of the
strategic weakness of all the Arab parties, including the Palestinians, at
that time.[20]

For their part, the Arab leaders, even in the front-line states, fully recipro-
cated the Palestinians' new desire for an alliance. In the case of President
Nasser, this leader of the weightiest of the front-line regimes became, once
his original fears regarding Fateh had been overcome by a face-to-face
meeting with some of its leaders in 1968, transformed from being Fateh's
'enemy number one', to being its 'supporter number one in active politics,
and in military support and training'.[21] In the recollection of Nasser's
confidant Muhamed Hassanain Heikal, who had played a key role in

bringing Nasser and the Fateh leaders together, the terms of this alliance were that the Palestinian guerrillas could be the Arab world's 'Stern Gang or Irgun' – presumably, to Egypt's and the other Arab states' Jewish Agency.

If some members of the guerrilla movement thought the post-1967 alliance with the front-line Arab regimes meant they would now be allowed to dictate these regimes' strategy, then in September 1970 they received a rude shock when the front-line regimes, with Jordan at the forefront, acted ruthlessly to circumscribe the guerrilla movement's power. The responses of all the different Arab regimes to the 1970-71 fighting in Jordan provided a textbook case of the nuances of Palestinian-Arab relations which remained virtually unchanged throughout the 12 years which followed, despite the broad shifts which occurred in the Middle Eastern balance of power in that period.

As Hussein's bedouin troops moved in September 1970 to snuff out the guerrillas' independent military base in Jordan, the Iraqi troops stationed in that country did nothing to help the guerrillas, while the effectiveness of the Syrian troops who did intervene briefly on the Palestinians' side was undercut by the refusal of the man who was shortly to become President of Syria, Hafez al-Asad, to commit his air force to the intervention. For his part, Egypt's President Nasser seemed to be moved by a desire to see the guerrilla movement cut down to size or, at least, as President Sadat was to describe Egypt's aim in July 1971, 'to give a chance to the clean fedayeen elements, such as Fatah ... and to cleanse ... the suspect elements'.[22] In the weeks preceding September 1970, Nasser announced his acceptance of the American Rogers plan. When the PLO's broadcasting house in Cairo continued to criticise the plan, Nasser closed it down, starting a crisis in relations with the Fateh/PLO leaders.

Nevertheless, as tensions mounted in Jordan in the early days of September, it was Nasser who hosted a summit meeting of Arab kings and presidents, at which the situation in Jordan was the major topic under discussion. While Arafat, Khalaf, Qaddumi and most other members of the Fateh Central Committee were busy in Jordan trying to limit the damage from the showdown there, Khaled al-Hassan was working in Cairo trying to line up the summiteers to give them effective support. In his view, while Iraq, Syria and Egypt were all happy to one degree or another to see the Palestinians 'taught a lesson' in Jordan, the response of other Arab heads of state was different:

In September [1970], I think we had an Arab support, in a political way, their own way...

The Saudis, they were supporting us, but in their own way. You know the Saudis do not take initiatives...

It's the same with the Moroccans, for instance. They were very clear with Hussein. They told him, 'It's impossible for you to rule the educated Palestinians by the uneducated others. So either you let them rule with you, or it's better for you to leave, alive, by your own wish; which is much better than leaving either kicked out or killed.'... The Tunisians were 100% against the behaviour of the King.[23]

This weight of Arab political support for the Palestinians, expressed in Cairo by a group of states which included the main contributors of outside aid to the Egyptian (and Jordanian) national budgets, meant that the consensus of the summit was basically supportive of the Palestinians in its diplomatic overtures with the protagonists in Jordan. On 19 September, President Nasser despatched his Chief of Staff, Muhammed Sadeq, to Amman to oversee a cease-fire, in order to be able at least to contact Yasser Arafat. On that and each of the succeeding two days Nasser addressed urgent cables to Hussein calling for immediate implementation of a cease-fire. In the cable of 21 September he stressed that

The United Arab Republic [i.e. Egypt] believes in the importance of the role of the Palestinian resistance, in its legality and in its effectiveness in the constant struggle against the enemy...
I must honestly tell you that we shall not allow the Palestinian resistance to be liquidated.[24]

The following day, the summit despatched a mediation commission to Amman made up of Sadeq, Sudanese President Jaafar Numairy, the Tunisian Premier, the Kuwaiti Defence Minister, and lower-ranking Saudi and Egyptian representatives. The days the eminent members of the commission spent in Amman were fraught with danger. They were fired upon by the Jordanian forces, who also shelled the site of their planned meeting with Arafat, and they were eye-witnesses to some of the most terrible parts of the carnage in Amman. As Numairy reported to a press conference afterwards,

On our way back from the Hummar Palace to the UAR Embassy in Amman after this meeting [with Hussein] and after the [cease-fire] announcements had been made over the radio, shelling was continuing and guns were firing in various sectors of Amman, being particularly alarming in the Palestinian areas... The Ashrafiyeh hospital was shelled and hundreds of children, women and disabled people were taken and put on the street, where motorised vehicles were brought to crush them. They kidnapped doctors and nurses and threatened to kill them unless the fida'iyin and Palestinians evacuated the whole area.[25]

Numairy's conclusion was:

We came out of Amman with the collective conviction that there was a full plan to exterminate all men of the valiant Palestinian Resistance and all the Palestinians in Amman. The plan is being carried out despite all promises and agreements... The

Jordanian authority has been and still is resorting to falsification and deception for the purposes of gaining time so that it can carry out its plan.[26]

Since this report was given wide prominence on Egyptian government radio and in many other Arab media, it was clear that the scale of his army's actions had left Hussein with little Arab political backing. But the general political support the Arab summiteers were affording the Palestinians was still not transformed into enough concrete military or logistic support to save their forces from extinction in Jordan. As Nasser himself reportedly explained it to Arafat on 27 September;

I have told you from the very first moment that we cannot help you by direct military intervention on our part, because that would be a mistake, because it would mean that I was abandoning the fight with Israel to make war in Jordan. *Also it would open the door to foreign intervention which can be expected at any moment.*

I am trying to gain time so that I can increase your capacity to resist and reach a reasonable solution.[27]

That same day, the summiteers were finally able to broker a cease-fire between Hussein and the PLO which had more effect than its many predecessors. But the political backing which the summit had expressed for the Palestinians was not sufficient in the months ahead to deter Hussein from resuming, and completing, his campaign against such guerrillas as remained in his Kingdom.

A year and a half after September 1970, and in the context primarily of the continuing Jordanian-PLO contest for influence inside the West Bank, but also of the shadowy terror exploits aimed against Jordanian targets by the Black September Organisation (BSO), Hussein was to launch his United Arab Kingdom plan for the reunification of the East and West Bank regions under his own crown. While the PLO Executive Committee met to map out the Organisation's official reaction to the plan, Fateh's Revolutionary Council was also discussing the same subject. As a result of these meetings, on 17 March 1972 Fateh issued a communiqué which denounced the Jordanian plan, saying, 'Neither the King nor any other outside party has any right to speak in the name of this [Palestinian] people.' But the Fateh statement went further than that when it said, 'The overthrow of the monarchy in Jordan now imposes itself as the provisional aim which will return matters to their natural status and will place the relations between the Palestinian and Jordanian peoples in their true framework'.[28]

This was the first time ever that Fateh had committed itself to the overthrow of the Jordanian regime – or of any Arab regime – and it should be noted that this step was taken not in response to all the harsh military attacks to which the guerrillas and their supporters had been subject for 18 months in Jordan, but as a reply to the overt political threat posed by Hussein's claim to represent a substantial part of the Palestinian consti-tuency. The bitterness caused by the whole United Arab Kingdom affair then continued right up until October 1974, when Hussein reluctantly submitted to the ruling of the 1973 and 1974 Arab summits that the PLO was the 'sole legitimate representative' of the Palestinian people. He and Arafat were not to meet face to face until January 1977.

Throughout all the years of the Jordanian-PLO power contest which followed September 1970, it is noteworthy that the other Arab regimes lessened the support they professed for the Palestinians only on one occasion – after the bloody BSO operation in the Sudanese capital, Khar-toum, in 1972 which left a Saudi diplomat and the U.S. Ambassador dead and Sudanese President Numairy's national honour sorely wounded. Apart from the criticisms raised by that affair, which led directly to the Fateh leaders' imposition of strict sanctions against the BSO, the consensus of official Arab political support for the PLO remained solid. It was, as we saw in chapter 3 above, in collaboration with the PLO/Fateh leaders, rather than with Hussein, that Egypt and Syria launched their offensive against Israel of October 1973.

By the middle of 1976 the Palestinian guerrilla movement again found itself at odds with an Arab regime: this time, Hafez al-Asad's Syria. The reaction of the other Arab states was complicated by the fact that two of them in particular – Egypt and Iraq – appeared to be providing quite hefty encouragement to those parts of the Palestinian movement which were inclined to force the confrontation with Syria to the utmost. The Syrian-Palestinian contest in Lebanon thus had deep-seated inter-Arab ramifica-tions. Thus, while on this occasion, unlike 1970, the role played by non-Arab interventions or threats of intervention was minimal, and inter-Arab diplomacy thus had the potential of being far more effective than in 1970, nevertheless, the obstacles to arriving at an inter-Arab consensus were this time correspondingly greater.

This time, again, the 'division of roles' between the Fateh leaders meant that while Khalaf and to a lesser extent Arafat were kept busy directing affairs at the scene of the battles in Lebanon, Hassan was again orchestrat-ing the campaign for support from Fateh's rearguard base of Arab support in the Gulf. Only this time the 'division of roles' also masked very real differences between, at the extremes, Khalaf and Hassan, with the other senior Fateh leaders taking various different positions in between these two. Hassan had even registered his disapproval of the policies being followed by such as Khalaf, Saleh and others in Lebanon to the extent of formally resigning from the Fateh Central Committee (see chapter 4 above). But as the situation in Lebanon worsened through the autumn of 1976, and in response to special pleas from Khalil Wazir once he had taken over the military command in the Lebanese mountains, Hassan started activating his official Arab contacts to work towards the only kind of solution he saw as effective in the circumstances: a reconciliation between the Syrian and Egyptian Presidents.

I started working again to have a meeting between Asad and Sadat. Then at that time [mid-October 1976] there was an Arab League meeting, to discuss the Lebanese question, and [King Hassan of Morocco's special advisor] Ben Souda came here to Kuwait with letters from the King for the same purpose, and we started co-ordinating with each other. Then the word No was always said. I convinced Sadat to say Yes, but I could not convince Asad to say Yes.

Then we went to [Saudi Arabia's] Crown Prince Fahd and King Khaled. Finally, when I was in the plane from Kuwait – it was the private plane of the Kuwaiti Emir – going from Kuwait to Cairo to participate in the Arab League meeting... I got a cable that Fahd finally succeeded in taking the Yes of Asad, and so now Sadat and Asad were ready to meet...

The next day, the summit started. There were a lot of discussions between Prince Fahd and Sadat, Prince Fahd and Asad. Finally they agreed to let them both meet. It took them only 10 minutes, and they came out of the room hand to hand, smiling, and the first session of the conference started immediately after that. Instead of discussions we started drafting the cease-fire immediately: I wrote it in my hand-writing.

When we finished, it was agreed... The next day, the war stopped.[29]

In other words, in 1976 as six years previously, the Fateh leaders were able to use their special relationship with such 'rearguard' Arab regimes as Saudi Arabia, Kuwait and Morocco to put pressure on a front-line Arab regime which was fighting their followers right up near the front line against Israel. The results in 1976, inasmuch as they did not include the total annihilation of the Palestinians' forces in Lebanon, were more successful than had been the results in 1970.

Nevertheless, as chronicled in chapters 5 and 6 above, the overall strategic strength of the Arab state system was eroding rapidly from the seeming high point it attained in late 1973, when Egyptian-Syrian unity at the battlefront had been backed up by nearly solid-front economic sanctions imposed against Israel's supporters in the West by the rearguard states of the Gulf. The effective 'defection' of Egypt from Arab ranks which resulted from Sadat's unilateral pursuit of his peace initiative with Israel was only the most egregious in a series of developments which weakened the Arab states' strategic position in the years from 1974 to 1982. Other such developments included the ever multiplying inter-Arab disputes, changes in the structure and organisation of the world oil market, and the success of Dr Kissinger's strategy of weaning the 'nationalist' Arab regimes away from their previous links with the Soviets.

By 1982, the Palestinian guerrillas again found themselves in an all-out confrontation. Once again, the basic parameters of the battle had shifted: this time, the adversary was not an Arab state, but Israel itself, though acting in co-ordination with local Lebanese allies. Given the terms of this confrontation, Arab rulers, including even King Hussein, could not but express their general political support for the Palestinians, but the very fact of direct Israeli involvement in the battle denied them any of the possibilities for the discreet but direct political mediation between the battling parties which they had employed in their political efforts of 1970 and 1976. If the Arab states were to put their political weight behind the PLO in 1982, they would have to do so through the United States; and this they did, most notably through the lightning visit of Saudi Foreign Minister Prince Saud al-Faisal to the Western summit meeting at Versailles, and then the visit of Prince Saud and his Syrian counterpart, Abdel-Halim Khaddam, to Washington in late July. They were accompanied on this visit by Khaled al-Hassan. He remained in a nearby hotel room while the two Ministers met President Reagan, but at one point Prince Saud wanted to clarify a point with him and telephoned him from the White house.

However, at no point during the two and a half months of the Israeli-Palestinian fighting in Lebanon did the Arab states or their representatives ever breathe so much as a word about bending the vast weight of their economic resources to their diplomatic initiative over Lebanon, and so the U.S. administration never really saw that it was in its own interest to apply much more than cosmetic pressure on the Israeli government at stages where the American public's horror at Israel's widely publicised excesses in Lebanon made it seem expedient, in U.S. terms, to be seen to be 'doing something'. So long as the attempts by the Arab states, including even Egypt, to intercede on the Palestinians' behalf with the U.S. administration were limited to purely rhetorical pleading, the most they could achieve was an undertaking that, *following a PLO evacuation from Beirut*, the U.S. government would start to address the broader issues of Middle East peace. That pledge was redeemed in President Reagan's comprehensive peace initiative of 1 September 1982, but the initiative met a blanket Israeli rejection, and over the months which followed the Reagan administration appeared unwilling to press forward into an open confrontation with Israel on this issue.

A second (and secondary) way in which the Arab states could hope politically to affect the balance in Lebanon in 1982 was through whatever influence they could still exert on Israel's principal allies in Lebanon, the Phalangist militia led by Bashir Gemayyel. This card they attempted to play during the meeting of Foreign Ministers of six Arab states held in the Saudi summer capital of Taif at the end of July 1982. According to Khaled al-Hassan, the Taif conferees repeatedly came up against a blank wall when they tried to negotiate with the Lebanese government representative at the talks, Joseph Skaff, since he stressed that he was not empowered to negotiate at all over the text of the statement he had brought with him. The conferees then tried to contact President Sarkis, but he was reported to be 'sick' and unable to talk to them, and Lebanese Foreign Minister Fuad Boutros, when contacted, said that he too was unable to negotiate 'without the agreement of all parties'.

At that point, the conferees decided to invite Bashir Gemayyel to come to Taif in person to do his own negotiating. He arrived forthwith, and met with the Kuwaiti and Saudi representatives. They reported back to the conference that

the stand of Bashir was very positive to our suggestions... He left on the Sunday, and news came later that Sharon was waiting for him in Beirut and he said, 'Look, Bashir, if you want to go on with the Arab League you will be one of seven in the political bureau of the Ketaeb [Phalangists].' That was kind of a threat that he would not be President. 'Otherwise, you will have to deal with us.'[30]

Within a month, Gemayyel had indeed been elected to be his country's next President, and the first official Israeli reactions to this news accorded it an extremely warm welcome.[31]

Thus, neither of the two major strands of the 'rearguard' Arab states' political intervention in the PLO's 1982 crisis appeared by early 1983 to have achieved very much, while the military intervention of the Syrians in the battles of 1982 was widely blamed by the Palestinians for having itself contributed to many of their woes.

Nevertheless, the failure of the 'rearguard' Arab states to take any effective action to save the PLO fighters' position in Lebanon was still not translated, as some American commentators had hoped, into an abandonment of their general political support for the PLO/Fateh leaders. Indeed, within the intricately nuanced web of relations tying the PLO/Fateh leaders to the Arab states, the very failure of the latter to make much impact on the situation in Lebanon, standing as it did in strong contrast to the effectiveness of the defence of Beirut mounted for ten long weeks by the PLO fighters and the Lebanese allies against the full force of the Israeli army, only strengthened the Palestinians in their political dealings with the Arab governments throughout the months following their evacuation from Beirut. This effect was apparent in the case of members of both major classes of Arab regime, 'front-line' and 'rearguard'.

In the months following the PLO's evacuation from Beirut it became clear that, although the basic modes of the Fateh leaders' interaction with the Arab governments remained basically unchanged, several changes had occurred in the delicate balances of forces within these modes of interaction.

At the level of the ability of the Arab regimes to intervene within the Palestinian body politic, the dispersal of the main fighting body of the Palestinian national movement away from the centre of concentration it had enjoyed in Lebanon (and before that, in Jordan) clearly decreased the capacity of the Fateh leadership to defend their hegemony over the Palestinian movement. The clearest internal threat this permitted to the Fateh/ PLO leaders was that backed by Syria and Libya in the last months of 1982 and the early months of 1983. This threat was not limited to the two allied regimes attempting to line up a new front of oppositionist non-Fateh groups inside the PLO; they were also able to sponsor a schismatic movement inside Fateh itself at a considerably higher level than any other previous attempt of this nature. When Nimr Saleh started, in the latter months of 1982, to mount his open challenge to the main body of Fateh leaders from Damascus, he did so from the authority of his seat on the Fateh Central Committee, and with his history as one of the earliest generation of Fateh organisers behind him.

In January 1983, Saleh's colleagues in the Central Committee 'froze' his membership in the Committee and stripped him of all the duties which had been his inside the Fateh military. The following month, at the sixteenth PNC session, they appeared to be celebrating the victory of their attempts to stave off the Syrian- and Libyan-backed challenges both from Saleh and from non-Fateh Palestinian figures such as Ahmed Jibril. But even the mood of Palestinian national unity which was celebrated in that PNC session carried undertones of fear for the future, with further challenges to the traditional Fateh leaders' position still considered possible, especially from either of the two front-line regimes still remaining within the Arab camp – Syria and Jordan.[32]

The extent of the Palestinian leaders' ability to capitalise, in their dealings with the various Arab governments, on the pro-Palestinian sentiments of these governments' own constituencies had also changed in the period leading up to and following the 1982 Battle of Beirut. Some Fateh leaders expressed disappointment, in early 1983, that 'the Arab masses' had not been moved more by the Palestinians' sufferings in Beirut.[33] One Palestinian in Beirut remarked that the only demonstration which took place in the Arab world during the entire Battle of Beirut had been a parade of football supporters celebrating a notorious win for the national team in Algiers. He exaggerated, a little, for there were demonstrations in support of the Palestinians in both Egypt and Kuwait in that time. No other Arab community actually went as far as those members of the Maronite community in Lebanon who had so viciously repudiated the Palestinians in their midst, but many sections of the 'Arab masses' were so stunned by such local developments as the Syrian government's huge-scale attack on its own citizens in Hama in early 1982, or the continuing bloodshed in the Gulf war or in the Sahara, that they had few reflexes still intact for the Palestinians.

The major exception to this trend as of early 1983 appeared to be the internal situation in the Arab world's weightiest society, the Fateh leaders' old *bête noire*, Egypt. Concomitant with his 1977 peace initiative towards Israel, and partly perhaps in reaction to his subsequent isolation from the other Arab states, President Sadat had tried to turn Egypt's 43 million people away from the omnipresent pan-Arabism of Nasser's day, and towards a greater stress on purely Egyptian nationalism. This move had been accompanied by officially sanctioned public criticisms of the Palestinians exactly similar to those directed in an earlier era against the Jews in Egypt (that they controlled all the real estate, paid others to do their dirty work, etc., etc.). But through the political crisis of 1981 in Egypt, the great majority of opinion-formers inside Egypt were able to affirm their rejection of Sadat's new cultural line, and it seemed clear, from the moment of his succession in October 1981, that President Hosni Mubarak felt himself to be under considerable internal pressure to keep Egypt within the general cultural milieu of Arabism and pro-Palestinianism. Fateh leaders such as Revolutionary Council member Nabil Shaath thus expressed themselves optimistic in early 1983 concerning the prospects of harnessing this internal Egyptian pressure to help steer the Egyptian government back towards more pro-Palestinian positions.

Meanwhile, the support offered the Palestinian movement at both the official and the popular level in the traditional rearguard countries continued to be apparently solid and well-intentioned. That support had always played precisely a rearguard and never – either militarily or politically – an up-front role in aiding the Palestinians' struggle. With no one effectively playing such an up-front role, it appeared, as of early 1983, that the Palestinians were, for a longer or shorter time, to remain trapped in the chronic impotence to act decisively which had afflicted the Arab world since early 1974. It was ironic that the major points of potential dynamic for the Palestinians, at the Arab level, remained the internal situations in the two front-line states whose populations the Israelis had hoped, by early 1983, to have 'pacified': the Arabs' *Umm ad-dunia* (the Mother of the World), Egypt, and tiny Lebanon, where the indigenous armed resistance to the Israeli occupation continued to simmer more than half a year after the evacuation of the PLO fighters from Beirut.

Chapter 10

International relations

Ever since the issuing of the Balfour Declaration in 1917 and its subsequent endorsement by the League of Nations, Palestinian Arab community leaders have understood that, in common with other victims of colonial systems, their chances for political development would be subject to a vast input from external forces. Vital decisions affecting the political balance in Jaffa, Lydda or Jerusalem would henceforth be made in London, in Geneva or (later) Washington. The Zionist colonisers of Palestine understood this fact as well. Since the very birth of modern political Zionism, the Zionists' efforts to build up the Jewish community in Palestine had proceeded hand in hand with attempts to influence the decision-making process in the Western centres of power. Themselves generally of European origin, the pioneers of pre-1948 Zionism could move easily in British or other imperial circles, relying on a wide range of local Jewish and non-Jewish contacts to back up their efforts.

The Palestinian Arabs' diplomatic efforts in those years, by contrast, were feeble, timid, supplicatory and hampered by the bare fact that the Palestinian Arab supplications to the imperial power were always coming from outsiders. Unable to beat back the Zionist-imperialist challenge either on the ground in Palestine (though they made a staunch try in 1936-39) or in the chanceries of world power, the Palestinians lost their land in 1948. Though several of their previous diplomatic supplicants continued to make almost routine appeals to the United Nations or other bodies in succeeding years, their voices were lost because their hearers knew they represented nothing: Palestinian political society had been broken by the 1948 disaster.

With the rise of the guerrilla movement a decade and a half later, it is scarcely surprising to find that from the very beginning the guerrillas linked their emphasis on direct armed struggle with tentative first efforts at international diplomacy. Veteran Fateh organiser Hani al-Hassan was only repeating a basic element of the movement's founding ideology when he repeated, in 1980, 'In the Palestinian arena we should not forget that the armed struggle sows and the political struggle reaps.'[1] As described in chapter 2 above, Fateh sent its first recorded communication to the Secretary-General of the United Nations back in June 1965, only a few months after launching its armed struggle. Throughout the following 18 years, the Fateh leaders responded creatively to any overtures made to involve them in a political settlement of the Palestinian problem and also sought to launch a number of their own initiatives towards the same end.

The Fateh leaders' declared ideology, as described in chapter 2 above, was always one of avoiding any identification with potentially divisive social or political ideologies, in pursuance of the national cause, and this approach was carried over as the basis for its approach to world politics. Nevertheless, the fact that most Palestinians perceive their condition to have been caused by the interventions of successive Western powers in their political process has predisposed a clear majority of Palestinians, including the leaders of the modern nationalist movement, towards an anti-imperialist stance of a more or less radical nature – though it should be stressed that only in a small proportion of cases did this lead Fateh activists to embrace much of a pro-Soviet or even generally 'leftist' outlook. A commoner reaction than this, and one entirely consonant with the political traditions of the Muslim society which is a majority in the Palestinian community, was a tendency towards asserting the viability of a third ideological position, neither capitalist nor communist.

In international as in Arab relations, a very basic pragmatism was always the order of the Fateh day. 'Are they with us or against us?' 'How could we benefit from this relation?' 'Is there a danger the costs might outrun the benefits?' These, rather than any weighty ideological issues, are the types of question the Fateh leaders ask when approaching international questions. This approach has taken their diplomacy around the world, adding to the existing base of political support they enjoyed in the Arab world, at successive stages, relations with the People's Republic of China, the Soviet Union, Western Europe and – extremely tentatively – the United States, gathering a wide base of support from the countries of the Third World on the way.

China since 1964

On 17 March 1964, two of the men who had founded Fateh in the preceding years, Yasser Arafat and Khalil al-Wazir, travelled to Beijing under Algerian auspices. Their visit laid the basis for a relationship with the People's Republic of China which was to prove strategically vital to Fateh for the whole of the following decade. Though by the early 70s the strategic importance of the Chinese link to the Palestinians' struggle had been diluted somewhat by the multiplication of the Palestinian movement's other international connections, it was to remain an object of general Palestinian goodwill at least until the early 80s. One source estimated at $5 million the value of the Chinese arms shipped to the Palestinians in the four years between 1965 and 1969 alone.[2] In early 1983, Fateh co-founder Khaled al-Hassan was to recall that Saudi Arabia and China were still the only sources of donated arms which the Palestinians had found to be totally reliable and regular.[3]

Arafat and Wazir's first visit to Beijing took place just as Fateh was starting to prepare for the armed struggle which it was to launch the following January. The two visitors did not, however, make a direct request to their hosts for arms, but, after talks with Liao Ch'eng-chih, the Chairman of the Chinese Committee for Afro-Asian Solidarity (CCAAS), both sides agreed that Fateh should station a permanent semi-official representative in Beijing to serve as a channel for continuing communication.[4]

The Chinese were not limiting their Palestinian contacts to Fateh. In February 1964, the month before Arafat and Wazir arrived in Beijing, Ahmed Shuqairy had been in touch with the Chinese Embassy in Cairo, as part of his preparations for the establishment of the PLO. When the First Palestinian National Council convened in Jerusalem in May 1964, the CCAAS sent it a message of greeting. In March 1965, Shuqairy – now Chairman of the PLO – undertook his first visit to China. While there, he and the delegation accompanying him were able to meet Chairman Mao Tse-tung and other high state and party officials. In a statement published at the conclusion of the visit, the two sides revealed that they had agreed that the PLO should set up a mission in Beijing, 'to strengthen mutual co-operation'. The Chinese side promised to 'make every effort to support the Arab people of Palestine in their struggle to return to their homeland by all means, political *and otherwise*'.[5]

Shuqairy, unlike his Fateh predecessors in Beijing, showed no hesitation in asking his hosts for military aid for the PLO's Palestinian Liberation Army, though he was less than well prepared in the key area of planning the logistics of any future arms deliveries.[6] Some Chinese military matériel nevertheless later did find its way to the PLA prior to the Middle East war of 1967.[7]

As we have seen already, the defeat of the front-line Arab states in the 1967 war weakened the political standing of both the states themselves and the official PLO structure, while providing a unique opportunity for the Palestinian guerrilla movement to grow in numbers and in power. On the Chinese side, the period 1967-70 saw the height of China's own radical 'Cultural Revolution'. Throughout these years, the Chinese saw the Soviets and the U.S. as working together in the Middle East, in their support of the cease-fire ordained in Security Council resolution 242 of November 1967. The new power of the guerrilla movement with which the Chinese had already been in contact for two years must therefore have presented an interesting opportunity to try to confront these two-power efforts in the region. The policy the Chinese leaders advocated for the Middle East at that time therefore centred on the Arab people, particularly the Palestinians, waging a 'continuous popular struggle until victory' against Israel, the U.S. imperialists and the 'Soviet revisionists'.

The explosive growth of the guerrilla movement must meanwhile have been pushing them to reconsider the duality of, and the balance in, their relations with Fateh and with the PLO. By the first anniversary of the start of the war, on 5 June 1968, the official New China News Agency was referring openly to Fateh's 'leadership' of the Palestinian struggle.[8] Indeed, as Fateh's Khaled al-Hassan recalled it, some of the crucial mid-1968 meetings at which Fateh's takeover of the PLO apparatus was planned were held in the home of the Chinese Ambassador to Cairo, who went as far as supporting Hassan's own theory that Fateh should undertake this political coup on its own, without associating any other Palestinian groups in the move.[9] The Chinese then sent a high-ranking delegation, led by an up-and-coming Chinese diplomat called Huang Hua, to the proceedings of the Fourth PNC (July 1968), at which Fateh's takeover bid showed its first signs of success.[10] China was the only non-Arab country to receive a special tribute in the resolutions of this important PNC session. Throughout the whole of the period of Fateh's explosive growth in Jordan in 1968-70, Chinese weapons supplies provided many of the basic military staples for the movement's multiplying guerrilla formations.[11]

The first major test of the Chinese 'continuous popular struggle' policy in the Middle East, as put into practice by the Palestinians, came in Jordan in September 1970. However, there is some indication that the Chinese side's apparent advocacy, in Jordan, of continued armed struggle was slightly removed from that of the Fateh leaders, the majority of whom were still trying to hold back their rank and file in an attempt to avoid a final showdown with the King. According to Hashim Behbehani's sources, the events of September 1970 caused the Chinese to reconsider their previous wholehearted support for Fateh within the Palestinian movement, 'because the latter was unable to sustain the Palestinian revolution and presence in Jordan'.[12] However, Fateh veteran Khaled al-Hassan was later to deny that the Chinese had ever diluted their support for Fateh.[13]

Whatever the truth of this, the China-Fateh relationship which had been so close in the immediate aftermath of 1967 showed some signs of becoming less exclusive after 1970-71. The Fateh leaders came to see their interests as broadly parallel to those of the major confrontation states –

Egypt and Syria – and in the late 60s and early 70s most of these parallel lines seemed to be leading towards Moscow. The Chinese, meanwhile, the heat gone out of their Cultural Revolution, were shifting in the early 70s back towards a more 'responsible' stance in international politics – a development linked to their acceptance into the United Nations in October 1971, after 22 years of American boycott of their membership. Once safely installed in their permanent member's seat in the Security Council, the Chinese did not once wield the veto this seat afforded them to block any resolutions opposed by the Palestinians.[14] In 1972, the Chinese discontinued the practice they had first instituted in 1965, of holding a week-long celebration of 'solidarity with Palestine' every May.[15]

On 17 July 1972, Yasser Arafat arrived in Moscow at the head of the second PLO delegation officially invited there and, shortly afterwards, the first Soviet arms shipments were reported to be reaching the Palestinian guerrillas through Syrian ports. The Chinese were obviously watching the development of Soviet-Fateh relations carefully, and in July 1973 a Chinese 'people's friendship association' invited the first DFLP delegation to visit Beijing. In the years which followed, the Chinese capital was to host a constant flow of delegations (at varying levels) from non-Fateh Palestinian groups.[16] The Fateh leaders, meanwhile, appeared to have made some kind of decision that whilst Arafat would be the person primarily in charge of the developing relationship with Moscow, most questions regarding Beijing would continue to be handled by Khalil al-Wazir.

During the 1973 Middle East war, the Chinese representative in the Security Council – the same Huang Hua – 'did not participate' in voting on the cease-fire resolution (no. 338), since he considered its terms insufficient in providing for 'the restoration of the national rights of the Palestinian people'.[17] In the diplomatic manoeuvring which followed the consolidation of the cease-fire, Dr Kissinger was able largely to ignore any Chinese input into the Middle East situation as he grappled with the larger problem of trying to limit and even eradicate Soviet influence in the region.

The decision taken by Fateh and the rest of the PLO mainstream in the aftermath of the 1973 war, to opt for inclusion in the postwar diplomatic process, is one which might at first have caused some concern to Chinese decision-makers, for it would surely take the mainstream of the Palestinian movement closer into the orbit of the two superpowers, and, in the case of the Soviet Union at least, this development was already apparent. But Fateh was pretty rapidly able to demonstrate that it could command clear majority support in Palestinian ranks for its new diplomatic initiative, so any Chinese misgivings were necessarily somewhat muted. They were demonstrated through such gestures as Beijing's notable silence on the whole topic of Arafat's November 1974 appearance at the United Nations in New York, and the presence in Beijing on that very day of a delegation from the PFLP, whose opposition to the PLO's diplomatic initiative had now been made public.[18]

Chinese-Palestinian relations continued in a low key throughout the latter half of the 70s. One Western author noted, for instance, that during the events of summer 1976 in Lebanon, 'China ignored its cue to likewise support the Palestinians. Instead, Peking ... raised a hue and cry over Soviet intervention in Lebanon and did not comment on the Syrian incursion into Lebanon at all.'[19] In general, however, the PLO/Fateh leaders expressed understanding of the constraints on the political support the Chinese could give the PLO. As Khaled al-Hassan noted in early 1983,

For sure, in the political scene they did not offer us much because they are not active as a big power in the political scene. But they always supported our stand in the Security Council, for example... They never harmed us anyhow; and when they abstained, we understood: it was because of their bilateral relations with the Soviets.[20]

China's response towards President Sadat's peace initiative with Israel found its initial focus on the opportunities this might offer for the diminution of the Soviet role in the Middle East, rather than on its effects for the Palestinians and the other Arabs. The Chinese reaction at all stages of the initiative was carefully to abstain from pronouncing either clear support for it or opposition to it.[21] The period following the conclusion of the Camp David accords thus saw the first criticisms of Chinese policy ever to be voiced openly by any Fateh leader. In this case it was Nimr Saleh, who in March 1979 issued a statement openly critical of Beijing. Three weeks later, the official PLO weekly, *Filastin al-Thawra*, carried an article headed 'Implicit Chinese support for the Egyptian-Israeli treaty'.[22]

However, the Chinese were also meanwhile going to great lengths to point out to the Palestinian leadership that their refusal publicly to condemn the Sadat initiative did not imply a lessening of support for the Palestinian movement in itself. In the period following the conclusion of the Camp David accords, Chinese-PLO contacts multiplied, with three major PLO/Fateh delegations visiting Beijing between November 1978 and August 1980.

In June 1979, Chinese Premier Hua Guo-feng (who also chaired the powerful Communist Party Central Committee) delivered a keynote speech to the Chinese People's Congress, in which he reiterated his country's support for the Palestinians' national rights, spelling out that these included 'the right to return to their homes and to create their own national state'.[23] In other words, China now appeared to be giving open backing, however qualified, to the PLO leaders' pursuit of a political settlement, however qualified. The following year, Beijing reinstituted its annual celebration of Palestine Week.

In October 1981, Yasser Arafat underlined the importance which the PLO leadership continued to attach to its relations with China, when he made his first return visit to Beijing for 11 years. He met the new chairman of the Communist Party Central Committee, Deng Xiao-ping, and other leading dignitaries of the Chinese hierarchy, and reportedly was able to conclude new agreements for arms deliveries.

True to expectations, the Chinese did not play a very important role during the diplomatic process which surrounded the 1982 Battle of Beirut. But the following February they restated their continued support for the existing PLO leadership and its policy emphases when Premier Zhao Ziyang sent a message to the Sixteenth PNC session. The message spelt out that

Under the leadership of the Palestine Liberation Organization, their sole legal representative, the Palestinian people are now making tremendous new efforts to regain their legitimate national rights after having frustrated the Israeli authorities' scheme to wipe out the Palestinian armed forces last year... I believe that the Palestinian people will *close their ranks*, persevere in struggle... and win final victory.[24]

Zhao's emphasis on the internal unity of the PLO must have been welcomed by the Fateh leaders, for whom this question constituted the major issue at stake in the PNC session.

The Soviet Union since 1968

It was in the middle of 1968 that Egypt's President Nasser first introduced Yasser Arafat to the Soviets. According to Nasser's confidant Mohamed Heikal,

I suggested to Nasser that, as the Fedayin's arms requirements seemed to be getting beyond the range of what Egypt could easily supply, the best plan would be to introduce them to the Russians so that they could conduct their own negotiations. Thus it was that Arafat went with Nasser to Moscow in July 1968.[25]

In the Soviet capital, still according to Heikal, Nasser was able to introduce Arafat to Premier Alexei Kosygin, Communist Party Chairman Leonid Brezhnev and President Nikolai Podgorny. Two or three weeks after those discussions, the Soviet Ambassador in Cairo informed Nasser that 'the Soviet Central Committee, *on Nasser's recommendation*, had decided to give the Palestinian resistance movement arms worth $500,000'.[26]

Despite that auspicious beginning to their relationship, both the Soviets and at least some members of the Fateh leadership continued to entertain

221

serious doubts about the intentions of the other. Such Soviet arms supplies as did reach the Palestinian guerrillas over the next four years continued to do so under the strict supervision of the Egyptian authorities, and, for quite some time even after 1968, the Soviets' Chinese rivals continued to be the guerrillas' most generous non-Arab source of weaponry.

On the Soviet side, the prior existence of this relationship between Fateh and the Chinese was an important cause contributing to their doubt and distrust of the Palestinian guerrilla movement. A typical Soviet view of the guerrilla movement in the pre-1970 period was that provided by this commentary, published in April 1969 in a Soviet English-language publication:

The policy conducted by the Maoists in the third world of stirring up conflicts and encouraging extremist, nationalistic circles has been clearly manifested in the Arab countries, where the Mao Tse-tung group is attempting to strengthen its influence on Palestinian organisations which come out against a political settlement of the Middle East conflict.[27]

For their part, the Soviets had supported the attempt to find a political settlement as enshrined in Security Council resolution 242. Indeed, the Soviets' policy towards the Arab-Israeli conflict was probably already, in the years which followed the Middle East war of 1967, being determined according to the criteria described much later by the Israeli scholar (and veteran Kremlin-watcher) Galia Golan, in the following terms: 'The cost, particularly to Soviet global interests, presented by this ever-erupting conflict may well outweigh the benefits ... especially in view of the subsidiary or supportive role played by the Middle East in Soviet global policy'.[28] In short, the Soviets would not risk being dragged into a global confrontation for the Palestinians' or the other Arabs' sake. That this was true was amply demonstrated during the 1973 war.

On the Palestinian side, meanwhile, there seem seldom to have been many illusions but that Soviet support for the guerrilla movement was mainly motivated (and therefore also limited) by the Soviets' own strategic self-interest. Few Palestinians, inside or outside the resistance movement, ever forgot that in 1948 the U.S.S.R. had been one of the first states to accord formal recognition to the State of Israel, or that Jewish emigration from the Soviet Union formed a significant source for the growth of Israel's Jewish population throughout much of the 70s. Back in 1969, even Salah Khalaf (often regarded as a leftist among the Fateh leaders) was asking, 'Is it not strange that Western information media are more open to the resistance movement than socialist media for instance?'[29] That same year, another Fateh leader also generally regarded as being on the left, Farouq Qaddumi, also felt able to expostulate on the 'state capitalism' of the ruling system in the Soviet Union.[30]

However, such reservations expressed on the ideological plane did not prevent the Fateh leaders, in the years of their rise to prominence after 1967, from actively seeking to strengthen their political links with the Soviet Union. These efforts bore fruit in February 1970, when Arafat made his first visit to Moscow at the head of a formal PLO delegation.

In the Tass statement issued at the conclusion of that visit, the Soviets' previous policy emphasis, that all that was feasible (or perhaps even necessary) in the post-1967 period was to 'eliminate the consequences' of the Arabs' 1967 defeat, was still evident. But the statement also, in clear contrast to earlier Soviet characterisations of the Palestinians' activities, now accorded the Palestinian movement a Soviet seal of ideological legitimacy by describing it as a 'national liberation and anti-imperialist struggle'.[31] The following month, the pro-Soviet communist parties in the Arab world jointly set up a military formation called Al-Ansar (The Partisans), dedicated to aiding the Palestinians' armed struggle. In what must have been a blow to the Soviets, the Ansar were not at first admitted into the PLO Central Council, because their programme called only for an Israeli withdrawal from the lands seized in 1967, with no mention of the liberation of the rest of Palestine. (The Ansar were admitted to the Council in 1971, however, but in 1972 the grouping was dissolved altogether.)

On 8 July 1972, in a move which took nearly all those concerned completely by surprise, Egypt's President Sadat told the Soviet Ambassador in Cairo that some 17,000 of the Soviet experts serving in his country – that is, over 80% of the total – were to leave Egypt within the next ten days. This move was extremely damaging for the Russians, in view of the long-term strategic investment they had made in Egypt. On the very day Sadat's deadline expired, Yasser Arafat was in Moscow at the head of a large delegation representing all the Palestinian guerrilla groups except the PFLP-General Command. The implication was clear: the Soviets were indicating that Egypt's rebuff had caused them to throw new emphasis on their support for the Palestinians.

In Moscow, Arafat's delegation held talks with Boris Ponomarev, a candidate member for the Communist Party Politburo. In the joint statement issued after the visit the Soviets promised increased aid to the resistance movement. A political deal was reportedly worked out during that visit under which the communist Ansar guerrilla organisation would be absorbed into Fateh, in return for political co-ordination between Fateh supporters and communist supporters inside the Israeli-occupied territories within the framework of a Palestinian National Front.[32] Soon after Arafat concluded his Moscow visit, the first Soviet arms shipments were reported arriving for the Palestinians through Syrian ports.[33] Syria had now replaced Egypt as principal godfather of the Soviet-PLO relationship.

The essential content of the Soviets' growing interaction with the Palestinian guerrilla movement – as opposed to its diplomatic form – had already been explained in detail in a discussion in May 1971 among Ponomarev, the leading Soviet theoretician Mikhail Suslov and the Syrian Communist Party leader Khaled Bekdash, a convincing account of which was later published in Beirut. The comments reportedly made by the Soviet team on the Palestinian question included the following:

Israel is a fact. There was not a Jewish nation or a Jewish nationality – this is obvious. But now an Israeli nation is arising. Israel has arisen on artificial foundations, and I do not want to justify it historically. But let us start from existing facts...

It is permissible to struggle against the racialism of the State of Israel, its reactionary qualities, its colonialist character, but *it is not permissible to talk about eliminating the State of Israel...*

Through Zionism Israel is an instrument of world imperialism. The important thing is to cut this link, *which can be done through a political settlement* of the problem when Israel is denied the possibility of appealing to world public opinion and world Jewry to rescue it from its alleged danger.[34]

It was in line with this approach that at least some of the Soviet media had been discussing, since as far back as 1969, the advisability of establishing a Palestinian state alongside Israel.[35] This kind of solution was still some distance from the 'secular democratic state' idea espoused by Fateh and the other guerrilla groups since 1968-69. But there is some evidence in the carefully documented researches of Galia Golan and others which suggests that from the earliest days of the Soviet-Palestinian relationship the Soviets were trying to nudge the Palestinians towards considering some kind of two-state solution which would *ipso facto* mean the continued existence of the Jewish state.[36]

The new regional balance wrought by the October War of 1973 provided a rare opportunity for all those actors on the Mideast scene who sought to cajole the Arab-Israeli conflict towards some kind of peaceful resolution. If Dr Kissinger ultimately proved himself better able to take firm advantage of this opportunity than his Soviet opponents, that does not mean that the Soviets too did not try also to transform the new facts created by the war into their own vision of a negotiated settlement. Thus we find that as early as 29 October 1973 the Soviet Ambassador in Beirut was handing urgent letters to Yasser Arafat, George Habash and Nayef Hawatma asking them to clarify what they read into the PLO's stated pursuit of the Palestinians' 'legitimate rights', and recommending to them the idea of pushing for a Palestinian state in the West Bank and Gaza areas.[37]

The following July, the PNC did indeed vote to pursue the diplomatic option under the slogan of establishing a Palestinian 'national authority' in the occupied territories. During the intense internal PLO discussions which preceded this vote it was noteworthy that most of the groups which the Soviets would have characterised as 'leftist' and 'democratic', primarily the DFLP and the Palestinian National Front, proved to be strong advocates of this option.[38]

The year 1974 was a year of intense Palestinian-Soviet contacts, with Arafat taking two fully fledged PLO delegations to Moscow, this time at the official invitation of the Soviet government. At the end of the second of these, in November 1974, the Soviet side announced its clear support for the idea of establishing an independent Palestinian state. The new, higher degree of warmth evinced by the Soviets towards the PLO mainstream throughout 1974 was probably not wholly dissociated from the danger of the new developments the Soviet leaders must have perceived under way in Syria, where President Asad had received Dr Kissinger's first attentions in the last weeks of 1973, only to succumb to them sufficiently by June of 1974 to have followed President Sadat into signing a bilateral disengagement agreement with Israel under his auspices. At that stage, the Soviets must have feared that Damascus, too, might slip out of their orbit, just as Cairo had two years before. As on that earlier occasion, one Soviet response was to step up contacts with the Palestinians.

In addition, the Soviets apparently feared that the successive Kissinger-brokered bilateral agreements would sound the death knell for any possibility of reconvening the Geneva conference on which they had pinned most of their hopes for retaining their influence in the Middle Eastern diplomatic arena. Thus, even in the midst of all the new attention they were according their Palestinian guests, they also appeared to be stepping up their pressures on them further to moderate their negotiating stance, in the hopes that this would be the key which could unlock the door to Geneva.

Before the problems connected with a resumption of Geneva could be addressed, however, the Soviets found themselves confronted with another conundrum: that constituted by the fighting in Lebanon in 1975 and 1976, and in particular the spectacle of the conflict which developed there between the PLO and Syria, which still remained the Soviets' two closest allies in the region. As Salah Khalaf recalled the Soviets' policy during the Lebanese war,

At the beginning, the Soviets didn't understand very clearly the nature of the civil war, taking it to be a sectarian conflict... The Soviet leaders advised us 'not to get mixed up' in a 'family affair'. It was only after the massacres of Dbayeh and the Qarantina in January 1976 that they began to grasp the dimensions of the conflict. They openly rallied to our side after the Syrian military intervention in Lebanon. Of course, their communiqués and newspapers only criticised the Syrians by allusion. But President Asad later confided to me that Moscow interrupted the delivery of spare parts to the Syrian army as of June 1976. At the same time, he received a number of messages from the Soviet government encouraging him to rebuild his bridges with the Lebanese left and the Resistance.

However, to our deep regret, the USSR did nothing to break the sea and land blockade to which we were subjected by Israel, the Christian separatists and Syria... *I don't think Moscow wanted to become implicated in the conflict for fear of being dragged into a confrontation with the United States. The imperatives of security and détente must have taken precedence over the desire to help us.*[39]

The Soviets' main goal during the summer and autumn of 1976 was somehow to bring an end to the fighting between Syria and the PLO. They were thus probably relieved when this was achieved by the Riyadh mini-summit of October 1976, though wary that the heavily pro-American slant of the states which engineered the conciliation might affect the stance of the two former antagonists. Within a few months, however, it became clear that the new Israeli/Phalangist threats to the presence of both the PLO and the Syrians in Lebanon would ensure their continued reliance on such strategic help as the Soviets could afford them, while the diplomatic manoeuvrings over the question of reconvening Geneva, which resumed with Jimmy Carter's accession to the presidency in Washington in 1977, ensured their resumed reliance on the Soviet Union's diplomatic weight.

President Carter's declared commitment to a resumption of the Geneva conference must have been extremely welcome to the Soviet leadership, for whom this highly visible manifestation of détente was infinitely preferable to Kissinger's manoeuvres to bar them from any effective diplomatic role in the Middle East. Much of the Soviets' behaviour throughout 1977 appeared to be governed by a kind of tacit understanding that if they could persuade the PLO to clarify and moderate its position – particularly by offering some kind of recognition of Israel, or at least of resolution 242 – then the United States might reasonably be expected to be able to persuade the Israelis to sit down at the same table in Geneva with PLO representatives of some undefined status. Other efforts to the same general end were also continuing through the pro-American Arab governments in Egypt and Saudi Arabia (and tentatively, through some European capitals), but the PLO leaders always saw a clear need to co-ordinate closely with the Soviets in this whole process because of the Soviets' special role as co-chairmen of the (however distant) Geneva conference.

By 1 October 1977, the Soviets must have been optimistic that, with the agreement reached in New York between the U.S. Secretary of State and their own Foreign Minister (see chapter 5 above), they were near to achieving their objective. But four days later, Israeli Foreign Minister Moshe Dayan had negated the work of his Soviet counterpart. The conditions for participation in Geneva were now made so strict that the PLO would be extremely unlikely to attend. It would perhaps have been interesting to see if the Soviets might have continued to pursue a resumption of Geneva, even on Dayan's terms, that is at the expense of PLO participation. In the event, the rapid developments of the following weeks, with President Sadat's surprise visit to Jerusalem, quickly rendered totally redundant any talk of a Geneva conference along the lines envisaged since late 1973.

For the Soviets, the unfolding of the Sadat initiative represented further successive blows to their strategic position in the Middle East. Ever since 1972 Egypt, the weightiest of all the Arab countries, had been moving away from the close links with Moscow it had upheld since 1955, but now Sadat was taking his country right into a strategic and economic relationship with the U.S. which was, if anything, even closer than the previous Egyptian-Soviet links. The Soviet view of Sadat's peace initiative three years after its launching was summed up in an article in the Moscow journal *International Affairs* which described it as a 'surrender' which, 'as expected, did not bring peace to the peoples of the Middle East'.[40]

True to established pattern, the Soviets reacted to Sadat's moves by giving new stress to their links with the PLO leadership, culminating in the decision of the end of 1981 to accord embassy status to the PLO office in Moscow. Soviet policy in the period following the start of the Sadat initiative focussed on strengthening the Steadfastness Front, while continuing to stress Moscow's desire for the convening of an international peace conference, to be attended by all relevant parties including the PLO, which it continued to describe as 'the sole and lawful representative of the Palestinian Arabs'.[41]

The Israeli-Palestinian war of 1982 found the Soviets once again acting according to established form. On 14 June 1982, the Soviet government issued a statement saying,

The Soviet Union takes the Arabs' side not in words but in deeds, and presses to get the aggressor out of Lebanon. The present-day Israeli policy makers should not forget that the Middle East is an area lying in close proximity to the southern borders of the Soviet Union and that developments there cannot help affecting the interests of the USSR. We warn Israel about this.[42]

Strong words! But once again there was no sign, in the days which followed, of any concrete Soviet move to challenge the siege imposed around Beirut. The Soviet government made no further high-level comment on the fighting until 8 July, when the possibility of a deployment of U.S. troops in Lebanon stirred the chronically ailing Soviet leader Leonid Brezhnev into warning the U.S. President that 'if that [deployment] really occurs, the Soviet Union will build its policy taking this fact into account'. However, in the same statement Brezhnev could do no more than 'appeal' to the U.S. President 'to halt the barbaric destruction by Israeli troops of

Lebanese and Palestinian women, children and old people'.[43]

On 20 July, in an interview with *Pravda*, Brezhnev had some words of encouragement for the defenders of Beirut. He also reiterated past Soviet policy by stressing that the problems of the Middle East

can be resolved only as a result of collective efforts of all sides concerned, including PLO, as the sole legitimate representative of the Palestinian people. Looking forward, it is precisely in that perspective that we see the value of the proposal put forward by us on the convocation of an international conference.[44]

On 15 September 1982, the Soviet President expanded on this theme when he set out a six-point peace plan which closely paralleled the one the Arab Summit had endorsed a few days before (see chapter 6). But within weeks, on 10 November, the 75-year-old Soviet leader finally passed away, ushering in the era of Yuri Andropov. First Palestinian reactions to the new leader in Moscow were positive. PLO/Fateh leaders who visited Moscow after Andropov's succession returned to the Middle East hopeful that the crisis of inaction which had marked the last years of Brezhnev's rule, and especially the presumed succession struggle of the last months of his life, would now be replaced by a brisker and more forceful era in Soviet Middle East politics.[45]

Despite the low tenor of Soviet interventions in the Battle of Beirut, in February 1983 the Sixteenth PNC reiterated its previous expressions of special recognition of the Soviets' role. The PNC spelt out its 'appreciation and support' for the September peace plan enunciated by Brezhnev. The section of PNC resolutions on international relations was headed by a clause calling for 'Developing and deepening relations of alliance and friendship between the PLO and the socialist states, led by the Soviet Union'.[46]

For their part, the Soviets' reaction to this PNC session was, understandably, to lay prime stress on the support the session expressed for Soviet positions, and the stance it took critical of the U.S. President's peace proposals of 1 September 1982. Significantly, the second stress in Soviet commentaries was placed on the achievements the session had revealed in terms of the PLO leadership's attempts to safeguard 'Palestinian national unity'.[47] In other words, the Soviets, like the Chinese, still gave firm political support to the existing PLO/Fateh leadership and its priorities.

The United Nations and other international organisations since 1970

As we saw in chapter 2 above, the Fateh leaders had since early 1965 followed a policy of addressing their cause directly to the United Nations. With the dynamism they injected into the PLO when they took over its apparatus in 1968, and with the breadth of their contacts with Arab and other Third World governments, the Fateh-dominated leadership of the PLO was able to start following up these contacts with increasing effect from about 1970 onwards. In 1970, for example, a PLO representative participated in a discussion of the question of Palestine by the Special Political Committee of the U.N. General Assembly. And in December of that year, the General Assembly adopted two resolutions affirming the Palestinian people's right to self-determination.

The first of these resolutions, no. 2649, twinned a condemnation of the Palestinians' denial of this right with its denial to the peoples of southern Africa. In the second resolution, no. 2672, the General Assembly spelt out that it '*Recognizes* that the people of Palestine are entitled to equal rights and self-determination, in accordance with the Charter of the United Nations'.[48] The vote on the section containing this clause was passed by 47 votes to 22, with 50 abstentions. Supporters included Arab, Eastern bloc and some African nations; opponents included Israel, the U.S., nine South American countries and a handful from Europe, Africa and the British Commonwealth.

Over the years which followed, the Palestinians' right to self-determination was reiterated again and again by the General Assembly. Meanwhile, the PLO was winning an ever wider base of international support, both through bilateral contacts with the Chinese, the Soviets, and others, and through its increasing activities in other, non-U.N., transnational groupings.

One of the first of these groupings to give the PLO its support was the Islamic Conference, which at a meeting in Lahore in the early 70s gave its endorsement to the Organisation, despite the stated secularism of its programme.[49] Then, in the aftermath of the October 1973 war, the PLO participated in the Algiers summit of the Non-Aligned Movement and soon afterwards it became the only non-African national liberation organisation to enjoy observer status with the Organisation for African Unity. By the late 70s, PLO diplomats in several African and other Third World nations – who were nearly all Fateh people – had acquired considerable experience in mediating a range of Arab-African issues far broader than purely Palestinian issues. Meanwhile, the PLO's political links with South African and some South American national independence movements grew stronger throughout the 70s, as Israel stepped up its links with South Africa and with totalitarian governments such as the Somoza regime in Nicaragua.

Already, in October 1974, the coalition of international support for the PLO and its programme which had been built up by the political efforts of the Palestinians and the other Arabs had broadened to such an extent that when the General Assembly invited the PLO to participate in its discussions on Palestine, the vote was carried by 105 to 4. Only Israel, the U.S., Bolivia and the Dominican Republic voted against this invitation, which provided the basis for Yasser Arafat's appearance before the Assembly the following month.[50]

Following Arafat's address to the Assembly, on 22 November 1974 it passed resolution 3236, which was used by the PLO as a bench-mark definition of Palestinian rights throughout the years which followed. This resolution, passed by 89 votes to 7, stated that the Assembly

1. *Reaffirms* the inalienable rights of the Palestinian people in Palestine, including:
a) The right to self-determination without external interference;
b) The right to national independence and sovereignty;
2. *Reaffirms also* the inalienable right of the Palestinians to return to their homes and property ... and calls for their return.[51]

In the following resolution, the Assembly invited the PLO to participate in its future works 'in the capacity of observer'.

The General Assembly provided an extremely valuable rostrum from which the Palestinians could explain their strategy to representatives of all the world's nations. Its resolutions and other expressions of support for the PLO were to help, in the late 70s, in giving the PLO a valuable *entrée* to public opinion in Europe, which was largely supportive of the concept of the United Nations as a world forum. However, the Palestinians always realised that the General Assembly did not wield the real power in resolving international disputes which was the stated prerogative of the Security Council, and the structure of the Security Council, with its four (and after 1971, five) permanent great-power members each wielding a veto, would not permit the passage of any pro-Palestinian resolutions to which the U.S. objected. In January 1976, in what was for the PLO a notable diplomatic victory, a PLO representative was actually invited to address the Security Council. But his intervention could not secure the passage of the resolution he supported. As always, for the Palestinians and their Arab allies, the question then was one of trying to calculate at each point whether it would be better to take whatever crumbs of support the U.S. might be offering in the Security Council or to try to embarrass the U.S. in the strength of its support for Israel by forcing it to use its veto. On occasion, the PLO and their allies chose the latter course, but when it came to major substantive security issues, such as the many votes on clashes with the Israelis in Lebanon, they generally chose to go along with whatever the U.S. could offer.

In the view of Hassan Abdel-Rahman, who from 1974 to 1982 was the deputy head of the PLO's observer mission at the U.N., 'The U.N. can only really be effective in a period of superpower détente.' Speaking in early 1983, he said he considered that the concept of détente had had some applicability to Middle Eastern issues from the early 70s 'down to 1977, that is until the issuing of the U.S.-Soviet joint communiqué on the Middle East in October of that year' (see chapter 5 above). But in Abdel-Rahman's view, the Carter administration's reversal of support for the communiqué signalled the end of superpower détente on the Middle East, and this fact was then underlined by the U.S.'s subsequent support of President Sadat's peace initiative. 'Since then, the effectiveness of the U.N. in the Middle East has been limited,' he concluded, 'though this could change at any time if the two superpowers resumed a process of détente.'[52]

Western Europe since 1974

By the mid-70s, propelled by the impetus of the October 1973 war, the Palestinian nationalist leaders were able to start moving their diplomatic efforts closer to the heartland of world support for Israel, when they became able to address governments and public opinion throughout West Europe.

According to English researcher David Allen, it was in October 1973 that, 'outraged at the superpowers' disregard for European interests in their resolution of the immediate crisis', French President Georges Pompidou called for a summit meeting of the nine member states of the European Economic Community (EEC). The summit duly convened in the Danish capital, Copenhagen, that December and, 'Although doubts remain as to who, if anybody, actually invited them, four Arab foreign ministers added to the already divided Nine's confusion by presenting themselves at the Summit and suggesting that the relationship between the Community and the Arab world be placed on a new basis'.[53] In July 1974, the Arab ministers' suggestion was finally acted on, when a meeting of European and Arab foreign ministers was held in Paris. That meeting instituted a body to be called the General Commission (or General Committee) for the Euro-Arab Dialogue, to be composed of envoys of the member states of the EEC together with their counterparts from the Arab League states.

From the very beginning, the European initiative ran into the unyielding opposition of Secretary of State Kissinger. U.S.-European relations were already strained in autumn 1973, following the breakdown of talks aimed at the drafting of an 'Atlantic Charter'. These strains were then considerably aggravated by the fact that the steep rise in OPEC oil prices hit the European (and Japanese) economies far, far more harshly than they hit the U.S. economy. Kissinger did not want the Europeans meddling in his game-plan for the Middle East. As he explained it later,

The European initiative ... threatened to sabotage our carefully elaborated strategy. We were proceeding step by step; the European Community had committed itself publicly to a comprehensive solution. We dealt with each of the principal Mideast parties separately; the Europeans were aiming at a conclave assembling all Arab countries, a forum I was convinced would give the whip hand to the radicals.[54]

Kissinger was soon able to outmanoeuvre the Europeans and relegate their initiative to a back seat in the diplomatic order of things. By early March of 1974, he was reported as predicting that 'The Europeans will be unable to achieve anything in the Middle East in a million years.'[55] The first meeting of the General Commission was delayed until May 1976 and even then the Europeans were able to deflect suggestions from the Arab participants that the PLO be allowed to participate. In addition most of the political content the original participants might have envisaged for the forum was largely superseded on the agenda by economic, financial and technological matters. Nevertheless, the first glimmerings of the West European governments' interest in playing their own role in the Middle East, unified among themselves but separate from the American role, were sufficient to alert some of the PLO/Fateh leaders to the new possibilities inherent in making direct contact with Europe.

Fateh as such had, since its first coalescence as a unified movement in the early 60s, had its own organisational base among the many Palestinian students in European universities, and the Palestinian 'guest-workers' in European factories. A decade later, many of these students and workers had progressed, professionally, to positions of some security as university lecturers or businessmen in their host societies, acquiring increased circles of local contacts (and in some cases local passports and/or local spouses) along the way. The position of the Arab communities in West Germany was threatened for a while during the mass expulsions of Arab workers and students which followed the Black September operation at the 1972 Munich Olympic Games, but, overall, by the early 70s the Palestinian communities in Europe had done much to decrease the Palestinians' historic disadvantage, compared with Zionist and later Israeli envoys, of being 'outsiders' when addressing the European body politic.

In 1974, Fateh veteran Said Hammami was sent to London, where he operated a (government-tolerated) 'PLO Information Office' out of the Arab League's official building. In October 1975, the French government was the first in Western Europe to give explicit official authorisation for the opening of a PLO Information Office, which was directed by Ezzeddine Qalaq. (Both Hammami and Qalaq were later assassinated at their posts by operatives of Fateh renegade Sabri al-Banna, who bitterly opposed the PLO's European contacts.) Offices in all other major West European capitals, except Amsterdam, followed quickly. In mid-1980, the

Austrian government took a new step, for Western Europe, when it accorded the PLO full diplomatic recognition. After this, the Fateh/PLO leaders held out, in the negotiations for the opening of offices in other, smaller European countries, for some kind of equivalent recognition of the PLO's representativeness.

Co-ordinating all this activity from PLO headquarters was Political Department chief Farouq Qaddumi, who saw the PLO's diplomatic advance in Europe mainly as a way in which to influence the U.S. government.[56] But Qaddumi's predecessor in the Political Department, Khaled al-Hassan, also took on a special role in pushing the European initiative forward, in his capacity as Chairman of the PNC's Foreign Relations Committee. In this capacity, he attended a meeting held in London in September 1975 of the Inter-Parliamentary Union, a body linking more than 80 Parliaments from different countries. Throughout the eight years which followed, he was to criss-cross Europe providing a high-level, open Palestinian presence at parliamentary and other political gatherings. His efforts were counterpointed by those of the permanent PLO representatives in Europe – who were all, except the representative in Scandinavia and later the one in Austria, Fateh people – and by the network of more discreet contacts built up by Isam Sartawi. Sartawi (who was assassinated in early 1983) had been a latecomer to Fateh ranks. This, his shadowy stature within the movement even after he had supposedly joined it, and the fact that in 1970 he had been the most prominent Palestinian supporter of President Nasser's decision to accept the Rogers plan, all meant that he could never enjoy the standing in internal Fateh ranks accorded, for example, Said Hammami, who himself had pioneered many of the same contacts which Sartawi later nourished.

On 19 April 1980, Hassan addressed a meeting of the 350-member Parliamentary Association for Euro-Arab Co-operation, held at the Palace of Europe in Strasbourg. Four days later, the parliamentary Council of Europe, which had its headquarters in the Palace, passed a resolution which: judged the Camp David accords an insufficient basis for reaching a comprehensive peace in the Middle East; called for recognition of the 'right of self-determination of the Palestinian people'; sought some amendment of those aspects of Security Council resolution 242 which consider the Palestinian question merely a refugee problem; and called for mutual recognition between Israel and the PLO.[57] Two months later, a summit meeting of European Economic Community government leaders, held in Venice, issued an official declaration, which again mentioned the Palestinian people's 'right to self-determination' and called for the PLO to be 'associated with' Middle East peace negotiations.[58]

Between 1974 and 1980, the balance in Europe's relations with the U.S.

had changed. On coming into power in 1977, President Jimmy Carter and his Secretary of State, Cyrus Vance, had adopted an attitude towards Western Europe very different from the jealous staking out of diplomatic turfs which had marked Kissinger's days of power. They were probably genuinely pained that the Europeans never shared their own enthusiasm for the Camp David peace process. As it became clear in Washington by early 1980 that Camp David was not, indeed, a panacea for total Middle East tranquillity, there were increasing suggestions that European leaders were being given an unofficial green light by the Carter administration to explore – if not necessarily to pursue – alternative approaches. Nevertheless, by mid-1980, Hassan still considered that considerable American pressure was being applied on the Europeans. 'It is not because they do not want to that [the European states] do not recognise the PLO officially,' he told an interviewer in summer 1980, 'but it is as a result of American pressure on them.'[59]

Public opinion in Europe had meanwhile also been shifting away from the generally pro-Israeli feelings which had dominated in Europe before the Palestinians launched their initiative. The Europeans' solid understanding of their economic interests no doubt played a role in this, but other factors were also involved. In Hassan's view, these included the effect on the Europeans of the successive U.N. resolutions on the Palestine question, and then – after 1977 and 1978 respectively – vivid recollections of the past history of new Israeli Premier Begin and the daily contacts of peace-keeping troops from three European nations with the Israeli-Palestinian conflict in south Lebanon.[60]

By mid-1982, much of European public opinion was ready to sympathise openly with the plight of the Palestinians and their allies during the Battle of Beirut, and at least two European nations, France and Greece, gave the PLO leaders there special political support in their search for a solution. It was the French special envoy in Beirut who provided one key opening in the indirect U.S.-PLO negotiations over withdrawal, and the French also contributed to the Palestinians' diplomatic efforts with the initiative they launched jointly with the Egyptians at the Security Council. Meanwhile, during the siege itself, the PASOK (Socialist) government in Greece signalled the extent of its support for the PLO by granting diplomatic recognition to the Organisation. It was in response to this Greek support, and as a way of highlighting the inactivity of the Arab states by contrast, that Arafat and other PLO leaders chose Athens as their first destination after evacuating the Lebanese capital.

Though both these states were EEC members in 1982 their support was still not firmed up into a full-blown EEC diplomatic initiative. EEC leaders attended a summit meeting in Brussels on 29 June 1982, and issued a statement calling for a disengagement of forces in Beirut prior to the evacuation of all foreign forces. The statement called, too, for the PLO's inclusion in negotiations for an overall peace settlement in the Middle East, and the summit's participants signalled their displeasure with Israel by postponing signing a 22 million financial protocol with it.[61]

But, in the end, none of these actions did anything to deflect Israel from its course or to persuade the U.S. to try harder to moderate Israeli actions. Hassan, as protagonist of much of the PLO's European initiative, had always understood the (mainly American) constraints on independent European action but in the months following the Battle of Beirut, he indicated that the Europeans could have achieved much more than they had done:

We know that the Europeans cannot do much. But in the meantime, they do not do what they can do. They can do two things: first, they can use their economic relations and the facilities given to Israel by the Common Market. They didn't use that at all. Secondly, Europe, as the closest ally to the United States, can influence the U.S. in one way or another, through quiet diplomacy. They are still very weak in this, because they are not united in it... Still, they have developed a lot.[62]

The United States

As related in chapters 3 to 6 above, a major part of the story of the Palestinian movement in 1970 and throughout the dozen years which followed was the story of its antagonistic relations with the United States, for it was the United States which from the late 50s onwards had been – in anti-colonialist terms – Israel's 'metropolis'. Despite all the hard feelings involved in this, from at least the middle of 1973 onwards the PLO leadership was, according even to Henry Kissinger's account, trying to establish a direct dialogue with Washington.[63] A decade later, despite all their many other diplomatic gains elsewhere, they had failed to achieve this objective, which they still saw as the key to unlocking the chronic dilemma of their statelessness.

In the spring of 1970, Kissinger, who was then President Nixon's National Security Advisor, listened to a report made by Assistant Secretary of State Joseph Sisco after a trip to the Middle East. Sisco argued for a major re-evaluation of American policy, and Kissinger wrote that he agreed with Sisco, because 'major assumptions about American strategy' in the region 'had been wrong across the board'. Among the four wrong assumptions Kissinger listed was: 'We had assumed that the Palestinians could be dealt with in a settlement purely as a refugee problem. Instead, they had become a quasi-independent force with a veto over policy in Jordan, and perhaps even in Lebanon.'[64] Kissinger's role later that year in encouraging King

Hussein to combat the guerrillas, as detailed in chapter 3 above, was presumably motivated by a desire to reverse this situation.

Three years later, in the worrying circumstances which faced the U.S. at the height of the October 1973 Middle East war, Kissinger (by then President Nixon's Secretary of State) momentarily responded to the diplomatic overtures the PLO leaders had offered earlier that year. According to Kissinger's account, which is tacitly endorsed in its bare outline by senior Fateh leaders, a meeting ensued, on 3 November 1973, in Rabat, between Deputy CIA Director Vernon Walters and 'a close associate of Arafat's'. Kissinger relates that following one further meeting the following March, the contacts were halted. 'This was no accident,' he wrote in his memoirs. '... Walters's meeting achieved its immediate purpose: to gain time and to prevent radical assaults on the early peace process.'[65]

In June 1975, in a meeting with American Jewish leaders, Kissinger was to spell out his attitude towards the Palestinians in these terms: 'I have left the Palestinian question alone in order to work on frontier questions hoping eventually to isolate the Palestinians. And this could work.'[66] A few weeks later, in September 1975, the U.S. was to give new meaning to the concept of 'isolating' the Palestinians, with its promise to Israel that it would not negotiate with the Organisation so long as it rejected resolution 242 and Israel's right to exist (see chapter 4 above). Although political contacts with the PLO – which might have held out the possibility of some ultimate political gain for the Organisation – were thenceforth formally ruled out by the September 1975 promise, secret technical contacts with the PLO/Fateh leadership at the security level nevertheless continued.

Through these 'security contacts', the Palestinian side had already co-operated in assuring the safety of Dr Kissinger during his December 1973 visit to Lebanon. During the Lebanese fighting of 1975-76, it was Fateh's security apparatuses which accorded vital protection to American and other diplomats in the areas controlled by the Palestinians and the Lebanese opposition. This protection continued well after the formal cessation of Lebanese hostilities in late 1976, and possibly right up until the Palestinians in Beirut themselves were besieged by the Israelis in June 1982. The Palestinians' role in protecting the Americans' sea evacuation of Westerners from Beirut in June 1976 had even received open recognition from President Ford himself.[67]

On the Palestinian side, the official policy of the PLO towards the U.S., at the time of Arafat's 1973 overture to Kissinger, had been that laid down by the Eleventh PNC, held in January of that year. The political programme agreed at that session referred to continuing 'American-Zionist-Hashemite schemes' and it accused 'American imperialism' of entertaining 'a broad plan to securely contain and liquidate both the Palestinian revolution and the Arab revolution'. Under these circumstances, the programme committed the PLO to 'Solidarity with the world struggle against imperialism, Zionism and reaction'.[68]

This programme certainly did not, on the face of it, leave much room for the kind of diplomatic initiative which Arafat launched later that year, though it should not be forgotten that leaders of nearly all national liberation movements in modern times, operating under a similarly strident anti-imperialist code, on occasion conducted contacts with the 'imperialists', in some cases bringing about significant political gains for their cause. But the Palestinians never really adequately formulated the groundrules under which contacts with the U.S. could be conducted. Thus, when George Habash's PFLP learnt of the 1973 overtures to Washington, they cited these secret contacts as one reason for the distrust for the PLO leadership which caused them to resign from the PLO Executive in October 1974.

For many Palestinian activists, the accession to power of Jimmy Carter's administration in Washington, in January 1977, seemed to hint of the possibility of change in the American position, and Carter's first nine months in office did indeed see a flurry of diplomatic activity aimed at trying to open the U.S.-PLO dialogue (see chapter 5 above).

So how close did the PLO and the Carter administration come, in 1977, to breaking through the barriers to direct contacts between them? No one could tell at the time, although it was significant that Secretary Vance continued for some weeks after the launching of the Sadat initiative to work towards a resumption of Geneva,[69] which may have indicated that he still thought that this part at least of the U.S.-PLO tangle was still open to resolution.

Two years later, a much feebler replay of the activities of 1977 was enacted, mainly in New York, where Kuwait's Ambassador to the U.N. made an attempt, in conjunction with some of the European representatives, to obtain a new Security Council resolution which would include all the essentials of resolution 242 along with a new reference to establishing a Palestinian state. The idea would be to secure the agreement of both Palestinians and Americans to the new resolution, thus effecting a simultaneous exchange of Palestinian recognition for the essentials of 242 for American commitment to a Palestinian state. But the U.S. Ambassador to the U.N., Andrew Young, was forced to resign when it was revealed that he had tried to deny that he had participated in a discussion on the new resolution which was attended by the PLO's chief Observer at the U.N. Faced with the prospect of an American veto in the Security Council, the Arab states first postponed, then quietly dropped their initiative.

When it subsequently appeared that the Syrians had also been adamantly opposed to the 1979 Kuwaiti initiative, it seemed that the constraints on both the U.S. and the PLO sides had in 1979 been too strong to permit the opening of a dialogue, and the same constraints would probably have obtained back in 1977 to an equal or even greater degree. To make this judgement, however, is to ignore the role that clear statesmanship, as exercised by the President of the world's strongest superpower, could have played in this regard. It is, at the very least, an interesting phenomenon that the American Presidents of the 70s came to realise the role statesmanship should play in opening up a dialogue with the PLO only when they no longer headed the ship of state.

At the time of the Kuwaitis' 1979 initiative, as at every point from 1977 to 1982 when it seemed that a U.S.-PLO dialogue was imminent, the PLO leaders were operating under the extreme duress of heavy attacks on their people by the Israelis, who were using American weapons. Thus, in August 1979, at the height of the drama over the Andrew Young affair in New York and despite the PLO leaders' continued desire to open up the dialogue with the U.S., Yasser Arafat was describing heavy and sustained bombardments of south Lebanon as 'organised American-Israeli terrorism' and a 'scorched earth policy'.[70]

On that occasion in 1979, as on other occasions, the main thrust of Arafat's reaction to this policy was to hint, repeatedly and in many different ways, of a linkage between Palestinian and Lebanese casualties and world oil supplies. 'Would Lebanese and Palestinian blood become more precious if it were mixed with oil?' he asked. 'Definitely, it will be... The Americans are supplying Israel with everything from flour to Phantoms: America should understand that Palestine is linked to petrol.'[71] However, for all the alliteration of this approach, the Arab states never did effectively establish the link that Arafat was seeking. Throughout the latter half of 1979, the Saudis pumped a million barrels a day more oil than previously, which helped to make up for the loss of Iranian supplies to the world market. Though they nominally linked this gesture of goodwill to vaguely defined 'progress' on the Palestinian issue, by the time they had ascertained that such progress was not forthcoming, the dynamics of the world oil market had turned against them. By 1983, Khaled al-Hassan concluded, 'We have to say that "the Arabs" as a united power does not exist, and therefore the Americans are at ease: their interests are not touched.'[72]

In Hassan's view, the relationship between the U.S. and Israel could be described as that of 'a weak lover' (the U.S.) and his girlfriend:

Israel is a part of the global strategy of the U.S., as a military base, cheap and efficient... Now the Israelis know how important they are in the strategy of the Pentagon: so they play, they demand a lot of things, and they play so many games where the Americans finally cannot say No – not because they agree but because they want Israel. It's like a lover who loves a girl so much, and she knows that, but she also knows that he cannot say No to what she asks for; and finally his reputation is ruined and she is getting everything out of him.[73]

Yasser Arafat's most frequent characterisation of the U.S.-Israeli relationship meanwhile used another analogy from family life, with Israel cast as the 'spoilt child' of its indulgent American parents. 'Is it more important for the American administration to indulge its spoilt child than to consider its own interests?' he asked in 1979.[74] Other Palestinian characterisations of the relationship include textbook marxist analyses from the annals of Lenin's studies of imperialism (mainly from nominally marxist groups such as the PFLP and DFLP) and blunt descriptions of the U.S. as, for example, 'the head of the snake'.

All these characterisations imply in themselves, of course, the ways in which the Palestinians should seek to deal with the U.S.-Israeli relationship. The 'head of the snake', for example, is presumably the part that should be hit, rather than its body or tail – though, as detailed above, the mainstream leaders of the PLO acted consistently between late 1973 and 1982 to protect U.S. interests located within their sphere of influence from the sporadic attacks launched by the (relatively powerless) radicals inside the Palestinian and Lebanese leftist movements. Indeed, the pattern had already been set in 1968: when George Habash took what some leftists considered the only effective action against U.S. interests in the region by blowing up the tapline pipeline in Syria, Fateh's newly named spokesman Yasser Arafat was subsequently reported as describing that action as 'contrary to the general interests of true fedayeen action'.[75]

In the case of 'spoilt child', the first tactic to be adopted by a neighbour whose windows the unruly infant keeps breaking would presumably be to try to speak to his parents about it, and have them co-operate in disciplining the child (while hinting that they should modify their own indulgence of him). Failing this, the aggrieved neighbour might call the police (given that the child is physically stronger than the neighbour, the option of disciplining him directly does not exist), but if the police – the U.N.? – can never get there on time the neighbour has no alternative but to continue pleading for the help of the delinquent's parents.

The 'weak lover', on the other hand, will continue to be manipulated by the object of his infatuation until something can break that infatuation. In Khaled al-Hassan's view,

That depends on another beautiful girl... This is Arab policy... But the Arabs cannot offer the unlimited loyalty of the people to the Americans.

The Israelis know that without the American support they will dry up and their whole state will finish without a bullet [being fired]... And because of that, the

Americans are very sure that the loyalty of the people of the whole state will not change.

But who can guarantee the Egyptian people? ... Or the Iraqis? Because those are self-sufficient countries. They can live without American support.

The only thing we can counterpose is [American] interests in the area.[76]

In this regard, Hassan had to admit that, as of early 1983, the Arabs still appeared impotent.

The PLO/Fateh leaders always considered the failure of their efforts to open up direct talks with successive American administrations as due, in the end, to the bad faith or lack of political understanding of the Americans. Privately and publicly, they admit that they themselves were nearly always acting under some pressure from their own hard-liners not to give too much away in negotiations without something concrete in return, and they themselves, arguing from their own experiences at the hands of the Americans over the years, shared much of the hard-liners' caution in this regard. The problem ultimately came down to a question of trust: if the Palestinians were to make the commitments required by the Americans, would the Americans then deliver something worthwhile in return? The Palestinians argued consistently, in 1977 and again in 1979, that for them to take the drastic step that recognising resolution 242 constituted for them it would not be sufficient to be rewarded only by the opening of vaguely defined 'talks' with Washington; but they would do so on the basis of an American commitment to support their demand for an independent Palestinian state, or at least a commitment to Palestinian 'self-determination'. But who should take the first step? On the basis of their own experience with the Americans the PLO leaders never felt justified in taking it themselves, and they rapidly came to see it as unrealistic to require that the Americans should do so. Yet the Carter administration would never in the end endorse the kinds of formula being considered, which would have allowed for a simultaneous exchange of commitments.

The experiences of 1977 and, to a lesser extent, 1979 were important because they revealed much about the dynamics of the Palestinian-U.S.-Israeli(-Arab) tangle, and they helped to inform Palestinian expectations concerning future initiatives towards the U.S. When Ronald Reagan's new administration took power in Washington in 1981, it did so with very different intentions towards the Palestinians from those expressed by Carter when he came into office four years earlier, but by mid-1982 the dynamics of the Middle Eastern situation had once again brought the U.S. administration up against the question of having to define its own policy towards the Palestinians more clearly. The result was the Reagan plan of September 1982 (see chapter 6 above). During the first seven months of the diplomatic movement which followed the announcement of the plan,

many of the realities, problems and ambiguities of the U.S.-PLO relationship which had been revealed three and five years earlier rapidly
emerged again.

This time round, the American plan ruled out the possibility of establishing an independent Palestinian state from the very start. Nevertheless,
the PLO leaders undertook much of the basic political footwork required
by the plan – working out formulas for a future confederation with Jordan,
and so on – with a view to exploring both the potentials of the scheme itself
and the intentions of its American authors. Still they saw no sign that the
Americans were prepared to do anything to follow up on implementing
their own peace plan in the face of the Israeli government's outright
rejection of it. By April 1983, when Yasser Arafat took the proposals of the
joint declaration he wanted to make with King Hussein in furtherance of
the Reagan plan back to the Fateh Central Committee in Kuwait, it was the
veteran leaders of his own organisation who stopped him from going
ahead with it. Khaled al-Hassan said of the American position at the time,
'I don't think there is a way to deal with it... How can we deal with it? We
cannot accept it, that's all. Even when we offered the confederation with
Jordan – this is a very big step from our side. And they still say No to
self-determination.'[77]

The gap, the complexities, the Israeli, Arab, American and Palestinian
constraints and parameters were all virtually unchanged from 1977.

Conclusions

Chapter 11

The irresistible force and the immovable object

If, in the late 70s or the early 80s, you were to ask any Fateh leader – or come to that, any member of any other Palestinian organisation, or practically any Palestinian at all – what the resistance movement had achieved after two decades of struggle, the first answer would be to the effect that the resistance movement *had re-established the Palestinian identity*. 'In the 50s,' Yasser Arafat recalled in 1979, 'John Foster Dulles used to say that the new generation of Palestinians would not even know Palestine. But they did! The group that made the [March 1978] operation against Israel were nearly all of them born outside Palestine, but they were prepared to die for it.'[1] 'Palestine,' said Khaled al-Hassan, 'had been eliminated from the books and maps; the Palestinian people had been eliminated. The problem was called the Arab-Israeli problem: it was a border problem between states, not a question of a people whose rights had been infringed. Now there is a Palestinian people which is recognised – there is strong recognition everywhere except the United States and Israel. This was our first achievement.'[2] Indeed, by the early 80s, not only was there a world-wide recognition that 'the Palestinian question' as such would have to be addressed, but also, inside the many different Palestinian communities themselves, both inside and outside historic Palestine, the people's identification with their own Palestinian-ness had become far deeper than – though still not at odds with – their self-identification as Arabs, Muslims or Christians.

The present-day Palestinian movement's assertion of Palestinian-ness had, at the beginning, to be made as against the existing claims of both the Israelis and the Arab states. The new generation of Palestinian activists which was emerging in the 50s saw the Israelis as having usurped their homes and their land – and along with that, given the overwhelmingly agricultural basis of pre-1948 Palestinian society, the major part of their identity. The Palestinians' revitalised assertion of their Palestinian-ness, and the Palestinian-ness of the land on which their society had been based, could not but remind some Israelis of the short span (and thus by implication the fragility) of the establishment of their own roots in Israel/Palestine, and perhaps, too, of the morally troubling way in which this had been achieved. It was thus fiercely opposed by the Israelis, most notably in Premier Golda Meir's famous words of 1969, 'It was not as though there was a Palestinian people ... and we came and threw them them out and took their country away from them. *They did not exist.*'[3]

The new Palestinian activists saw the Arab states, meanwhile, as having contributed to the disaster of 1948. Further, they saw them as having broken the previously existing leadership of Palestinian society, and as trying to complete the suppression of the Palestinian identity through the heavy control they exerted both on those parts of Palestine not taken by Israel and on all the other communities of Palestinian refugees dispersed throughout the Arab world. The Arab nationalist ideologues who came to power in the Arab states in the 50s were no better, from the Fateh/ Palestinian point of view, than their more traditionalist predecessors. Indeed, because of the brute force and wide appeal of their pan-Arabism, which in most cases opposed any assertion of Palestinian-ness as schismatic, in some ways the Fateh people considered them worse.

With the tides of pan-Arabism running high against them throughout the 50s and early 60s, the men who founded Fateh were virtually powerless to confront the pan-Arabists in any open arena. In the harsh and fragmented circumstances of the Palestinian diaspora, they still had no integrated popular base from which to do so. So what they set about doing instead – and this proved to be their most solid contribution to the Palestinian renaissance – was patiently to weave back together the torn threads of the Palestinians' own internal socio-political entity.

By 1964, when Ahmed Shuqairy was making the preliminary contacts for the holding of the First PNC, he found (as Hassan was to recall that Shuqairy himself later admitted) that the 'flowers' (*zahrat*) of Palestinian political society had already all been organised by Fateh. Nineteen years later, the Sixteenth session of the Fateh-dominated PNC, with its videotaped messages of support from community leaders in the Israeli-occupied territories as well as the direct participation of Palestinians from throughout the diaspora, truly reflected the continued existence of a specifically Palestinian body politic. The continuing importance of Fateh's role in this was pointed up at the 1983 PNC session when even bitter Fateh critic Ahmed Jibril apparently felt he needed the standard embrace of support from Fateh symbol Yasser Arafat to legitimise his intervention.

The Fateh leaders' attempt to carve out and define a piece of specifically Palestinian 'political space' was doubtless aided by the general phenomenon of the waning of the pan-Arabists' appeal throughout the 70s, but their success was due also to their own continuous organising efforts. By the mid-60s these efforts had extended throughout the many communities of Palestinians, both in the Arab world and further afield. The circumstances which followed the Arab states' defeat of 1967 then permitted the Fateh leaders to spin many new threads to their web of support at the Arab level. These connections – particularly those with the once-feared Arab regimes, but also those with popular movements such as the Lebanese National Movement – were to cushion them against the successive blows they suffered in 1970, 1971, 1975-76, 1978 and 1982. Starting in the 60s, the Fateh leaders had also been able to start weaving international connections into their network of support, starting with the Chinese, and later embracing also the Soviets and East Europeans, most of the Third World, and (to a considerable extent, by the early 80s) Western Europe as well.

Given the Palestinians' lack of their own territorial base, this network of external (i.e. non-Palestinian) connections was vital to the maintenance of the movement once it had reached a certain size and degree of visibility, and thus also of vulnerability. While the contribution the individual Fateh leaders could make to the collective leadership was at first primarily based on the influence and support they could wield within Palestinian society, as the leadership's influence broadened the contributions of its various members became a function also of their roles in maintaining these external bases of support.

In practice, by the early 70s, each of the individual leaders brought to the Fateh Central Committee a wide range of both internal support and external contacts. Thus, Salah Khalaf, for example, who was generally regarded as a leftist and a Palestinian populist, did bring a wide base of popular support from the refugee camps and elsewhere to the leadership, but he also brought contacts with many Arab regimes right across the political spectrum from Syria (on occasion) to Morocco (more consistently). Khaled al-Hassan, who was sometimes considered by outsiders as contributing 'merely' his excellent contacts with the Saudis and the other Gulf regimes to the Palestinian leadership, also brought a solid base of support and respect from successive generations of Palestinian intellectuals, again, right across the political spectrum. Farouq Qaddumi contributed the broad range of international contacts he came to build up through his service as PLO 'Foreign Minister' from 1973 on, and also the internal influence he wielded as overlord of Fateh's internal cadre-training programme. Khalil Wazir had his twin internal bases of support through his responsibilities in the Fateh military and for activities in the West Bank, but he also retained his importance in the lengthy and stable relationship with China, and built up a surprising range of other international contacts. Yasser Arafat, of course, contributed his unequalled position as symbol of the Palestinians' national renaissance, both internally and externally.

247

Other members came to the Fateh Central Committee with their own dual internal/external contacts and support, but the collective's success in having already established the Palestinians' own political arena meant that the internal, Palestinian support each enjoyed was still paramount.

The Fateh leaders succeeded over the years in building up their own organisation into a carefully controlled series of interlocking networks, which came to mesh internal support and external links into a flexible and unified whole, commanded from the centre by a tight-knit and relatively homogeneous group of leaders with a long experience of working together. Of the members of the Central Committee elected in 1980, all without exception belonged to the 'historic' generation of those who had been active in Fateh continuously since before the launching of the armed struggle in January 1965. Conversely, of all the original leaders of that historic generation, none had ever led any open schism against the rest of the movement's leaders until Nimr Saleh adopted his pro-Syrian stand in late 1982, and even then the rest of the Fateh leadership were apparently easily able to isolate the effects of his secession. The continuity between the historic generation and the leadership of Fateh in the early 80s was thus extremely strong.

In most Fateh leaders' and Fateh-watchers' view, the second generation of activists was the one that joined after January 1965 but prior to the 1968 Battle of Karameh. By the time of the 1980 Fateh conference, some members of this generation were starting to reach the second echelon of movement leadership in the Revolutionary Council, but the Council still continued to be dominated by members of the historic generation. Because of the nature of the period in which they joined Fateh, many members of this second generation made their greatest contribution to its military activities, where by 1982, and through their performance in the Battle of Beirut, they showed that they constituted a tough, experienced and sophisticated military cadre. All but a tiny handful of the 23 representatives of the Palestinian military who were elected into membership of the Sixteenth PNC in 1983 were Fateh people, and most of these came from Fateh's second generation.

After the 1968 Battle of Karameh, there was a flood of new members into Fateh and, as we saw in chapter 3 above, the standards required of new members, and their indoctrination procedures, perforce were relaxed drastically. This fact, plus all the caution imbued in members of the preceding generations whose political formation had taken place while their struggle was still waged in extreme secrecy, meant that members of the first two generations of Fateh were always reluctant to devolve too much power or responsibility to members of the post-Karameh generation.

In other words, by 1983 the fact was that only very few activists could hope to wield much real power inside Fateh unless they already had a solid record of over 15 years of continuous service in the movement. 'We don't have ideological levels inside Fateh,' said Khaled al-Hassan, 'because for us that doesn't exist. What we do have is levels of experience.'[4] The net result was that, far from being unstable and fractious as the Palestinian movement was often portrayed in Western media, the leadership of Fateh, i.e. the core of the Palestinian movement, was if anything too stable, to the point of imminent ossification, by many Western standards – though this had proved an effective and probably necessary form of leadership for the Palestinians in the stage of reasserting their national identity.

The social and educational backgrounds of the members of Fateh's first two generations reflected two key conditions of the Palestinian diaspora in which they matured: the overturning of existing social classes which the disaster of 1948 had wrought in Palestinian society, and the extreme hunger for education which the refugees saw as the only way out of their misery. Thus, few members of Fateh's historic generation came from the 'big' families which had wielded influence in Palestine prior to 1948. Arafat came from a minor branch of the Husseini family – and through his mother, too – and the Hassan brothers came from a family which had wielded some influence in Haifa. But in general, the historic Fateh activists came from the class of small traders who had been financially ruined in the disaster, rather than from the 'aristocracy' whose standing in the Palestinian community had been gravely damaged by the failure of its leadership in 1948.

But the historic Fateh activists were all people with a strong drive to travel 'up', out of the misery their parents knew. Of the leaders of that generation, all except Khalil al-Wazir had a university degree, and he had failed to complete his time at Alexandria University only because he was deported from Egypt in 1955 after undertaking some unauthorised guerrilla activities. At the time of Karameh, Hassan reported that no fewer than 99 of the 120 Fateh activists killed in the battle there were university graduates. The strong role of university students/graduates in the movement was pointed up again in the early 70s, when it was Fateh students and graduates from European universities who spearheaded much of the Palestinians' diplomatic initiative in Europe, and then in the 1976 fighting in Lebanon, when the Fateh Students' Brigade made a significant contribution to the battles against the Syrian army in the mountains behind Beirut.

The historic leaders of Fateh, most of whom, with the exception of Arafat, were addressing or had already addressed the question of higher education for their own children by the early 80s, always seemed to grasp the role of education in their task of reconstituting the Palestinian socio-political entity. What they felt they did not need were brash young outsiders coming up anew with all the old ideological arguments they had shed blood over and solved to their own satisfaction many years before. This, and the generally strict operation of the 'generation system' described above, meant that there were often a few Palestinian 'bright young things' who did not feel at home in Fateh. In addition, from the early 70s on, an ambitious young Palestinian could far more easily acquire a grandiose-sounding title in a small organisation than reach even the (actually more powerful) middle rungs of Fateh.[5] But, overall, Fateh has continued to attract, as Shuqairy had remarked back in 1964, the flowers of the Palestinian people.

Whilst all the members of the Central Committee elected by Fateh's General Conference in 1980 brought solid contributions to the leadership, the core of this core still remained the fascinating triangular relationship among Arafat, Hassan and Wazir. As Fateh's activities had first coalesced in the late 50s and early 60s, the relationship between Hassan and Wazir became cemented with a closeness which was to last more than two decades. Hassan, on the basis of the experience he had gained in his solid base in Kuwait, turned his sharp analytical mind to developing and propagating the ideology of the emerging movement; Wazir, eight years younger, was despatched nearer the front lines in Beirut to start using the guerrilla experience he had already gained in Gaza in the mid-50s to develop ideas for the movement's coming military struggle, and to serve as Fateh's organisational pivot through the *Filastinuna* post office box.

But in late 1967 it was Arafat (intermediate in age between the other two) who went into the West Bank to try to rouse the flame of rebellion, and even after he had failed the fact that he had attempted it at all increased the solidity of his credentials within the movement. However, Fateh retained the anonymity and collective nature of its leadership until, in the early summer of 1968, when the leadership felt the necessity of naming an official spokesman, it was Arafat who was thrust into the limelight – or, in the parlance of secret movements, which is what Fateh still was, put 'up front' – by being thus designated.

In 1968, there was a fundamental disagreement between Hassan and Arafat over how Fateh should handle its move into the PLO (see chapter 7 above). Arafat contended that Fateh should not seek to take over the PLO on its own, and he was supported in this argument by Khalaf and Qaddumi. Once this view had won out in the discussions of the Fateh leadership, it was therefore Arafat who in February 1969 became Fateh's nominee as Chairman of the PLO. Over the years which followed, the prestige and power of this position further strengthened his position inside the Fateh leadership. Despite his disagreements on the manner in which Fateh had entered the PLO, Hassan nevertheless also entered the PLO Executive

Committee in 1969, where he headed the Political Department ('Foreign Ministry') for the following four years. In January 1973, however, fundamental disagreements with the political programme adopted by the Eleventh PNC in January 1973 prompted him to resign. He then continued his PLO activities only from the relatively low-profile position of Chairman of the PNC Foreign Relations Committee, while maintaining his activities in the Fateh leadership as before.

In 1976, Hassan again found himself in deep disagreement with Arafat, Khalaf and other Central Committee members, this time over policy in Lebanon. He felt despairing enough over the course the others were taking to resign from the Central Committee of the movement (Fateh) with whose birth and development he had been so closely associated. According to Hassan's own account, it was only after Wazir contacted him from Lebanon that he agreed to try to intervene and save the situation there.[6] After Hassan's diplomatic intervention (and, as Hassan himself stressed, the success of the military strategy employed in the Lebanese mountains by Wazir) had proved successful in halting the continuation of the agony in Lebanon, his counsels were once again more closely heeded within the Fateh Central Committee (to which he had returned, if indeed he had ever really effectively left). By the time of the Fifteenth PNC, in April 1981, he was the near-unanimous choice of the Fateh caucus at the PNC session to take up the additional seat Fateh had won in negotiations for the PLO Executive list. The main opposition to this, according to some insiders' accounts of the Fateh caucus deliberations, came from Arafat, who staunchly opposed Hassan's return to the Executive Committee; but none of the other Fateh leaders present at the PNC would agree to enter the PLO Executive in Hassan's place.[7] It was only some time later that Mahmoud Abbas, who had been absent during the PNC session and the caucus meetings, consented to be nominated to the position, and he did so only after consultation with Hassan.

The net effect of the 1981 affair was to underline the continuing vitality and power of the collective leadership of Fateh, and of the core relations within it, to the extent that despite the considerable personal support Arafat enjoyed in the movement by the early 80s, it was still the historic collective leadership of Fateh which provided the central direction and leadership of the Palestinian movement. In 1982, Arafat's personal position in the movement was certainly further enhanced by the leadership he provided during the Battle of Beirut. But it was still the collective leadership of Fateh, rather than any other group, which was to pull him back from the agreement he had hoped to reach with King Hussein in early April 1983 in the continued discussions over the September 1982 Reagan peace plan.

One can only speculate as to what the results might have been if the majority in the Fateh leadership had not decided, back in 1968, to take the other smaller guerrilla groups with it into the PLO. By doing so, however, they ensured that not only the other, smaller guerrilla groups but also the Arab states which stood behind most of them would continue to have a 'legitimate' voice inside the Palestinian decision-making process in the years ahead.

The legitimacy these groups gained within the PLO, and their growth under its umbrella, caused undoubted problems for the Fateh leadership in Jordan in the late 60s and in 1970. The appeal of their radical slogans meant it was impossible, in some cases, for Fateh to ensure the observance even of its own base for its traditional policy of non-intevention in the Arab states' affairs. And the radical actions of the smaller groups, culminating in the PFLP's multiple hijacks of September 1970, drew the Fateh leaders into the open confrontation with the King's forces which ensued. The Palestinian radicals caused further serious problems for the Fateh leaders in 1974, with their opposition to the PLO's pursuit of a diplomatic settlement. But the Rejection Front, as we saw in chapter 7 above, was considerably weakened by the end of 1976, and was dead and buried by 1978. Thereafter, there was no significant Palestinian challenge to the Fateh leadership in the PLO. Indeed, the PFLP's Habash became, as we have seen, almost a political mascot for the Fateh/PLO leaders.

If the Palestinian challenges to Fateh's leadership had been beaten back by the end of the 70s, however, the Arab interventions in PLO afairs which the decision of 1968 had also allowed were still very much in existence in the years thereafter, for through 'their' groups inside the PLO, including inside the PLO leadership, the Syrians, the Iraqis and the Libyans were still easily able to affect PLO decision-making. Although the real strength of the PFLP-GC's Ahmed Jibril in the Palestinian movement was defined by the few dozen (at most) GC fighters who took part in the Battle of Beirut, Syrian and Libyan sponsorship of him meant that he would have to continue to be allowed a say in PLO affairs unless the Fateh leaders wanted to risk a complete showdown, and perhaps the security of the entire Palestinian communities, in both those two countries. By openly criticising Jibril and these two regimes at the Sixteenth PNC, the Fateh leaders demonstrated that they still felt self-confident in their dealings with them. But the majority of Fateh leaders continued to be unwilling to risk a complete showdown – or at least without some tangible hope of a commensurate gain in return.

In the end, perhaps, this problem of outside intervention in Palestinian affairs is insoluble so long as the Palestinians have no territory to call their own. The Palestinian activists will always have to be dependent to some degree on their relations with the host regimes, and especially those in the front line against Israel, while even minimally active communities of Palestinian civilians (where they exist) will continue to be effective hostages in those relations. But the fact remained, in early 1983, that the continued existence of the 'pro-regime' groups in the PLO leadership institutionalised and legitimised the regimes' interventions, leading to a situation where it was these regimes, rather than any significant internal Palestinian opposition, which provided the main brake on the PLO/Fateh leadership's ability to act decisively.

Simply asserting the Palestinian identity was never, of course, the Palestinian activists' sole goal. Nobody ever joined the movement just to sing patriotic songs or enjoy slightly solid socialist-realist art portrayals of Palestinian themes, important though these activities may have been in themselves. They joined to get their land back, and this, by early 1983, they had signally failed to do. 'Ours is the hardest revolution of modern times,' Yasser Arafat said in 1979, 'because it is not just a movement for national liberation, it is also one waged by a people 40 percent of whom are in exile.'[8]

From the beginning, the Fateh organisers realised that the Palestinians' own guerrilla activities would not in themselves lead directly to the collapse of the State of Israel, though they argued that these activities would be a necessary part of the process, inasmuch as they would galvanise the Arab societies into joining the struggle (see chapters 2 and 9 above). The question of the credibility of the guerrilla struggle was thus never so much a function of its immediate military results as of its longer-term political effects, both in contributing to the Palestinians' reassertion of their political identity and in forcing the other Arab societies to face their 'historic responsibilities' towards the Palestinian cause. In a certain sense, one was meant to marvel (as Dr Johnson regrettably said of women preaching, as of dogs standing on their hind legs) not so much at how well they did it, but at the fact that they did it at all.

And do it they did. In the period down to September 1970, the Palestinians were able to sustain a long-term level of guerrilla operations which the Israelis were not to suffer again until they found themselves bogged down in Lebanon after their 1982 invasion. Throughout 1969 and 1970, by the Israelis' own reckoning, the guerrillas were inflicting casualties on them at a rate higher than 35 per month. This rate of activity was reduced to less than half after King Hussein sent his army against the guerrillas in September 1970.[9] But the Jordanians' action was not the sole factor responsible for cutting back the guerrillas' effectiveness. Their own organisational and ideological disorder in that period also contributed, as of course did the harsh and rapid responses evinced by the Israelis. In the late

253

70s, one American military expert testified that 'An analysis of Israel's antifedayeen program from a counterinsurgency point of view leads to the conclusion that it was generally successful.'[10]

Hounded out of Jordan, the Palestinian military turned to reinforcing its existing support bases in south Lebanon, transforming them into its new 'principal forward line'. The dynamics of the situation inside Lebanon, which was already a constant target for Israeli reprisals, prompted this development. Many Palestinian activists continued to argue right through to 1982 that the great weight of the Palestinian military apparatus in Lebanon was needed for purely defensive purposes, that nothing else could protect the refugee camps from Israeli retribution. This argument held some persuasion, at least until the events of 1982 made it clear that no amount of heavy artillery the PLO could amass could protect the camps from a determined assailant prepared to use the latest technological dirty tricks from air, sea and land against them.

The total effect of the elaborate military fortifications laboriously dug around the Palestinian refugee camps in Lebanon throughout the 70s was not really that desired by the diggers. They might have imparted a psychologically necessary sense of security (although this was ultimately revealed as a false security), but they also transformed the Palestinian military presence in Lebanon from an essentially guerrilla formation into something which could never make up its mind whether it was a guerrilla formation or a regular army. The Palestinians found themselves sitting ducks in fixed defensive positions in Lebanon, in blatant contravention of the whole guerrilla military canon. That might have been a viable posture so long as there was some hope of movement on the diplomatic front. But once it became clear that this was not to be, it left them extremely overexposed and vulnerable; and of course, regardless of what local alliances they might forge, they were still 'guests' in somebody else's country.

So in some senses, and despite the terrible amounts of pain involved, the Israelis could even be considered as having done the Palestinian movement a favour by pricking the balloon of its development into a quasi-regular army in Lebanon. The events of 1982 forced the PLO/Fateh leaders to reconsider their strategy, and inevitably most of these re-evaluations resulted not in any startlingly new military theories, but in a return to the origins of the Fateh theory, which had always centred on the importance of the Palestinian guerrilla. One percipient foreign correspondent wrote from Israel on the first anniversary of the June 1982 invasion: 'Small bands of guerrillas ... may in the end pose a greater threat [to Israel] than a PLO mini-army that had much to lose by risking open incursions across the border from its base in southern Lebanon.'[11] Some senior Fateh strategists

254

had already voiced voicing this same conclusion – not just since the events of 1982, but for several years before that.

The military challenge, in the post-Beirut period, was to transform the acknowledged experience and capabilities of the 8,000 PLO fighters evacuated from Beirut in August 1982 into an effective guerrilla force, and to devise a realistic strategy in which they could operate. In the latter respect, many of the same limitations which the Fateh leaders had faced when they first launched their armed struggle in 1965 were once again operational: primarily, the lack of any politically favourable area contiguous with the Israeli front lines in which to maintain their own forward bases.

In comparison with 1965, the guerrillas' military prospects in 1983 showed both new strengths and new problems. By 1983, they had acquired new funds of military, political and organisational experience, along with much greater access to arms and money. In 1965, they had still faced the wrath and repression of the Arab governments abutting Israel, but by 1983 the importance of retaining and fostering political links with their governments acted equally to brake the Palestinian leaders' desire to use these countries as guerrilla springboards. By 1983, also, Israel and some of its Arab neighbours wielded far more advanced technologies of population control against those living under their respective aegises than had been theirs in 1965.

The latter factors would necessitate innovations in guerrilla strategy compared with those which had been followed in 1965, but one constant military/political theme of the Fateh leaders' thinking after the departure from Beirut was their new stress on developing military aspects of the struggle inside the Israeli-occupied areas. It should be noted that by 1983 the support enjoyed by the Palestinian nationalists in these areas was greater than it had ever been before. Different views continued to be expressed within the home-based resistance movement over the importance to be attached to developing their own military activities. The threat of wide-scale deportations was perceived by all members of the West Bank and Gaza communities as a very real possibility in the event of effective military resistance getting under way, but whereas this persuaded some parts of the resistance movement of the need to stress political alternatives to the military struggle, it persuaded others merely that sensitive timing and the formulation of a clear overall political and military strategy were what was called for. Regardless of the eventual outcome of these debates, it seemed as of mid-1983 that long-term structural changes in the political emphases of the Palestinian movement would indicate that a large proportion of the expertise of the former members of the PLO's mini-army in Lebanon would be put to use in the years ahead mainly in a support role for

255

such military activities as would be planned inside the Israeli-held areas, rather than by being reconstituted as another mini-army anywhere else.

The original game-plan of the Fateh leaders had been to set up far more extensive political networks of supporters at both the Palestinian and the Arab levels before launching their armed struggle. The Arab states' establishment of the PLO in 1964 forced them, despite all their studied public indifference to this development at the time, to take some kind of dramatic action to assert their own claim to leadership of the emerging Palestinian movement: hence, the rush into armed struggle well before the previously-conceived political networks were in place. Once launched, of course, the armed struggle did tend to take on a dynamic of its own, until in the aftermath of the Arab states' defeat in 1967 the 'guerrilla idea' threatened to overwhelm all other thinking in the Palestinian sphere – despite the fact that the historic leaders of Fateh still fully realised the limitations on its effectiveness at the purely military level. Since popular outrage at the Arabs' defeat of 1967 absolutely demanded that something – anything – be done to protest it, the Fateh leaders with their keen eyes for popular psychology could not stand aside, but instead developed their successive theories of trying to light the flame of struggle inside the newly occupied areas, and, when that failed, of at least showing that the Arabs could still stand and fight, which they did at Karameh.

The explosion of popularity which Fateh won through its stand at Karameh brought, as we have seen, its own problems to the movement. It also brought heavy new responsibilities of political leadership, forcing it to define more closely its eventual political aims.

The development in the political thinking of the PLO/Fateh leaders, from describing their goal as the 'liberation of Palestine', through the 'secular democratic state', to the 'independent Palestinian state' was described above in chapter 1; so was their parallel move into seeking a negotiated settlement of their national cause (chapter 4). It should be noted, however, that even after declaring themselves ready to pursue a negotiated settlement, so long as they were not invited to do so they insisted on retaining a 'military option', however symbolic, and that even after espousing the mini-state they stressed that this would not imply the liquidation of the right of the Palestinian refugees of 1948 to return to their original homes and properties.

The PLO/Fateh leaders' decision to join the Arab states' peace process in the post-1973 period was based on the idea of the Arab parties *all together* seeking a comprehensive peace settlement in the region. In the new circumstances obtaining in the region immediately after the war this might perhaps have been a realisable aim. But Dr Kissinger was already busy, even before the guns of October 1973 had all fallen silent, chipping away at the foundations both of the united Arab stand and of a comprehensive settlement. With each successive partial disengagement agreement he reached, the Palestinians' political strategy became harder and harder to pursue. At some stage, it must then be said, the Palestinians' political goal changed qualitatively from being merely hard to pursue to being actually unrealisable in the given circumstances. If this stage had not already been reached by late 1977 – and there is some indication, as seen in chapter 10 above, that it may not have been – then once Sadat was firmly launched on his unilateral peace initiative by the end of that year, surely this moment had come.

One might even venture to judge that at this point, given too the parlous condition of the rest of the Arab world, the failure of the Palestinian leadership to be able to present a realisable strategy, either military or political, for the attainment of its goals might have meant that the Palestinian national movement was on its way to being relegated to the long catalogue of lost Middle Eastern national causes – were it not for the continued existence and rising resistance movement of the Palestinian communities inside historic Palestine in this period. For the key political achievement of the armed national movement of the Palestinian exiles proved in the long run to be its role in defining a Palestinian renaissance around which the Palestinians remaining in Palestine could also organise. From the early 70s onwards, nearly all the previous ambiguities in these people's various self-identifications – 'Arabs', 'Palestinian-Jordanians', 'Jordanian-Palestinians', 'Israeli Arabs' and the like – had been resolved, thanks in great part to the guerrilla movement's military and political activities, in favour of straightforward identification with the powerful and unifying Fateh-defined idea of Palestinian-ness.

The years from 1977 onward were marked by an accelerated shift in the centre of gravity of the Palestinian movement from those of its components operating outside the Israeli-held areas closer towards those resisting Israel from within. Indeed – and this is a point of which Menachem Milson seemed to have some understanding – by the end of the 70s the single most important part of the Palestinian national movement was no longer that operating outside historic Palestine, but had become located precisely at the series of political junction-points between the wings of the movement inside and outside historic Palestine. Despite the efforts of Milson and his colleagues in the Israeli administration, from 1974 until at least early 1983 the inherent strengths of these junction-points meant that they were operating with considerable effectiveness to co-ordinate the activities of the two wings. By 1983, one of the most important co-founders of the Palestinian national movement operating from the outside, Khaled al-Hassan, was even saying, 'I think now that the people inside, they have more weight than we have. Their support to us gives us the international legality... They are the only source left to resist.'[12]

Throughout their pursuit of a negotiated settlement in the years 1974 to 1983, the PLO/Fateh leaders directed their efforts primarily to trying to persuade the U.S. government to use its undoubted influence over Israel to bring the Israelis to the negotiating table with them. The details in this strategy were of course many, but in broad outline it consisted of the Palestinians attempting to use three major parallel diplomatic levers – Arab, Eastern bloc and West European – to bring this about. On the basis of this strategy a whole vast diplomatic edifice was created, touching nerve-centres throughout all these regions.

Yet still the U.S. government refused even to talk to the PLO leadership, and there developed in Palestinian-American relations a whole sub-diplomacy of nuance, faulty and faltering mediations, and, on both sides, a very basic mistrust. In 1977, for example, even as the Fateh/PLO leaders were girding themselves to revamp their diplomacy after the end of the Lebanese fighting, the Fateh leader in charge of Palestinian diplomacy, Farouq Qaddumi, was saying of the Carter administration's first overtures, 'We believe that the United States is going through the motions, not really taking action. We do not expect anything from this operation, because it is an American manoeuvre.'[13]

On the U.S. side, meanwhile, members of successive administrations in Washington expressed an apparently deeply held fear that even if they did come to some kind of political agreement with Yasser Arafat, they had no reason to trust him to carry out his side of it. Even if he wanted to, how could he impose implementation on all the other branches of the Palestinian movement, fractious and unstable as it was 'known' to be?

It was the first aspect of these fears that was addressed by the (non-official) American politico-psychologist Herbert C. Kelman in a study he made of Arafat in late 1982. Kelman considered that 'Arafat's refusal until now to make explicit commitments makes it difficult to conclude with certainty that he has the will to make peace, but it does not constitute conclusive evidence of a lack of will.' U.S. policy, Kelman said, 'can play a crucial role in providing a meaningful test of Arafat's will and capacity to negotiate a settlement'.[14]

What Kelman missed, however, was the fact that throughout the latter half of the 70s, and right up until June 1982, the Fateh/PLO leadership had indeed been submitted to a series of tests of its ability to implement different commitments to the U.S. From late 1973 onwards, the two sides made a series of agreements through the semi-clandestine 'security channel' between them, as described in chapter 10 above, and in nearly all these cases the Palestinian leadership showed itself capable of following through on its undertakings. Then in 1978 the PLO leadership made a commitment, indirectly through and to the U.S., of a completely higher order in the political scheme of things: for the first time ever, it committed itself to a formal, public cease-fire with Israel; and this cease-fire, as described in chapter 5 above, was brokered jointly by the United Nations and by the U.S. On that occasion, the PLO leadership showed itself ready and able to use force against those Palestinians who sought to prevent implementation of the cease-fire agreement; and the cease-fire continued in force for three years, until the devastating Israeli air strike of July 1981 against the heart of the Palestinian-populated areas of Beirut forced the PLO leaders to respond.

The upshot of the 1981 escalation in Lebanon was the conclusion of the first cease-fire the PLO leaders had ever reached with Israel *under the direct auspices of special U.S. presidential envoy Philip Habib* – although the Americans' continued refusal to talk openly to the Palestinians meant that this agreement too was partly dressed in U.N. clothing. Once again, the PLO leaders were able to enforce implementation from their side, and despite successive large-scale Israeli infractions they abandoned the 1981 cease-fire only after Israel massively bombarded Beirut in early June 1982.[15]

The U.S. administration would thus seem to have had ample opportunity to judge the PLO leadership's honesty and effectiveness by the end of 1982, but still it gave little sign of any willingness to make the kinds of overture that would have drawn the PLO into the diplomatic process. Thus, by early 1983, the U.S. administration's refusal to have any direct political dealings with the PLO seemed to constitute, not the result of an understandable reluctance to take a leap in the dark towards an unknown destination, but a political 'immovable object' in its own right.

The major question facing the Fateh Palestinian leaders in early 1983 appeared to be whether some 'external' factor – radical political change in Egypt? a move back towards great-power détente? – might intervene to salvage the hopes they had pinned for nearly a decade on attaining at least a mini-state (i.e. two-state) solution for the Palestinian-Israeli problem. Broad hints were meanwhile being dropped, by members of the U.S. administration and others, that the gathering momentum of Israeli settlement activity in the 1967-occupied areas meant that time was running out for the Palestinians. In spite of this, Palestinian leaders both inside and outside those areas hung together in their refusal to enter a peace process under the terms spelt out by the Reagan administration, which they considered an insufficient basis for starting talks. For some Palestinians, at least, the pace of Israel's colonisation of the West Bank meant only that

259

time was running out not for the Palestinians as such but for the hopes of a two-state solution in Israel/Palestine. For with the increased demographic mingling of the two peoples in the whole of Mandate Palestine, and the rise of nationalist feeling and activity among the Palestinians of 1948 Israel, over time the only viable solution left to a situation increasingly resembling the demographic and political entanglement of Northern Ireland would have to be a single-state formula – that is, the 'secular democratic state'. Perhaps, a persistent minority continued to feel, this would anyway, despite all the sufferings to be expected over the intervening period, prove preferable to creation of a 'rump' Palestinian state.

Within both the two-state and the one-state perspectives for a solution, it seemed certain by early 1983 that a cardinal role would continue to be played in the years ahead by the resistance movement inside Mandate Palestine.

The role of the PLO/Fateh leaders thus seemed bound to change, as the new circumstances of the post-Beirut period shifted them (for a while, at least) away from the direct cutting-edge of the daily struggle against Israel. In immediate operational terms, they would perforce move into more of a support role for their brothers and cousins inside the Israeli-held areas. This support would continue to have both political and military aspects. In broad terms, the very fact of their freedom from the constraints of Israeli control would continue to give the PLO/Fateh leaders a key role in co-ordinating all the many different wings and aspects of the Palestinians' national struggle, while the close association of the historic Fateh leaders with the whole reassertion of the Palestinians' national identity in the decades following 1948 assured them a continuing ideological role of unequalled importance in the movement.

Around this reassertion of identity, the Fateh leaders had painstakingly reconstructed an entire Palestinian socio-political community, with its fellowship, leadership and financial bonds retained intact even after the terrible losses the movement suffered in the 1982 Battle of Beirut. Palestinian businessmen in the Gulf, in the other Arab countries and in Europe continued to offer money to the movement and jobs to its supporters; their wives continued to organise social programmes for the families of those who had fallen in battle; Palestinian families with branches both inside and outside the Israeli-held areascontinued to look for a way out of the terrible. dilemma of their dispersal that would satisfy the best interests of all of them; and the towns of the occupied territories continued to ring to the demonstrators' haunting chants of *Filastin arabiyya* (Palestine is Arab!). And weaving through all these activities, the ubiquitous networks of the many Fateh apparatuses continued to tie them all together within the reconstituted Palestinian nation.

By 1983, the fact and vitality of this nationhood seemed incontrovertible, as did the role of the PLO/Fateh leaders in having achieved this. The continued existence of the Palestinian people, as a people, no longer seemed to be in doubt, nor its leadership in jeopardy. Palestinian nationalism had become an irresistible force, but the results of its encounter with the seemingly immovable object of American policy had still to be ascertained.

Appendixes
Notes
References and select bibliography

The political programme of the Sixteenth PNC, Algiers, 22 February 1983 (extracts)

Source: FBIS, Middle East Section, 23 Feb. 1983, pp. A14-16, and 24 Feb. 1983, p. A1.

Palestinian National Unity:

The battle of steadfastness and heroism in Lebanon and Beirut epitomizes Palestinian national unity in its best form. Out of this leading Palestinian experience, the PNC affirms the need to bolster national unity among the revolution's detachments...

Independent Palestinian Decision:

The PNC affirms continued adherence to independent Palestinian decisionmaking, its protection, and the resisting of all pressures from whatever source to detract from this independence.

Palestinian armed struggle:

The PNC affirms the need to develop and escalate the armed struggle against the Zionist enemy. It affirms the right of the Palestine revolution forces to carry out military action against the Zionist enemy from all Arab fronts. It also affirms the need to unify the forces of the Palestine revolution within the framework of a single National Liberation Army.

The Occupied Homeland:

The PNC salutes our steadfast masses in the occupied territory in the face of the occupation, colonization, and uprooting. It also salutes their comprehensive national unity and their complete rallying around the PLO, the sole legitimate representative of the Palestinian people, both internally and externally. The PNC condemns and denounces all the suspect Israeli and American attempts to strike at Palestinian national unanimity and calls on the masses of our people to resist them.

. . .

Contacts with Jewish Forces:

In affirming resolution No. 14 of the political declaration of the PNC at its 13th session on 12 March 1977, the PNC calls on the Executive Committee to study movement within this framework in line with the interest of the cause of Palestine and the Palestinian national interest.

. . .

Arab Relations:

D. Rejection of all schemes aimed at harming the right of the PLO to be the sole legitimate representative of the Palestinian people through any formula such as assigning powers, acting on its behalf, or sharing its right of representation.

. . .

The Resolutions of the Fes [Fez] Summit:

The Arab Peace Plan:

The PNC considers the Fes summit resolutions as the minimum for political moves by the Arab states, moves which must complement military action with all its requirements for adjusting the balance of forces in favor of the struggle and Palestinian and Arab rights. The Council, in understanding these resolutions, affirms it is not in conflict with the commitment to the political program and the resolutions of the National Council.

Jordan:

Emphasizing the special and distinctive relations linking the Jordanian and Palestinian peoples and the need to develop them in harmony with the national interest of the two peoples and the Arab nation, and in order to realize the rights [passage indistinct] the sole legitimate representative of the Palestinian people, both inside and outside the occupied land, the PNC deems that future relations with Jordan should be founded on the basis of a confederation between two independent states.

. . .

The Steadfastness and Confrontation Front:

The PNC entrusts the PLO Executive Committee to have talks with the sides of the pan-Arab Steadfastness and Confrontation Front to discuss how it should be revived anew on sound, clear, and effective foundations, working from the premise that the front was not at the level of the tasks required of it during the Zionist invasion of Lebanon.

Egypt:

...The Council calls on the Executive Committee to define relations with the Egyptian regime on the basis of its abandoning Camp David policy.

. . .

On the International Level:

Brezhnev's Plan:

The PNC expresses its appreciation and support for the proposals contained in President Brezhnev's plan of 16 September 1982 which asserts the established national rights of our people, including the right to return and the right to self-determination and to set up the independent Palestinian state under the leadership of the PLO, this people's sole legitimate representative...

Reagan's Plan:

Reagan's plan, in style (an-nahj) and content, does not respect the established national rights of the Palestinian people since it denies the right of return and self-determination and the setting up of the independent Palestinian state and also the PLO – the sole legitimate representative of the Palestinian people – and since it contradicts international legality. Therefore, the PNC rejects the considering of this plan as a sound basis for the just and lasting solution of the cause of Palestine and the Arab-Zionist conflict.

. . .

The Palestinian National Charter as revised by the Fourth PNC meeting, July 1968 (extracts)

Source: Leila S. Kadi, *Basic Political Documents of the Armed Palestinian Resistance Movement*, Beirut: PLO Research Center, 1969, pp. 137-142.

Article 1: Palestine is the homeland of the Arab Palestinian people; it is an indivisible part of the Arab homeland, and the Palestinian people are an integral part of the Arab nation.

Article 2: Palestine, with the boundaries it had during the British mandate, is an indivisible territorial unit. . .

Article 4: The Palestinian identity is a genuine, essential and inherent characteristic; it is transmitted from parents to children. The Zionist occupation and the dispersal of the Palestinian Arab people, through the disasters which befell them, do not make them lose their Palestinian identity and their membership of the Palestinian community, nor do they negate them.

Article 5: The Palestinians are those Arab nationals who, until 1947, normally resided in Palestine regardless of whether they were evicted from it or have stayed there. Anyone born, after that date, of a Palestinian father – whether inside Palestine or outside it – is also a Palestinian.

Article 6: The Jews who had normally resided in Palestine until the beginning of the Zionist invasion will be considered Palestinians. . .

Article 8: The phase in their history, through which the Palestinian people are now living, is that of national struggle for the liberation of Palestine. Thus the conflicts among the Palestinian national forces are secondary, and should be ended for the sake of the basic conflict that exists between the forces of Zionism and of imperialism on the one hand, and the Palestinian Arab people on the other. . .

Article 9: Armed struggle is the only way to liberate Palestine. Thus it is the overall strategy, not merely a tactical phase. The Palestinian Arab people assert their absolute determination and firm resolution to continue their armed struggle and to work for an armed popular revolution for the liberation of their country and their return to it. . .

Article 10: Commando action constitutes the nucleus of the Palestinian popular liberation war. . .

Article 12: The Palestinian people believe in Arab unity. In order to contribute their share towards the attainment of that objective, however, they must, at the present stage of their struggle, safeguard their Palestinian identity and develop their consciousness of that identity, and oppose any plan that may dissolve or impair it. . .

Article 15: The liberation of Palestine, from an Arab viewpoint, is a national duty and it attempts to repel the Zionist and imperialist aggression against the Arab homeland, and aims at the elimination of Zionism in Palestine. Absolute responsibility for this falls upon the Arab nation – peoples and governments – with the Arab people of Palestine in the vanguard. . .

Article 19: The partition of Palestine in 1947 and the establishment of the state of Israel are entirely illegal, regardless of the passage of time, because they were contrary to the will of the Palestinian people and to their natural right in their homeland, and inconsistent with the principles embodied in the Charter of the United Nations, particularly the right to self-determination.

Article 20: The Balfour Declaration, the mandate for Palestine and everything that has been based upon them, are deemed null and void. Claims of historical or religious ties of Jews with Palestine are incompatible with the facts of history and the true conception of what constitutes statehood. Judaism, being a religion, is not an independent nationality. Nor do Jews constitute a single nation with an identity of its own; they are citizens of the states to which they belong.

Article 21: The Arab Palestinian people, expressing themselves by the armed Palestinian revolution, reject all solutions which are substitutes for the total liberation of Palestine. . .

Article 22: Zionism is a political movement organically associated with international imperialism and antagonistic to all action for liberation and to progressive movements in the world. It is racist and fanatic in its nature, aggressive, expansionist and colonial in its aims, and fascist in its methods. . .

Article 27: The Palestine Liberation Organisation shall cooperate with all Arab states, each according to its potentialities; and will adopt a neutral policy among them in the light of the requirements of the war of liberation; and on this basis it shall not interfere in the internal affairs of any Arab state. . .

Article 33: This Charter shall not be amended save by (vote of) a majority of two-thirds of the total membership of the National Congress of the Palestine Liberation Organisation [i.e. the PNC] at a special session convened for that purpose.

Members of the PLO Executive Committee elected February 1983

		Secretary-General of the group
Yasser Arafat	Fateh (Chairman)	—
Farouq al-Qaddumi	Fateh	—
Mahmoud Abbas	Fateh	—
Yasser Abed Rabboo	DFLP	Nayef Hawatma
Ahmed al-Yamani	PFLP	George Habash
Muhammed al-Khalifa	Saiqa	Issam al-Qadi
Talal Naji	PFLP-GC	Ahmed Jibril
Abder-Rahim Ahmed	ALF	Abder-Rahim Ahmed
Abdel-Muhsin Abu Maizar	Independent	—
Hanna Nasir	Independent	—
Muhammed an-Nashashibi	Independent	—
Jamal Surani	Independent	—
Hamid Abu Sitta	Independent	—
Ahmed Sidqi al-Dajani	Independent	—

The following two tiny PLO member-groups have no member in the Executive Committee:

	PLF	Talaat Yaaqoub
	PPSF	Bahjat Abu Gharbiyya

List of regular sessions of the Palestinian National Council, May 1964 to February 1983

	Venue	*Date*	
1st	Jerusalem	May/June 1964	
2nd	Cairo	May/June 1965	
3rd	Gaza	May 1966	
	(Middle East war)		
4th	Cairo	July 1968	Guerrilla groups
5th	Cairo	February 1969	take over PLO
6th	Cairo	September 1969	
7th	Cairo	May/June 1970	
8th	Cairo	February 1971	
9th	Cairo	July 1971	
10th	Cairo	April 1972	
11th	Cairo	January 1973	
	(Middle East war)		
12th	Cairo	June/July 1974	
13th	Cairo	March 1977	
14th	Damascus	January 1979	
15th	Damascus	April 1981	
16th	Algiers	February 1983	

Fateh Central Committee elected April/May 1980

Previous members re-elected
Yasser Arafat (Commander-in-Chief of the military)
Khalil al-Wazir (Deputy Commander-in-Chief)
Mahmoud Abbas
Hayel Abdel-Hamid
Muhammed Ghunaym
Khaled al-Hassan
Salah Khalaf
Farouq al-Qaddumi
Nimr Saleh[1]
Selim al-Zaanoun

New members
Samih Abu Kuwaik
Majd Abu Sharar[2]
Hani al-Hassan
Rafiq al-Natsheh
Saad Sayel[3]

1 Saleh's membership in the Committee was frozen in January 1983 (see chapter 6).

2 Abu Sharar was killed in Rome in October 1981.

3 Sayel was killed in eastern Lebanon in late 1982.

Notes

Note: where a reference is made to a *despatch* to a newspaper, but the title and page reference of the article as published are not given, the final published version of this despatch will have appeared in the issue of the newspaper one or more days after the date given.

1. The PLO in the 1980s

1 For example, Ariel Sharon reportedly said in June 1982, 'The more we damage the PLO infrastructure the more the Arabs in the West Bank and Gaza will be ready to negotiate with us and establish coexistence' (*Times* (London), 19 June 1982). See also David K. Shipler, 'Israel steps up drive against PLO on West Bank', *New York Times*, 11 July 1982, p. 12.

2 See, for example, David K. Shipler, 'Rising worry for Israelis', *New York Times*, 12 July 1982, pp. 1 and 6.

3 Indeed, the Lebanese events of summer 1982 sparked considerable anti-Israeli protest among the Palestinian population of the occupied territories, including those who had remained inside Israel's 1948 borders. See, for example, *New York Times*, 5 July 1982, p. 4 and Sa'di, 1983, pp. 86-115.

4 See, for example, Kiernan, 1976, p. 33. He locates Arafat's birthplace in either Cairo or Gaza. However, some of the most substantial of Kiernan's other 'revelations' in this work have been disproved by reputable scholars: see, for example, Behbehani, 1981, pp. 32-37 and pp. 362-64. Sources in Arafat's own family say the family did not establish a household in Cairo before 1932.

5 It is a common feature of Palestinian society that a man is called 'father of —' (Abu —) with the name of his eldest son; a woman is likewise called 'Umm —' ('mother of'), again with the name of the eldest son. A man who has no son is often, as a mark of respect, called Abu plus the name he might be expected to give to a son. Yasser Arafat is not married, but is called 'Abu 'Ammar' as an inversion of the name of the heroic early Muslim warrior 'Ammar bin ('son of') Yasser. The idea, presumably, that if Yasser Arafat had a son, he would or should be as heroic as the earlier 'Ammar.

6 For details of the Arab states' roles in the dissolution of the Palestinian political leadership in this period, see Samih Shabib, 'Muqaddamat al-musadara al-rasmiyya lil-shakhsiyya al-wataniyya al-filastiniyya, 1948-1950', *Shu'un Filastiniyya*, Aug./Sept./Oct. 1982, pp. 72-88.

7 *Report of the Commissioner-General of the United Nations Relief and Works Agency for Palestine Refugees in the Near East, 1 July 1981 – 30 June 1982* (United Nations, General Assembly Official Records: 37th Session, Supplement No. 13 (A/37/13)), p. 47.

8 For more details of Fateh's organisational structure, see ch.2 below. A list of the members elected to the Fateh Central Committee in June 1980 can be found in Appendix 5; that Committee remained in control of the movement's affairs at least until early 1983 with only minor changes in personnel.

9 A list of the PNC sessions down to early 1983 is found in Appendix 4.

10 *Malaff watha'iq filastin, al-Juz' al-thani, 1950-69* (Cairo: Al-Markaz al-ʿArabi lil-Maʿlumat, n.d.), p. 1287.

11 My computing, from attendance at Sixteenth PNC session.

12 See fig. 1.

13 On the two occasions (at the Fourth and Fourteenth PNCs) where no agreement was found possible on the composition of a new Executive Committee, the old Executive was returned into office with only minor changes. The underlying problem was solved in each case at the following PNC session: at the Fifteenth PNC, for example, conditions were agreed for the return to the Executive Committee of George Habash's Popular Front for the Liberation of Palestine, and a new Executive was voted in with little further disagreement on that issue.

14 A list of the members of the PLO Executive Committee is given in Appendix 3.

15 *Fiches du monde arabe*, No. 1658 (6 August 1980). Some smaller Palestinian fighting groups, notably Ahmed Jibril's PFLP-GC, acquired more advanced weaponry than this during the following two years. But the Palestinian mainstream complained that the PFLP-GC never allowed these weapons, which they said included SAM-9 surface-to-air missiles supplied by Libya, to be put into operation.

16 Interview with Khaled al-Hassan, October 1982.

17 Habash's behaviour throughout all the Battle of Beirut and at the Sixteenth PNC reflected this. For more details on the PFLP and the Rejection Front, see ch.7 below.

18 My notes from Arafat's meeting with Jesse Jackson's delegation, September 1979.

19 Interview with Salah Khalaf, February 1983.

20 Interview with Khaled al-Hassan, October 1982.

2. The phoenix hatches (1948-67)

1 Other early leaders of the Cairo student organisation who were later to play an important role in the development of Fateh included Salim al-Zaanun, Abdel-Fattah Hammoud and Zuhair al-ʿAlami (interview with Zaanun, April 1983).

2 Abou Iyad, 1981, p. 20. My emphasis.

3 *Ibid.*, p. 21.

4 *Ibid.*, p. 23.

5 Most of the material for this paragraph came from my interview with Khaled al-Hassan, October 1982.

6 Interview with Salah Khalaf conducted by Lutfi al-Kholi: *Al-Tali'a* (Cairo), June 1969, pp. 51-87. Fateh official translation as published in *International Documents on Palestine, 1969*, pp. 699-733.

7 See ch.1, n. 5 above.

8 Abou Iyad, 1981, p. 29.

9 Interview with Khaled al-Hassan, October 1982.

10 *Ibid.*

11 *Ibid.*

12 The members of the Central Committee were all *ex officio* members of the Revolutionary Council, as were the commanders of the major Al-'Asifa military brigades and directors of important Fateh institutions. In addition, Arafat was reportedly given the right to appoint 15 Council members himself, from a list of 45 names provided by the Conference.

13 The source who provided this analysis wished to remain anonymous.

14 'Alush, 1964, pp. 180-82. Although 'Alush was not at that point at all in favour of *Filastinuna*'s ideas, and in fact reproduced them in his book only to criticise them, his rendering of them appears quite faithful, and could possibly have been a direct quotation. Later on, however, 'Alush joined Fateh, where he became a leading figure on its left wing and rose with Fateh's help to the presidency of the General Union of Palestinian Writers and Journalists. Then, in 1978, he was accused of collaborating with a conspiracy against the Fateh leadership orchestrated by Fateh renegade Abu Nidal (see ch.5 below).

15 'Alush gives the following reference for his quotation: *Filastinuna*, No. 23: 4th year, March 1962, p. 3.

16 'Alush, 1964, pp. 180-82.

17 Actually, two summit meetings of Arab heads of state had preceded the 1964 gathering, in May 1946 and November 1956. But the January 1964 summit has gone down in history as 'the First Arab Summit', and subsequent summits have been numbered accordingly.

18 *Malaff*, n.d., p. 1273.

19 See, for example, *Al-Kitab al-Sanawi lil-Qadiyya al-Filastiniyya, 1964*, pp. 95 and 98.

20 *Ibid.*, p. 96. The ANM later founded the Popular Front for the Liberation of Palestine as its Palestinian wing. See ch.7 below.

21 Interview with Khaled al-Hassan, April 1983.

22 Abou Iyad, 1981, p. 21.

23 Interview with Khaled al-Hassan, April 1983. Khalaf wrote that it had been he who had made these contacts with Shuqairy (Abou Iyad, 1981, p. 41).

24 Interview with Khaled al-Hassan, April 1983.

25 For the text of the National Charter as it emerged after some revisions in 1968, see Appendix 2 below.

26 *Malaff*, n.d., p. 1362. This claim has been rejected by the groups which have dominated the PLO since 1969. But it was later revived, interestingly enough, by Israeli Defence Ministers Moshe Dayan and Ariel Sharon. By mid-1982, the latter was claiming volubly that the Palestinians already had one homeland, in Jordan, so they should not lay claim to another (in the West Bank and Gaza).

27 *Malaff*, n.d., p. 1363.
28 See, for example, the footnote to *International Documents on Palestine, 1967* (henceforth *IDP, 1967*), p. 570, and Helena Cobban, 'Shukairy shuns contrived solutions in Mideast', *Daily Star* (Beirut), 22 August 1975.
29 *Al-Kitab al-Sanawi lil-Qadiyya al-Filastiniyya, 1964*, p. 102.
30 *Ibid.*, p. 103.
31 Yaari, 1970, p. 37.
32 Abou Iyad, 1981, p. 42.
33 For more details on Palestinian-Chinese relations, see ch.11 below.
34 Abou Iyad, 1981, p. 42.
35 See an expression of Sweidani's views on this subject in, for example, *Al-Watha'iq al-filastiniyya al-'arabiyya, 1966*, p. 209.
36 Some Israelis, for their part, also tacitly admit this. See, for example, Yair Evron, *An American-Israeli Defense Treaty* (Tel Aviv: Tel Aviv University Center for Strategic Studies, 1981), p. 44, where the author refers to Israel as 'the guarantor of Jordan and Lebanon'.
37 *Al-Watha'iq al-filastiniyya al-'arabiyya, 1965*, p. 1.
38 *'Al-Tali'a'*, 1969, in *IDP, 1969*, p. 709.
39 Interview with Khaled al-Hassan, October 1982.
40 *Al-Watha'iq al-filastiniyya al-'arabiyya, 1965*, p. 353.
41 *Ibid.*, pp. 482-83. One instance of the official 'news blackout', imposed even in 'democratic' Lebanon, occurred when the Press Union in Lebanon circulated newspaper publishers in early September 1965 with a request, which they attributed to the Lebanese army command, that all news related to Al-'Asifa be considered military news and therefore not be published (*ibid.*, p. 467).
42 In Khaled al-Hassan's view 'We had nothing to do with the 1967 war at all' (interview, April 1983).

3. The joy of flying (1967-73)

1 Abou Iyad, 1981, p. 52.
2 The fullest account of the Arafat group's exploits in the West Bank, which assigns them considerably more importance than is given even in much subsequent Arab mythology, is contained in Yaari, 1970, pp. 125-50. See also Abou Iyad, 1981, pp. 55-56.
3 This man, 'Azmi al-Sughayr, was later despatched by the Israelis on an espionage mission to the East Bank area, where he turned himself over to the guerrillas. After eliciting from him details of precisely what information the Israelis now had on their activities, he was rehabilitated into guerrilla ranks, and served in sensitive military posts within the guerrilla forces until he was killed in south Lebanon in summer 1982.
4 Interview with Yasser Arafat, November 1979.
5 Yaari, 1970, p. 133.
6 *Ibid.*, p. 150.
7 See, for example, Tawil, 1979, p. 126.
8 *Rose El-Youssef* (Cairo), 20 May 1968, p. 3.
9 See, for example Erskine Childers, 'The other exodus', *Spectator* (London), 12

May 1961; Dimbleby and McCullin, 1980, pp. 88-90; Kimche and Kimche, 1960, pp. 227-28; Sayigh, 1979, pp. 64-97.

10 The American researcher Ian Lustick wrote, 'In the first massive wave of [Jewish] immigration, nearly 200,000 Jews were able to obtain housing by moving into abandoned Arab towns and villages' (Lustick, 1980, p. 58). For a comprehensive listing of 385 Palestinian villages (out of a pre-1948 total of 475) destroyed by Israel after its founding in 1948, see *The Shahak Report*, produced by Dr Israel Shahak, Chairman of the Israeli League for Human and Civil Rights in Tel Aviv, on 15 February 1973.

11 Israeli Arabist Yehoshafat Harkabi quotes Professor Haim Hillel Ben-Sasson as describing the 'feeling of diaspora' as 'expressed in the sense of being foreign in the strange land, longing for the political and national past, and haunted by penetrating questions as to the causes, reasons and purpose of the present situation'. The Palestinians, Harkabi adds, 'had something of this feeling, although their diaspora was in no way comparable to the Jewish diaspora' (Ma'oz, 1975, p. 60).

12 Sayigh, 1979, p. 102.

13 Of course this theory, like all global theories, encompasses seemingly contradictory details. Fateh's leadership core is made up predominantly of intellectuals who 'succeeded' in making a new life in the Gulf; but their earlier experiences in the refugee camp communities in Gaza and elsewhere cannot be forgotten. And Dr George Habash, intellectual and co-founder of the ANM and the PFLP, did enjoy considerable personal prestige in refugee camps. But Sayigh's general rule does still appear to have some value, at least up to the time of the 1974 oil-boom when large numbers of additional refugee camp residents started being drawn directly into the petrodollar economy.

14 Interview with a Palestinian guerrilla, late 1979.

15 Sharabi, 1970, p. 21.

16 For the text of the statement, see *International Documents on Palestine, 1967* (henceforth *IDP, 1967*), pp. 723-26. For details of the PFLP's development see ch.7 below.

17 Abou Iyad, 1981, p. 57.

18 *Ibid.*, p. 58.

19 For another account of the battle, which largely corroborates Khalaf's, see Cooley, 1973, pp. 100-01.

20 Quoted in Sharabi, 1970, p. 8.

21 Interviews with Khaled al-Hassan, October 1982 and April 1983.

22 Rashid Hamid, 'What is the PLO?', in *Journal of Palestine Studies*, Summer 1975, pp. 99-100. For more details of these political developments see the rest of Hamid's article, and Quandt *et al.*, 1973, pp. 67-73. I am also grateful to Judith Perera for sharing some of her material on this period.

23 Kadi, 1969, p. 138. All the quotations used here from the Palestinian National Charter use this text, which was published by the PLO's own Research Center. For the text of the amended National Charter, which remained unchanged up to early 1983, see Appendix 2.

24 *Fiches du monde arabe*, No. 1901 (20 May 1981).

25 Hassan resigned from the PLO Executive Committee in January 1973, after failing to persuade the Fateh/PLO leadership to adopt a more realistic diplomatic strategy. His place as 'Foreign Minister' was then taken by Najjar. In April 1973, Najjar was killed in Beirut by the Israelis (see below); he was succeeded in the post by Qaddumi.

26 Khalaf interview in *Al-Tali'a* (Cairo), June 1969. English translation in *IDP, 1969*, p. 701. My italics.

27 The main source for this and the next two paragraphs is Abou Iyad, 1981, pp. 53-55 and 62-63. For further analysis of the development of Fateh's relations with the Arab regimes in this period see ch.9 below.

28 Interview with Khaled al-Hassan, April 1983.

29 Abou Iyad, 1981, p. 55.

30 Heikal, 1975, p. 64.

31 *Ibid.*, p. 65.

32 Cooley, 1973, p. 104.

33 Abou Iyad, 1981, p. 47. According to other accounts, Arafat's Fateh colleague Abu Ali Iyad was also arrested with him on this occasion.

34 For an English translation of this text see *IDP, 1969*, p. 804.

35 *Financial Times* (London), 25 March 1968.

36 See Abou Iyad, 1981, p. 77. Khalaf recalls that at a meeting of the PLO Central Council in July 1970, comprising representatives of all guerrilla groups, 'only a handful of delegates from organisations other than Fateh' agreed with his proposition that the guerrillas should negotiate a *modus vivendi* with Hussein.

37 Interview with Khaled al-Hassan, October 1982.

38 Kissinger, 1979, pp. 595-96.

39 *Ibid.*, pp. 596-97.

40 *Ibid.*, p. 606. Seymour Hersh wrote, 'The hijackings did more than jangle nerves in Washington. Nixon, deciding that the time had come to destroy the *fedayeen*, ordered American Navy planes from the Sixth Fleet in the Mediterranean to bomb the guerrillas' hideaways... There is no evidence that Kissinger raised any objections to the order, which the President himself verbally gave to Laird. But Laird did. 'We had bad weather for forty-eight hours,' Laird recalled years later, with a grin. 'The Secretary of Defense can always find a reason not to do something. There's always bad weather.'... The exact date of Nixon's order is not known, but the evidence – and Laird's recollections – suggest that the most critical moment came on or before September 8, two days after the first hijacking, and before the deadline for the release of the jailed PLO members' (Hersh, 1983, pp. 235-36).

41 It should be noted that Kissinger viewed almost the entire Jordan crisis primarily as a test of wills with Moscow, and he appears to have viewed the Palestinian guerrillas of all different tendencies simply as Moscow's 'clients' – regardless of Moscow's deep disagreements with PFLP tactics and lingering reservations even about Fateh's (see ch.11 below). But Kissinger's chapter on the Jordan crisis is nonetheless worth reading, not least to notice the nuance of his views about the Hashemite regime.

42 Kissinger, 1979, p. 609.

43 *IDP, 1970,* p. 907.

44 *Fiches du monde arabe,* No. 54 (21 August 1974).

45 Kalb and Kalb, 1974, pp. 199-200. Kissinger himself says he only learnt of the incursion on 19 September (Kissinger, 1979, p. 618).

46 Kalb and Kalb, 1974, p. 200.

47 *Ibid.* The Kalbs do not say here what the Israelis were doing that might have worried Hussein.

48 *Ibid.,* p. 202.

49 Kissinger, 1979, p. 623.

50 For details of these developments, see *Fiches du monde arabe,* No. 826 (14 December 1977).

51 The power of Palestinian-related developments to affect state affairs in a wide circle elsewhere throughout the Arab world should not be underestimated. The September 1970 events in Jordan probably also contributed greatly to President Nasser's death from a heart attack on the 28th of that month. Contrary to his doctors' express orders to rest, he had thrown himself into the efforts to find a peaceful settlement between the two sides, and on the day of his death he had spent six hours on his feet at Cairo Airport seeing off the participants in his emergency Arab summit (Heikal, 1975, pp. 103-04). On hearing of the death of their old adversary, Arafat, Wazir and Mahmoud Abbas 'all three burst into tears' (Abou Iyad, 1981, p. 90). Certainly the passing of the Egyptian leader, and his succession by Anwar Sadat, was to usher in an era of change for the whole Middle East.

52 Cooley, 1973, pp. 131-32.

53 Abou Iyad, 1981, p. 98.

54 *Middle East Monitor,* Vol. 3, No. 8 (15 April 1973), pp. 7-8, quoted in Amos, 1980, p. 316.

   Awda's career subsequent to his release by the Jordanians in September 1973 continued to be colourful. Travelling to Paris on official PLO business with the Quai d'Orsay in early 1977, he was arrested by the French secret police on the request of the Israelis, who filed an order for his extradition. Released once again, amidst many red faces in Paris, he returned to PLO headquarters in Beirut. But in 1978 he was also heavily implicated in the same Iraqi plot within Fateh in which Naji 'Alush was involved (see ch.2, n.14 above). However, by February 1983 he was back in favour with the Fateh leadership, who sponsored his re-election into the Palestinian National Council.

   Salameh was also an interesting character. His first wife was from the Husseini family, his second the Lebanese-born 'Miss Universe' of 1970. He was killed by an Israeli car-bomb in Beirut in January 1979.

55 *Fiches du monde arabe,* No. 26 (24 July 1974).

56 From 1978 onwards, Banna was to collaborate with the Iraqis and, on occasion, the Syrians in a punishing campaign against PLO diplomatic representatives in Western Europe (see ch.5) plus repeated attempts to infiltrate the Fateh/PLO security apparatus. In June 1982, it was reportedly one of his agents who fired the shot against the Israeli Ambassador in London which sparked Israel's invasion of Lebanon (see ch.6).

57 Abou Iyad, 1981, pp. 121-22.
58 *Ibid.*, pp. 122-23. The PLO, despite all its internal soul-searching on the issue, was the sole party in this list which was never even invited to Geneva (see ch.4 below).
59 Heikal, 1975, p. 28.
60 Abou Iyad, 1981, p. 126.
61 Heikal, 1975, pp. 221 and 236.

4. Caught in the Lebanon net (1973-76)

1 Kissinger, 1982, p. 602.
2 Abou Iyad, 1981, p. 129.
3 *Ibid.*, p. 132.
4 *Ibid.*
5 *Ibid.*, p. 127. In Egyptian chief of staff General Sa'd Shazli's memoirs there was no mention of the Israelis' Deversoir penetration before 16 October. But he wrote that already, on the 12th, he had been ordered, over his own protests, to make a forward deployment which stripped the total reserves in the Egyptian war zone down to a single brigade of tanks. 'It was a grave error,' he wrote (Shazly, 1980, pp. 167 and 170).
6 'Document: To isolate the Palestinians', *MERIP Reports*, No. 96 (May 1981), p. 27. For more on Kissinger's views on the PLO see ch.10 below.
7 For further light on Kissinger's view of Hussein see Sheehan, 1976, p. 99.
8 Kissinger, 1982, p. 976.
9 *International Documents on Palestine, 1974* (henceforth *IDP, 1974*), p. 525. My emphasis. The previous Arab Summit (Algiers, November 1973) had called for 'Commitment to the recovery of the national rights of the Palestinian people in conformity with the decisions of the Palestine Liberation Organisation, the sole representative of the Palestinian people'. But King Hussein had been able to record his reservations on this point in the (confidential) official text of the summit's decisions (*IDP, 1973*, p. 525). In 1974, Hussein had to accept the summit resolution's wording with what grace he could muster.
10 Kissinger, 1982, p. 847.
11 Abou Iyad, 1981, p. 138. For a description of Fateh's internal structure see ch.2 above.
12 Abou Iyad, 1981, pp. 139-40.
13 Interview with Khaled al-Hassan, April 1983.
14 *IDP, 1974*, p. 411.
15 *Ibid.*, p. 449. My emphasis.
16 The groups which constituted the Rejection Front were the PFLP, the PFLP-GC, the Arab Liberation Front and the Palestinian Popular Struggle Front.
17 *IDP, 1974*, p. 143.
18 For a good account of Lebanon's modern history in English see Salibi, 1965.
19 *Fiches du monde arabe*, No. 1699 (24 September 1980). The figures quoted here are those provided by Y. Courbage, given on the back of the card. These figures do not appear to include: the Lebanese Armenians, all of whom had

been granted Lebanese citizenship, and whose numbers in 1975 were probably around 300,000; or the Jews, who in 1968 were counted at 6,204; or atheists, agnostics, etc., the possibility of whose existence the Lebanese system does not allow of; nor, of course, the Palestinians.

20 Sunni Arab communities have an inbuilt kind of pan-Sunnism left over from the days of the Sunni caliphs and the glories of past Arab Islamic empires; this is often transformed almost painlessly into a kind of gut pan-Arabism. The Greek Orthodox (which here is the name of a religious group, not an ethnic group) are those descendants of Christ's first converts who have remained in the area ever since, resisting all blandishments to convert, from the Islamic rulers to the south and east, and from the Catholic popes or Protestant churches to the west. Identifying themselves as true *indigènes*, their communities in the Arab East tend to identify with pan-Arabism: Baath Party co-founder Michel Aflaq is an Orthodox, as are the PFLP's Habash and the DFLP's Hawatma. The Maronites, originally followers of an obscure Monothelite doctrine, have identified with Rome since the fifteenth century; and the Greek Catholic church was a schism from Greek Orthodoxy which transferred its allegiance to the Vatican.

21 For details of the security regime inside the Palestinian refugee camps in Lebanon down to 1969 see Sayigh, 1979, pp. 130-36. For details of the Cairo agreement see ch.3 above.

22 The question of how many Palestinians there actually were in Lebanon in 1975 was itself hotly controversial, with Lebanese right-wing spokesmen on occasion inflating the Palestinian 'demographic threat' to as high as 750,000 people. The 400,000 figure used here is that estimated by the U.S. State Department in 1982 (assuming only minor net changes between 1975 and 1982). Given the large numbers, particularly of Christian Palestinians, who had gained Lebanese nationality and become integrated into Lebanese society by the 70s, all figures used should also take into account people's self-definitions as to nationality.

23 Michael Hudson, 'Developments and setbacks in the Palestinian resistance movement, 1967-71', *Journal of Palestine Studies*, Spring 1972, pp. 64-84.

24 Khalidi, 1979, p. 81.

25 Interview with Khaled al-Hassan, October 1982.

26 No one can devise a set of labels acceptable to all participants in the Lebanese conflict. I have tried to use some which combine an honest attempt at accuracy with suitable brevity. Some Phalangist Party members claim that their party is neither Christian nor right-wing; I consider that, broadly speaking, it is both.

27 *IDP, 1975*, pp. 267-68. My emphasis.

28 Helena Cobban, 'Gunmen in hotel area', *Daily Star* (Beirut), 6 November 1975.

29 Helena Cobban, 'Abu Iyad interviewed', *ibid.* 17 November 1975.

30 *Fiches du monde arabe*, No. 1774 (24 December 1980). This *fiche* estimates that between 600 and 1,000 of Karantina's residents were killed during this operation. The *fiche* also gives a figure of 500 for those killed during the Palestinian/oppositionists' storming of Damour.

31 Interview with Khaled al-Hassan, October 1982.

32 For details of the reforms see *Fiches*, No. 1781 (31 December 1980).
33 Abou Iyad, 1981, p. 181. My emphasis.
34 The original Syrian plan had presumably relied on units of the pro-Syrian Lebanese and Palestinian organisations aiding the tanks' advance. But these organisations had been routed the previous day, and the Syrian commanders were apparently unwilling to expose their own men to the dangers of infantry operations.
35 Some press correspondents covering the siege of Tel al-Zaatar from the right-wingers' operations rooms noted the occasional presence there of Colonel Ali Madani, Syria's commander in Lebanon at that time.
36 Helena Cobban, 'Horror trip to the camp of corpses', *Sunday Times* (London), 15 August 1976.
37 The Egyptians shipped in some military supplies to the Palestinians in this period, as well as arranging the transit to Beirut of some Iraqi 'volunteers' to the Palestinians' fighting units. (There was some question whether these reinforcements were Iraqis or merely Palestinians raised and trained in Iraq. The two captured members of this force I interviewed under Phalangist auspices in East Beirut certainly described themselves as Iraqis.)
38 It was at this stage that the Syrians briefly tried to promote a Fateh breakaway called 'Revolutionary Fateh' (Fath al-Thawra), under the leadership of one Abu Sa'id.
39 This term was reportedly originally used by Wazir to describe the strategy he was to implement. For Khalaf's version of these events see Abou Iyad, 1981, pp. 195-96.
40 *Ibid.*, p. 196. My emphasis.
41 For the text of the Riyadh mini-summit's resolutions see *IDP, 1976*, pp. 492-93.
42 See n. 37 above.
43 Muhsin was killed by unknown assailants in July 1979 in Cannes. For more details about Saiqa see ch.7 below.
44 For an early expression of this analysis see my despatch to the *Christian Science Monitor* (Boston), 12 December 1976.

5. The net tightens (1977-80)

1 The Israelis had originally drawn this 'Red Line' as a limit for the Syrian troops who entered Lebanon in early 1976. They continued to apply the same concept even after these troops had been transformed into the backbone of the ADF, though the exact geographic limits of the 'Red Line' were never publicly defined and apparently remained open to any interpretation the Israelis cared to place on them at any particular time. For example, see Randal, 1983, p. 195.
2 Since the early 70s, the Israelis had nicknamed this region 'Fatehland'.
3 Despatch to *Christian Science Monitor* (Boston) (henceforth *CSM)*, 28 February 1977.
4 See, for example, *ibid.*, 2 January 1977.
5 See, for example, Farouq Qaddumi's interview in *Shu'un Filastiniyya* of June

1977, as translated in *International Documents on Palestine, 1977* (henceforth *IDP, 1977*), p. 367.

6 See ch.4 above. The members of the committee were Syria, Egypt, Kuwait and Saudi Arabia.

7 *IDP, 1977*, p. 337. My emphasis. Some other Fateh leaders would probably have disagreed with the emphasised portion. Resolution 3236 had been passed by the General Assembly in November 1974 after Yasser Arafat's address there.

8 Despatch to *CSM*, 13 March 1977.

9 *IDP, 1977*, p. 349.

10 *Ibid.*, p. 364.

11 Despatch to *CSM*, 20 March 1977.

12 *IDP, 1977*, p. 343.

13 *Ibid.*, p. 366.

14 Despatch to *CSM*, 24 March 1977.

15 Interview with Khaled al-Hassan, October 1982.

16 For details of the Kissinger commitment see ch.4 above. For more details of U.S.-PLO relations in this period see ch.10 below.

17 Conversation with William Quandt, April 1983.

18 *IDP, 1977*, p. 172.

19 Interview with Khaled al-Hassan, October 1982.

20 *Ibid.*

21 Despatch to *CSM*, 14 September 1977.

22 *IDP, 1977*, p. 244.

23 Despatch to *CSM*, 25 September 1977.

24 *Ibid.*

25 For the text of the statement see *Department of State Bulletin* (Washington, D.C.), LXXVII, 2002 (7 November 1977), pp. 639-40; reproduced in *IDP, 1977*, pp. 255-56.

26 Despatch to *CSM*, 2 October 1977.

27 Dayan, 1981, p. 65.

28 *IDP, 1977*, p. 258. For further light on Dayan's thinking on these points see Dayan, 1981, pp. 67-71.

29 See Dayan, 1981, pp. 70-71.

30 Conversation with William Quandt, April 1983.

31 Despatch to *CSM*, 17 October 1977.

32 Interview with Khaled al-Hassan, October 1982.

33 Dayan, 1981, p. 43.

34 See, for example, Abou Iyad, 1981, p. 202.

35 *Ibid.*, pp. 206-07.

36 *IDP, 1977*, p. 444.

37 An analysis of how Egypt's removal from the Arab side of the Middle Eastern military balance affected this balance in the years following 1977 is given in Helena Cobban, 'The strategic balance in the Middle East', *CSM*, 2 and 3 March 1982.

38 The Libyan President, Colonel Qadhafi, tried at first to have PFLP leader

George Habash included in the Tripoli talks on a more or less equal footing with Arafat, but the PLO Chairman was able to abort this plan.

39 *Al-Hawadith* (London), 7-13 July 1978. My emphasis.

40 *Fiches du monde arabe*, No. 951 (10 May 1978).

41 Despatch to *CSM*, 20 March 1978.

42 For more details on Awda, see ch.3 n.54 above.

43 That this continued to be the case in 1982 was indicated by evidence from the London trial of the gunmen who had tried to kill the Israeli Ambassador there in June 1982, that the operation was organised by the Iraqi secret services (*Washington Post* (Washington, D.C.), 8 March 1983, p. A10). Israel's retaliation for that shooting was its 1982 invasion of Lebanon, which seriously weakened the Syrians.

44 My contacts with Irish and Norwegian diplomats in Beirut. This effect was also said, by numerous Dutch non-diplomats, to be particularly marked in Holland, a country where opinion had previously been overwhelmingly pro-Israeli.

45 The whole point of the army's going through Khiyam and Marjayoun was to reassure the Lebanese Muslims and leftists, as well as their Syrian and Palestinian allies, that the Sarkis government still intended to reassert its authority over those areas held by Haddad, although (with ample reason) the army command did not feel confident of challenging Haddad to the extent of seeking to set up permanent positions inside his sector.

46 Despatch to *CSM*, 31 July 1978.

47 *Ibid.*, 28 March 1978.

48 The full text of the accords can be seen in Dayan, 1981, pp. 321-31.

49 Despatch to *CSM*, 19 September 1978.

50 *Ibid.*

51 *Fiches du monde arabe*, No. 1118 (15 November 1978).

52 Despatch to *CSM*, 20 November 1978.

53 'The mood of the West Bank', *Journal of Palestine Studies*, Autumn 1979, p. 114.

54 Despatch to *CSM*, 19 March 1979. My emphasis.

55 *IDP*, 1979, p. 26.

56 There was only a slightly cynical sense of *déjà vu* from some Palestinians who remembered the slogan of 1975: 'Today Vietnam! Tomorrow Palestine!'

57 See Randal, 1983, p. 220.

58 For an excellent round-up of the security situation in Lebanon from January 1980 to March 1981 see *Keesing's Contemporary Archives*, 19 June 1981, pp. 30917-27.

59 *Al-Burnamij al-siyyasi al-sadir 'an al-mu'tamar al-'am al-rabi' li-harakat al-tahrir al-watani al-filastini 'fath', ayyar 1980* (unpublished), pp. 3, 5 and 7.

6. The broken wing (1981 – February 1983)

1 The 'Joint Forces' was the joint military command set up in Lebanon in 1976 by the PLO and the militias of the Lebanese Nationalist Movement (see ch.4

above). By 1981, the LNM had a handful of ministers sympathetic to it in the Lebanese government, but such governmental power as was still exercised in the country was still far from their control.

2 Despatch to *Christian Science Monitor* (Boston) (henceforth *CSM*), 23 April 1981.

3 Jean Gueyras, 'Beirut's search for consensus', *Guardian Weekly* (London), 7 June 1981.

4 Despatch to *CSM*, 21 April 1981.

5 The 1958 U.S. intervention in Lebanon had ostensibly been aimed at shoring up Camille Chamoun's presidency during the civil war then raging there. But another important consideration behind the marines' landing had been to try to put the U.S. in a position to influence events throughout the region after the recent Iraqi coup (Malcolm Kerr, 'The Lebanese civil war', in Evan Luard, ed., *The International Regulation of Civil Wars* (London: Thames and Hudson, 1972), p. 78).

6 In July 1981, Israeli air force commander David Ivri was to define this 'threat' in the following terms: 'Today part of the Lebanese sky is barred to us. As a result, our capability as regards intelligence and our offensive ability against the terrorists is restricted as well.' (*Ha'aretz* (Tel Aviv), 22 July 1981; translated in *FBIS*, 22 July 1981).

7 Carter would even reportedly have accepted a qualified PLO acceptance of 242 as satisfying his terms for opening the dialogue (see ch.5 above).

8 Ben-Zvi, 1982, pp. 14-15.

9 *Facts on File, 1981*, p. 324.

10 Ben-Zvi, 1982, p. 16.

11 For an account of these incidents by the U.N. Secretary-General see U.N. Security Council document S/14789 (11 December 1981), pp. 12-13. The casualty figures given here are taken from *Fiches du monde arabe*, chronology for July 1981. For details of the casualties of the Beirut raid see Helena Cobban, 'The building called Mercy', *New Statesman* (London), 24 July 1981, p. 8. 'Lebanese sources' were quoted as estimating the total casualty toll that day at 300 (*Facts on File, 1981*, p. 510); but Palestinian sources, probably closer to the events, had told me the figure was over 400.

12 VOP, 20 July 1981; translated in *FBIS*, 20 July, pp. A5-A6.

13 *Fiches*, chronology for July 1981.

14 Jerusalem domestic radio, 24 July 1981; transcribed in *FBIS*, 24 July 1981, p. I1.

15 VOP, 24 July 1981; translated in *FBIS*, 24 July 1981, p. A6.

16 *As-Safir* (Beirut), 26 July 1981, and VOP, 28 July 1981; translated in *FBIS*, 28 July 1981, p. A1, and 29 July 1981, p. A6.

17 Computed from U.N. Security Council documents S/14789, pp. 9-13, and S/15194, pp. 9-11.

18 The text of the Fahd plan is printed in *FBIS*, 10 August 1981.

19 Radio Monte Carlo (Arabic), 8 August 1981; translated in *FBIS*, 11 August 1981, p. A1.

20 Middle East News Agency (Cairo), 13 August 1981; translated in *FBIS*, 14

August 1981, p. A1.

21 Kuwaiti News Agency (KUNA), 13 August 1981; translated in *FBIS*, 13 August 1981, p. A1.

22 *Fiches*, chronology for August 1981.

23 Interview with Khaled al-Hassan, April 1983.

24 KUNA, 4 November 1981; translated in *FBIS*, 4 November 1981, p. A1.

25 KUNA, 12 November 1981; translated in *FBIS*, 13 November 1981, p. A2. My emphasis.

26 *El Pais* (Madrid), 18 October 1981, p. 6; translated in *FBIS*, 23 October 1981, p. A6.

27 Conversation with Khaled al-Hassan, March 1983.

28 See *FBIS*, 24 November 1981, p. A1. One can only guess that the 'responsible source' worked not far from Arafat's office at the time.

29 It was to reconvene in September 1982.

30 See, for example, Eric Rouleau, 'The Saudi plan for a Middle East settlement...', *Le Monde* (Paris), 27 November 1981, as translated in *FBIS*, 30 November 1981, pp. A1-A3.

31 Conversation with Khaled al-Hassan, March 1983. Hassan also expressed his conviction that in November 1981 'the *Americans* really did not want a decision from Fez'. He likened the U.S.'s attitude then to its attitude in 1969, when he said the U.S. had discreetly opposed the convening of any Arab summit to discuss the Rogers peace plan.

32 *Monday Morning* (Beirut), 19-25 October 1981, p. 60.

33 *Ibid.*, 12-18 October 1981, p. 19.

34 The only part of Sinai still held by Israel after April 1982 was a stretch of coast adjacent to Eilat, on which Israeli contractors continued to build a tourism and marine facility.

35 The text of Israeli Military Government Order No. 947, under which the 'civilian administration' was established, is given in Kuttab and Shehadeh, 1982, pp. 23-26.

36 See Menahem Milson, 'How to make peace with the Palestinians', *Commentary*, May 1981, pp. 25-35, and 'The Palestinians and the peace process', *Forum*, Nos. 42-43 (Winter 1981), pp. 119-27.

37 For further details of the development of the resistance movement inside the occupied territories see ch.8 below.

38 *Fiches*, chronology for March 1982, p. 9.

39 *Facts on File, 1982*, p. 121.

40 *Fiches*, chronology for April 1982.

41 *Facts on File, 1982*, p. 279.

42 The would-be assassin was apprehended and identified as a young West Bank Palestinian. He and another young Palestinian arrested nearby were thought by prosecutors in the trial which ensued to have been acting under the orders of a third, older accomplice also arrested. The older man, an Iraqi businessman, received a substantially longer sentence than the two youths. Unidentified British officials later hinted strongly that the older man was an operative of his country's secret service (*Washington Post*, 8 March 1983, p. A10).

43 It is outside the scope of the present work to provide a detailed account of the Israeli-Palestinian war in Lebanon of summer 1982.

44 *Lubnaan 1982: Yawmiyyat al-Ghazu al-Isra'ili* (Beirut: Dar al-Andalus, 1982 (henceforth, *Yawmiyyat*), pp. 66-67.

45 Many of Sadr's followers blamed the Libyan leader, Colonel Qadhafi, for Sadr's disappearance. For some details of the tensions between the Shi'ite group, Amal, and the JF see *Fiches*, chronology for April 1982.

46 Unfortunately, this source has insisted that he not be named, but the author remains grateful to him for much of the material in this and the next section of the chapter.

47 For some new details of the degree to which Sarkis had been supporting Phalangist militia leader Bashir Gemayyel since at least early 1982 see Randal, 1983, pp. 143, 145 and 236.

48 *Yawmiyyat*, p. 69.

49 Carole Collins, 'Chronology of the Israeli invasion of Lebanon June-August 1982', *Journal of Palestine Studies*, Nos. 44/45, Summer/Fall 1982, p. 146.

50 In fact, the U.S. veto was only threatened and never used against this proposal. On 24 July, the Security Council members decided to delay convening a meeting to discuss the French-Egyptian proposal, so as to save the public embarrassment of an American veto.

51 See n. 46 above.

52 U.S. State Department, Bureau of Public Affairs,'Lebanon: Plan for the PLO Evacuation from West Beirut' *Current Policy*, No. 415 (August 1982), pp. 8-10.

53 See n. 46 above.

54 Conversation with a Fateh commander, Algiers, February 1982. For a reference to Israeli soldiers' surprise at the Palestinians' military proficiency in Beirut see Amnon Kapeliuk (Kapeliouk), 'Begin and the "beasts"', *New Statesman* (London), 25 June 1982.

55 Sayel had chaired the Higher Military Committee since the late 70s, and was credited by most Palestinian activists with having brought new vigour and purpose to its previously shaky structure. He was killed in an ambush in eastern Lebanon in late 1982.

56 *Yawmiyyat*, p. 233.

57 For the text of the plan see *New York Times*, 2 September 1982.

58 *Yawmiyyat*, pp. 236 and 237. The PLO had reportedly been informed of the existence of Reagan's 1 September speech in advance (comment from William Quandt, June 1983).

59 *New York Times*, 10 September 1982; *Yawmiyyat*, pp. 442-43.

60 In the terminology of the U.N. relief agency UNRWA there was no refugee camp called 'Sabra'; that was really the name of a poor Lebanese quarter adjacent to the UNRWA refugee camp in Shatila, but over the decades the populations of the two areas, Lebanese and Palestinian, became ever more mingled.

61 Kapeliouk, 1982, p. 34.

62 *Ibid.*, p. 35.

63 The 'Lebanese Forces' was the joint military command grouped around the Phalangist militia since 1976. Bashir Gemayyel had been its first commander; Fadi Ephram (Frem) had been named to succeed him shortly after his election to the presidency.

64 Kapeliouk, 1982, p. 38.

65 *Ibid.*, pp. 47-48. Kapeliouk's book needs to be read in full for its full horror and political meaning to emerge.

66 *Ibid.*, p. 61.

67 *Ibid.*, p. 94.

68 For the text of Khalaf's speech, see *FBIS*, 23 February 1983, pp. A1-A12.

69 *Ibid.*, p. A6.

70 Many Palestinian activists had summed up the contrast between the support the PASOK government in Greece accorded the PLO throughout the Battle of Beirut with what they saw as the Arab regimes' inaction, by describing Athens as 'the only real Arab capital left'.

71 *Al-Qabas* (Kuwait), 4 February 1983, pp. 10 and 17; translated in *FBIS*, 7 February 1983, pp. A2-A3.

72 For a fuller description of the PLO's relations with Syria and Jordan as of January 1983 see Helena Cobban, 'Palestinians find new woes in Syria', *Boston Globe* (Boston, Mass.), 7 February 1983, p. 1, and 'The friendship grows between PLO, Jordan', *ibid.*, 8 February 1983, p. 1.

73 Associated Press despatch from Damascus, 21 January 1983.

74 *FBIS*, 23 February 1983, pp. A2 and A4. My emphasis.

75 *Ibid.*, p. A9. My emphasis.

76 *Ibid.*, p. A10.

77 *Ibid.*, p. A11. My emphasis.

78 *Ibid.*, p. A16.

79 For one early report of West Bank reaction to the Battle of Beirut see Christopher Walker, 'Fall-out of invasion hits West Bank', *Times* (London), 19 June 1982. See also ch.8 below.

7. Non-Fateh guerrilla groups

1 Jabhat al-Quwa al-Filastiniyya al-Rafida lil-Hulul al-Istislamiyya (Front of Palestinian Forces Rejecting Surrenderist Solutions).

2 As regards the PFLP, which was the guiding light of the Rejection Front, there is considerable evidence that replacing the Fateh leadership of the PLO was less their intention in forming the Rejection Front than was pressuring the Fateh leadership not to go to Geneva.

3 Kubaisi worked with Habash from the late 50s to at least the mid-60s. In 1971, he presented a doctoral thesis in the American University in Washington, D.C., which, though as yet unpublished in English, remains the best first-hand account of the origins of the Habash group. Most of the material in this and the following five paragraphs is taken from this thesis, pp. 48-77.

4 Kubaisi, thesis, p. 54. In fact, so distant was the early ANM from any leftist sympathies that one source who was an ANM activist in the 50s and early 60s

recalled to me that in those years ANM members used to try to break up Communist Party demonstrations in Damascus with violence.

5 See, for example, Kazziha, 1975, pp. 75-81. Much of the information in this and the succeeding paragraphs comes from my discussions with a participant in the events mentioned who preferred not to be named.

6 Kazziha, 1975, p. 79.

7 Khurshid, 1971, p. 111. For an English translation of the first political statement issued by the PFLP see *International Documents on Palestine, 1967* (henceforth *IDP, 1967*), pp. 723-26.

8 My private sources.

9 *IDP, 1967*, p. 724.

10 Most of the information in this paragraph comes from my own private sources. For an account of these developments at the 'official' level, see Rashid Hamid's article 'What is the PLO?', *Journal of Palestine Studies*, Summer 1975, pp. 98-101.

11 In 1979, Yasser Arafat told me, 'of 52 representatives of the mass organisations in the PNC [at that time], 44 or 45 of them are from Fateh' (interview with Arafat, November 1979).

12 At the following PNC session, held in February 1969, the PFLP decided not to risk a repetition of this debacle, and decided to stay away altogether, but Fateh was able, to a certain extent, to use even that abstention as a political weapon against it.

13 For the text of the Statement, see *IDP, 1968*, p. 425.

14 See the conference's ruling on this issue in *IDP, 1969*, p. 621.

15 One account of the PRFLP's short history is given in Amos, 1980, pp. 87-88.

16 See, for example, Khaled, 1973, pp. 112 and 116. Independent eye-witnesses have also remarked on the popularity of the PFLP's first hijacks in Palestinian communities.

17 For details of the PFLP's operations against Israeli and Israel-related aviation, as well as the Israeli counter-measures, see Phillips, 1973, pp. 130-73, or Cooley, 1973, pp. 146-55.

18 This Israeli action also considerably aggravated the political polarisations inside Lebanon at the time (see ch.3 above).

19 Phillips, 1973, p. 138.

20 For one full account of these developments, see Cooley, 1973, pp. 111-14.

21 *IDP, 1972*, p. 288.

22 *IDP, 1974*, p. 500.

23 *Ibid.*, p. 501.

24 *Ibid.*, p. 503. One corroboration of this accusation came from Dr Kissinger (Kissinger, 1982, pp. 503 and 626-29). See ch.10 below.

25 *IDP, 1974*, p. 513. My emphasis.

26 A good description (in Arabic) of the circumstances surrounding the Rejection Front's foundation appears in *Al-Kitab as-Sanawi lil-Qadiyya al-Filastiniyya li-'Am 1974*, pp. 27-29.

27 My despatch to *Christian Science Monitor* (Boston) (henceforth *CSM*), 7 August 1978.

28 *Ibid.*, 29 October 1978.
29 My private archives.
30 The DFLP's original name was the Popular Democratic Front for the Libera-
    tion of Palestine; it dropped the word 'Popular' from this in 1974.
31 *IDP, 1969*, p. 777. My emphasis.
32 *Ibid.*, p. 806.
33 *IDP, 1970*, p. 897. The debate over the attitude to adopt towards Jordan
    continued inside PLO ranks for many years. In 1972, after Hussein announced
    plans to take the West Bank back under his crown, the PNC hit back by calling
    for the formation of a joint Palestinian-Jordanian 'national liberation front'
    (see ch.4 above). But after Hussein agreed in 1974 to the Arab Summit's
    designation of the PLO as the 'sole legitimate representative' of the Palestinian
    people, this call was notably cancelled. The question of PLO-Jordanian rela-
    tions arose again with the announcement of President Reagan's peace plan in
    September 1982. See ch.1 above.
34 Interview with Khaled al-Hassan, April 1983.
35 *Fiches du monde arabe*, No. 1246 (18 April 1979).
36 For an English translation of this see *IDP, 1974*, p. 419.
37 *Fiches*, No. 1246 (18 April 1979).
38 *Ba'th* means 'renaissance'. A full translation of the name of the Baath Party,
    which has been split into pro-Syrian and pro-Iraqi factions since 1963, would
    be 'the Arab Socialist Renaissance Party'.
39 Khurshid, 1971, p. 85.
40 Rashid, 'What is the PLO?', p. 99. For further details of this period see ch.3
    above.
41 Petran, 1972, p. 247.
42 *Ibid.*, p. 253.
43 *IDP, 1974*, p. 421.
44 See, for example, Muhsin's comments in a November 1975 interview with
    Al-Tala'i (Damascus), translated in *IDP, 1975*, pp. 504-05. For Muhsin's own
    explanation of Saiqa's role in the Lebanese war of 1975-76 up to August 1976
    see *IDP, 1976*, pp. 463-66.
45 Broadcast on Damascus Radio in Arabic, 25 March 1975; translated in *IDP,
    1976*, p. 388. My emphasis.
46 At least some of the defectors had been infiltrated into Saiqa by the other
    groups in the weeks preceding the June debacle, presumably with some such
    eventual defection in mind. With all the money Saiqa had available for new
    recruits in the first half of 1976, it was apparently difficult for the group's
    leaders to vet all those attracted. (One source told me that, in the months
    preceding June 1976, Saiqa's leaders in Lebanon had been collecting a monthly
    payroll subvention from Damascus sufficient for over 30,000 full-time mem-
    bers and fighters.)
47 The Saiqa units in Tel al-Zaatar were, for example, accused of withdrawing
    prematurely from the anti-aircraft position on Tellat al-Mir, which comman-
    ded the whole camp.
48 My despatch to *CSM*, 15 March 1977.

49 This killing was apparently linked to an action some days earlier, launched by the Saiqa front organisation Nusour al-Thawra al-Filastiniyya (Eagles of the Palestinian Revolution) against the Egyptian consul in Turkey.

50 See Khurshid, 1971, p. 197.

51 For details of this, and of Jibril's role at the Sixteenth PNC, see ch.6 above.

52 Interview with Khaled al-Hassan, April 1983.

53 For an account, in Arabic, of the founding and early development of the ALF see Khurshid, 1971, pp. 173-94.

54 Kayyali later left active politics and founded a successful publishing venture. He was killed in Beirut in 1981.

55 For an account, in Arabic, of the founding and early development of the PPSF see Khurshid, 1971, pp. 215-26.

56 Interview with Khaled al-Hassan, April 1983.

57 *Ibid.*

58 *Ibid.*

59 *Ibid.*

60 Interview with Salah Khalaf, April 1983.

61 Kadi, 1969, p. 128.

62 Interview with Khaled al-Hassan, April 1983.

63 Interview with Yasser Arafat, November 1979.

8. The movement inside historic Palestine

1 For more details of this period see Amnon Cohen's essay 'Political parties in the West Bank under the Hashemite regime', in Ma'oz, 1975. Cohen based his work on archives of the Jordanian Security Services captured by the Israelis in 1967.

2 Interview with Muhammed Milhem, January 1983. Raymonda Tawil wrote, 'All our sympathies lay with the guerrillas. They emerged at a time when our morale was low, when we had lost our self-respect' (Tawil, 1979, p. 126).

3 Many houses in East Jerusalem's Mughrabiyyeh quarter had been bulldozed immediately after June 1967 to make way for the vast plaza the Israelis wanted in front of the Wailing Wall.

4 Ann M. Lesch, 'Israeli deportation of Palestinians from the West Bank and Gaza Strip, 1967-78', *Journal of Palestine Studies*, Winter 1979, pp. 101-31, and Spring 1979, pp. 81-112. The figure quoted here is the total for the West Bank districts listed in table 2 (*Ibid.*, Winter 1979, p. 103). Lesch's figures contain no mention, however, of the mass deportations from Gaza in the immediate aftermath of the June 1967 war.

5 *Ibid.*, Winter 1959, p. 105. I have computed the percentages from the figures given by Lesch.

6 Shaul Mishal, 'Nationalism through localism: some observations on the West Bank political elite', *Middle East Studies* (Tel Aviv), Vol. 17 (October 1981), pp. 477-91. This quotation is from pp. 485-86; My emphasis.

7 Major-General Shlomo Gazit, 'Early attempts at establishing West Bank autonomy', *Harvard Journal of Law and Public Policy*, Vol. 3 (Summer 1980),

p. 143. My emphasis.

8 *Ibid.*, pp. 148-50.

9 *International Documents on Palestine, 1973* (henceforth *IDP, 1973*), p. 459.

10 *IDP, 1974*, p. 449. My emphasis.

11 Much of the material from this and the following four paragraphs comes from Ann Lesch's excellently documented study *Political Perceptions of the Palestinians on the West Bank and the Gaza Strip* (Lesch, 1980).

12 *Ibid.*, p. 60.

13 Selim Tamari, 'The Palestinian demand for independence cannot be postponed indefinitely', *MERIP Reports*, Vol. 11 (October-December 1981), p. 29.

14 Quoted in Lesch, 1980, p. 83.

15 W. F. Abboushi, in Nakhleh, 1980, pp. 7-8.

16 *Ibid.*, p. 8.

17 The quotations are taken from 'The mood of the West Bank', *Journal of Palestine Studies*, Autumn 1979, p. 114.

18 Interview with Muhammed Milhem, January 1983.

19 Benvenisti, 1982, p. 66.

20 Menahem Milson, 'How to make peace with the Palestinians', *Commentary*, Vol. 71 (May 1981), pp. 30, 34 and 35. My emphasis.

21 Michael Precker, 'West Bank village official bucks PLO', *Boston Globe*, 22 November 1981, p. 2.

22 Sa'di, 1983, pp. 185 and 186.

23 Interview with Muhammed Milhem, January 1983.

24 Tamari, 'The Palestinian demand', p. 30.

25 Interview with Muhammed Milhem, January 1983.

26 Conversation with Raymonda Tawil, June 1983.

27 For Salah Khalaf's account of his experiences in Gaza in 1957-59 see Abou Iyad, 1981, pp. 25-28.

28 Interview with Selim al-Zaanoun, April 1983.

29 Kennet Love, quoted in Neff, 1981, pp. 420-21.

30 Interview with Selim al-Zaanoun, April 1983.

31 Quoted in Neff, 1981, p. 421. Six days later, Bayard was reporting that the Israelis had forcibly induced four Gaza notables to sign a statement calling on Israel to 'take over and administrate [*sic*] the Gaza Strip'.

32 Interview with Selim al-Zaanoun, April 1983.

33 *IDP, 1971*, p. 649 (U.N. document A/8383).

34 Lesch, 1980, p. 21.

35 Lustick, 1980, p. 138. This well-documented study, by an author claiming that 'All my life I have been involved, as a participant, leader, and resource person, in Jewish and Zionist organizations' (*ibid.*, 'Preface'), contains a wealth of detail on how the Israeli state controls its Arab minority.

36 *Ibid.*, p. 139.

37 For more details of this demographic and housing/property situation see *ibid.*, pp. 51-64.

38 Edward Walsh, 'Despite officials' fear of violence, Israeli Arab land day is calm', *Washington Post*, 31 March 1983, p. A25. Details of the lands lost by

various other Israeli Arab villages up to 1976 are given in Tawfiq Zayyad, 'The fate of the Arabs in Israel', *Journal of Palestine Studies*, Autumn 1976, p. 96.

39 Jiryis, 1968, p. 154. This book gives a clear and comprehensive picture of how the Military Government affected the lives of the Israeli Arabs between 1948 and 1966. Jiryis left Israel soon after writing this book, and later became Director of the PLO's Research Center in Beirut.

40 *Ibid.*, p. 155.

41 Mark A. Tessler, 'Israel's Arabs and the Palestinian problem', *Middle East Journal* (Washington, D.C.), Vol. 31 (Summer 1977), p. 317.

42 Such a map, for the year 1979, is given in John Stebbing, 'The demographic jigsaw puzzle in northern Israel and the West Bank', *International Relations* (London), Vol. 6 (November 1980), p. 926.

43 The text of the Koenig memorandum is printed in *Journal of Palestine Studies*, Vol. 21 (Autumn 1976). For a discussion of the memorandum in its Israeli policy-making context see Lustick, 1980, pp. 255-57.

44 See also the view of the Israeli Arabs' poetry expressed by Fateh's Salah Khalaf – himself a former littérateur – in *IDP, 1969*, pp. 717-18. He said, 'Every one of them has enriched the Arab revolution in general and the Palestinian revolution in particular.'

45 Ori Stendel, 'Political currents among Israeli Arabs', in Ma'oz, 1975, p. 127.

46 Saleh Baransi, 'All this time we were alone', *MERIP Reports*, No. 96 (May 1981), p. 18.

47 *Ibid.*

48 *Ibid.*, pp. 19 and 20.

49 *Ibid.*, p. 20. My emphasis.

50 Stendel, 'Political currents', p. 117.

51 Tawfiq Zayyad, 'The fate of the Arabs in Israel', *Journal of Palestine Studies*, Autumn 1976, p. 103.

52 The names of some of these groups can be found in Mohammed Kiwan, 'Sons of the Village assert Palestinian identity in Israel', *MERIP Reports*, No. 68 (June 1978), p. 15.

53 *Ibid.*, p. 16.

54 *Ibid.*

55 Edward Walsh, 'Despite officials' fear of violence, Israeli Arab Land Day is calm', *Washington Post*, 31 March 1983, p. A25.

56 These figures are from Saʿdi, 1983, p. 89.

57 *Ibid.*, pp. 91, 106 and 110.

58 Tessler, 'Israel's Arabs', p. 325.

59 Baransi, 'All this time we were alone', p. 21.

60 Saʿdi, 1983, p. 87. My emphasis.

61 Lustick, 1980, pp. 269 and 271. My emphasis.

9. Arab relations

1 Sayigh, 1979, pp. 98-136. Read especially her very perceptive analysis of the distinctions in attitudes towards pan-Arabism among different social classes in the Palestinian diaspora (p. 102).

2 Rosemary Sayigh, 'Sources of Palestinian nationalism: a study of a Palestinian camp in Lebanon', *Journal of Palestine Studies*, Summer 1977, p. 21.

3 Interview with Khaled al-Hassan, October 1982.

4 *Ibid.*

5 Kadi, 1969, p. 102. My emphasis.

6 For details of the Gaza raid, see Neff, 1981, pp. 30-33. For details of the situation along the Egyptian-Israeli border in 1955-56, especially as it pertained to the Palestinians, see the important n. 43 in Livia Rokach's book *Israel's Sacred Terrorism*, pp. 58-59.

7 Interview with Khaled al-Hassan, April 1983.

8 *Ibid.*

9 Ibn Haifa, 'Nathra lil-wad' al-'arabi min khilal nuqtat al-intilaq fi ma'rakat al-tahrir wal-'awda', *Filastinuna*, November 1964, p. 11.

10 For further details on Jibril, see ch. 7.

11 *Ibid.*, April 1983.

12 For Salah Khalaf's account of his part in these contacts see Abou Iyad, 1981, pp. 53-55 and 61-64.

13 One open expression of this reproach in English, representative of many which have been voiced over the years in private, is found in Samir Franjiyyeh, 'How revolutionary is the Palestinian resistance? A marxist interpretation', *Journal of Palestine Studies*, Winter 1972, pp. 52-60.

14 The only significant exception to this rule is that provided from the late 70s on by a sizeable part of Lebanon's 700,000-strong Maronite Christian community.

15 Interview with Khaled al-Hassan, April 1983.

16 After Fateh had taken over the PLO in the late 60s, it was able to establish something called the Arab Front Participating in the Palestinian Revolution, but Khaled al-Hassan described this Front as 'a very pale reflection of the original idea: very pale, and a very big mistake' (interview, April 1983).

17 Taher Abdel-Hakim, 'Fateh: the birth and the march; a discussion with Kamal 'Udwan', *Shu'un Filastiniyya*, No. 17 (January 1973), pp. 49-50. Udwan was one of the three PLO leaders killed by the Israelis in Beirut in April 1973 (see ch.3).

18 Abou Iyad, 1981, p. 221.

19 Interview with Khaled al-Hassan, October 1982.

20 Salah Khalaf's position in 1969, as described by Munah Solh in conversation in Algiers, February 1983.

21 Interview with Khaled al-Hassan, April 1983.

22 *Al-Ahram* (Cairo), 24 July 1971; quoted in Quandt *et al.*, 1973, p. 209.

23 Interview with Khaled al-Hassan, April 1983.

24 *International Documents on Palestine, 1970*, p. 932.

25 *Ibid.*, p. 947.

26 *Ibid.*, p. 948.

27 *Ibid.*, p. 955. My emphasis.

28 Bilal al-Hassan, 'The Palestinian resistance and the response to King Hussein's plan', *Shu'un Filastiniyya*, No. 9 (May 1972), pp. 249-50.

29 Interview with Khaled al-Hassan, April 1983.
30 *Ibid.*
31 Gemayyel never took up the presidency, but was killed in a bomb explosion on 14 September 1982. See ch.6 above.
32 In May 1983, the Syrians and their Libyan allies tried to fan a further dissident movement inside Fateh, this time among the Fateh military in eastern Lebanon. Some of the same figures were involved in this as had headed the movement inside Fateh in 1976 to take a tough line towards the Syrians. In 1983, as in 1976, the consensus of Fateh's political leadership then sought to isolate them.
33 Comment from Salah Khalaf, April 1983.

10. International relations

1 Hani al-Hassan, 'A pause at the fifteenth anniversary of the Palestinian revolution', *Shu'un Filastiniyya*, No. 98 (January 1980), p. 32.
2 Lillian Craig Harris, 'China's relations with the PLO', *Journal of Palestine Studies*, Autumn 1977, pp. 123-54.
3 Interview with Khaled al-Hassan, April 1983.
4 Behbehani, 1981, pp. 34-35. I have relied, for much of the material in this section of the chapter, on this work by the Kuwaiti scholar Dr Hashim S. H. Behbehani, who has the unusual accomplishment of combined fluency in Arabic, Chinese and English.
5 *Ibid.*, pp. 38, 40 and 45. My emphasis.
6 *Ibid.*, p. 46.
7 John Cooley, 'China and the Palestinians', *Journal of Palestine Studies*, Winter 1972, pp. 19-34.
8 Xinhua (New China News Agency) commentary, 'Raging storm of Arab people's struggle against U.S. imperialism', 5 June 1968; quoted in Behbehani, 1981, p. 64.
9 Interview with Khaled al-Hassan, April 1983.
10 Huang then enjoyed wide responsibilities for Chinese policy in Africa. In January 1966 he was to be named Ambassador to Cairo; in 1971 he was China's first Ambassador at the U.N.; and five years later he became Foreign Minister of the world's most populous nation (Donald W. Klein and Anne B. Clark, *Biographic Dictionary of Chinese Communism, 1921-1965* (Cambridge, Mass.: Harvard University Press, 1971), Vol.I, p. 395).
11 Some details of these shipments are given in Cooley, 'China and the Palestinians', pp. 26-27.
12 Behbehani, 1981, p. 87.
13 Interview with Khaled al-Hassan, April 1983.
14 Harris, 'China's relations with the PLO'. Behbehani computed that between December 1971 and November 1974, China voted for eight Security Council resolutions criticising Israel, while it abstained from voting on seven others (Behbehani, 1981, p. 98).
15 Musallam, 1982, p. 27.
16 Behbehani, 1981, pp. 109 and 132.

17 *International Documents on Palestine, 1973* (henceforth *IDP, 1973*), p. 163.

18 Behbehani, 1981, pp. 120-21.

19 Harris, 'China's relations with the PLO'.

20 Interview with Khaled al-Hassan, April 1983.

21 For details of China's reaction to the Sadat initiative, see Musallam, 1982, pp. 8-15.

22 Some Palestinian activists were also upset, in this period, by reports that Egypt was obtaining replacement parts and engines for its ageing fleet of Soviet military aircraft from China, following the decision of the pro-Soviet bloc to cut off further military supplies to the Sadat regime.

23 Musallam, 1982, p. 25. Material for the next paragraph comes from *ibid.*, p. 28.

24 Xinhua in English, 14 February 1983, as reprinted in FBIS (China section), 15 February 1983, p. I1. My emphasis. For the text of a commentary in *Renmin Ribao* (Beijing) on the results of the Sixteenth PNC see FBIS (China section), 25 February 1983, pp. I1-2.

25 Heikal, 1975, p. 64.

26 *Ibid.*, pp. 65 and 82. My emphasis.

27 *Soviet News* (London), 29 April 1969, as reprinted in *IDP, 1969*, p. 74.

28 G. Golan, 1977, p. 19.

29 Salah Khalaf interviewed by Lutfi al-Kholi in *Al-Taliʿa* (Cairo), June 1969, as translated in *IDP, 1969*, p. 729.

30 Kadi, 1969, p. 105.

31 *IDP, 1970*, pp. 46-47.

32 *Fiches du monde arabe*, 24 July 1974 (No. 25). For more on the fate of the Front see ch.8 above.

33 G. Golan, 1980, p. 14.

34 *Journal of Palestine Studies*, No. 5 (Autumn 1972); also reproduced in *MERIP Reports* (Washington, D.C.), No. 55 (March 1977). My emphasis.

35 See, for example, Cooley, 1973, p. 169.

36 Khaled al-Hassan, however, denied that the Soviets had ever tried to push the PLO leadership towards any particular political position (interview, April 1983).

37 G. Golan, 1980, p. 53.

38 George Habash's PFLP, which also professed itself a friend of the Soviet Union, notably did not favour the PLO's switch to diplomacy. But the Soviets had long had disagreements with Habash, dating back to their open criticisms of the PFLP's skyjacking tactics, and in September 1974 they openly accused Habash of 'co-operating with the imperialists' in his efforts to dissuade the PLO from participating in a Geneva conference (*ibid.*, p. 115).

39 Abou Iyad, 1981, pp. 193-94. My emphasis. Khalaf added, 'If the Soviets were slow to seize all the implications of the Lebanese conflict, our Chinese friends never did understand anything about it' (*ibid.*, p. 194). For another assessment of the Soviet role in the Lebanese fighting see Robert O. Freedman, 'The USSR and the Lebanese Civil War, 1975-1976', *Jerusalem Journal of International Relations*, Vol. 3, No. 4 (Summer 1978), pp. 90-91.

40 V. Konstantinov, 'The Palestinian problem and the Middle East settlement', *International Affairs* (Moscow), Vol. 7 (July 1980), p. 50.

41 See, for example, *ibid.*, p. 55.

42 FBIS (Soviet Union), 15 June 1982, p. H1.

43 *Ibid.*, 8 July 1982, p. H1.

44 *Ibid.*, 21 July 1982, pp. H1-2.

45 Conversation with Salah Khalaf, February 1983.

46 FBIS (Middle East), 23 February 1983, pp. A16-17. It may be noted that, as at a number of the immediately preceding PNC sessions, no explicit mention was made of China in the resolutions of the Sixteenth PNC.

47 See, for example, the Radio Moscow commentary (in Arabic) of 23 February 1983, translated in FBIS (Soviet Union), 25 February 1983, p. H4.

48 Tomeh, 1975, pp. 78 and 80.

49 According to Khaled al-Hassan, the endorsement of the PLO provided at the Islamic Conference by Hajj Amin al-Husseini played a significant part in winning its support for the PLO, despite the latter's openly secularist programme (interview, April 1983).

50 Tomeh, 1975, p. 109.

51 *Ibid.*, p. 111.

52 Conversation with Hassan Abdel-Rahman, April 1983.

53 David Allen, 'The Euro-Arab dialogue', *Journal of Common Market Studies*, Vol. 16 (June 1978), p. 325. Allen suggests it was France and Britain which had invited the Arab ministers to the summit. Alan R. Taylor, in 'The Euro-Arab dialogue: quest for an inter-regional partnership', *Middle East Journal* (Washington, D.C.), Vol. 32 (Autumn 1978), p. 431, wrote that the Arab ministers concerned in this meeting were those of Algeria, Tunisia, Sudan and the United Arab Emirates.

54 Kissinger, 1982, p. 900. For further details of Kissinger's war against the Euro-Arab dialogue, read pp. 898-900 and 926-31 of this work.

55 *Daily Telegraph* (London), 8 March 1974; quoted in Allen, 'The Euro-Arab dialogue', p. 327. See also pp. 328-29 of the Allen article.

56 Conversation with Farouq al-Qaddumi, mid-1977.

57 Council of Europe, *Texts Adopted by the Assembly*, Parliamentary Assembly, 32nd Ordinary Session (Strasbourg: Council of Europe, 1980), document I17 749 (Resolution 728), pp. 2 and 3. The Council of Europe is not to be confused with the directly elected European Parliament, whose seat was also in the Palace of Europe.

58 The text of the Venice Declaration is printed in *New York Times*, 14 June 1980, p. 4. For the text of Hassan's address in Strasbourg (in Arabic), see Hassan, 1981, pp. 73-81.

59 Faisal Hawrani, 'Dialogue with Kahled al-Hassan', *Shu'un Filastiniyya*, July 1980, p. 48. Also reprinted in Hassan, 1981, p. 149.

60 Interviews with Khaled al-Hassan, October 1982 and April 1983.

61 *Lubnaan 1982: Yawmiyyat al-Ghazu al-Isra'ili*, p. 398; FBIS (West Europe section), 29 June 1982, p. B2; and Carole Collins, 'Chronology of the Israeli invasion of Lebanon June-August 1982', *Journal of Palestine Studies*, Nos.

44/45 (Summer/Fall 1982), p. 156.
62 Interview with Khaled al-Hassan, April 1983.
63 Kissinger, 1982, pp. 503 and 626-27.
64 Kissinger, 1979, p. 573.
65 Kissinger, 1982, p. 629. For Kissinger's whole account of this saga see *ibid.*, pp. 503 and 624-29, which also throw much light on the way the Secretary viewed the PLO at that time.
66 'Document: "To isolate the Palestinians"', *MERIP Reports*, No. 96 (May 1981), p. 27.
67 *New York Times*, 21 June 1976, p. 13. For further details of U.S.-PLO 'security contacts' from 1973 onwards see Doyle McManus, 'U.S., PLO: seven years of secret contacts', *Los Angeles Times*, 5 July 1981; and David Ignatius, 'PLO operative, slain reputedly by Israelis, had been helping U.S.', *Wall Street Journal*, 10 February 1983.
68 *IDP, 1973*, pp. 404-05 and 407.
69 Conversation with William Quandt, April 1983.
70 Interview with Yasser Arafat, August 1979. (Two colleagues from the *Christian Science Monitor*, John Cooley and Ned Temko, also participated in this joint interview.)
71 *Ibid.*
72 Interview with Khaled al-Hassan, April 1983.
73 *Ibid.*, October 1982.
74 Interview with Yasser Arafat, August 1979.
75 *Al-Hayat* (Beirut), 13 June 1969, quoted in Fuad Jabber, 'The Arab regimes and the Palestinian revolution 1967-71', *Journal of Palestine Studies*, Winter 1973, p. 80.
76 Interview with Khaled al-Hassan, October 1982.
77 *Ibid.*, April 1983.

11. The irresistible force and the immovable object

1 Interview with Yasser Arafat, November 1979.
2 Interview with Khaled al-Hassan, April 1983.
3 *Sunday Times* (London), 15 June 1969, quoted in Hirst, 1977, p. 264 (my emphasis). See also the other examples Hirst gives here.
4 Interview with Khaled al-Hassan, April 1983.
5 Salah Khalaf once remarked of the leader of a tiny PLO member-group: 'Secretary-General! He would not even make deputy secretary of an *iqlim* [region] in Fateh!' (conversation with Khalaf, mid-1979).
6 Interview with Khaled al-Hassan, April 1983.
7 My despatch to *Christian Science Monitor* (Boston), 21 April 1981. Hassan's own subsequent interpretation of Arafat's position in 1981 was more diplomatic than that in my original notes referred to here, which had come from a different source.
8 Interview with Yasser Arafat, November 1979.
9 O'Neill, 1978, p. 242.

10 *Ibid.*, p. 99.
11 Edward Walsh, 'War's value splits Israel a year later', *Washington Post*, 5 June 1983, p. A20.
12 Interview with Khaled al-Hassan, April 1983.
13 Farouq Qaddumi, quoted in *International Documents on Palestine, 1977*, p. 337. See ch.5 above.
14 Herbert C. Kelman, 'Talk with Arafat', *Foreign Policy* (Washington, D.C.), No. 49 (Winter 1982-83), pp. 136-37 and 138.
15 It has been argued that, in contrast to the instances listed here of the PLO leadership sticking to commitments it made to the U.S., in 1977 and early 1983 it apparently failed to deliver on a diplomatic undertaking. I would argue that these two instances were of a completely different order: they occurred during the pre-negotiating process itself, rather than subsequent to a formal, public (if still indirect) agreement, as was the case with the 1978 and 1981 cease-fires. In both 1977 and early 1983, both sides blamed the other for the breakdown; and the indirect nature of the process made it impossible ultimately to apportion the responsibility in this between them. For more details on the indirect diplomatic dances of 1977 and 1979 see ch.10 above.

References and select bibliography

Books and booklets in English

Abou Iyad (Abu Iyad) with Eric Rouleau,1981. *My home, my land.* New York: Times Books.

Abu-Jaber, Kamel S., 1966. *The Arab Baath Socialist Party.* Syracuse, N.Y.: Syracuse University Press.

Amos, John W., 1980. *The Palestinian resistance: organisation of a nationalist movement.* New York: Pergamon Press.

Behbehani, Hashim S. H., 1981. *China's foreign policy in the Arab world, 1955-75: three case studies.* London and Boston: Kegan Paul International Ltd.

Beirut massacre (The), press profile: September 1982, New York: Claremont Publications.

Benvenisti, Meron, 1982. *The West Bank data project.* Jerusalem: privately produced.

Ben Zvi, Abraham, 1981. *The United States and the Palestinians: the Carter era.* Tel Aviv: Center for Strategic Studies, Paper No. 13.

1982. *The Reagan presidency and the Palestinian predicament: an interim analysis.* Tel Aviv: Center for Strategic Studies, Paper No. 16.

Bertelsen, Judy, 1976. *The Palestinian Arabs, a non-state nation systems analysis.* Beverly Hills/London: Sage Publications.

Budeiri, Musa, 1979. *The Palestine Communist Party, 1919-1948: Arab and Jew in the struggle for internationalism.* London: Ithaca Press.

Carter, Jimmy, 1982. *Keeping faith.* New York: Bantam Books.

Chaliand, Gérard, 1972. *The Palestinian resistance.* Harmondsworth: Penguin Books.

1977. *Revolution in the Third World: myths and prospects.* New York: The Viking Press.

Cooley, John, 1973. *Green March, Black September.* London: Frank Cass.

Darwish, Mahmoud (moderator), 1974. *Palestinian leaders discuss the new challenges to the Resistance.* Beirut: PLO Research Center.

Dayan, Moshe, 1981. *Breakthrough.* London: Weidenfeld and Nicholson.

Dimbleby, J., and D. McCullin, 1980. *The Palestinians.* London: Quartet Books.

Golan, Galia, 1977. *Yom Kippur and after: the Soviet Union and the Middle East crisis.* Cambridge: University Press.

1980. *The Soviet Union and the Palestine Liberation Organisation.* New York: Praeger.

299

References and select bibliography

Golan, Matti, 1976. *The secret conversations of Henry Kissinger.* New York: Quadrangle/New York Times Book Co.

Haley, P. Edward, and Lewis W. Snider, 1979. *Lebanon in crisis: participants and issues.* Syracuse, N.Y.: Syracuse University Press.

Harkabi, Yehoshafat, 1979. *The Palestinian covenant and its meaning.* London: Vallentine Mitchell.

Heikal, Mohamed, 1973. *The Cairo Documents.* New York: Doubleday and Co.
  1975. *The road to Ramadan.* New York: Quadrangle/New York Times Book Co.
  1978. *The sphinx and the commissar.* New York: Harper and Row.

Hersh, Seymour M., 1983. *The price of power: Kissinger in the Nixon White House.* New York: Summit Books.

Hiro, Dilip, 1982. *Inside the Middle East.* New York: McGraw-Hill Book Co.

Hirst, David, 1977. *The gun and the olive branch.* London: Faber and Faber.

Hudson, Michael, 1977. *Arab politics: the search for legitimacy.* New Haven and London: Yale University Press.

Israeli invasion of Lebanon (The), press profile: June/July 1982. 1982. New York: Claremont Publications.

Jiryis, Sabri, 1968. *The Arabs in Israel.* Beirut: Institute for Palestine Studies.

Jureidini, Paul A., and William E. Hazen, 1976. *The Palestinian movement in politics.* Lexington, Mass.: Lexington Books.

Kadi, Leila S., 1966. *Arab summit conferences and the Palestinian problem, 1936-50 and 1964-66.* Beirut: PLO Research Center.
  1969. *Basic political documents of the armed Palestinian resistance movement.* Beirut: PLO Research Center.

Kalb, Bernard, and Marvin Kalb, 1974. *Kissinger.* Boston: Little, Brown and Co.

Kapeliouk, Amnon, 1982. *Sabra et Chatila, enqûete sur un massacre* (French). Paris: Seuil.

Kazziha, Walid W., 1975. *Revolutionary transformation in the Arab world.* London and Tonbridge: Charles Knight.
  1979. *Palestine in the Arab dilemma.* New York: Barnes and Noble.

Kerr, Malcolm H., 1971. *The Arab cold war.* London, Oxford and New York: Oxford University Press.

Khaled, Leila, 1973. *My people shall live: the autobiography of a revolutionary.* London: Hodder and Stoughton.

Khalidi, Walid, 1979. *Conflict and violence in Lebanon: confrontation in the Middle East.* Cambridge, Mass.: Harvard Center for International Affairs.

Kiernan, Thomas, 1976. *Arafat, the man and the myth.* New York: W. W. Norton.

Kimche, Jon, and David Kimche, 1960. *Both sides of the hill.* London: Secker and Warburg.

Kissinger, Henry, 1979. *White House years.* Boston: Little, Brown and Co.
  1982. *Years of upheaval.* Boston: Little, Brown and Co.

Kuttab, Jonathan, and Raja Shehadeh, 1982. *Civilian administration in the occupied West Bank: analysis of Israeli Military Government Order No. 947.* Ramallah, West Bank: Law in the Service of Man.

Lesch, Ann Moseley, 1980. *Political perceptions of the Palestinians on the West Bank and the Gaza Strip*. Washington, D.C.: Middle East Institute.

Lustick, Ian, 1980. *Arabs in the Jewish state: Israel's control of a national minority*. Austin, Texas: University of Texas Press.

Ma'oz, Moshe (ed.), 1975. *Palestinian Arab politics*. Jerusalem: Jerusalem Academic Press.

Migdal, Joel S., *et al.*, 1980. *Palestinian society and politics*. Princeton, N. J.: Princeton University Press.

Nakhleh, Emile A. (ed.), 1980. *A Palestinian agenda for the West Bank and Gaza*. Washington, D.C.: American Enterprise Institute.

Nazzal, Nafez, 1978. *The Palestinian exodus from Galilee 1948*. Beirut: Institute for Palestine Studies.

Neff, Donald, 1981. *Warriors at Suez: Eisenhower takes America into the Middle East*. New York: The Linden Press/Simon and Schuster.

O'Neill, Bard E., 1978. *Armed struggle in Palestine: a political-military analysis*. Boulder, Colo.: Westview Press.

Owen, Roger (ed.), 1976. *Essays on the crisis in Lebanon*. London: Ithaca Press.

Petran, Tabitha, 1972. *Syria*. London: Ernest Benn Ltd..

Phillips, David, 1973. *Skyjack: the story of air piracy*. London: Harrap.

Porath, Yehoshua, 1974. *The emergence of the Palestinian Arab national movement, 1918-29*. London: Frank Cass.

Quandt, William B., 1977. *Decade of decisions*. Berkeley: University of California Press, 1977.

Quandt, William B., Fuad Jabber and Ann M. Lesch, 1973. *The politics of Palestinian nationalism*. Berkeley and Los Angeles: University of California Press.

Randal, Jonathan C., 1983. *Going all the way: Christian warlords, Israeli adventurers, and the war in Lebanon*. New York: The Viking Press.

Rokach, Livia, 1980. *Israel's sacred terrorism*. Belmont, Mass.: Association of Arab-American University Graduates.

Salibi, Kamal S., 1965. *The modern history of Lebanon*. Delmar, N. Y.: Caravan Books.

Sayegh, Fayez A., 1971. *Palestine: concordance of the United Nations resolutions, 1967-71*. New York: New World Press.

Sayigh, Rosemary, 1979. *Palestinians: from peasants to revolutionaries*. London: Zed Press.

Seale, Patrick, 1965. *The struggle for Syria*. London: Oxford University Press.

Shahak, Israel, n. d. *The Shahak Report*. Washington, D.C.: Free Palestine.

Shamir, Shimon, 1974. *Communications and political attitudes in West Bank refugee camps*. Tel Aviv: Shiloah Center for Middle East and African Studies.

Sharabi, Hisham, 1970. *Palestine guerrillas, their credibility and effectiveness*. Washington, D.C: Georgetown University.

El-Shazly, Saad, 1980. *The crossing of Suez*. London: Third World Centre for Research and Publishing.

Sheehan, Edward R. F., 1976. *The Arabs, the Israelis, and Kissinger.* New York: Reader's Digest Press/Thomas Y. Crowell.

Shukairy, Ahmed, 1966. *Liberation – not negotiation.* Beirut: PLO Research Center.

Tawil, Raymonda Hawa, 1979. *My home, my prison.* New York: Rinehart and Winston.

Taylor, Alan R., 1982. *The Arab balance of power.* Syracuse, New York: Syracuse University Press.

Tomeh, George J. (ed.), 1975. United Nations resolutions on Palestine and the Arab-Israeli conflict, 1947-74. Beirut: Institute for Palestine Studies.

Toward Peace in the Middle East, 1975. Washington, D.C.: Brookings Institution.

Van Arkadie, Brian, 1977. *Benefits and burdens.* New York: Carnegie Endowment for International Peace.

Yaari, Ehud, 1970. *Strike terror: the story of Fatah.* New York: Sabra.

Yodfat, Aryeh, and Yuval Arnon-Ohanna, 1981. *PLO: strategy and tactics.* New York: St Martin's Press.

Books and booklets in Arabic

ʿAlush, Naji, 1964. *Al-Masira ila filastin.* Beirut: Dar al-Taliʿa.

Dajani, Ahmed Sidqi *et al.*, 1978. *Al-filastiniyyun fi al-watan al-ʿarabi.* Cairo: Maʿhad al-buhuth wal-dirasat al-ʿarabiyya.

al-Hassan, Khaled, 1981. *Filastin wa ʾuropa.* Beirut: Dar al-Kalima.

Khurshid, Ghazi, 1971. *Dalil harakat al-muqawama al-filastiniyya.* Beirut: Markaz al-Abhath al-Filastiniyya.

Lubnaan 1982: Yawmiyyat al-Ghazu al-Israʾili, 1982. Beirut: Dar al-Andalus.

Malaff wathaʾiq filastin, al-Juzʾ al-thani, 1950-69, n.d. Cairo: Al-Markaz al-ʿArabi lil-Maʿlumat.

Muhsin, Zuhair, 1973. *Al-thawra al-filastiniyya.* Damascus: Manshurat al-Talaʾiʿ.

Musallam, Sami, 1982. *Al-Sin wa al-qadiyya al-filastiniyya, 1976-1981.* Beirut: Muʾassasat al-dirasat al-filastiniyya.

al-Saʿdi, Ghazi, 1983. *Taqrir ʿan al-awdaʿ fi al-aradi al-ʿarabiyya al-muhtalla.* Amman: Dar al-Jalil.

al-Shuqairi, Ahmed, 1959. *Arbaʿun ʿam fi al-hayat al-ʿarabiyya wal-dawliyya.* Beirut.

Serials in English

Facts on File. New York, weekly and annual.

Fiches du monde arabe (English edition). Beirut, weekly.

Foreign Broadcast Information Service (cited as *FBIS*) (mainly Middle East volume; also used China and Soviet Union volumes). Washington, D.C., daily.

International Documents on Palestine. Beirut, annual.

Keesing's Contemporary Archives. London, weekly.

Report of the Commissioner-General of the United Nations Relief and Works Agency for Palestine Refugees in the Near East. United Nations, New York, annual.

Serials in Arabic

Al-Kitab al-Sanawi lil-Qadiyya al-Filastiniyya. Beirut: Mu'assasat al-Dirasat al-Filastiniyya, annual.
Al-Watha'iq al-filastiniyya al-'arabiyya. Beirut: Mu'assasat al-Dirasat al-Filastiniyya, annual.

Articles in English

Allen, David, 'The Euro-Arab dialogue', *Journal of Common Market Studies*, Vol. 16 (June 1978).
Baransi, Saleh, 'All this time we were alone', *MERIP Reports* (Washington, D.C.), No. 96 (May 1981).
Collins, Carole, 'Chronology of the Israeli invasion of Lebanon June-August 1982', *Journal of Palestine Studies* (henceforth *JPS*) (Beirut), Nos. 44/45 (Summer/Fall 1982), p. 146.
Cooley, John, 'China and the Palestinians', *JPS*, Winter 1972, pp. 19-34.
'Document: To isolate the Palestinians', *MERIP Reports*, No. 96 (May 1981), p. 27.
Farah, Tawfiq, 'Political socialization of Palestinian children in Kuwait', *JPS*, Summer 1977, pp. 90-102.
Franjieh, Samir, 'How revolutionary is the Palestinian resistance? A marxist interpretation', *JPS*, Winter 1972, pp. 52-60.
Freedman, Robert O., 'The USSR and the Lebanese Civil War, 1975-1976', *Jerusalem Journal of International Relations*, Vol. 3, No. 4 (Summer 1978), pp. 90-91.
Gazit, Shlomo, 'Early attempts at establishing West Bank autonomy', *Harvard Journal of Law and Public Policy*, Vol. 3 (Summer 1980), p. 143.
Hamid, Rashid, 'What is the PLO?', *JPS*, Summer 1975, pp. 90-109.
Harris, Lillian Craig, 'China's relations with the PLO', *JPS*, Autumn 1977, pp. 123-54.
Hudson, Michael, 'Developments and setbacks in the Palestinian resistance movement', *JPS*, Spring 1972, pp. 64-84.
Ignatius, David, 'PLO operative, slain reputedly by Israelis, had been helping U.S.', *Wall Street Journal* (New York), 10 February 1983.
Jabber, Fuad, 'The Arab regimes and the Palestinian revolution 1967-71', *JPS*, Winter 1973, pp. 79-101.
Jiryis, Sabri, 'On political settlement in the Middle East: the Palestinian dimension', *JPS*, Autumn 1977, pp. 3-25.
Khalidi, Walid, 'Thinking the unthinkable', *Foreign Affairs* (New York), Vol. 56, No. 4 (July 1978), pp. 695-713.

References and select bibliography

Kiwan, Mohammed, 'Sons of the Village assert Palestinian identity in Israel', *MERIP Reports*, No. 68 (June 1978), p. 15.

Konstantinov, V., 'The Palestinian problem and the Middle East settlement', *International Affairs* (Moscow), Vol. 7 (July 1980), p. 50.

McManus, Doyle, 'U.S., PLO: seven years of secret contacts', *Los Angeles Times*, 5 July 1981.

Milson, Menahem, 'How to make peace with the Palestinians', *Commentary*, Vol. 71 (May 1981).

'The Palestinians and the peace process', *Forum*, Nos. 42-43 (Winter 1981).

Mishal, Shaul, 'Nationalism through localism: Some observations on the West Bank political elite', *Middle East Studies* (Tel Aviv), Vol. 17 (October 1981), pp. 477-91.

'Mood of the West Bank, The' (interviews with Muhammed Milhem, Fahd Qawasmeh and Bassam Shak'a), *JPS*, Autumn 1979, pp. 112-20.

Sela, Abraham, 'The PLO, the West Bank and the Gaza Strip', *Jerusalem Quarterly*, No. 8 (Summer 1978), pp. 66-77.

Stebbing, John, 'The demographic jigsaw puzzle in Northern Israel and the West Bank', *International Relations* (London), Vol. 6 (November 1980), p. 926.

Tamari, Selim, 'The Palestinian Demand for independence cannot be postponed indefinitely', *MERIP Reports*, Vol. 11 (Oct.-Dec. 1981), p. 29.

Taylor, Alan R., 'The Euro-Arab dialogue: quest for an inter-regional partnership', *Middle East Journal* (Washington, D.C.), Vol. 32 (Autumn 1978), p. 431.

Tessler, Mark A., 'Israel's Arabs and the Palestinian problem', *Middle East Journal* (Washington, D.C.), Vol. 31 (Summer 1977), p. 317.

Articles in Arabic

(These are all in the PLO monthly *Shu'un Filastiniyya* (SF) unless otherwise identified.)

Abdel-Hakim, Taher, 'Fath: al-milad wal-masira, hadith ma' Kamal 'Udwan', SF, No. 17 (January 1973), pp. 49-50.

'Ahadith ma' qadat al-muqawama hawla mashakkalat al-'aml al-fida'i al-filastini', SF, No. 4 (September 1971) (Khaled al-Hassan and George Habash), and No. 5 (November 1971) (Salah Khalaf and Nayef Hawatma).

'Alush, Naji, 'Harakat al-tahrir al-watani al-filastini wal-'aml al-jamahiri', SF, No. 17 (January 1973).

al-Hassan, Bilal, 'Al-Majlis al-watani al-filastini: hazimat al-mukhawif wal-shukuk', SF, No. 66 (May 1977).

'Al-Muqawama al-filastiniyya wal-jawab li mashru' al-malak husayn', SF, No. 9 (May 1972), pp. 249-50.

al-Hassan, Hani, 'Waqfa 'and al-thakra al-khamisa 'ashra li-intilaqat al-thawra al-filastiniyya', SF, No. 98 (January 1980), p. 32.

Hawrani, Faisal, 'Hiwar ma' Khaled al-Hassan: hawla mawqaf 'uropa al-gharbiyya wal-tawajjuh al-filastini nahwaha', SF, July 1980, p. 48.

'Munaththamat al-tahrir al-filastiniyya wal-ittijah nahwa al-taswiyya', SF, No. 99 (February 1980).

Ibn Haifa, 'Nathra lil-wad' al-'arabi min khilal nuqtat al-intilaq fi ma'rakat al-tahrir wal-'awda', *Filastinuna*, November 1964, p. 11.

al-Khatib, Husam, 'Khawatir fi al-'unf al-filastini', SF, No. 7 (March 1972).

'Al-Muqawama al-filastiniyya fi wad'iha al-rahin' (round table discussion with Bilal al-Hassan, Ahmed Khalifa, Munah Sulh, Shafiq al-Hut, Nabil Sha'th, Sadiq al-'Adhm and Ghassan Kanafani), SF, No. 2 (May 1971).

Shabib, Samih, 'Muqaddamat al-musadara al-rasmiyya lil-shakhsiyya al-wataniyya al-filastiniyya, 1948-1950', SF, Aug./Sept./Oct. 1982, pp. 72-88.

Shafiq, Munir, 'Limatha yurfud al-filastiniyyun mashru' al-dawla al-filastiniyya fil-daffa al-gharbiyya wa qita' ghazza', SF, No. 7 (March 1972).

Nabil 'Ali Sha'th, 'Al-Thawra al-filastiniyya wal-taswiyya al-siyasiyya', SF, No. 23 (July 1973).